MAKEUP TO BREAKUP

MY LIFE IN AND OUT OF KISS

PETER CRISS

WITH LARRY "RATSO" SLOMAN

Scribner
New York   London   Toronto   Sydney   New Delhi

Scribner
A Division of Simon & Schuster, Inc.
1230 Avenue of the Americas
New York, NY 10020

Names and identifying details of some of the people portrayed in this book have been
changed.

First Scribner hardcover edition October 2012

SCRIBNER and design are registered trademarks of The Gale Group, Inc., used under
license by Simon & Schuster, Inc., the publisher of this work.

For information about special discounts for bulk purchases,
please contact Simon & Schuster Special Sales at
1-866-506-1949 or business@simonandschuster.com.

The Simon & Schuster Speakers Bureau can bring authors to your live event.
For more information or to book an event, contact the Simon & Schuster Speakers Bureau
at 1-866-248-3049 or visit our website at www.simonspeakers.com.

Designed by Carla Jayne Jones

Manufactured in the United States of America

10   9   8   7   6   5   4   3   2   1

Library of Congress Control Number: 2012014597

ISBN 978-1-4516-2082-5
ISBN 978-1-4516-2084-9 (ebook)

All photographs courtesy of Peter and Gigi Criss, except for the following: page 1 of the
photograph insert, middle, courtesy of Donna Many; page 4, bottom left and right, ©Bob
Gruen/www.bobgruen.com; page 5, top left, courtesy of Eddie Rhines; bottom right,
courtesy of Joe Marshall; bottom left, courtesy of Amy Cantrell; page 7, left center, *OZ*
photograph courtesy HBO®; lower middle, on the set of *Detroit Rock City*, courtesy of Tim
Sullivan; page 366, photograph collage, third row, left, courtesy of John 5.

For Loretta and Joe, my parents

To the fans.

What you are about to read is my account of my journey through life — complete with all the highs and lows. It was a world saturated with sex, drugs, and Rock and Roll. You may hate it or you may love it. But if this book in any way gets you in touch with your true feelings, then all my soul searching and the long hours spent documenting my life would have been worth it. Anyway, you always wanted the best and I did my best! Enjoy the ride!

Thank you for a wonderful life and God Bless you all!

Always
The Cat Man

ACKNOWLEDGMENTS

*P*eter would like to thank:

My wonderful wife Gigi, whom I love to death and who is so very loving to me. You do so much for me. Your respect, positive outlook, clarity, and love for Jesus have helped me so much through life. You're always doing things for others, never thinking about yourself. You are my hero.

My collaborator Larry "Ratso" Sloman. We spent long days and nights together at the Breakers hotel in our rooms overlooking the ocean. Ratso helped me through the sometimes painful process of documenting my life. I couldn't have done it without the best, and he is. I love this guy; he's truly unique. And thanks also to Christy, his lovely wife, who helped Ratso keep his sanity . . . well, at least attempted to.

Michael Harriot, my agent; Joel Weinstein, my lawyer; Brant Rumble, my editor; Brian Belfiglio, my publicist; and all the people at Scribner, my publisher. Thank you all for making one more of my dreams come true. I am truly grateful for all your hard work. Thanks also to my great personal publicist Lori Lousararian from Rogers and Cowan.

Charlie Kipps, who helped ignite the fuse for this book.

Mark Elliot. Thanks for the autographed book and your honesty and help.

Joey Scardino, his family, and everyone at the Breakers hotel in Spring Lake, New Jersey. I couldn't have picked a better place to search my heart and soul with Ratso. The generosity and respect you gave Ratso and me is hard to find today. Joe, you are one of a kind. Thank you. I really love this hotel. It's a place that always makes me feel at home. When you stay here you will find true peace of mind. It doesn't get better than this.

Thanks to my family: my mom and dad, my daughter Jenilee, my granddaughter Jordan, my nanna Clara, my grandpa George and his wife Pauline, my grandpa Peter and grandma Nancy, my uncle George and aunt Rosie and their daughter, Roseanne, my brother Joey and his wife Margie, my sisters Donna Donna and her husband Joe, Nancy and her husband Joe, Joanne and her husband Billy, the Criscuola, Brown, and Henry families, all my nieces and nephews, my ex-wives Debra McMurray and Lydia Criss, my mothers-in-law Georgia and Betty and Betty's husband Paul Svensk.

A special thank you to Tall Man and Angel, two of my bandmates in Criss. God bless you for being there when I needed a friend. Also special thanks to Tom Fontana, who always kept his word. He's a man of dignity and honor. I'm proud to be his friend. And thanks for *Oz*! And to John Eyd, the greatest acting coach around. I couldn't have done *Oz* without you. ATI is the best!

Thanks always to the godparents of my daughter: Jeanette Frehley and Chris Lendt.

Thanks also to my Kiss family. Of course, Ace, Gene, and Paul, Bill Aucoin, Sean Delaney, Neal Bogart, Joyce Biawitz, Rosie Licata, John Hart, Eddie Balandas, Fritz Postlethwaite, J. R. Smalling, Moosey, Frankie Scinlaro, Billy Miller, Alan Miller and Ken Anderson, Tim Rozner, David Matthews, Baby Beth, and Trish, Lonnie Stoner, Eric Carr, Mark St. John, the Kulick brothers, Vinnie Vincent, Monique Frehley, Larry Harris, Don Wasley, Bucky, Susan Muneo, Jeff Franklin. Thanks to all our road crews, our truckers, our grips, and the lighting and pyro crews. Thanks always to Scott Shannon, whose support made "Beth" KISS's biggest hit single. Thanks to Bill Starkey and Jay Evans, who founded the great KISS Army, and to each and every fan and member who started the ball rolling on our amazing trip and who keep the flame alive today.

I can't forget my longtime writing partner Stan Penridge and his wife Nell and son Jesse, along with all the members of the Barracudas, the Sounds of Soul, Nautilus, Chelsea, Lips, and Criss.

Thanks to the great producers I've worked with—Bob Ezrin, Eddie Kramer, Vini Poncia, David Wolfert, Kerner and Wise and Dito Godwin and the great musicians who've played with me, including Phil Naro, Paul Shafer, Will Lee, and Clifford Carter. Thanks to the legendary bands who've played with us, including Rush, Aerosmith, Cheap Trick, AC/DC, Ted Nugent and his band, Skid Row, and Bob Seger and the Silver Bullet Band.

Thanks to the great photographers who have shot me over the years: Bob Gruen, Annie Leibowitz, Barry Levine, Norman Seeff, Francesco Scavullo, Lynn Goldsmith, and Eric Stephen Jacobs.

Thanks to my record labels over the years: Decca, Casablanca, Phonogram, Universal, Mercury, Sony Red, and Megaforce, and to the late Tony Nicole of TNT Records. And to New Line Cinema, Hanna-Barbera Productions, and NBC.

Thanks also to the Lombardi family at DW Drums, along with John Good and his wife Esther, and Garrison. Thanks to Pat Brown from ProMark drumsticks, Mr. Remo for his great drumheads, everyone at Zildjian Cymbals, Roxanne and everyone at Audiotechnica, and *Modern Drummer* magazine and the Guitar Center.

Thanks to my unions and associations: Local 802, ASCAP, SAG-AFTRA, AFM, and Actor's Equity.

Thanks to my great musician friends: Carmine Appice, Tommy Lee, Johnny 5, Vince Neil, Richie Scarlett (and his wife Joanne), and Markie Ramone, Rob Affuso, Chad Smith.

Thanks to everyone at Madison Square Garden, Larry London, Walt Johnson from Pearl, and everyone at Hawk Radio. Thanks to Mark Newman of Sony, everyone at MTV and VH1, especially Ed Trunk. Respect to Dick Clark, Bill Boyd, Charlie Hernandez from Aerosmith, Jim Chapin, and Sandy Gennaro.

Thanks to my friends Jerry Nolan and his mom Charlotte, Edward Mulvihill III (whom I miss dearly) and his wife Dottie, my number one fan Vinnie Gonzales and his wonderful mother Nancy, Marie Mullowney, Peter Arquette, John and Judy Belushi, Ernie Hudson, Tim Sullivan, Bob Nelson, Carol White, Bill Dooley and his wife, Eddie Rhines, Josselyne Herman-Saccio and her family, Tom Perkins, Chris Jennings, Jen Johnson, childhood friends Carol and

Elvira, Tommy Gannon, George Davidson, Louie Demando, Peter Cudereski, George Saskus, Frank Doogan, the Rosploch family, the Cotter family, John, the 3rd of July gang—Sweet Richard, Richard and Maureen, Joyce, Ralph and Janine, John and Anita, also Carleen Tobin, and John Percuoco from Ladder 5 and his wife Sue. Thanks to Steve Ascione at Moto Photo in Wall Township and to Gail Winterstella at Gail's Optical Shoppe. Thanks too to Helena and Dan, the Lortz family, Roseanne Barr and Tom Arnold.

I wouldn't be in one piece if it weren't for all my (and Gigi's) wonderful doctors. Thanks to my dearest friend and doctor Terry Hammer and his daughter Katie, my angel Dr. Alex Swistel and his wife Pat, Dr. Alton Barron and his wife Carrie, Dr. Steven Glickel, Dr. Gae Rodke, Dr. Lowe, Dr. Ray Hanbury, Dr. Daniel Smith, DeDe, Dr. Brian Klohn and his wife Robin, and Dr. Karen Lindsay.

Always thanks to Mother Mary.

*R*atso would like to thank:

The Catman, who opened his heart and plumbed his memories and who always told the truth, warts and all. Your journey has been truly epic and I'm privileged to have been able to chronicle it.

Gigi Criss, for all your help, and your great home cooking and hospitality!

Mike Harriot, agent extraordinaire, Brant Rumble for his judicious editing, Joel Weinstein and Eric Rayman, the voices of reason, and everyone at Scribner for shepherding this book to the marketplace.

Special thanks to Tim Sullivan, Chris Lendt, Tim Rozner, Paul Marshall, and the Tall Man for taking time out of their busy schedules to regale me with some great stories of the Catman.

Extra special kudos to Jill Matheson who pored over hundreds of hours of tapes and transcribed them in superhuman time.

Thanks to Lach for his encouragement and his wonderful song "Kiss Loves You," and to Evan Zimmerman for all his research help.

And, as always, thanks to my wife Christy for all her support and infinite patience and to Lucy, for keeping her company while I was catting around in New Jersey.

MAKEUP TO BREAKUP

PROLOGUE

Have you ever tasted the barrel of a .357 Magnum that's halfway down your throat? It's a really unforgettable sensation, like a piece of iron dipped in oil, with sort of a coppery aftertaste. I got my first and (hopefully) last taste of one on January 17, 1994, sitting on the floor of my debris-strewn bedroom in Los Angeles.

Just twelve hours earlier I had been lying in bed, watching TV. It was around three A.M. and I was cozy under the covers when I feel a little tremor. I'd been through quite a few "shakers" in California. Chandeliers rattling, traffic lights swaying. But this was different. The tremors started getting more frequent and I started to hear a rumbling noise, so I sat up in the bed and all of a sudden the whole place shook big-time and the TV flew off the dresser, tumbled down, and blew up. I was like, "Motherfucker!" Then the lamps fell over and I was like, "Holy shit!" Turned out this was the beginning of the Northridge earthquake, a massive catastrophe that killed thirty-three people and injured more than eighty-seven hundred.

I'm a Brooklyn boy: I knew about cockroaches and rats and zip guns, not earthquakes. So I started to panic. I heard glass shattering in the bathroom. I was hearing all this devastation, and just then another big jolt came, and my bed collapsed and the huge wooden armoire started dancing across the bedroom and then tipped over. Behind the armoire, on a nail, I had hung a bag that was filled with $100,000 cash. That was all the money I had to my name. I wasn't going to put it in a bank—didn't trust them—and I was in trouble with the IRS then, so I figured I'd keep the cash nearby and if someone was going to rob it, that's a big piece of motherfucking shit to move. But now the huge armoire was lying on the floor and the bag was hanging from the nail, exposed.

My fear of death set in. Lamps were flying through the air. I got up and ran into the living room and I saw all my KISS gold albums falling off the walls and shattering. I also had a full cabinet of Steuben crystal that I had managed to pry from my ex-wife's hands, and all that precious crystal busted up. All of a sudden, the couch flew through the air, the armchair went over, and I got thrown into the bathroom wall. I was thinking, "Jesus, I'm going to fucking die in some shithole apartment in Hollywood. I just don't believe you're going to take me this way."

So I found my .357 Magnum, tucked it under the waistband of my sweatpants, threw my bathrobe on, pulled on some sneakers, grabbed my bag with the cash, and ran. I knew enough not to take the elevator, so I rushed down the steps. It was still dark out and people were screaming, running half naked out of their apartments into the street. Outside, it looked like a war zone. Cars were overturned; a water hydrant had blown up and there was water gushing out into the street. People were running around screaming that it was the end of the world. Then, like in a movie, I heard a rumbling sound and I saw the tar separate and the street crack open. Everybody was panicking, but suddenly I got strangely calm. I was scared, but once I had my footing and my money and my gun, I knew no one was going to take them from me.

I just kept walking around in circles; I didn't know where to go. By then the sun was coming up and there was an aftershock and everybody screamed again. I had circled back to the front of my building, where hundreds of people had congregated. All the windows of the health-food store on the ground floor had shattered, and the food was all over the ground. Our underground garage had collapsed and lots of cars got totaled.

By late afternoon, they let us back into the building. I walked into my apartment and I couldn't believe it. Everything I had of value was leveled. I had no bed. The rod in the walk-in closet had collapsed and my clothes were on the floor. The refrigerator had toppled over and all the food was going rancid. The kitchen cabinets broke open and there was sugar everywhere. In the living room, all my records were shattered on the floor. The top of my People's Choice Award, which I had won for "Beth," had broken off. My daughter's pictures had fallen off the wall and smashed into a million pieces. Everything that I used to look at and cherish was destroyed.

I didn't have electricity yet, so I lit a few candles. I was filthy, covered with the dirt and grime of the streets, but I couldn't shower because the whole shower had fallen apart. Even if it hadn't, there was no water. I couldn't even run the sink and wash my hands. I walked back into the bedroom and sat down on the mattress on the floor. I had to brush away the soil from my flowerpots, which had all broken. It was dusk and a huge wave of depression rolled over me and I almost threw up. I felt like there was a hot poker plunged into the pit of my stomach. I thought I was taking a stroke. I couldn't even breathe right: The air felt thin from the dust and the dirt in the apartment and the rotting food. The whole room stank from death.

I thought to myself, Why should I keep going? I was in the middle of recording a new album, but fucking whoop-de-do; I was on TNT, a clown label. Then I started talking to myself, like in that Peggy Lee song "Is That All There Is": "What do you really have to live for? Your two marriages have gone to shit. You hardly see your daughter. You got a hundred grand, but you were worth twelve-some-odd million at one point in your life. If this had happened when you were in KISS, your manager Bill Aucoin would have been there with fifty cop cars, twenty ambulances, and a helicopter. When you're on top and you're making everyone rich, they all love you, babe. Life is wonderful. But now you're really just a has-been. No one cares about you, especially in Hollywood."

I looked around the room. I once had money to burn. I'd fly to Barbados for the weekend. I lived in a twenty-two-room mansion and had my pick of four luxury cars. And now I was sitting on the floor in the middle of the debris of my former exalted life. It was then that I realized that I didn't want to live. Life had been just a fucking nightmare, nothing but ups and downs and drugs and fighting, and I was sick of it all.

So I pulled out the .357 Magnum and put it in my mouth. The barrel is about six inches long, and I easily put three inches in. The gun is an inch in diameter, so I began to gag a little. When I hammered the gun back with my finger on the trigger, I started shaking. I knew if I slipped, it was all over. I also knew that I had straight flat-head bullets in the gun, so if I pulled the trigger, my brains would wind up somewhere across the street. I was a lucky bastard: I had cheated death a few times, but that wasn't going to happen with a .357 Magnum in my mouth. That gun would literally take a man's head off. If you shot an elephant in the head, it would go down. That's why Clint Eastwood loved it. It's the most powerful handgun in the world.

They say that in situations like this, your mind just starts racing, and you see your whole life before you. But for me, everything seemed to be in slow motion. I had cried wolf many times in my life, especially with KISS. I was known for quitting the band a million times. But this was different. This was far from a bluff, because there was nobody there that I was bluffing. Just me and the rubble.

Then I thought about my mother. There's not a day that goes by that I don't bless myself with holy water and then get in my car and rub the medal of the Virgin Mary that she gave me and say a Hail Mary for my mother. And then I kiss her Mass card that's right there on the dashboard.

My mother had died three years earlier, on New Year's Day, 1991, and I still hadn't gotten over it. I had been very close to my mother; we had a very strange, deep relationship. We were more than mother and son: She was my closest friend. I was still hurt and grieving her. I had been concerned my whole life about letting her down. I always realized how hard she had worked for me to be something, how much it meant to her that I *became* something. And if I offed myself, how could I ever meet her again in heaven?

And what about my father? He was still alive; he'd be devastated. And I thought of the KISS fans, the greatest fans in the world. And then my eyes wandered a bit and I looked over at the fallen armoire, and next to it was a picture of my daughter. It was my favorite picture of her: Jenilee was about ten when it was taken, and she looked like a saint. And, miraculously, the glass wasn't cracked, it wasn't broken—the frame was standing up defiantly in the midst of all the rubble. That's when it just clicked. I had been going through some real bullshit, but no matter what, I still had my kid, man.

Suddenly there was an immense feeling of faith in that room. I began to believe that God didn't want to take me in the midst of this massive lunacy—that he had more in store for me. But the depression was so dark and so deep and the pain so acute; I was in the middle of a tug of war, almost like a battle for my soul. I could feel the force of the power I had holding back the trigger with the gun in my mouth. I had the power of life and death, right there and then. And *I* was in full control of me dying or living. It was very, very heavy.

But how could I do this to my little angel in the picture? So I pulled the barrel of the gun out of my mouth, put it back in its holster, and then locked it back up. And I resolved to go and finish the album and take my young band on the road and see what the future would bring. I cheered myself up and took my pillows and made a bed out of the mattress on the floor and slept right through the night. And then I woke up the next morning and got on with my life.

CHAPTER ONE

I *entered the world on December 20, 1945, feet first, ass backward,* a breech baby. They didn't have C-sections in those days so they had to take me out with a forceps, like you would use for salad. My mom, Loretta, said the whole process was so painful that she didn't want any more kids after me. Of course, she had four more.

I was also impatient, exiting my mother's womb two months prematurely, a tiny little thing with long black hair down my neck. The nurses would dote over me; they had never seen a baby with that much hair. The cool thing is that I was a love child. My mom got pregnant, and then she and my dad got married a few months after. But my dad, Joe, wasn't really ready to settle down. He was a handsome young Italian guy who loved ballroom dancing. My mother told one of my sisters that my father left for three years when I was young and then came back to the family. But I was never told that.

What a family. I was named Peter after my father's father. He and his wife, Nancy, moved to the U.S. from Naples and settled in Hartford, Connecticut, where they had a farm. Besides their own kids, they adopted a bunch, so there were something like twenty kids in the family. My dad was born on the farm, but eventually his dad bought a six-family tenement building in Brooklyn, where he got a job as a mason. He was a real Italian who spoke only Italian, so one of the guys on the job, to bust his balls, would teach him English phrases like "Fuck you.

Kiss my ass. I'd like some pussy." He didn't understand what it meant. One day he came home from work and my grandmother was cooking and he said, "Hey, fuck you, eat my dick." My grandmother flipped out and my father had to tell him that wasn't nice stuff to say, so the old man got furious and the next day he went to work and kicked the shit out of his coworker.

I loved to visit my grandfather. In his backyard he grew grapes, eggplants, and tomatoes. I'd sit on his lap in the yard and he was like the Godfather. He'd have the big hat, the big pants with the belt, and the big sweater with the holes in it. He was tall, about six foot one, a really good-looking man. He kept pigeons in the back, and in the cellar he had all these rabbits in cages that I used to play with. My mother told me that one day she was eating his pasta sauce and she said, "That's delicious, Pa. A little greasy, but tasty." Then she found out it was made with rabbit, and she never ate the sauce again.

He was a tough man. He didn't believe in doctors. He used to pull his own teeth with pliers. He was a religious Catholic until one day he went to church and caught a priest screwing a nun, and that was it. He gave up his religion after he got a real dose of reality. I really loved him, and I was proud to be named after him.

But I disliked his wife, Nancy. She used to beat the shit out of me. My mother told me that when I was really young, she yanked me up upside down by my feet and I started hemorrhaging and literally bled from my penis. I got my revenge eventually. My grandmother moved in with us toward her last days. She'd sit in the kitchen bitching, complaining, her feet always soaking in warm Epsom salt water. She always wanted things, and she'd curse me in Italian. One day my friend Vinnie came over to play cowboys and she was all pissed because we were having fun, so we went to the back end of the railroad flat, got naked, and ran around the house, taunting her. She couldn't do a thing about it because she was in her wheelchair. Finally my father came home and she mumbled something to him. He came over to us. "What! You got naked in front of your grandmother?"

"Why would I do that, Dad?" I said, all innocent. "I came home to drop off my books. We had lunch and we left. She's seeing things." She was getting a bit senile, so he bought it and she was furious. I got even for all those years she abused me as a baby.

Growing up, I never really knew my mother's dad, my grandfather George, whom I was also named after. He was a real gigolo who left my grandmother when my mother and her brother were really young. Her brother, my uncle George, never forgave his father for deserting them. The old man rarely showed up in New York, but he used to send me things from all over the world: cowboy boots, trinkets. He was globe-trotting because he kept getting married to different rich women. After a few years he'd divorce the first one and then marry another one. He was a real smart guy. He'd read the dictionary for fun. When he moved to San Francisco in his seventies, he wound up smoking weed with all the professors in Berkeley and they gave him an honorary degree to put on his wall.

When I was living in Canarsie with my first wife, he came to visit us with this really rich woman from Amarillo. She was an art collector. She had bought him a saloon. Then he dumped her and he got another rich one to buy him a restaurant in Albany. When he was staying with us, he'd get up in the morning, put on a white shirt and a tie, and place a rose on my wife's side of the table. "Good morning, darling. How are you feeling today?" He knew the magic words.

I visited him years later in San Francisco when he was much older and he had met a nice woman and they were living in an RV. We took a shower together in the trailer park facility and when he turned around, the guy was hung like a horse. He didn't have a dick, he had a baby's arm! My grandfather saw the surprise on my face and he said, "This is why I do so well in life. I'm a cocksman." I had never heard that word before. "That's a man who knows how to use his dick. I haven't worked a day in my life, because once a woman gets some of this thing, it's all over," he explained.

My grandmother Clara never seemed to get over his desertion. She was from a large Irish family of major drinkers. Her family would come over to my grandma's joint, get her drunk as a skunk, and then leave. By the time my granddad got home from work, they were gone and my grandma was passed out cold. Her drinking got so bad that my mom and her brother started missing school, and when my mother was ten, the state took them away and put them in a home. My mother hated it there.

She never really got into it with me, but certain things would set her off. For the rest of her life, if she so much as smelled marmalade, she'd go off. "Don't ever bring that shit around. They served me that every day of my life when I was a little girl." My mother never forgave her mother's sisters and brothers for not stepping up and helping them out before the state took her and her brother away. They had a very hard life, and when they were finally reunited with their mother, Clara had stopped drinking heavily, and they tried to resume a normal family life.

So this was the crazy world that Peter George John Criscuola was thrust into. I just made it crazier. I was a sickly child, and I put my mother through living hell. I caught everything—measles, mumps, whooping cough, a swollen testicle, chicken pox, ear infections, the works. I even caught ringworm from my grandma's cat. When I started school, I was so anemic I'd go every week for a transfusion of fresh blood and vitamins. I was a mess. I must have weighed all of sixty pounds, a skinny kid with a big head and big baggy eyes and big ears. Thankfully, the priest at my school paid for the doctor visits. We couldn't afford them.

When I wasn't getting sick, I was getting hurt. When I was seven, my mom went to visit a friend. They were having coffee and somehow I wandered away from her and went into the backyard. There was a little dog out there. The dog was eating, and I poked my face into what was going on and the dog figured I was going to take its food so it ripped at my mouth and tore my top lip half off. My mother heard the screaming and she saw I was bleeding profusely and rushed me to the hospital. My parents didn't have money or insurance, so it was off to the emergency room, my second home in my younger years.

I must have had an angel looking over me because there was a major plastic surgeon from Germany who was there to give a seminar. He saw me in the hallway bleeding to death and he immediately said, "Bring this kid in." They didn't even put me out. They just strapped my legs and my hands down and went to work on my face. It felt like a million bees stinging me in the face. I was hallucinating, the pain was so intense.

I was bandaged for months, eating through a straw. My father and my grandmother both blamed my mother for me getting fucked up. They thought I would be disfigured for life. Finally it was time to take the bandages off. We went back to the hospital, the doctors and nurses surrounded me, and my mother was biting her nails as she always did. They removed the last bandage and I remember everybody staring at me—either in amazement that I was so ugly or because the lip looked so good, I didn't know. My mom started crying, and I looked in the mirror and could kind of notice the gash in my lip, but it didn't look horrendous, and over time it went away completely. But from that day on, I wouldn't go into a house if there was a dog.

My mother kept me close to her after that. I was always in the bed with her; she was always holding my hand. We were inseparable. My dad was another story. He was either working or trying to find work, or he'd be upstairs on the roof with his pigeons. He seemed not to want to get involved in other people's lives. He was into his own world and he was very childlike, a trait I inherited from him. As tough an Italian street kid as he was, I think he was scared most of the time. He had no education. He had dropped out of school after the third grade so he was illiterate. He worked a succession of odd jobs when he did work. And eventually he had five kids to raise, so he had an enormous amount of pressure on him. He was just a very conservative, uptight guy. He would not allow bad language in the house at all. Except for my mother, who cursed like a sailor.

At times I think my father should never have been married or had kids. He never seemed to be happy. I think he wanted more for himself in this world and it never worked out, so he just retreated into his own little world. But despite his remoteness, he had a heart of gold. If you came over to the house and admired something, he'd say, "Take it, it's yours."

His job situation was never stable. He worked in a factory for a while making car parts. He fixed cars at a garage. But the best job he ever had was buffing the floors at the UN building. He got paid a lot of money under the table, working the night shift, and he loved it. My mom was afraid to be home alone, so I'd get in bed with her and she would keep me up all night watching the late show and then the late, late show and even the late, late, late show. I had huge black circles under my eyes from not sleeping. Christmastime, my dad would take me to see the big Christmas display at the UN and I'd think, "Wow, my dad's the shit. He works at the UN." Little did I know he was a floor buffer.

Among the few times my dad and I would bond would be over his pigeons. I remember many summer days when the sun was going down, I'd go and sit with him up on the roof and we'd share an apple and he'd point out the different types of birds and tell me about the races he would enter.

My dad didn't dig sports; he liked staying home. But my mother's brother, my uncle George, was always available for me. He was an ex-marine who was childless then because my aunt Rosie had had two miscarriages, so my Unc, as I called him, became my surrogate father. I really loved him. We'd go fishing or go to ball games or to Sunnyside Gardens to see the wrestlers. Sometimes on a Sunday he'd take me crabbing and we'd bring back all these blue claws. My mom would cook up a big batch and I'd grab a Pepsi and sit outside for hours, eating crabs and daydreaming. Life seemed so easy then.

For such a loner, my father depended on my mother for everything. My mother paid the bills, did the shopping, fixed things around the house. When they were first married they went to a movie occasionally, or maybe a Chinese restaurant, and my grandmother would babysit me. But that didn't last. Once he had four more kids his leisure time was shot, and it seemed that once he came back from work to that apartment, he never left. His joy for life seemed to be fading, and he didn't give a fuck about going anywhere.

I don't want to make it sound like there was no love between them, though. I know they loved each other deeply, but they just didn't know how to show it. My father wasn't a kissy-huggy guy. Even my mom didn't like to be touched. I was the opposite of them. I was very emotional, and I'd hug everyone I got near. But when I grabbed my mother and went to give her a big kiss, she'd kind of shy away and say, "Come on, Georgie." I never did get those hugs and kisses that I wanted from my mom and dad. They protected me and did all they could, but they just weren't emotionally available. They both had hard lives, but they loved me to death. Even though I was the oldest child, they called me "the baby," or sometimes "Bubba."

I'd have to say that I grew up poor, but it didn't seem like that at the time. We lived in a tenement building, six families per house. We had a four-room railroad flat. There was a belly stove in the parlor and a coal stove in the kitchen. I remember my dad and I would go scrounging for wood in the middle of the winter, going down into people's basements and breaking their bins up and stealing the wood so we could bring it home and throw it into the fire to keep warm. If you wanted to take a bath, the tub was in the kitchen, so you'd heat a pot of water and throw it into the tub and jump in.

We didn't really go hungry, but we didn't eat like kings either. On the way to school, I'd have a spartan breakfast. My mother would make a cup of coffee for me and then she'd put a fork into a slice of white bread, put it over the fire on the gas stove—when we finally got gas—and she'd toast it and butter it and that was breakfast.

When I was young, we had to share a bathroom with the family next door. They were an Irish family and they were clean but they were as poor as we were. Sometimes you'd go into the bathroom and there was no toilet paper, just a newspaper cut into slices. Trust me, wiping your ass with the funnies is a painful situation. The only upside was that the family next door had a couple of hot teenage girls. I used to go out on the fire escape and look in through the bathroom window and watch them pee. Growing up with these privations was just the way life was to us. If you were poor, so were the people upstairs, and the people downstairs were even poorer. So everybody helped everyone else out. It was always "Have some milk" or "Can I borrow a potato?" or "Take some butter." There was a potpourri of nationalities in Williamsburg, a true melting pot of Irish and Italians and Polish and Jewish, and everyone got along fine.

The only time I got a taste of how other people lived was when I would visit some of my relatives who were better off and lived in nicer neighborhoods. My great-aunt May, my grandmother's sister, married a really nice guy named John who made orthopedic shoes and was worth a lot. She would have my grandmother come out and clean her house, and my Nanny would bring me along sometimes. They had one boy, Johnny, who was in college, so I'd get to stay in his room. It was the typical *Leave It to Beaver* room: the perfect desk, college banners over his bed, model airplanes hanging from the ceiling. They had a basement with a bar and a television and I'd look at my grandmother and say, "Someday, if I ever get rich, Nanny, I'm going to have all this, too." Meanwhile, I was wearing hand-me-downs that didn't fit. Before we left, May would give my grandmother a box of clothes and some leftover food and a couple of bucks. She was my godmother, but she was cheap. But then John would come home and he'd slip my grandmother a fifty-dollar bill.

All in all, Brooklyn was a phenomenal place to grow up in the fifties. At first all we had for entertainment was a radio. Besides music, I'd listen to *The Lone Ranger* and *Amos 'n' Andy* and *The Arthur Godfrey Show*. When I was five years old, we got a TV. The first show I ever saw was *The Howdy Doody Show*, and I'd sing along to the theme "It's Howdy Doody Time." All those shows were great—*The Liberace Show, Queen for a Day, I Love Lucy, Flash Gordon*. But my favorite was the cartoons.

Cowboy shows were huge in the fifties. I always had my cowboy hat, two six-shooters, and cowboy boots. Then I got my Davy Crockett coonskin cap and the long flintlock plastic Davy Crockett rifle. Maybe that's how I got into guns. I could morph into all these characters I'd watch on TV and my imagination would just soar. Even at that age, I started performing. I'd watch that dance routine from *Yankee Doodle Dandy*, and when my mother had people over I'd perform it for them in the kitchen. I slicked my hair into a pompadour and came out with a broom and did Elvis doing "Blue Suede Shoes." I wanted to be the center of attention at all times.

I was an only child until age seven, and I just built my own little world. I used to go through the stuff under my mother's sink and be like a mad scientist brewing up some chemicals. I made big tents out of tables with blankets and had wars in them. I could play with my soldiers for twenty hours, acting out make-believe battles. I was a dramatic kid.

On hot summer nights, everybody would sit out on the stoops and bring out food and stuff to drink. We'd turn on the fire hydrants—we called them Johnny pumps—and cool off. But when we put them up full blast, we'd soak the houses and get the adults wet and they'd scream at us and the cops would come with a wrench and turn them off. If it was hot all night, we'd even sleep out on the fire escapes under the stars.

We didn't have baseball fields like they had in the suburbs, so we played stickball in the street. If you hit the ball a distance of three sewers, it was a home run. It was tough catching a fly ball with the cars parked on the street and the bottles and the garbage cans in your way. All the old Italian guys would sit on the side and make bets on the games.

When I was a teenager, my mother talked me into joining the YMCA so I would stay out of trouble. I loved swimming, maybe because I had big, fat, flabby feet and I got good at it. I won a trophy for the freestyle, and they had a big chicken dinner at the Y and my grandmother and my mother came. I was so proud to go up and get my little trophy. It was the only thing that I had ever won in my life. I got into boxing at the Y and I fought Golden Gloves for two years. But the neighborhood began to change, and even the Y started to get a little dangerous: People didn't want to go because you'd get your ass kicked.

Christmas was really special at the Criscuola home. Even though we weren't that rich, we celebrated it to the nines. Christmas Eve, all of our relatives would go to church and then get real smashed and come home and we'd open up maybe a little teeny thing. Christmas morning, I'd get up and open my presents and play with them for months on end.

But the highlight of my youth had to be the trips we'd take to Coney Island. It was just the greatest place in the world. We would get up early Saturday morning, my grandmother would pack a suitcase full of sandwiches, and we'd hop on the train, which was still safe then. We spent the whole day swimming and running and eating. The beach was packed with what seemed like a million people jammed in like sardines as far as you could see.

Come sunset, my uncle George would drive out and meet us. Then we'd each get three rides and a hot dog and a drink at Nathan's. That hot dog tasted like no other hot dog in the world. Once a year Pfizer, the big chemical company, would have Steeplechase Day; my uncle Billy worked there, so he'd get us passes and we'd go to Steeplechase Park. They had the best rides, especially the Steeplechase, which was a ride with mechanical horses that raced around a track that encircled the building. After you rode the horses you had to exit the ride a certain way, and they'd have these clowns who would shock the guys with a shocker in their rear ends. And the women would walk over a vent and a blast of air would blow their dresses up.

But the best thing was to go under the boardwalk and look up the chicks' dresses as they walked by. Sometimes you'd get lucky and she wouldn't be wearing any underwear and we'd be like, "Holy mackerel, what was that?" We were still boys: We weren't familiar with a girl's sexual equipment. I could have lived at Coney. It blew Disneyland away. People came from all over the world, no one looking for trouble, everybody wanting to have a good time. No hate, no killing, no robbery, no rape. Just good vibes.

I had that experience all to myself until I was seven. That's when my sister Nancy came along, followed by my brother, Joey, and my sisters Joanne and Donna Donna. It was weird being a seven-year-old boy towering over a crib that contained this little girl. I immediately freaked out at my sister Nancy because she was a girl and everybody gave her a lot of attention. I was really jealous. That's probably why I took up the drums. I needed affection and I needed attention.

My grandmother would say to my mother, "Let Georgie come over to my house for the weekend. You got two infants there and it'll give you a break." Georgie was only too happy to go! I didn't want to hear the kids screaming and crying all night. That was a blessing for me. All that space was good for my brain. My grandmother lived downstairs in the same building, so I loved staying there. She'd buy me potato chips and she had a little TV set. I had my own room and my own bed. After a while, I just wound up staying at my grandmother's place and my mother didn't care, because she still saw me every day. It was almost like living two lives, sleeping at my grandmother's house but living with my mom and dad.

As they grew older, my sisters and brother hated me for it. They would say, "Spoiled little bastard. You got your own room, you come over here, you fucking fill your face, and you leave." But it wasn't always that simple. I helped my grandma out, too. I would undress her and put her to sleep. At that age, I would sleep next to her. For a ten-year-old boy, undressing an elderly woman and putting her to bed was not easy. But I loved her to death and she loved me. She was the best thing in my life.

My grandmother taught me how to sew, how to hem pants, how to iron clothes, how to do laundry. I resisted at first, but she would say, "Someday you may be all on your own in the world and no one will want you. Trust me, these are important things to know." I was so childlike, I think that she knew that I was going to have a tough time in the world.

When I was around fifteen, my grandmother moved to an apartment on the second floor of a nicer building. She had been working two jobs and got a raise, and these apartments were more spacious. Her new place was a five-minute walk from my mother's, and I was happy to be even farther away from my brothers and sisters. My Nanny was part German, so of course she kept this new place spotless. And she was tough. Once she bought me a nice coat, and one day I didn't hang it up. When I got back from school, all my clothes were in the street. My shoes, my socks, my underwear, and my new coat—she just threw them all out the window. People were laughing, watching me gather them up. And she stuck her head out the window and yelled down, "You get the message? You know how hard I worked to get you that coat? And you just throw it on the floor? Maybe now you'll hang it up." For the rest of my life, everything was hung, neatly folded, and put away in drawers. I was a tough little bastard, always getting in trouble, but my grandmother was tougher. My mom I could bamboozle, my dad was easy, but my grandmother, good fucking luck. She'd break my head with a bat.

Talk about tough love. When I was a teenager, I got drunk for the first time on Thunderbird wine. I got so high and dizzy that I stumbled home and banged on her door. She opened it and I just fell down on the floor, threw up, and passed out. When I came to, she was standing over me. "You want to drink? You think it's all fun and games? Well, this is the other side of it." To this day, the word *Thunderbird* makes my stomach turn.

When it came to school, it wasn't tough love I was getting: It was pure sadism, courtesy of the nuns at my Catholic school. I went to Transfiguration, about twelve blocks from my mother's house. I started there in kindergarten and I remember how scary it was the first day. I was petrified to look up and see these old sisters of Saint Joseph with the big black-and-white habits and the huge black crosses around their necks and the rosaries hanging around their waists. In the first grade, I actually had the same teacher that my mother had when she went there. This nun was ancient. She even smelled like she was dying. We used to throw chalk up at her, shoot spitballs at her, and she couldn't even hit you because she was so feeble. She'd try to hit your knuckles with a ruler and whap, she'd miss and hit the desk. But I did respect her even though we tortured her.

My closest friends at school were the biggest troublemakers: Peter Cud-ereski, George Davidson, Tommy Gannon, Louie Demando, and Jimmy Greer. We were always getting into mischief and fights. So of course we became altar boys. It seemed like a cool gig to me. You got to mimic the priests and wear the same clothes they wore. They'd show you a little more leniency, give you a little more freedom, because we were a little more godly, being that close to the priest.

Well, the experiment lasted about two years. Part of the responsibilities of an altar boy was to do the funerals, which meant you had to get there at six in the morning because the funeral started at seven. It was depressing as hell for a twelve-year-old boy. People were all in black, crying; there was a big coffin out there. One morning, my buddy Jimmy and I said, "Fuck it," and we went back to where the priest kept the wine and got drunk.

When the priest came in to get it, the wine was half gone and he looked at the two of us and we were slurring our words.

"I don't believe you two!" he screamed. "Get your robes off! Don't ever come into my church again. I'm going to call your moms the minute I'm done with this Mass." We knew we were fucked. And sure enough, when we went back to school, the nun marched us out to the playground and made us stand there for two hours under the most intense summertime sun. It was like *Stalag 17*. You don't send a kid out into the sun where he could take a sunstroke and die. Where did they get these fucking ideas?

So I hated school. To be honest, I wasn't a smart kid. I believe I might have been dyslexic. In the seventh grade I was left back one year. I didn't seem to grasp the stuff they were teaching. But I had other things on my mind. I would rather stay home with my mother and watch TV and go into my never-never land. I didn't want to deal with that ABC bullshit. Except for history. I always got an A+ in that.

I know I was deterred from wanting to learn by my fear of the nuns. It was definitely the old fire-and-brimstone shit in my Catholic school. *You jerk off, you go blind. You must never touch yourself.* They even tried to destroy my love of music. I was different: I had art and music in my blood. I'd walk home on my lunch break no matter what the weather was and play drums on my mom's pots and pans, listening to the radio. I even joined the drum corps at school but, being me, I was showing off to the guys when the drum teacher was standing there, and he threw me out.

Then they banned Elvis Presley. I remember my nun getting up there, going, "This Sunday, Elvis Presley is going to be on *The Ed Sullivan Show*. No one in this classroom can watch it." That was a dagger to my heart. I imitated Elvis. I'd have my hair long like Elvis and the girls would dig it, but the nuns flipped out. They put a pink ribbon in my hair and made me go to the girls' classrooms and stand in front of their class to show them what a boy who needed a haircut looked like. I wanted to die. Then they made me cut my hair. God, it was traumatic.

Plus I couldn't stand the hypocrisy. We'd go to see *The Ten Commandments,* and the nuns were all fixated on Charlton Heston on the screen. "Who are they kidding?" I whispered to my buddy Louie. "They got this guy half naked, sweating, everything hanging out. I think the nuns love it."

Some of the older nuns were very mean to me. Maybe because I was different, I was the kid who cut up in the room and made a fool of myself to get attention. I wasn't a great-looking kid. I was very skinny and sickly. I'm sure part of the reason I was getting sick so much was to escape the torture of these nuns: "I don't feel good." "My stomach hurts." It was a litany of excuses I'd give my mom so I wouldn't have to go to school.

Who could blame me? Let's say I had to go pee. I'd raise my hand: "Sister, sister, I gotta go to the bathroom."

"What's your problem, Master Criscuola?"

"I have to go, sister."

"Well, I think you could wait an hour, right, Master Criscuola?"

What! I'm ten years old. I gotta go *now.*

"Sit down, Master Criscuola."

So I peed my pants. I had to go through the whole day with wet, pissed-up pants, and it was freezing out. I remember walking home and my pants got stiff, and my mom screamed at me.

Another time—oh, God—I shit my pants.

"Sister, sister!"

"What's the problem, Master?"

"I gotta go number two."

"Wait."

Well, you can't wait: You're a kid. So I shit my pants. And it stunk. And I'm sitting in it. Then I walked down the steps at the end of the day and the shit was falling down my leg and everybody was laughing at me. It was one of the worst days of my life. I came home and said, "Ma, the nun is torturing me. She wouldn't let me go to the bathroom and I made in my pants and I had to sit in it all day."

Where did they come up with these tortures? One time a nun threw me into a pitch-black cloakroom for hours. Well, you're thirteen, and your imagination starts running, and the coats turn into monsters and the arms of the coats start moving. I was screaming bloody murder, but the nun wouldn't let me out. I had to sleep with the light on in my bedroom after that, I was so traumatized.

Their major punishment was cracking your knuckles with a ruler till they bled. I'd be talking or I didn't have my homework or whatever, so she'd march me up to the front of the room in front of the whole class. I'd put my hand out and she'd whack my knuckles four or five times. It hurt big-time. But if you moved, you'd get ten more smacks.

One time I made the mistake of bringing my toy soldiers to school. I was playing with them in the back of the class. The nun came up, took the toys, and then dragged me over to the metal wastepaper basket.

"Now you sit in it," she said.

"In the basket?"

"Yes."

My legs had rim marks around them when I got out. I couldn't walk: I was hunched over for hours. These were cruel and unusual punishments. Today, if you slap your own kid they put you in jail. But those nuns got away with all that shit. So after nine years of torture, I went to my mom.

"Ma, this ain't right. I got one more year to graduate. Let me go to public school, please!"

Thank the Lord, she agreed and I went to P.S. 122.

In retrospect, that might not have been the smartest move. Sure, I got away from those sadistic nuns, but now I was facing big black guys, huge Hispanic guys, tough Italian guys who were left back year after year. We were fifteen and they were nineteen! They always sat at the back of the room and called you out so they could kick your ass and get your lunch money. I wouldn't take shit from nobody. I would turn around and say, "What's your problem?"

"What's *my* problem, motherfucker? You'll see after school."

I was fucked. I'd try to go out the back way; they'd be waiting there. I'd try another way, but they'd have that covered, too. Then I'd get my beating. One guy would grab me in a headlock, another guy would punch me in the ribs a few times, punch me in the stomach, throw me to the ground, and then they'd both stomp on my head. I'd go home with a ripped shirt and black eyes and my mother would say, "What the hell happened to you?"

"I got beat up again."

My dad had his own advice.

"If he's bigger than you, hit him in the back of the head when he doesn't see it coming. If he doesn't go down, hit him in the head with a brick. I don't care what you got to do, there is no such thing as fair fighting. Fight to win."

My uncle George had the same attitude. "Get a bat. Wait until after school, come behind him, and break his knees with a bat." I got really good with a bat. In fact, I still carry a bat in my car to this day.

But what they didn't factor in was that these weren't one-on-one fights. I was going up against organized gangs. There were no gangs in Catholic school. In public school there were fourteen gangs and I was getting beat up almost every day, so I had to get into a gang for self-preservation. If you weren't in a gang, you were a pigeon.

I got in the Young Lords, along with my best friend, Jerry Nolan. Eventually, as you got older, you'd graduate to the Phantom Lords. They were one of the top gangs. The Phantom Lords were always in the news for killing other gang members, racketeering, robbery. They were really gangstery guys. That's what you'd aspire to. Isn't that great?

Gangs were all about turf. The Young Lords and the Phantom Lords were predominately Puerto Rican, but where we lived the kids were mainly Irish and Italian. If other gangs would try to come into our neighborhood, the word would get out to the Puerto Ricans and then they would come down and whoever had come, they'd get scared shitless and leave. You didn't want to fuck with the Lords. We were really like wannabes. They let us fight next to them, but we weren't as badass as these Puerto Rican guys.

One of the things we used to do was pick on the Hasidic Jewish who lived in the neighborhood. I was hanging out then with a bunch of asshole kids who were really prejudiced, so we'd chase the Hasids, knock their hats off, pull their curls, and kick their asses.

My aunt Rose, my uncle George's wife, was Jewish. She was an absolutely gorgeous woman with the body of a movie star and long black hair. I'd go over to her house and eat matzo ball soup and gefilte fish, and I loved it. I'd even visit her mom's house and eat herring with cream sauce. One day I was sitting there looking at her mom's menorah and the Sabbath candleholders and it dawned on me that they were the same as the Hasidic kids: They were all Jewish. I loved Rosie and her mom, so why was I knocking these Hasidic kids' hats off? "What a piece of shit," I thought. "What's wrong with you? Are you a Nazi, running around beating up people who don't deserve to be beaten up, just like you get beaten up after school?" I never messed with the Hasidic kids after that.

Don't get me wrong, I wasn't an angel. I got into a lot of fights when I was running with the Lords. I used a stickball bat and I would get my shots in. I hit a guy once with an aerial from a car, wrapped it really good around the neck. Got hit with one, too. This black guy snapped an aerial on my head and the ball from the top of it stuck in my head. I had to go to the hospital to get it pulled out. I still have a hole there that hurts when I touch it. I've been in knife fights, been cut by razors, cut by a meat cleaver.

Sometimes the wounds were self-inflicted. One time I was being chased by a bunch of guys on the south side of Brooklyn. I didn't know the neighborhood that well and it was dark. I ran down an alley between two buildings to escape them, and I ran right into a brick wall and knocked myself out. I woke up the next day with a big cut on my head.

Eventually I got a little reputation for being a tough guy and I worked my way up to war counselor. That was the guy in charge of the weapons that we'd use in our rumbles, whether it was bats or chains or switch-blades. I started thinking that there might be some money in this shit, and I began to build zip guns and sell them for five bucks a pop. I used to hide the zip guns I made in a vent in my grandmother's bathroom. I'd unscrew the four screws, put six or seven guns up there, and put the vent back on. Sure enough, my uncle George found them. I came home one day and he and my grandmother were sitting there with the guns on the table.

"This has got to stop," he said.

"Okay, Unc. I won't do it anymore, promise," I lied.

Then my grandmother, who knew me well, said, "Bullshit!" and she took a broom and broke it over my head. I thought I would have to go to the hospital, my head hurt so much. They dumped the guns in the sewer and my gun-toting, gun-selling days were over. But I still had my knives.

Sometimes I'd take a girl to the movies. The best movies were at the RKO theater on the south side. But that wasn't on our turf—it belonged to the Jesters, a tough all–Puerto Rican gang. If you went alone, just you and her, you didn't know if you'd get home alive. A lot of times on the way out, I'd take a beating with a bat. One time me and a bunch of the guys from the gang took our girls to the RKO to see Tony Curtis and Kirk Douglas in *The Vikings*. We figured we could see the movie, slip out at the end, and we wouldn't get snagged. It didn't work out that way. Sure enough, every member of the Jesters was watching the movie that particu-lar Sunday afternoon.

"We're fucking outnumbered. We're going to have to fight these guys, and we're gonna get killed. I'm not up for this shit," I moaned.

When it really got down to it, everybody got punky quick because we weren't really bad guys. I could fight with best of them, but I'd rather not: I'd rather just look like a badass and not really *be* the badass, but some-times you had to stand your ground.

We came out of the theater, and there were about thirty of them out-side waiting. They had aerials from cars, chains, and a baseball bat with a nail through it. So immediately it was like, *"Run!"* and everybody just took off. They didn't bother with the girls, but they ran right after us. I was running down the street and I tripped into a bunch of garbage cans and this Puerto Rican kid was right behind me and he grabbed a garbage can lid and started beating my head in with it. I was holding my hands up to protect my head and he was beating my hands and my knuckles started bleeding. There was blood all over my clothes. I popped my switchblade out, turned around, and boom, the blade went right up his armpit and out through his shoulder. He started screaming in Spanish and I just took off. I turned around and saw him pull it out, and there was blood squirting out of his shoulder. I couldn't believe it. He was the first and only guy I've ever stabbed. But it was him or me.

I wasn't raised in a violent family. The only two times my father beat me, I had it coming. I was basically a good Italian-German-Irish kid who didn't want to get his ass beat every day in school. Now I was seventeen years old and after three years of this shit, what did I have to look forward to? Becoming a member of the Phantom Lords? Those were the guys you see in prison for life with tattoos all over their necks and teardrops tattooed on their faces. They were real killers. Stealing cars, robbing stores, assassinating people. But my best friend Jerry Nolan and I weren't sociopaths. We certainly didn't want to die. And by then, both of us had found something to beat on besides other people's heads. We both had drum sets, and we both saw music as the antidote to these mean streets.

And as usual, my mother was right there, steering my moral compass. "Do you see Jimmy boy play drums?" she'd lecture me. "Does your friend Louie play drums? How about Peter Cudereski? No. The only person you know who plays drums is Jerry. Well, Jerry was born to play drums and so were you. You both got gifts from God. Don't waste it. You're going to break my heart if you stay with this gang stuff, because you'll wind up in jail or dead."

I don't know if she really believed that. I was working while I was in school, and whenever I got paid, I'd bring her my full paycheck; she'd take a few bucks out and give me the rest. That's how it was in Brooklyn. She's feeding you, she's raising you, you owed it to her. It was all about respect.

"God gave you a gift, your music," she'd continue. "I want to see you have a great life, hit the top. I want to see my son have everything a boy should have and more."

Who could argue with that?

CHAPTER TWO

"**Y**ou came out of my womb dancing," my mother would always tell me. Whether or not that's true, there was a bit of genetic predisposition for me to love music. My dad loved to dance. He was a great ballroom dancer, but when he got loaded he used to improvise and do the strangest dances I'd ever seen. Unlike my mother, he hated Elvis and rock 'n' roll. My father loved big-band music, Benny Goodman, Artie Shaw, Gene Krupa—that's what he called *real* music. He did like the Beatles, though.

My mom loved music, period. She could sing like an angel. She sounded just like Dinah Washington. For a German-Irish woman, she had a wild hair up her ass and she just fell in love with rock 'n' roll. She'd always have the radio blasting Elvis and Gene Vincent and Bill Haley and the Comets.

But when I was about almost ten, I heard a song that my father was playing, Benny Goodman's "Sing, Sing, Sing." And the rhythm of Gene Krupa's drums hit me like a lighting bolt from heaven. That was it for me. I wanted to be that guy playing the drums. Forget about being a fireman: I knew, deep down inside, that my destiny was to play drums. Even when I was five, I'd turn over my mother's pots and pans, took her forks, butter knives, or wooden spoons, and began banging away. I got addicted to it. My father would complain that I was making too much noise, but my mom really liked it. "Let him alone," she'd say. "There could be a lot worse things he'd be doing."

I became obsessed. When I wasn't banging on the pots, I'd figure out ways to play real drums. Whenever I'd go to a relative's wedding, I'd get my chance. They'd rent out the local Knights of Columbus hall and the women would bring cold cuts and potato salad and they'd hire out a little trio band. And as soon as they took their break, boom, I'd be up on the drums, banging away.

When I was seven, my parents bought me a toy set of drums, endorsed by one of my favorite TV programs, *The Rootie Kazootie Club*. It was a bass drum with two drums attached. I broke the toy, I played it so hard. My next set of drums was a makeshift set that my dad assembled. He bought a busted-up old army marching-band snare drum at a hockshop and rested it on top of a wooden box. For cymbals, he took two garbage-can lids, attached some nails to them so you'd get that sizzle when you hit them, and soldered each lid to a thin mop stick. Then he put the sticks into buckets of cement to keep them stable. I put some stars and glitter on the front of the box and wrote out the name STARS, which is what I named my imaginary band. I would then sit on a chair on top of some phone books and play the snare with brushes.

I set up the drums in my mother's bedroom and I practically never left the room, playing along to the songs on the radio. When I was twelve, I came across a white doo-wop group that used to sing down the street and I hung around them until eventually they let me sit in and back them with my brushes and my snare and the garbage-can lids. These guys would be down in the basement singing "Da-da dom, ba-da dom," and there'd be a little twelve-year-old kid back there playing away, those old C-F-G-minor oldies but goodies, over and over.

By the time I was fifteen, I got a job delivering meat on the weekends for a local butcher shop. The owner knew I was into drums, and one day he told me, "I've got a set of Slingerland Radio King drums down in my cellar that I don't play anymore. There's a twenty-four-inch bass drum, a trap case with a snare, a couple of cymbal holders, and a tom-tom. They were made in 1935, and they were originally mother-of-pearl, but they turned yellow."

Slingerlands! The brand that Gene Krupa used.

"You're kidding me! Would you sell them to me?" I burst out.

"Yeah, I'll sell them to you for two hundred dollars," he said.

I rushed home and I asked my mom and dad if I could get those drums.

"If you want them that bad, why don't you work for them?" my mom suggested. "We don't have two hundred dollars, but you can pay them off a little out of each paycheck."

So every weekend Joe would take fifteen bucks out of my pay, and he paid me a little more to mop the floors of the tenement building the shop was in, and eventually I paid them off. I'll never forget bringing them home to my grandmother's apartment. I was walking down the street with the bass drum on my back, kicking the trap case in front of me inch by inch with the tom-tom on top of it. I finally got the whole set up the stairs and into the kitchen. When I took them out of their cases and set them up, it was like an orgasm. If I could have slept with those drums, I would have.

But then I had a major problem. I didn't know how to play with a full set. I always just played on a snare drum. But my friend Jerry Nolan had a beautiful set of red sparkle drums and he gave me my first lesson. One hand kept a steady beat and the other was going pop, pop, pop. I worked on that beat everywhere I went, even on the train (which is a great place to hear unusual rhythms when the train wheels hit the tracks), and I finally got it. That was like opening up Pandora's box. I learned a million different beats from that one beat.

I was a slave to those drums. I cleaned them and buffed them, so proud that this was something I worked for and got. I'd come home from school for lunch and play the whole hour. I'd play them all night until I had to go to bed. The kids outside would say, "Oh, man, why don't you come on down and play stickball?" I'd say, "Nah, it's cool, I gotta just play." I wanted to play my drums much more than I wanted to be in a gang. Jerry and I began to cultivate other role models, guys who didn't have tattoos on their necks. Guys like Dave Brubeck and Miles Davis and Cal Tjader.

We found a way out of the gang life through social clubs. The clubs were a great institution. You'd rent out a store and get members to pay dues to cover the rent. Then you'd blacken out the windows so nobody could see in and put up some cool things on the walls. You'd put a juke-box in the front room and lots of couches all over, even in the back room. We found an old deli that went out of business, rented the space, and called our place Club Gentlemen. Jerry designed a logo with a top hat, a cane, and two white gloves. I became the president; Jerry was the vice president. Our rent was like sixty-five dollars a month, but it was easy to cover because we got the Mob to put a jukebox inside and we got a piece of the proceeds.

Once you entered, it was pitch black except for a few red and blue lights. Which was the perfect environment to start experimenting with sex and drugs. I was about fifteen when I got introduced to Mary Jane. Pot was spooky then—it was so taboo. This older guy we called the Dirty Swede would sell us a skinny little joint for a buck. That was okay money in the early sixties, so two guys would chip in and buy one. We'd go down in the basement and it would be pitch black and we'd light up. Immediately that eerie smell would hit you and you knew you were doing something forbidden. You feared that you might get addicted and get into heroin: All that propaganda was out then. I didn't even get high the first time we did it, but the second time was the charm. Jerry and I just laughed and ate a million Twinkies and listened to the jukebox. Music had never sounded so good before. Eventually I brought my drums into the club and I'd get high and play along to the jukebox, which was a lot more fun than playing to the radio.

Having the club was a godsend. It certainly kept us off the streets. But I'd be remiss if I didn't mention the biggest attraction to having a social club. You'd bring a chick to the club, turn on the jukebox, give her some wine or pot, dance a little bit, and then, if you were lucky, take her to a couch in the back room and get laid.

Now, if music was in my blood, so was sex. My dad was very horny. He was always chasing my mother around to get laid. She'd be like, "Get your dirty hands off me!" I was always incredibly open with my mother: We could talk about anything. One time, years later, I was visiting with my parents and my dad went off into the other room.

"Hey, Ma, did you ever give Dad head?" I asked her.

"What? Are you serious?" She frowned. "Do you think I would do something that filthy with your father? That's disgusting. Get away from the table, you're making me sick to my stomach. I think the music is making you crazy."

I knew that they had missed that boat. For them it was just do it and have a kid. They were old-school people.

I learned from an early age the difference between sex and love. The first time I fell in love was in summer camp. It was a Catholic camp, and it was really scary for a kid from the streets going out to the country by himself. I cried my eyes out that first night. This nun came around with a strap and slapped the shit out of whoever cried, so I had to stick my head in the pillow and muffle my sobs. But there was this nurse there who was just beautiful, and I fell in love with her. I was so crazy about her, I would scratch myself just so I could have her fix it.

But having sex itself was far from that romantic. My uncle George got me my first blowjob. I was around thirteen when he came over one night. He was loaded.

"I gotta go down to the bar," he said. "Why don't you come with me and I'll get you a Coke and some potato chips." I always dug visiting with my uncle at his bar, so I went.

My uncle would hang out with his friends at the end of the bar and I would sit at a nearby booth because it was illegal for a minor to sit at the bar. Right around the corner at the end of the bar were the bathrooms and a big phone booth and then the kitchen. I was sitting at the booth and I watched as one by one, my uncle's friends went back to the kitchen area. I wondered what they were doing back there. Then my uncle came over to me.

"Do you want to try something that you'll never forget? But you can't tell your mom or Nanny!"

"Sure, Uncle George," I said.

His friends were all laughing, getting a kick out of this. One guy said, "Send the kid in, break his cherry." So Unc told me to go back to the phone booth. In the booth was a forty-something dirty blonde, skinny, somewhat attractive. I was scared shitless. I'd never been with a girl, let alone a grown woman. She sat me down in the booth and got down on her knees and pulled down my little jockey shorts and I got my dick sucked for the first time in my life. It didn't take long, trust me. When I came back out to the bar area, I was white as snow and the men were hysterical.

I started getting a steady diet of blowjobs a few years later when I worked at the butcher shop. The three butchers were real horny Italian guys. They had *Playboy* centerfolds plastered all over the walls of the back room of the shop. That was the first time that I saw a centerfold with the big tits and great ass. I didn't have anything like that at home, so I'd always find an excuse to go to the back room and whack off looking at those pictures, keeping one eye on the door so I wouldn't get caught.

Every Friday night, after they cleaned up and prepared for the big Saturday rush, they'd bring a broad in to blow them in the back bathroom. A lot of these women came in, sadly enough, for food. I remember one who had kids and her husband had just left her and they would give her two huge shopping bags full of meat for blowing them. It was quite an education, that little shop.

One Friday night, one of the guys came over to me.

"We're going to get you laid."

I thought that was pretty cool. I had had a blowjob, but I'd never lost my cherry.

"Go in the bathroom in ten minutes and she'll be waiting for you."

I waited and then I went in and there was this thirty-something black woman sitting there. She was attractive but a little bit chunky with huge boobs.

"Hi, honey," she said. "I know you're a little nervous, but it's gonna be fine. Sit down."

I sat down on the toilet seat, petrified. She sat down on top of me and took my dick out and tried to put it in her but it wasn't even there. It disappeared. All I can think was that there was a big black naked woman sitting on top of this skinny little Italian boy. I couldn't get it up, but she just laughed and said, "Don't worry about it, honey. I'm gonna go out there and tell 'em you were the best, man. You put them to shame." And she did.

I eventually lost my virginity with a neighborhood girl and I went on to conquer quite a few of them on the couches of our social club. But I lost my real virginity to the first girl that I loved and didn't just fantasize about, like that nurse. Her name was Denicia and she lived downstairs from my friend Jerry Nolan. She was half Spanish and half Irish, a tall, willowy, blue-eyed blonde. I was smitten from the moment I laid my seventeen-year-old eyes on her. When I met her I was pretty wild, going to social clubs with Jerry, fooling around, but this was the real thing, I thought. This was love.

I'll never forget the first time we slept together. My grandmother was working, so I told Denicia to cut school that day and come over. Oh, my God, it was exciting. I didn't use protection, like an idiot. We didn't think of that, we just did it. I really got into it and the minute I put it in, I came. But I was young, so, boom, it popped right back up, and the fucking thing wouldn't stay down. We did it a couple of times more. I felt like this was a sacred screw, not just getting laid by some black whore who was coming in for some lamb chops. This was marriage screwing. And I wanted to get married.

As much of a rebel and an outcast as I was, I still believed in the notion that there was stability in family life. You get married, you have kids, you get a house on Long Island. I had those ideas instilled in me. So after going out with Denicia a couple of years, I started thinking that I wasn't going to be a rock star and I should get a good job and have the white-picket-fence life. And this was the girl to do it with.

So I went to a pawnshop and I bought an engagement ring for $150. Now we were engaged. My mother was ecstatic: She was crazy about Denicia. My sister Nancy, not so much. Denicia actually got into a fist-fight with my sister and my sister beat the shit out of her.

In the end, I was just kidding myself with the marriage thing. I was much too young to get married and settle down. And I was not nice to Denicia. Sometimes I'd get really nasty and treat her like shit. I thought I was Mr. Badass. But eventually she found a badder ass, a biker, and she gave me back my ring. I was crushed. I spent the whole summer crying in my grandmother's bedroom. It took me years to get over her.

I was so confused then. I was going to a vocational high school in downtown Brooklyn called George Westinghouse. The Vietnam War was heating up, and everybody told me that I had to have a trade, like an electrician or a plumber. So I went to Westinghouse and somehow I started taking dental mechanics. It seemed like an easy course, and I liked that you got to wear long white doctor-type coats.

I quit my job at the butcher shop and got a job at my uncle George's bar in the summertime. It was a nightmare. There I was, eighteen years old, and when I went to open at seven A.M. there were already barflies lined up to get some drinks before they went off to work. One of these guys would shake so bad that he'd have me pour him a drink, then he'd take his tie off, take the thin end of the tie and tie it around his wrist, then put the tie on around his neck and use the tie to get the glass to his mouth. By his third shot he'd get better and the shakes would go away and he'd say, "Okay, I got to go to work." He was there every fucking morning.

One time a black guy came in and had a few drinks. Then he said, "I'm not going to pay you."

"You'd better fucking pay me," I said, and I pulled out the machete that my uncle kept behind the bar.

So he pulled out a gun.

"Oh, yeah, fuck you," he said, and left.

I dropped the knife and peed my pants.

I wasn't into working at the bar, and I really wasn't into becoming a dental mechanic. Music was still in my blood, and I was soaking it up every chance I could. I'd go to the big Easter Sunday shows at the Brooklyn Academy of Music downtown. Murray the K was a big celebrity deejay then, and he would host the shows. For something like $3.50 you'd see fifteen acts, one after another, just constant music. You had Jan and Dean with the California sound, then Dionne Warwick and the girl groups like the Crystals and the Ronettes and the Shangri-Las singing "Leader of the Pack." I loved Smokey Robinson and the Miracles. I saw Little Stevie Wonder with his harmonica doing "Fingertips Pt.1," one of the first big Motown hits. And these great groups just totally took you out of the depression of Brooklyn, the gangs and the fighting and the illnesses. They just grabbed hold of your soul, and it soared and it was beautiful.

Jerry Nolan was my partner in crime on these musical expeditions. He was an Irish army brat. We would go to school together for a couple of years and then he'd disappear for a year or so and live in the Philippines and then he'd be back, a little more seasoned than I was from all his travels. When he was around we were inseparable. Deep down, we both wanted to be drummers and to be famous someday. Jerry's dad made money so he always had nice clothes, much nicer than mine. He would take me shopping and style me. He was very flamboyant and charismatic, and my father thought he was like Gene Krupa—that he was the greatest drummer on the planet. He'd go "Jerry this" and "Jerry that." I was so jealous that he thought Jerry was better than me.

Our first love was jazz. We'd dress up in our three-piece suits and slick back our hair and go to the Village Vanguard to see people like Brubeck and Mingus and Monk. But then as our musical palette expanded and Motown was coming in, we got into the Temptations and the Four Tops. Then Phil Spector blew me away. When I heard "Be My Baby," my balls hit the floor. The sound he got on drums was unbelievable compared to any recorded jazz drumming.

After a while, we started hanging out in Washington Square Park in the Village. Now, instead of suits, people were wearing sweatshirts with the sleeves cut off and chinos with sandals. We'd go to the coffee shops and you'd see Bob Dylan walking in, or Joan Baez. I got to meet the Loving Spoonful, and we'd sit in and play with them at the Night Owl Café. The Village was the place to be.

That's where we realized that Vietnam was *not* the place to be. People were going thousands of miles from home to die in some jungle. For what? We were savvy enough not to fall for that war. So when Jerry and I got our draft notices, that letter that began with "Greetings," we were petrified.

"Let's say we're gay," I suggested.

"Let's say we're junkies," he countered. "They'll never take us."

So we stuck needles in our arms, putting pinholes in the veins, and reported for our physicals at Whitehall Street. Jerry, being an army brat, had connections, and he was the only son in the family so he immediately got out on a hardship thing. But I was stuck. So I filed in and saw the army shrink.

"Are you gay?" he asked me.

"Absolutely," I said.

"Do you have any issues with carrying a gun?" he asked.

"Nope. If I had a gun I'd shoot the captain before I went over any hill."

I was full of bravado, but in the end what got me out of the service were my flat feet.

While I was exploring the city's musical scenes, I hooked up with a band back in Williamsburg. The Barracudas used to practice in the cellar of a building that the bandleader's parents owned. His name was Carlos Cancel, and he was about twenty-one. Carlos and his friend Alan Rosen both played guitar and they had a sax player and Carlos's brother played drums. I was only about seventeen, but I would stand outside and listen to them practice. One day I got to meet Carlos, and he told me that his brother had just gotten married and was quitting the group.

"Come on down and play with us," he told me.

I lived about fifteen blocks from them, so my mother helped me bring my drums over to the cellar. She waited outside on the street while I auditioned, and finally I came out.

"Ma, I got the gig!" I said.

Our first job was a bar mitzvah. I had to wear a yarmulke on my head and play "Hava Nagila." We got paid twenty-five dollars and we got to eat. It was great, my first professional gig. Of course, I gave my mom half of my earnings.

After that we played bars, weddings, everything. Eventually we got a steady job at a local Mafia hangout called the King's Lounge. The guys would come in with pinkie rings. "How you doin'?" they'd say, and they all had their gal with the big boobs.

Little did Carlos know it, but it was because of him I finally decided that I was going to make music my career. One night, he and I went up to see Joey Greco and the In Crowd play at the Metropole, on Broadway and Fifty-eighth Street. The Metropole was one of the hottest places to see music in the city. There was a long bar at the front of the place with a floor-to-ceiling mirror behind it and a bandstand where both the bands and these go-go girls would perform. It was nonstop music from morning to night, and a huge crowd would gather outside on the sidewalk to watch the girls and listen to the bands.

When we got there, I was talking to Joey, who I knew from the Village. He told me that his drummer broke his leg and asked if I'd replace him for this gig, which was going to run the whole summer. I didn't even care about the $125 a week I could earn. I was ecstatic because Gene Krupa was playing there at the same time.

Krupa was my idol. It was my dream to meet him, and now I had a chance to open for him! To me he was the gold standard, the greatest drummer in the world, greater than Buddy Rich, greater than Joe Morello, greater than Louie Bellson. I must have seen his biopic *The Gene Krupa Story* a hundred times. I used to go home and slick back my hair and try to move like him.

I started the gig and I got to see him up close. He was one of the nicest gentlemen you'd ever want to meet, but you could tell he was not happy at this juncture of his life. This was not the Krupa who played with Benny Goodman's big band, not even the Krupa who had his own forty-piece band. He had been busted for pot, for possessing two joints, in the forties, and he'd spent most of his money fighting the charge but still had to do a three-month sentence. That took a lot out of him. Then the swing era faded but he still did well in the bebop period. So now he was fifty-two but he looked like sixty-two. His hair was graying and he seemed a little bit broken. I remember walking past his dressing room one night and he was sitting in front of the mirror, smoking and drinking from a bottle of J&B scotch, slowly putting his bow tie on because he always wore a tux. It was a haunting, melancholy image, to see my hero like that. How the mighty could fall.

But I was still in awe of Gene. I must have been a pain in his ass, telling him how I worshipped the ground he walked on, but he was always cordial. He showed me a few things on the drums and he always encouraged me.

"You got it, kid," he'd say. "You could be something someday."

My heart swelled to hear that coming from his lips.

That was all I needed to hear. About halfway through that gig, I confronted my mother. I was in my second year of high school then.

"I want to quit school. I want to play in a band and I promise you, I'll make it," I said.

"You don't have to give me a whole spiel," she said. She really didn't have a problem with me not going back to school. She knew I hated it. She knew that playing in clubs would keep me off the streets. And she remembered a pledge I had made to her one day when we were walking past Madison Square Garden: "Ma, I'm going to play that hall someday," I vowed.

My father went along with it, too. He hated the aggravation of me going out late at night, not knowing where I was, especially when I came home with cheap wine on my breath and an attitude.

But my grandmother was having none of it.

"Don't worry, I'm going to make it with my music," I told her.

"Bullshit! Get a job! Get a haircut! Finish school. I don't want to hear about this drum stuff," she ranted. "You're nuts. Get a real man's job, become a cop or a fireman."

But there was no turning back now. I had gotten a taste of the night-life in the city. I was taking home a nice chunk of change, enough to buy my first chrome snare drum. Now I could get some cool threads. And I was meeting girls who were paying attention to me when I was up on that stage. Finally, no one was picking on me. I didn't have to fight to get attention. I was getting love through music, which was the only way to go.

CHAPTER THREE

I *had a taste of Broadway, but after the gig at the Metropole was over* I was back at the King's Lounge in north Williamsburg, playing for the boys with the pinkie rings. One night a guy came up to me during a break.

"I want my nephew to sit in and play," he said.

I was a cocky kid then. I had a Beatles haircut and I was wearing a black vest with a polka-dot tie and a white shirt and tight pants and Beatles boots.

"Nobody sits in on my drums," I dismissed the guy.

He threw a fifty-dollar bill on my bass drum. "The kid is going to sit in," he said firmly.

And then he gave me a look that could kill.

"No problem," I said meekly, and pocketed the bill.

It was harrowing playing at a Mob joint. I almost expected to see a bomb come in through the window. Every time the door opened and someone walked in, I was scared it might be a guy who was going to take a machine gun out from under his jacket and just level the joint. But one night in the summer of 1966, someone special walked through those doors. She was a tiny little thing with long, silky, beautiful black hair and a really cute face. I'd like to jump on that, I immediately thought. So I was all over her.

We talked between each break and she told me her name was Lydia DiLeonardo, a nice Italian girl. The next day was the Fourth of July, so I invited her to go to Coney Island with me. We got to the beach and I tried to be very cool. I lit a cigarette, the ash blew back in my eye, and I felt like an idiot. But once I got her on the sand, I was all over it. We were making out like crazy. I don't think it was love at first sight, but we kept seeing each other. She would come down on the weekends and see me play. We'd go to movies and hang out.

Eventually I asked her to go steady. Why not? She was really smart, going to school for bookkeeping. Back in Brooklyn, if you were going to bring a girl home to Mom and Dad, you wanted an Italian or an Irish or even a good Jewish girl. And Lydia to me was the Bella Donna, the Mother Mary. A real beauty. My parents loved her.

Her parents were another story. They were real Italians from Sicily. They had three sons and Lydia. She took me home for a Sunday dinner one night to meet them and it was right out of *Guess Who's Coming to Dinner?* The whole family was around the table, which had an abundance of food on it. Her dad was sitting at the head of the table with a gallon of homemade wine in front of him. Her mom and dad and her brothers kept looking me up and down. And they were seeing a skinny kid with hair down to his breast and they weren't liking the picture one bit. I may as well have been black or gay. I was the enemy. They despised everything that my long hair stood for. What's worse, I wanted to be a musician—not a dentist, not a car mechanic, not even a plumber. I was a bum in their eyes.

But we didn't care. After we started going steady, we had sex for the first time in Jerry Nolan's mom's bedroom. Then sometimes Lydia would cut school and come to my grandmother's house and we'd make love in the daytime. We had to keep things undercover back then, because if her family had found out they would have killed both of us.

And if Lydia had found out about Linda, she might have killed me. While I was dating Lydia, I was sneaking off to have fun with a foxy little blonde whose mother owned a funeral parlor. Linda was just sixteen, two years younger than Lydia, and I was crazy about her. I would take Lydia home, then sneak off to the funeral parlor where Linda and I would make out in the coffins, bizarre but true.

When I wasn't sneaking off to see Linda, I'd sneak off to see Jerry

Nolan. Lydia's parents lived just blocks from Jerry in Queens. After a date, I used to tell Lydia I was going home and then I'd go over to Jerry's house. We both wanted to be famous and we knew that image was everything, so we'd sit in front of a tanning lamp, then give ourselves facials with the creams and lotions that Jerry had. Jerry had gone to barber school and he'd razor-cut my hair. We looked like two gigolos!

When I met Lydia, I was still playing with the Barracudas. But that was getting old pretty quick. We were still playing instrumentals like "Tequila" and "Wipeout," along with some Motown and some Beatles and Stones. I was pushing to play Procol Harum or Hendrix. But Carlos was older, twenty-four or so, and he just didn't have that feel. He liked Motown but he wasn't that crazy about the British invasion bands.

Around that time I went to see my friend Joey Lucenti's band and he had a guy named Pepi Genneralli who played a mean Farfisa organ. Pepi was a great-looking blond, blue-eyed Italian chick magnet. He wasn't happy in his band either, so he joined the Barracudas and the two of us dominated the group. Eventually Carlos left and we got Joey Lucenti in on guitar and my friend Angelo Opper on bass and a guy named Tommy Ventimiglia on sax. We started doing Brit music along with Motown, and we called ourselves the Sounds of Soul.

We played all over the city. Trudy Hellers, the Night Owl, Café Wha?, the Purple Onion. We worked constantly, playing a month at each club. After a while, we all wore matching double-breasted suits and ties, and we looked sharp. We even got gigs out of town.

Back in 1967, it was amazing how much hatred and disdain you could generate just by wearing your hair long and dressing like Jimi Hendrix. But I didn't care. I wanted to look like a star all the time. Jerry called it "profiling." We'd sit in his apartment figuring out what to wear so that people would stare at us. We were total nonconformists, total rebels. In a way, we had just graduated to a different gang.

I'd leave my apartment wearing a purple satin shirt, gold pants, and a velvet jacket and walk to the subway. All along the way, the Puerto Ricans would whistle at me and call me *puta,* which means whore, or *paco,* which meant gay. They'd make kissing sounds and go, "Paco, paco, suck my dick, baby." But I didn't care. I was cool, as far as I was concerned.

Coming home it was a different story. My parents had moved to Greenpoint and they lived over a bar. I was back living with them and I had a cool room. I painted the ceiling black and put stars on it so it looked like a galaxy. My mom and dad even grew pot for me on their roof—that's how cool they were. (Of course, when I finally told them that that leafy green plant they were having so much fun cultivating was pot, they freaked out.) My dad would meet me at the subway at four in the morning when I was coming back from my gigs in the Village and help me with my drums. We had to push the drums fifteen blocks, and the Polish drunks who were coming out of the bars would ridicule me. If I didn't have a gig, if I had just been clubbing in the Village, they would chase me all the way home and if they caught up to me, they'd push me around and pull my hair, pull out a switchblade and threaten to cut it off. I used to think, You motherfucker, five years earlier I would have fucking broken your knees with a bat. But now I wanted to be a rock star, so I had to endure it.

I even got that shit on the road. One time the Sounds of Soul were playing in upstate New York and we got hungry. We pulled into a truck stop, and they sent me in to get some food. I sat down, ordered some hamburgers to go, and these two huge truckers sat down on either side of me. One of them leaned over to the other and said, "I bet you I could punch him so hard that my fist could come through his brains." Then the other guy described what torture he'd do to me. They started calling me Goldilocks, and I freaked out and ran out the door. And they ran after me.

Tommy was driving and he saw me running toward the van with these two huge truckers hot on my heels, so he started to take off. Meanwhile, Pepi opened the back door of the van and just as I caught up, he grabbed me and pulled me in. We turned around and gave those two assholes the finger.

The Sounds of Soul came to an end when our sax player, Tommy, got drafted and went to Vietnam. We were devastated, but we carried on. We wanted to play more originals, so we changed our name to the Brotherhood and began to slip some originals into our set. That didn't go over too well with the uptown clubs.

"What the fuck was that shit?" the owner would storm over to us after the show. "I told you guys I wanted to hear 'Green Tambourine.'" And then we'd get fired.

Nineteen sixty-eight was a great time to be a musician. You could see the greatest bands in the world play in the East Village at Bill Graham's Fillmore East and at the Anderson Theater down the block. I'll never forget sitting up in the balcony of the Fillmore and seeing the Jefferson Airplane. I saw the Who premiere *Tommy* there. I saw Hendrix, the Doors, Savoy Brown, Arthur Brown, Van Morrison. My brain cells would just blow up hearing all that great stuff.

But the best was Steve Paul's nightclub, the Scene. All us young musicians would hang out there in the peanut gallery and wait for all the stars to come in and jam. One night I went there with Jerry and I saw Hendrix jam with Buddy Miles and Johnny Winter. My fucking balls hit the floor. One night Janis Joplin walked in with Jim Morrison after they had played a double bill at the Fillmore and Janis pulled a bottle of Southern Comfort out of her bag and kept topping off the glass of bourbon she ordered.

Another time, Steve Paul had managed to get his hands on an advance copy of the Beatles' *White Album*. When I first saw the Beatles on *The Ed Sullivan Show*, I was not that crazy about them. I loved the Stones then. But then I really got into the Beatles and their lyrics, and they changed my life. I started to wear a Sgt. Pepper hairstyle, I grew a mustache like Paul McCartney's, and then I got into the Lennon image, all in white with white sneakers and my hair long and straight down with the wire-rimmed glasses. Waiting for a new Beatles album was like waiting for a gift from the gods.

They locked the door at midnight and Steve Paul came out and said, "Shut the fuck up, everybody." You could hear a pin drop in the whole nightclub. And he played that album from side one to side four straight through and it was like God was speaking through those speakers. We took those songs to be law.

We would make our own music too, informally. Every Sunday we'd meet up at the fountain in Central Park and there'd be people jamming with guitars and bongos, people talking about music and politics, passing around joints.

All of this propelled us toward wanting to do more originals. By then, Pepi and I had connected with a guitar player named Kevin Reese and a bass player named Peter Shandis and we started a band called Nautilus. Pepi and I were the best musicians in the band; we kept the foundation solid. I wasn't the front man, but I sang most of our songs. Kevin was half black and half white with green eyes. He was gorgeous. He couldn't play that great, but he reminded me of a young Hendrix and he had great stage presence. In those days, it seemed that how you looked was almost as important as how you played. And he looked great. And so did Peter Shandis. He lived in the Village, and that was impressive in itself. He was a true hippie nonviolent love child, with one of those Byrds-type haircuts with the bangs. Great image, not so great a bass player. So we played the same club circuit, only with a heavier British Invasion–based sound.

We gigged all around the East Coast, but one of our mainstays was a club on Forty-second Street and Third Avenue called the Headliner. One afternoon in the fall of 1969 we were rehearsing there and this guy walked in accompanied by a knockout babe. He was in his thirties, blond, with thinning hair but really built, easily a two-hundred-pound guy. He had a bulldoggish look about him, like he was a guy you didn't want to cross. His girlfriend was a little bit younger, a flaming redhead with a gorgeous face and a knockout body. He introduced her as Kathy and said his name was Jack O'Brien, which was odd because he looked about as Irish as I was.

But what immediately captivated us was that he said he was a close friend of Bob Seger, whose group, the Bob Seger System, had just had its first hit. He had helped produce the album and he was tight with all the music people in the Detroit scene, he told us. He and his girlfriend were living in New York now and he wanted to get involved with a group, maybe manage them like Brian Epstein had done with the Beatles, or maybe even sing with them since he was also a singer. He said he had heard us play and he liked what he heard.

So after buying us a round of drinks, he invited the band up to his penthouse apartment to continue the discussion. I took one look at his huge diamond ring, his gold Rolex and gold jewelry, and Kathy's even bigger rock and I knew he was the real deal. This was the jump connection we so desperately needed. We followed him past his doorman and up to his pad. Looking out the big picture windows, we saw a spectacular view of the cityscape. And we were lapping up everything he was saying. "I'm gonna get you guys a deal, you're great," he enthused. "First of all, we gotta get you a decent PA system. Then we'll go out to our place on Long Island and you guys can hole up there and write and rehearse. I'll be coming out periodically and I'll sit in with you. We'll put a show together and get a deal. And don't worry, I'll pay for everything."

A few days later, Jack called and told us to get a U-Haul van. We met him and he told us to drive to some parking lot where he made us take the license plates off two cars and put one of them on our van. As tough as I was, I had never done anything like that in my life. It should have been a tip-off to us that Jack wasn't who he appeared to be. Then he had us pull the van in front of Manny's music store on Forty-eighth Street, where Kathy was sitting in a limo waiting for us. Both Jack and Kathy were wearing wigs that day and it struck us as a little strange, but we didn't think much of it. And we certainly didn't give it a second thought when two guys who worked at Manny's schlepped out this great Altec Lansing PA system and helped us put it into the van. Then Jack gave us some pills that were like speed and downers at the same time. After we got the PA to Pepi's dad's warehouse, I felt so weird I thought I was going to die. I crashed big-time, but I still had this lingering feeling that something was really weird.

We took all our equipment, including Pepi's B-3 Hammond organ, my set of drums, two big amps, some big Fenders, and the PA system, and drove out to Jack's house on Long Island. It wasn't a mansion by any stretch of the imagination, but the house was nice enough and he had a big basement where we set up our stuff. We started working on songs and Jack would come out every weekend, drop off some money for us, and listen to the stuff.

"Whaddya got?" he'd say, and we'd play him the songs. "That's pretty good," he smiled. We kept asking him to sit in and sing, but he kept putting us off. "I don't feel like it this weekend, my throat is bugging me today. Next time," he'd say. "But keep practicing. I like what I'm hearing." Then he peeled some cash off his roll and dropped it on the table. This went on for months and months. I was seeing Lydia then, and she'd come out occasionally to visit, but we were consumed with our music. This was our big break and we certainly weren't going to fuck it up.

After about five months of this, some doubts about what we were doing began to creep in. Every time we'd asked Jack to sing with us, he had some excuse. And we were getting cabin fever. We all wanted to get out and gig and try out the material we had been writing and rehearsing. Plus we started questioning just who this guy Jack really was. Every time he and Kathy would come out to the house, they were driving a different luxury car. And they'd retreat into their room, which had a huge padlock on the door. Plus it didn't take a brain surgeon to realize that both of them were cranked up on meth most of the time.

We wanted to confront Jack, tell him that we wanted out of there, but we were afraid to bring the topic up. One day, just before Jack and Kathy were due out, we all smoked some weed and Pepi decided that he was going to talk to Jack. That night, we were all sitting around the dinner table. Me and Pepi and Kevin and Peter were stoned on pot, giggling, but Jack and Kathy were tweaked out on speed.

"Look, Jack," Pepi suddenly said. "We're getting tired of this shit. We came here to make it, but all we're doing is rehearsing in the basement. We want to get out of here and play." The table immediately grew silent. Pepi went on a bit more about how we were just going to leave. Jack just sat there and stared at Pepi.

"Really?" he finally said. And then he picked up his glass and threw it at Pepi, hitting him square in the forehead. The glass shattered and Pepi began to bleed profusely.

"Anybody else got something to say to me?" Jack stared at Kevin and Peter and me. We were in total shock. I'll never forget his piercing, weird eyes.

"Hey, man, that wasn't cool," I managed to protest.

"Shut the fuck up," he snapped at me. "You ain't fucking going nowhere. That's the way it's gonna be. My way or no way."

The four of us freaked out.

Jack and Kathy retreated into their locked room, and when they came out, Kathy was wearing a wig and an outfit that made her look like a fifty-year-old woman and Jack had a mustache that made him look completely different.

"You guys just stay here and play," he said, and then they left.

I called Lydia and said, "We're going to get out of here. My buddy told me about a gig up in Kennebunkport, Maine. We could be the house band for this fraternity, and they'll pay us a salary. We'll live in the back of the bar, they'll feed us. We've just got to get out of here—this guy Jack is dangerous."

We snuck out, rented a truck, loaded it up, and took off and drove up to Maine. We were thinking, "Wow, we're free, we got away from this fucking guy, thank you Jesus! That's the last we'll ever see of Jack."

About halfway through the summer, we were playing one night and I looked out at the audience and sitting there at a table was Jack and Kathy. We all turned as white as ghosts. I remember Pepi saying, "Holy shit, he's in the audience." I didn't know what to say. It was probably the worst we ever played, everything was out of key, and you could hear our voices trembling when we sang. When we finished, the waiter came over and said, "There's a guy over there at the table who wants to buy you a drink."

So we went over to the table and we sat down and Jack said, "You guys weren't home when we got back. What's the matter?" I said, "Well, you hit Pepi with a glass. We were there already four or five months working with you, you never really sang with us, you said you were going to help us get a record deal. We wrote all these new songs, we wanted to try them out on an audience." I was going on and on.

"Well, don't worry now, everything has changed," Jack said. "I'm going to sing in the band, I got us a deal, we're going to go to Detroit and do our first recording." He had everything nice and rosy again.

"When are you finishing up here?" Jack asked.

"A couple more weeks," I said.

"Good, I'll come back up with Kathy and we'll help you bring the stuff back to Long Island. I want you to meet some of these new producers I got." He had it down.

So we decided to try it again. We went back to the Long Island home, and as soon as we had loaded everything back in, he looked at us and said,

"Guess what? Now you can't go fucking anywhere. You think you could fuck Jack O'Brien over and escape out of here?"

His whole disposition had changed. The next day, after Jack and Kathy left, we broke the lock and went into their room. We wanted to know just who we were dealing with. The first thing we saw was this big machine that looked like a counterfeit printing press. Our suspicions were confirmed when we opened up a drawer and saw piles of big-denomination bills taped up and stuffed into bags. Then we opened another drawer and there were stacks of checkbooks there, each one with a different name on it—Mr. Jerry Jones, Mr. and Mrs. K. Lawton, on and on. We opened the closet and there were wigs, fake beards, fake mustaches, old people's clothing, and makeup. Then we opened up one more drawer and found his arsenal. He had six Winchester rifles, a shitload of .38s, .45s, and 9-millimeters.

That night, Jack and Kathy returned. When they saw that we had broken into their room, Jack came back out with a cocked Winchester.

"All you motherfuckers are going to sleep together on the fucking living-room floor tonight. I tell you what, I've even got something to make sure you don't leave." And then he went into the room and came out with these two big Doberman pinschers. I have a fear of dogs, so I instantly just started shaking and freaking out. Pepi was like, "You've got to relax."

"Fuck you, look at these fucking dogs," I said.

Imagine how I felt, cowering on the living-room floor with a cranked-up maniac right out of *Justice Files* clicking his Winchester as he walked around and his large, vicious Dobermans circled their prey. Every so often Kathy would join the scene, and even she was packing a .38 in her blouse. I was now convinced that they were just going to cut us up, bury us in the backyard, and steal our equipment. I figured that they had done this before to other unsuspecting ambitious bands.

That night we lay there and then the next day, somehow or other they went out again and I escaped—I got out through this back door, shimmying through the little doggie flap. I must have walked miles, but I got to a phone booth and called Lydia. "You've got to call an army and the troops. Get Billy, the cook from Maine. He's got a van. You've got to come up and get us, because this guy is going to kill us and you're never going to see me again." And they did. A day went by and we told Jack, "Our friends are coming up to get us." He said, "Oh really?" And we said, "Yeah, they're coming up tomorrow." He said, "That could be a big mistake for everybody." And we thought it was going to be like a mass murder, that he would let them come in and then kill us all and leave.

That night the dogs circled us again. They would come up to my face and I could hear them breathing. Nobody slept a wink that night. The next day we were waiting with anticipation when we finally heard a horn blowing outside. A few seconds later, there was a knock on the door, and Jack opened it. We looked out and there was Lydia and Pepi's girlfriend and Billy the chef from Kennebunkport, Maine, who was driving his old fifties Chevy panel truck.

Jack put his Winchester out of sight and then walked outside to confront them. When he saw them all lined up, he realized that he couldn't shoot everyone, so our friends came in. We rushed down to the basement and started moving all our gear out of the house into the truck. The whole time Jack was standing outside with his two dogs, looking confused. Just as we got the last piece out into the truck and we were ready to leave, Jack came up to me.

"Someday I'm going to fucking kill you," he whispered ominously. "You're never gonna know when, but I'm gonna fucking kill you someday."

For many years, when I got up behind the drums, I used to get a feeling that it was gonna be—*boom!* God, I hope this book doesn't stir up an old vendetta. But somehow I don't think Jack made it to senior citizenship.

Now that I was back in the city with Lydia, I got the feeling that she was getting serious about our relationship. My relationship with Jerry Nolan had pretty much diminished, thanks to Lydia. She didn't really like him and he didn't really like her. Jerry and I were used to going everywhere together, and now there was my girlfriend tagging along. They used to argue all the time. I think Lydia wanted me all for herself.

Life with Lydia wasn't a bed of roses. We fought a lot. Brooklyn chicks were a breed unto themselves, hard and tough, and Lydia was one tough girl. She was short, but she had a raging temper. If I bopped her, she'd pick up whatever was near her and I'd get whacked with it. She took no shit from me. I think back and wonder how I could have done something so disgusting as hitting a woman. I would never do something like that now. But I did then.

Getting married would have been like putting gasoline on a fucking fire. So naturally we did it. I proposed to her in May 1969, right after we saw *Romeo and Juliet*. That movie just got to me. The next thing I knew I was saying, "Do you want to get married?" We used the theme song from the movie as our wedding song.

I told Lydia that I wasn't going to get a nine-to-five job and, because I had no money, I wasn't going to pay for anything, even the wedding. I was going to single-mindedly pursue my musical career until I made it big. So if we were going to wed, she'd have to work a nine-to-five job. Lydia had no problem with that: She believed in me, and she was prepared to be a good wife.

We got married on January 31, 1970. Being Italian, she wanted a big wedding in a big church, so she got a second job at a clothing store in the Village to pay for it. We had the reception in a big hall and I remember I was smoking a joint with Jerry and the guys in a room upstairs. "This is a fucking mistake. What are you doing getting married?" Jerry said to me. He was right. I wasn't ready to get married.

But the party was great. Nautilus played, along with the Costello Brothers, who used to open for us at the Headliner. My grandmother was there in a wheelchair because she had had a diabetic stroke by then. She wasn't really with the program, but she was there, God bless her. We continued the party back at Lydia's house later, smoking and drinking.

In the spring, we finally took our honeymoon. We got a joint passport to save money and then got on a plane for the first time in our lives. We went to Spain first—Madrid and Barcelona. We would sit in the outdoor cafés and drink wine all day and then walk around the city at night. But we saved the best for last. I had been pushing for England. I had ulterior motives. I made up business cards and left them everywhere we went. I thought maybe I'd get lucky and find someone looking for a drummer.

In the meantime, I made pilgrimages to the places that the Beatles played. In Piccadilly Circus, we went to see *Let It Be*, the Beatles' last movie. They were in the process of breaking up then and I just started crying like a baby. "Oh, my God. It's over, it's really over," I was babbling. I recorded the whole movie on a little tape recorder and listened to it over and over again.

I hated the food in England, but I loved the clothes. I went to one little store near Carnaby Street and I picked out this beautiful black-and-gold velvet jacket. The owner was a nice man. I told him I was a musician and I was hoping to make it, and he took some of my cards and then he told us about a club called the Speakeasy, a private after-hours club that was *the* place to go in the music world. He got us in and we went to see some up-and-coming guy named Elton John.

Seeing Elton was an epiphany for me. He played "Your Song," and I started crying—he was just so good. Each new song was better than the last one. I had never heard music like that in my life. While I was watching him play, I realized that I could never play "Knock on Wood" or "Foxy Lady" again. I had to play songs that had never been heard before.

The next morning we were getting set to go home. I put on my new velvet jacket, a pair of blue velvet bell-bottoms that I had just bought, a white T-shirt with red stars, and a white satin scarf. My hair was teased up like Jimi's, and I slipped on my shades and stood in front of the mirror in the hotel room and I said, "You are going to go home and get into an original band and you're going to make it. You're twenty-four, you're getting too old for this shit. Now is the time."

As soon as I got back to Canarsie, I disbanded Nautilus and put an ad in the *Village Voice* and went on a bunch of auditions, but nothing panned out. Then I got a call from a guy named Mike Brand. He and his writing partner, Peter Shepley, had just gotten out of college and wanted to start a band. Mike was loaded: He lived in the Village in a beautiful brownstone with his wife, Beck, who also came from big bucks. Peter was married to a girl named Eleanor, but they didn't have as much money. They had hooked up with this kid named Barry Minsky who wanted to be a rock manager. His dad was the famous nightclub owner who was the basis for the movie *The Night They Raided Minsky's*.

Mike and Peter told me that this Minsky guy knew Lou Merenstein, who did *Astral Weeks* with Van Morrison, as well as John Cale from the

Velvet Underground. I was impressed. I went to meet them in the Village, and they played me some of their songs. I loved them. They were like Frank Zappa meets the Rolling Stones meets country and western. I brought a bongo along and I jumped in, and we clicked right from the start. We decided to add a bass player and a guitarist.

We found our bass player in Queens, a big fat kid named Michael Benvenga. He loved speed—he could take four black beauties and sweat his ass off but keep playing forever. He and I played so well together that we started calling ourselves the Machine. Michael knew a Greek kid named Chris Aridas who played lead guitar. He actually sucked and was a rich kid with a shitty attitude, but they brought him into the band, over my objections.

I really bonded with Peter and Mike at first. We would meet in the Village every day and grab some sandwiches and roll some joints and write all day and night. I'd come home and tell Lydia, "This fucking band is it! This is the band!" We named ourselves Chelsea and auditioned for Decca Records. They loved us and gave us a contract. We recorded our album with Lew Merenstein producing. He brought in Larry Fallon, who did all the strings for *Astral Weeks,* and had John Cale play electric viola. Our music was so different, everybody thought we had a real shot at hitting the jackpot.

The album came out in February and we played a gig a few weeks later at a high school. Peter got completely fucked up on booze and passed out because he was so nervous about playing in front of people. Mike, on the other hand, got blasted on weed and couldn't remember the chords. I was furious.

"This is a fucking disaster," I screamed. "We can't just make records, we have to go out and play fucking shows. Peter, you gotta be Mick Jagger. You're the lead singer. You can't come out wearing fucking khakis and a short-sleeved shirt and then pass out. You gotta be a rock star."

I hadn't realized that those two guys had no experience playing before audiences. After the live disasters, Chris left the band. I was ready to quit, but then Mike and Peter came all the way out to my house in Brooklyn with a guy named Stan Penridge. He was going to replace Chris. At first I didn't like Stan at all. There was something creepy about him that didn't sit right with me. He was a Greek kid, very slick, very smart; they wanted him in the band, and I was outvoted again.

The album had come out to great reviews in all the music trades, but it went nowhere. It was just devastating to me that this band didn't make it. But we went back to writing. Stan lived in the Village, and I would bring a conga to his house and we'd get high and write all day. Then later Michael, the bass player, would come by after he got off work and the three of us would jam.

We got a gig in New Jersey with the new lineup. Peter and Mike were late to the show, so Stan, Michael, and I started without them. And the audience went crazy. When Pete and Mike finally showed up, the place was in an uproar. We knew right then that we wanted to be a power trio. That night, Lips was born.

We rehearsed for a couple of months and then played a club in Oceanside in October of 1971 as Lips. Then, naturally, it was back to the Headliner with my new band. In January 1972 we played a club called the Saint James Infirmary at the Hunter ski resort in upstate New York. We weren't getting paid much, but they'd feed us these great hot dogs and we seemed content. But then I'd get flashes of "Why am I doing this again?" I still had that drive to be a star, and I was convinced that I was a better musician than Stan and Michael.

Things were getting stagnant with Lydia, too. She was working and I was playing. I was in love, I guess. That's a big word. People love their dogs and their cars; they love skiing. But I had gotten married, so I had to be in love. Lydia was a good cook and she kept a clean house. The problem was money. She was so tight. We didn't have all that much money, but she was giving me only a buck a day to live on. She stuck by me, paid the dues with me, did all the things a wife does, but I was wild.

Part of the reason was her jealousy, especially if I got close to other guys. She wanted me all for herself. When you cage someone like that, forget about it when you let him out. Temptation is all around in rock 'n' roll, especially on the road. You would call your girl and tell her how much you miss her and then go back and get laid. The road never changed.

Another reason I cheated was that Lydia and I didn't really click in bed. She had no real experience; she had only gone out with two other guys before me. And the sex was never enough for me. I always had to have more, and on the road I could have one-nighters every night. I know now that if you really love someone, that's just not acceptable. But at that time I was young and wild and hungry for everything.

By April, Michael had left Lips and gone to work at a bank. I started hanging at Stan's East Village pad, and that was a huge mistake. He had been selling pot, but then he started getting into heroin and speedballs. Stan was a very manipulative guy, and he could talk anybody into anything. My dream was shattering once again, and I was ripe for an escape. So when Stan asked me if I wanted to try skin-popping smack, I said, "Why not?"

It didn't seem dangerous when Stan was doing it. He didn't pass out on the floor. It was more like, "We'll shoot a little dope and then we'll write some more songs." It was exciting, too. Shooting dope is definitely taboo. And it did nullify the pain. After shooting up, I didn't feel any nagging doubts about whether I'd ever make it in music, no feelings that I was getting too old, no sense that my marriage was in a rut. Everything felt perfect for those few hours with him. Everything we wrote sounded genius, everything we did was great, everything we talked about was just right. We were living in a fantasy world. Then I felt guilty and was afraid that I would get hooked on heroin, so I confessed to Lydia that I had been shooting up. She freaked out and I stopped.

But I kept going over to Stan's place to write. And he kept dealing smack. One day we were sitting up there working, and somebody buzzed from downstairs. We snuck down the stairs to see who it was and saw four tall, skinny black guys waiting by the elevator. They looked like you didn't want to fuck with them. So we ran back upstairs and bolted the door. Stan grabbed a rifle and I picked up his wife's knife. The guys came off the elevator and started pounding on the door and attempted to break in. They were after his drugs. I thought, I'm in the wrong place at the wrong time and I'm going to die over a shoebox of heroin. Finally they gave up and split. I was shaking like a leaf and wondering what this had to do with music. That was the last time I hung out at Stan's place.

Around that time I got a call from my old bandmate Joey Lucenti. He had a new band called Infiniti, his drummer had broken his leg, and he wanted to know if I'd fill in. They were playing every weekend at the King's Lounge, that Mob joint in Williamsburg. I had just left a band that was associated with giants like John Cale and Lou Merenstein. I had a brief taste of what it was like to be a real artist, creating new songs, and then I'd be back in a Mob bar playing fucking jukebox music. But Lydia was on my case to work, so I took the gig. I went there my first night and I came in with skintight gold-lamé pants, a scarf, nail polish, and New York Dolls makeup on. I was a star, at least in my mind. Joey and the other guys were bald and fat by then, in front singing, "Louie, Louie, whoa, we gotta go," and I was in the back crashing and booming away at my drums because I was so fucking mad at the world.

I was drinking a lot and fucking every single chick who walked into that room on the weekends, and then I'd go home to Lydia. It was intolerable. But at least it got me away from Stan and got me playing in front of an audience again. I thought that maybe somebody would come into the club and say, "Jesus, look at that guy. He's got talent." So I had Joey print up some business cards for me that read HAVE DRUM WILL TRAVEL, PETER CRISS. I had shortened my name when I was in Chelsea to Peter Cris, but somehow Joey added an extra *s* to my last name and I liked it.

So I started from scratch again. I had just turned twenty-six and I was desperate. I would have worn pantyhose and high heels and a Lone Ranger mask, I wanted to make it so bad. It was my time. I knew I had something special. Every place I ever drummed we'd get a bigger and bigger crowd, and when it would come time for me to play, people would go crazy. I knew I had charisma, that I had something that no one else had. I'd put ads in the *Village Voice* before, but then I decided to run a classified ad in *Rolling Stone*. That was where musicians found other musicians.

So I took out an ad. Twelve simple words.

EXPD. ROCK & roll drummer looking for orig. grp. doing soft & hard music.

CHAPTER FOUR

We were having a party at our house in Canarsie one Saturday night in April of 1972 when the phone rang. Lydia picked it up and then called out to me. "It's some guy who wants to talk to you about your ad." I was half in the bag from drinking Mateus wine and smoking some pot, but I took the phone from her.

"Hello, this is Gene Simmons, and I read your ad and I'd like to ask you a few questions," this guy said. He had a deep voice and enunciated each word like he was a teacher talking to a student.

"Uh, sure, shoot," I said. To be honest, I wasn't expecting much from this call. I had gotten a few responses to the ad and gone on a few auditions in the Village and one in Yonkers, but they were all really bad bands.

"How tall are you?" Gene asked.

"I'm five foot ten."

"Are you fat?"

"No, I'm nice and skinny." I was a fucking toothpick. I was a starving musician.

"Do you have long hair?"

"Yeah, it's down to my tits," I said.

"Would you consider yourself handsome, good-looking, or cute?"

Now it was a multiple-choice test? This was getting ridiculous. So I turned to my friends in the apartment, who had been listening to my answers.

"Am I good-looking?" I asked them.

"Fucking A!" they shouted.

"I'm fucking gorgeous," I said.

I had to give it to this guy. He was meticulous in his line of questioning, and he seemed to know exactly what he wanted from our conversation.

"Would you be willing to dress in drag?"

"Would I be willing to dress in drag?" I repeated the question for my audience.

"Absolutely. I have no problem with that. As a matter of fact, I'll play naked. I have a nine-inch dick."

Everyone in the room cracked up. There was silence on the other end of the line.

"Uh, okay," Gene finally said. He told me that he liked that I would be willing to do anything to make it, because he felt the same way. We talked for a long time and during the course of the conversation, he told me that he had a band with his friend Paul named Wicked Lester. They'd just done some recording and had a deal for the album, but it didn't come out, they didn't like the guys in the band, and they were looking to regroup. Somehow he made all this sound very positive. When he told me that his producer was Ron Johnson, I got intrigued. Ron Johnson was the engineer on my Chelsea album. And when he asked if I could come meet him and Paul at Electric Lady Studios in the Village, where they had recorded, I was floored. That was the studio Hendrix had owned. Now I really wanted to meet this guy who had been asking me all these ridiculous questions on the phone.

A few days later I put on my black-and-gold velvet jacket, along with gold satin pants, an emerald-green ruffled shirt, and green-and-burgundy suede shoes I had picked up in Spain. My hair was teased up in an Afro. I was the shit. I took the train to the Village with my brother, Joey, who came along for moral support. We got to Eighth Street a little early, so we stopped in to Shakespeare's for a few beers. Then I left Joey at the bar and walked over to Electric Lady. As I was about to go in, I looked over my shoulder and saw two guys leaning on a car. They were really nondescript—both of them had long hair and were wearing flowered hippie paisley shirts and jeans. They were staring at me as I rang the bell and went down the stairs to the studio.

I went up to the receptionist. "Is there a Gene Simmons and Paul Stanley here?"

"Yeah, they're waiting right outside," she said.

I went back outside, and sure enough, they were the two guys leaning against the car. Immediately I thought, "This fucking guy put *me* through the ringer about looking cool? These guys look like two fucking hippie panhandlers."

When they saw me approach them, they lit up. They told me later that they thought I was someone famous going in to record. As far as Paul was concerned, I was hired on the spot. He didn't have to hear me play, he was so impressed by the way I looked.

We made our introductions and went back in to hear their music. I couldn't believe I was in Hendrix's studio! It still had the curved walls, that alien-spaceship feel to it. We went into one of the rooms and there was Ron Johnson, my old engineer from my Chelsea days.

"Wow, Peter, what are you doing here?" he said.

We gave each other a hug and I told him I was being considered for Wicked Lester.

"You don't even have to audition him," Ron told Gene and Paul. "This is your guy. He's the shit." They seemed to like the sound of that. Ron put on their tape. Almost anything sounds good on studio monitors, but this really was good. It wasn't the type of music that I loved or played. It was a little too heavy for my taste. They obviously were into Zeppelin. But I knew I could cut it, and I thought that I could change the songs around in a way that they'd go for. I heard potential, something in this music I could sink my teeth into.

I suggested that Gene and Paul come see me play that weekend at the King's Lounge. With their long hair and their jeans they stood out like sore thumbs in that joint. Everybody had their five-hundred-dollar suits on with their short hair and diamond pinkie rings. I was the only guy with long hair except for these two Jewish guys who were trying to look inconspicuous.

Before I went on, the owner, Vinnie, came over to me.

"Who are those two fucking fruits in the flowered shirts sitting in the back? You know them?"

"Yeah, they came down to audition me," I said.

"Audition what? You should be auditioning them. You want us to take them in the back and slap them around a little? Tell them you got the job?"

"No! Don't do that. I want this job," I said.

"Okay, okay. I just wanted to make sure you're okay. We love you in this place, Peter. You bring these fruits down, we don't know . . ."

It was time to go on. I got on the stage and then Joey and the other guys came on. Three 250-pound half-bald guys just standing there like lummoxes, and I was in the back, dressed like a star, thrashing and smashing the shit out of my drums. The whole place was watching me steal the show.

When we launched into Wilson Pickett's "Knock on Wood," I opened my mouth and began to sing and Paul later told me he leaned over to Gene and said, "That's it, that's our drummer."

Gene liked the savage way I'd beat those drums. He loved the aggressive vibe I gave off. They wanted a real animal on the drums, and I was their boy. But first we had to play together. We set up a date to play and I went over to this loft they had on Twenty-third Street. I had to play on their other drummer's set and I felt like I couldn't kick ass—they weren't my skins. At that point I had this childish notion that I could only play on my own drum set. We broke into a song that was a bitch to follow, really hard technically, and I just couldn't get it together. I could see on their faces that they were as let down as I was.

"I don't think we should let this go," I said. "Let me come back and bring my own drums and I know that'll make a world of difference."

The next time we got together, it was magic. I asked them to play something more rock 'n' rollish, like Chuck Berry, and we broke into "Strutter" and everything fell into place. We all looked at each other and smiled and we just knew we were dynamite together. And they said, "You're hired."

We started practicing like fiends. We'd get together every night from Monday to Friday for as many hours as we could and practice—their songs. I was a little frustrated, since I had original songs that I had written with Chelsea and later with Stan. I was in the same place as a songwriter as they were, but I thought I'd just zip it for a while and do their tunes.

I could see that they wanted things their way. Already I could feel a control issue with them. But I thought, "Okay, Peter, maybe you should back off a little. It's their record." I figured I'd get in that drummer's seat and then I could be a little more forceful. So for maybe the first time in my life, I thought about things rather than just opening my big mouth and losing my temper. This was an opportunity, and I didn't want to blow it.

It wasn't as if they were telling me how to drum. If they had done that, I would have walked immediately. They were happy with the way I changed the songs with my own unique style.

At first I gravitated to Paul. He had gone to art school and he had a real artistic sensibility. With Gene everything was so methodical, so cut and dried. We had to do A, B, C, D, E. Gene was a thinker. He'd plot everything out. Sometimes in our business, you didn't have time to think: You just have to jump in. Rock 'n' roll is an attitude, not a science.

I could understand why Gene was like that. He had come to this country at an early age from Israel. His mother was a concentration-camp survivor whose husband had left her for another woman. Gene hated his father for that and never spoke to him. He was a big, gawky, shy kid who had been picked on a lot when he was growing up in Brooklyn. I could see why—after all his mother had gone through, and then having his father leave, and then coming to a strange alien culture—money and power might be attractive to him.

I had more in common with Paul, even if he was six years younger. He had grown up in Manhattan. He had an older sister, so he wasn't an only child like Gene. His father was a hardworking guy who sold furniture. But then he shared a disturbing detail with me. When his family moved to Queens, he told me that even though he was a fat kid, he used to have fantasies that all the other kids would call him King Paul. Bingo. Looks like we had two Machiavellis in training in the band.

I liked Gene and Paul at first. There were much more professional than any of the other musicians I had worked with. For one, they weren't drug addicts. Most musicians I knew smoked pot or did a little blow now and then, but these guys were as clean as angels. They were crystal clear about where they were going and how they were going to get there. I felt that I had finally met my soul mates who would travel with me down the road to fame and stardom.

It was freezing in that loft in the winter—there was no heat—so I would buy a bottle of cheap Gallo sherry and Paul and I would share it. We played so loud that the neighbors were always complaining. The antiques dealer downstairs even claimed we were damaging his delicate pieces with the vibrations. So we went out and got a thousand egg crates and glued them to the walls to soundproof the loft. The problem was there was still egg residue in the crates, so we started attracting huge prehistoric cockroaches. Gene brought up a mattress because sometimes he would crash there, and then he began bringing up women and fucking them on this filthy mattress in this filthy freezing loft with monster cockroaches crawling all over.

I guess that was his prerogative. He was also working full-time in an office as a secretary, so he was paying the rent. Working in an office came in handy because Gene could make copies of the bios and press releases that we were starting to send out. The Wicked Lester record deal had gone south, and they didn't have a manager who they really liked.

I thought we were going to be the next great power trio. The only problem was we were playing for ourselves in our little loft. We had been practicing and rehearsing for six months, and I was getting itchy. I was older than they were, I had paid a lot more dues, and my musical biological clock was ticking a lot faster. I'd moan and complain that we weren't out playing, we'd fight, and then I'd say, "Fuck this group. I'm out of here tomorrow." Then the sun would come up and I'd get dressed and go back to rehearsing at the loft. That's how I was quitting. Did I really mean it? No, never.

We finally played a showcase for Don Ellis, the head of Epic Records, in November of 1972. We set up a few chairs in the loft, and Don came down with some associates. We didn't really have our look together yet. We wore whiteface and lipstick, and Gene was wearing some sort of sailor suit. But we cranked that volume up and Don's hair looked like it was waving in the breeze from the sheer magnitude of our sound, like that

TV ad for Maxell cassettes. It was so loud you couldn't even make out any chord changes.

Ellis couldn't wait to get out the door. The only problem was that my brother had just come home on leave in the real navy and was in his real navy uniform, standing by the door in the back of the room, drunk as a skunk. As Ellis beat a hasty retreat, my brother proceeded to projectile vomit all over the music mogul's shoes.

That was an eye-opener for us all. We realized that to get a record deal or even some good gigs, we needed a great lead guitar player. So we put an ad in the *Voice* and went through at least thirty guys. One day, a guy came in straight off the boat from Italy. He couldn't even talk to us: He was using this woman, who was his wife or maybe his mother, as an interpreter. He didn't even tune his guitar, he just took it out of the case and started playing. We were sitting there watching this fiasco when the next guy came in to audition. The first thing I saw about this new guy was that he was wearing two different-colored sneakers, one red, one orange. He had skintight pants, tight shirt, long hair, a polka-dot scarf, and he looked Mongolian to me, with real heavy-lidded eyes like John Wayne. A real character.

This guy proceeded to take his guitar out of his case and slide over to the amp. We were thinking, What the fuck is this guy going to do? We hadn't talked to him yet, we didn't even know his name, and the other guy was in the middle of his audition. But this new guy just plugged in to the amp and wham! He started playing over the other guy! We were all stunned. He just cut the other guy to pieces, he was so good. The first guy packed up his gear and left in tears, so we started to jam with the interloper. He was fantastic.

After a while, we stopped and talked. He told us his name was Ace and he was from the Bronx but he really was an alien from a planet named Jandel. I was loving this guy. I'd never talked to anyone like him. He had the balls to literally move a competitor out of the fucking way to play because he knew that guy was a piece of shit and he wasn't. That, to me, was a winning fucking attitude.

After he left, the three of us talked. Their main concern was that we couldn't have a Chinese guy in the band. Because we were creating a certain look with our makeup, we felt that all the band members had to be white. Earlier we had auditioned a great guitar player but he was black, so he didn't get hired. But I maintained that Ace wasn't Chinese, he was Mongolian.

"This is the guy," I said. "He's from another fucking planet, he even says he is."

But they were still hesitant.

"I know we're looking for Jimmy Page, but we ain't finding him. This guy's got it," I urged.

We talked about Ace for days, and then we finally called him back in. We started jamming, and the sound that was happening was like nothing I'd ever heard in my life. We all knew Ace was the guy.

With Ace in the band, we were a lot more balanced. It turned out that he wasn't even Asian: He was of German descent. He was the black sheep of his family, running with a gang in the Bronx called the Ducky Boys. Being from Brooklyn, I didn't know how badass a gang that specialized in using slingshots could be. But at least he had a semblance of being a street kid, and I found that we had a lot in common. He was fun to be with, he had a great sense of humor, and he loved to party. I never met a guy who loved beer as much as Ace did, and he could drink a ton of it. He just loved to get a buzz on and tell jokes in his weird high-pitched voice.

Maybe all that booze contributed to Ace's offbeat beliefs. He was convinced that extraterrestrials had colonized this planet and he was one of them. In fact, he was working on a radio to communicate with his home planet—as least that's what he told us. He believed in ghosts, karma, and lucky numbers that totaled twenty-seven.

He also had a gigantic ego. Perhaps his belief that he was an alien gift to this planet made him think that he was above doing manual labor, but I just think he was fucking lazy. When we started playing around town, he would come up with any kind of excuse to get around loading out the equipment. He'd move his amp a few feet and then say, "Curly, I can't work, I sprained my arm." Or, "Curly, I have a problem breathing. I feel dizzy." Everyone was Curly to Ace. Most guitar players are prima donnas: They just want to walk up, plug in, and play. But Ace took it to new levels.

He wasn't lazy, however, when it came to beating his meat. Every chance he got, he'd jerk off. We would be loading out and Ace would be standing in the corner because it was too cold and he didn't want to hurt his hands. So he kept them warm by pulling out his huge dick and whacking off.

One time we were driving away from a gig in our converted milk truck. Paul would stand up behind the wheel and drive. Gene would sit shotgun, and Ace and I would be in the back with all equipment. We were all shivering in our coats and all of a sudden, we heard the familiar sound of slapping. We looked back and Ace was sitting on one of the amps, jerking off.

The only time Ace had a legitimate reason not to load the equipment was when we were storing our gear in Gene's mother's basement in Queens. For a time, we kept our equipment there, but Gene's mother wouldn't let Ace and me into the house because we were gentiles. Maybe it was because we were not only gentiles, but part German too. She wouldn't even let Paul into the house because he was German Jewish. Rain, snow, sleet, storm, it didn't matter, we couldn't enter those portals. We had to stand in the cold or the rain and hand the equipment to Gene, who then had to schlep it all downstairs. Ace would always give Gene shit about it, too.

Now that we had our full lineup, we had two more things to do: come up with a name and start playing gigs. One night Paul and Gene and I were driving to the loft and trying to come up with a name for the group. We wanted it to be sexual and hard yet also convey the spirit of rock 'n' roll. "Let's call the band Fuck," I said as a joke. Okay, that was the bottom line. But how do you get to that point? I mentioned that I had been in a band called Lips.

Suddenly Paul said, "Kiss."

"Get the fuck out of here," I fumed. "That's a terrible pansy name."

I looked at Gene, and the wheels seemed to be turning in his head. He knew me like a book.

"Well, Peter, there *is* the kiss of death."

Hmm. He had me there with the whole Mafia thing. How could a street guy not like the Kiss of Death?

So we started breaking it down. Before you get in her pants, you gotta kiss her. Warm her up to get to second base. Good kissing makes for good laying. It's sexual, it's cool, let's go with it, we thought.

When Ace came in a week later with his sketch for a KISS logo, the name was confirmed in heaven. Ace is a great artist, and his KISS rendition, with the last two letters as lightning bolts, was totally bitching. And contrary to some people's opinions (and later the opinion of the government of Germany), the S's didn't symbolize the Nazi SS. Despite the fact that Ace would get drunk and run around in a full SS uniform, complete with a monocle, and scream, "You vill die! Give me your papers! I vill kill your family," those were lightning bolts from space. Then Paul refined the logo, made the K a little straighter, and we had a name and a logo.

Now it was time to play. At the end of January 1973, we booked ourselves in a little rock club in Queens called Popcorn (the name was later changed to Coventry). Of course we had no following then, so the audience, all four of them, was Lydia, Gene's girlfriend Jan, her friend, and a friend of Ace's. But we played our asses off. We played like the place was packed, and afterward I realized that this band was *the* band. I was so proud of the guys. We were all drenched in sweat, and we had given the performance of our lives for four people.

Over the next few months we played a lot at a little club in Amityville on Long Island called the Daisy. We had gotten a few write-ups, and they were uniformly negative, but we didn't give a shit. I actually liked the fact that we were so obnoxious and crazy that people hated us, although it did bug me a little because I thought we were absolutely dynamite.

When we first started at the Daisy, we drew a sparse crowd. But for some reason Sid, the owner, kept bringing us back, and by the fourth time we were pulling up to the club in our milk van and there were a few people waiting outside to get in, and inside the place was crowded. We knew we were on the right track. The club itself was a dump, and we changed into our costumes in the owner's office, which was barely bigger than a closet. We hadn't formulated our characters by then: We were just experimenting with different makeup and costumes. I wore a long-sleeved spidery black shirt with studs going down the chest, black studded cutoffs that my mom had sewn, and a scarf. I bought a couple of pairs of light-green Hush Puppies and brought them home and my mother soaked them in glue and poured silver sparkle over them and they were my stage shoes. The other guys improvised as well, trying to keep to our silver-and-black motif.

One night we were about to go on, but before we left the office, I said, "Let's go out and make believe it's Madison Square Garden and we're going to rock the house, because we're the greatest!" I said that because I knew deep in my bones that one day we would play the Garden. And that became our mantra. No matter what toilet we were playing, we'd say, "Let's go out like it's Madison Square Garden." And there was no stopping four guys who had that incredibly positive energy.

Gene would jump into the audience and grab people at random and make them clap their hands to the music. That took some major balls. He'd go up to huge, scary-looking guys and force them to clap. I was convinced he was going to get floored one night because what he did was so humiliating. But it never happened. And after every show, I was ecstatic.

At the time, we were managing ourselves. When we had a gig coming up, Gene would print up some pamphlets at work and then we would divide up the city and put them up wherever people could see them. We were a band of brothers, all thinking the same way, all pulling in the same direction. What was great about us then was that we were so open-minded. You want to wear nylons? Sure, no problem. You want to put on greasepaint? Fine. You're going to wear a dress? Great. Anything we had to do to make it, we all were willing to do.

Now we had to work on our images. Androgyny was really big then, with guys like Bowie and even my friend Jerry's band, the New York Dolls. So at first we just dressed in drag and wore women's makeup. That was a disaster. Gene looked like an old drag queen in a blond wig and lipstick. Ace looked just like Shirley MacLaine. Paul was a little chunky then, so he looked like some hooker working the corner of Bowery and Delancey. I was a skinny little bastard, so I could get away with dressing in women's clothes, but in the end we weren't as cute as the Dolls. In fact, we all looked like bad transvestites. That's when we realized that we had to come up with something no one else had.

The KISS epiphany happened the night we went to Madison Square Garden to see Alice Cooper play. Alice and his band came on, and Ace and Paul ran all the way to the front of the stage like groupies. Gene and

I sat in our chairs in the back, but we were all equally impressed by Alice. It was amazing theater. Alice was in full makeup, and the kids in the audience were freaking out over this guy who came out with a huge snake and got hung onstage. The four of us got together after the concert, and it all started coming to us. We wanted the Beatles' wit, the same type of fun paired with a high level of creativity, too. But we wanted to be tougher than the Beatles—more like the Stones, but not quite the Stones. We had been battling to be more gangish in a way, a tougher, almost biker don't-fuck-with-us attitude. After that concert, I forgot who said it, but someone said, "What if we have four Alice Coopers?" Alice was the star attraction and the only one in makeup in his band. But what if the whole band wore makeup, and each guy's makeup expressed some aspect of his persona?

So Alice inspired us to go from the garish drag makeup the Dolls used to more theatrical Kabuki-type makeup. Little by little, we'd start bringing shoe polish, whiteface, and other makeup elements to the rehearsals. Now we were using the makeup to each develop a unique character. Gene loved horror films, so he became the Demon, evil incarnate. Paulie was always a star, so he had to be the Starchild. Ace was definitely a space cadet, hence the Spaceman.

My Catman character came to me one night. I was designing one of my stage costumes at home. I was sketching it out and smoking a joint and then I just kind of zoned out and started staring at my wife's black cat, who was named Mateus. I realized that we both shared a lot of personality traits. We were both wild, independent, aggressive, powerful—yet also soft, gentle, warm, and comforting at the same time. I loved cats. I found them to be the most mystical, mysterious animals on the planet. They either loved you or scratched your eyes out. And like me, they had nine lives. So becoming a cat was a no-brainer for me. I brought the idea back to the guys, and they loved it.

By March of 1973 it was time to do a demo tape. Through Gene and Paul's connections we were going to record at Electric Lady, which was really exciting for me, but better still, Eddie Kramer, Hendrix's old producer, was going to be behind the board. That was really heavy for me. He was known for the great sound he got from drums and guitars on his records. I couldn't sleep the night before the sessions, I was so excited to get to work. We recorded three songs in one day: "Strutter," "Deuce," and a song called "Black Diamond." By the time we were ready to tackle "Black Diamond," Eddie had already heard me singing harmonies on the other tracks and I think he dug my raspy voice.

"Black Diamond" was a song Paul wrote, and he sang the first take. Eddie was behind the board listening to the playback and I said, "Man, I could sing the shit out of that song."

"Really?" he said in his thick British accent. "Well, go ahead, mate, go give it a crack."

I went into the studio and belted it out. "Out on the street for a living . . ." I killed it. Eddie loved it.

"Why don't we have Peter sing this? This song was made for him," he said.

"That sounded pretty good," Paul admitted.

I put everything I ever had into that song because I had waited so long for that magical moment at Electric Lady. So I finally had a lead vocal all to myself.

When I got home that night, I played the demo tape twenty-four hours a day for weeks, I was so proud of it. I brought it to my mom, who was always my most trusted critic with my music.

"Baby, this is it. This is your break," she said. "This band has it."

Everything seemed to be falling into place. We had a hot demo; we were gigging in the region. But we needed management to help get us a record deal. By the summer of 1973, I was getting antsy again. I was still playing on the weekends with Infiniti, doing covers, and they were getting more gigs than KISS was. So I started complaining again. I'd been up and down the New York City music roads, and except for Ace, who had once played the Purple Onion, the other guys didn't have any of that experience.

We finally lined up a gig for August 10 in the ballroom of the Diplomat hotel in Manhattan, which, despite being a sleazy shithole, was a very cool place to play. So I was a little placated. The night of the show, Paul and Gene did something really nice for me. They rented a brown stretch Mercedes limo to take us to the show so I would feel like a star making his entrance. They hoped that would change my mood. Well, it worked for a couple of minutes. But then everybody started loading into the limo. Instead of it just being the four of us, Lydia was in there, and the sound guy was in there, some friends piled in, and then the roadies put some of our equipment in the trunk and squeezed in. Suddenly the limo had become a cab. I got furious.

"We're going to pull up in front of the place and all these people are going to come out of the limo like it's a circus car? That's not cool."

But when we got to the hotel entrance, the sidewalk was deserted! There was nobody there to make an entrance for.

Gene was promoting this show and had made the wise decision of putting us on in the middle slot, even though the bands that opened and closed were much more popular than we were at the time. A lot of people would leave before the last band went on to go someplace else, so it was a shrewd move. We were getting ready to go on, and I saw an older guy standing next to my sisters up front near the stage. He was getting ready to leave before we played, but he was intrigued that the girls next to him were wearing homemade KISS T-shirts, so he struck up a conversation with them—and my sister Donna Donna told this guy that we were the most incredible band in the world. So he decided to stay.

That gentleman was Bill Aucoin, and he went on to manage us into worldwide superstardom. Of course, we didn't know that Bill was in the audience that night. Gene was relentless in sending out invitations to hundreds of people who were somehow connected to the music industry on the odd chance that one of them might come see us and decide to manage us.

That night Bill did come, and after the show he arranged to meet with Gene and Paul later that week. That day, I got a call from Gene while they were in Aucoin's office.

"This guy is great, he should manage us," Gene said. "He could get us a record deal."

"He's probably just another asshole who's promising to make us rich and famous," I said.

"No, no, he's not what you think," Gene said. He told me that Aucoin had a music show on TV called *Flipside.* I remembered seeing John Lennon on that show once, so I thought that maybe this guy just might be legit.

"In fact, he says that if he can't get us a record deal in six months, he's out of here," Gene said. He urged me to go meet Bill.

I drove my Vega into the city a few days later and met Bill at his office. I was in my wise-guy stance, not showing any emotion, but I was really impressed. Bill was incredibly nice, soft-spoken, meticulous, and very, very smart. I left that office knowing that this was it. I didn't let on to the guys, I actually kind of gave them a hard time about it, but I was excited.

The following weeks only confirmed what a great decision we had made. Bill was a wonderful person. Unlike most of the people in the music industry, he was sensitive and sentimental. In fact, I had signed our contract with a pen that I had found in the gutter on the way over to his office, and he kept that pen and framed it! As we got to know Bill, we saw that he had an artistic sensibility. He was classy. He dressed immaculately. He really seemed like he was the guy who had the knowledge and the wherewithal to make us famous.

Bill's first advice to us was that we should honor our previously made bookings at Coventry in Queens. Then we were instructed not to play anywhere else. He also told us that we were going to play a showcase at the end of the summer for a major player in music who was starting his own record label.

That man was Neil Bogatz, otherwise known as Neil Bogart. Neil was a Jewish kid from Brooklyn who was born to be in show business. He started out as an actor under the name Wayne Roberts, then had a hit record called "Bobby" as Neil Scott. When his career didn't take off, he became a music executive and became known as the Bubblegum King when he was running Buddah Records. Bill had known him for a while and had inside information that Neil was leaving Buddah to start his own label, Casablanca, which would be distributed by Warner Bros.

So just weeks after signing with Bill, we were going to audition for Neil at a small dance studio in midtown. Bill had a partner named Joyce Biawitz, a very cute girl who was constantly bugging Neil to come see us. For days before the date, Bill and Joyce were hyping the audition, telling us how important it would be to our careers. We got all dressed up as if we were going to play a club and set up our equipment in that little rehearsal room. Bill set up a few chairs for Neil and a couple of people from his label. We turned off all the lights before we began, and then we cranked it up and all hell broke loose. They probably heard us over in Jersey. After the first song there was no reaction, so Gene came down off the makeshift stage, walked over to Neil, and grabbed his hands and forced him to clap, just like he'd do at the Daisy. Then during "Firehouse," Paul did his usual gimmick. He ran up to Neil with what looked like a bucket of water in an old red fire bucket and threw it in Neil's face. But the bucket contained confetti, not water. And Neil started laughing hysterically.

When we finished, Neil seemed to be in total shock. But I noticed that Joyce had her arm around Neil, who was a married man, and they looked pretty chummy.

"I can't hear myself talk, you guys play so loud," Neil told us. "But Joyce was right, you guys are totally different from everyone else. I certainly wasn't expecting this."

A few days later, Bill called us into his office. "Neil loves the group. He wants you guys to be the first signing on Casablanca."

I couldn't wait to get home to tell Lydia and my mother that I had a record deal again.

We knew we were on our way. We had two wild men, Bill and Neil, behind us, guys who would do anything to break an act. Guys who didn't think out of the box: They fucking smashed the box to smithereens. But what we didn't know, and what would have blown Gene and Paul's oh-so-straight minds, was that our futures were now in the hands of two men who, in a few years' time, would both become major coke addicts.

CHAPTER FIVE

We were in the middle of playing when Paul started scratching his head. That was all Sean Delaney needed to see. He blew his whistle and stopped the rehearsal.

"You can't look like a rock star and scratch your head," Sean barked.

"But my head itches from the dye you used," Paul pouted. "What am I supposed to do?"

Sean walked up to Paul.

"Make it into a move," he said. And he took Paul's guitar and put the strap over his shoulder.

"Throw the guitar behind you," he demonstrated dramatically. "Then take both of your hands and just rip into your scalp like it was on fire. Then throw your hands up in the air and walk forward like some kind of beauty model." Sean demonstrated, very accurately, a model walking the runway. And Paul's first signature stage move was born.

Sean Delaney was, in my estimation, the fifth member of KISS. He was a tremendously talented creative force. He wrote great songs. He had a voice you could die for. He had flair and style. He was a great dancer. He knew theater. He had worked with Tennessee Williams. In his spare time, he was a transvestite. And he was our manager Bill Aucoin's live-in lover.

We didn't know that Bill was gay when we first met him. In those days, especially if you were on the business side of music, you had to stay in the closet. But as soon as Bill became our manager, he brought Sean in to refine and expand upon our act. That's putting it mildly.

Bill had met Sean at a bar in the East Village when Sean was putting together a gay band called Manhole. For some reason that project fell through, and all Sean was left with was the earrings in his nipples. The music world's loss was our gain. He was perfect for us, a multitalented musician who knew how to create an image and put it across. He was way, way ahead of us at that point.

The first thing Sean did was convince us to dye our hair blue-black.

"You're a band. All of you should have the same color hair. And blue-black will really pop against the white makeup," Sean said.

He took all of us down to the apartment of one of his gay friends in the Village. One by one, he dyed our hair in the bathtub. When we were finished, the apartment was in shambles, but we felt great. We hit Eighth Street, and everybody was looking at us. Who had ever seen a band where all four guys' hair color was exactly the same?

Sean wanted to dress us in gold and black, but gold changes color under lights, so we changed it to silver and black. And the black, of course, would be leather. We used to wear studded dog collars that we'd get from pet shops, but Sean marched us to the Pleasure Chest, an S&M clothing store in the Village that had a large gay clientele. That's where we got heavy studded leather dog collars and bracelets and leather vests, studded leather cock pouches and chains.

Paul was chubby at that time, and Sean knew you couldn't have a fat rock star, so he had the owner of the Pleasure Chest design a custom lace-up corset to squeeze Paul's love handles in. Paul would put this leather contraption on and we would go behind it and pull the laces tight.

Then Sean began to work on our stage moves. He brought us to a loft in Chinatown where his old band used to practice. Paul put up the most resistance. The two of them fought for hours.

"I can't move like that—I don't look good," Paul would say.

"Sure you do," Sean would respond. "Pucker up your lips a little more. It'll drive the girls wild."

We had to block out elaborate choreography because Sean had made our platform shoes taller. They were now more than half a foot high and the guys kept falling, so he taught them how to do parachute-landing falls—and when that didn't work, he taught them how to make the falls look like part of the show and how to surreptitiously pick each other up. At first we wanted Sean to bring in a professional choreographer, so he found a famous gay guy who worked on Broadway. The guy knew nothing, so Sean intervened. His moves blew the guy away.

We had come up with some great moves on our own, but the guys didn't even realize they were doing them. Ace would be sideways with his legs spread apart, then Gene would come over and put his leg between Ace's legs, and then Paul put himself at the back and they all gyrated together. Sean immediately saw that it was a dynamite move and he even named it, I think, calling it the KISS Swerve. Sean said it was a physical representation of a musically charged orgasm.

These moves weren't just for aesthetics. Sometimes Ace would get so drunk, he'd pass out while he was doing a solo. Gene and Paul would see it happening and quickly jump over him and do a little move and, by the end, lift him up. It was hard for me to play and keep a straight face: I couldn't believe what they were getting away with, making Ace's passing out part of the act.

The sexual element of the stage show wasn't lost on a writer from *Mandate* magazine, a gay magazine that gave us one of our first positive reviews. The guy said that Paul "bi-modulates bi-sexually" across the stage, and Paul was upset. But what did he expect? He used to do a move where he'd wear a red garter belt like a stripper and come up to the lip of the stage and stick his leg out. Everyone in the audience, both male and female, would grab at it. He loved it—he couldn't wait for that moment.

Paul's sexuality became a topic of speculation even for us guys in the band. Paul always loved to doodle. And he drew the best cocks in the universe: He could have gotten a job working at a gay porno magazine. He had the veins down, he had the balls just perfect. Ace would say, "You gotta suck a dick to draw a dick that good." Gene would just sit there and not say anything but smile as if to say, "You think?"

Of course, one of the reasons that Paul drew such perfect penises was that he was surrounded by some great models to work from. We were young crazy guys then, and Ace and I became famous for taking our dicks out at the drop of a hat. Then we'd grab each other's dicks. It wasn't sexual, just stupid adolescent tomfoolery.

Sometimes we did it to provoke Gene. We'd be putting our makeup on, I'd get a huge boner, and I'd pull my pants down and go over to Gene as he was applying his makeup and lay my boner on his shoulder. Then Ace would do the same thing on his other shoulder. Gene would scream and flip out and yell, "Get the fuck away from me!" But he dug the joke.

"Go over to Paul," he'd say.

When we'd do that to Paul, he'd cringe.

Gene and Paul never whipped their dicks out. In fact, Gene had a thing about never getting naked in front of us. He'd never shower with us after a show. Paul didn't care, but he wasn't as exhibitionistic as Ace and I were. Maybe that's because Paul and Gene came in a distant third and fourth place to Ace and me when we had a contest to see who had the biggest dick. Mine was the longest, Ace's was the fattest, and then Paul and Gene were lagging far behind. They actually named my dick. They called it the Spoiler, presumably because once a woman had me, she'd be spoiled forever. Writing about this now as a sixty-six-year-old man, it all seems so stupid. What the fuck was I thinking? But we were young and it was fun and everybody enjoyed it at the time.

Ace and I were smart enough not to take our dicks out in front of Bill or Sean. Maybe because they might have videotaped them. One of Bill and Sean's great innovations when we were practicing in that loft was to video our performances and play them back to us and critique us as if they were football coaches breaking down plays. Bill had done some television directing, and he was really into the visual aspects of the show. So Sean would set up two cameras on either side of us, we'd get onstage in full costume and makeup and rehearse for hours, and he'd video it. When we were finished, we'd watch the whole tape back and Sean would lecture us.

"Paul, you see when you do that? That's fucked up. Don't do that again. Don't open your mouth there." Or: "Peter, do you see when you do that with the sticks? I like that. Keep that in there."

We'd eliminate anything that wasn't cool and keep whatever was great.

It may have looked spontaneous, but every little move was planned in our band.

Sean understood and loved theatricality. We had just developed our stage characters with our makeup, but Sean made sure that we stayed in character throughout the whole show. Sean really worked with Gene to develop his whole demon persona. One time Gene stuck out his pro-digious tongue at Sean to be obnoxious, and Sean claimed he had an epiphany right then and there. Gene should be a monster the whole show. So they worked on walking like a monster and not deviating from that character. Whenever Gene would break character, Sean would pull out his whistle, blow it, and stop the rehearsal. I didn't get away with anything either. The same went for Paul and Ace. Sean didn't need to do much to make sure that Ace consistently acted like a space cadet, though.

What's scary is that the more we got into our roles and the makeup, the more we actually became our alter egos. Once we ditched the female eye shadow and eyeliner and lipstick and actually created these four charac-ters with full-on theatrical makeup, we transformed into different entities. Gene morphed right into a demon. That little Hasidic boy was nowhere to be found when the Demon took over Gene's brain. He would spit right into our roadies' faces. Just plodding around on those platform shoes, which added to his natural height, he exuded menace. People would liter-ally cringe in fear when he came near. Especially when he whipped out that tongue. His tongue was so long, there were rumors that he had had it cos-metically enhanced. With his tongue flicking in and out of his mouth, he looked like some demonic lizard. Gene once told me that if he could leave his makeup on all the time and never leave that persona, he would do it.

Paul would literally become the Star. Ta-da! This chubby little kid from Queens became Liza Minnelli, Rod Stewart, Mick Jagger, all beamed into one. He knew he could have any woman he wanted. He has very feminine hands, but he would use them like a Svengali onstage. Like Dracula, he'd gesture to a girl in the audience as if he was commanding her. He'd grab his face dramatically and walk along the lip of the stage and look down on the people as if they were nothing, because he was the Star. And then the white light would hit him and I could see that his brain was bubbling, because everything was "Look at me! Look at me!"

Ace was a true Spaceman, a guy who tripped and fell over himself because he could never quite adjust to the gravity on earth. He actually used to say that to us, and not even when he was in costume!

When I put on that Cat makeup, I truly was transformed. Forget about Peter Criscuola, the kid from Brooklyn. He didn't exist. I believed I was a superhero, the most iconic cat of all cats, sitting up there overlooking my prey. I was a nasty little alley cat, ready to grab whatever I wanted. Don't get too close to me, because I might just attack. It was insane power tripping. I felt taller. My arms felt stronger. I was really transformed into this powerhouse of energy. I couldn't hit my drums hard enough. It was almost scary to feel that much power.

Sean fed on that energy. I remember so many times in rehearsals when Sean would be screaming in my face to kill those drums, break those motherfuckers. It was almost militaristic: Everything we did onstage was meant to annihilate. When we opened shows, our goal would be to kill so bad that the headlining act wouldn't want to come on after us. Sean helped us develop that animal instinct, and all of it began with the drums. The other guys had to keep up with me playing fifty million miles an hour.

Sean worked 24/7 with us. He was like an obsessed drill sergeant. When we'd get in that rehearsal room and were all up together on that stage, he would get in front of us and it was like he was leading the largest orchestra in the world, he was so into it. I was a nobody then, but when I was around Sean, I felt like royalty, like I was the greatest drummer in the world. Both Sean and Bill knew instinctively that it was important to treat us all like stars, and they absolutely did.

Sean was also protective of us.

"I'll kill any fucking body that touches you four," he told us. "I will cut their fucking throat from ear to ear. You're my babies."

Sean was a tough bastard, too, and if he had to get a little tough and show his butch side to protect us, he'd put on a game face that would scare the shit out of anyone who tried to fuck with us.

He also kept the peace among us. We each spent a lot of time alone with Sean, and he knew which buttons to push for each guy. He helped me with my temper, he helped Gene work on his attitude. Gene had a patronizing way of talking to the rest of us, almost as if he was back teaching sixth grade, which he had done years before. Sean saw that Paul was developing a rock-star arrogance about him way before we had even released our first album. That would piss Ace off, so Sean had to be like a referee and keep the peace all the time. But when it came time to get honest feedback, we relied on Sean. He'd tell it like it was. He never bullshitted us.

I got really close to Sean, or Seana, as I used to call her when she was in drag. At first I was a little gun-shy around him because I was this macho kid from Brooklyn—God forbid I should be hanging around with a fag, much less a tranny. He showed us photos, and he was hot when he dressed in full drag. But little by little we got close, and Sean used to love to take me to all the gay clubs in the meatpacking district of the city. One time he took me to a club and we went into the back room and there was a naked guy down on all fours. This other guy greased him up and then he rammed his fist all the way up his ass up to the elbow.

"Welcome to the Fistfuckers Club," Sean said.

"Uh, I gotta go now," I said to Sean.

I was out of there in a flash. I will never forget that scene until the day I die.

Sometimes Sean went too far around me. He would grab my ass, or grab my dick, and crunch me over. I'd chase him around and wrestle with him and throw him to the ground.

Bill would do the same thing once we got to know him well. We'd be at a party at a club and I'd be in the bathroom and I'd feel somebody's hand going across the back of my butt and I'd hear, "Oh, what a cute ass you got." It would be Bill.

"Get the fuck out of here," I'd say.

"You've got the cutest little toilet. I just love your butt," he'd persist.

But Bill had such a sweetness to him, it just seemed playful.

Sadly, Sean never got the credit he deserved for making us into superstars. If you listen to Gene or Paul, they were the driving engines behind our success, and Sean maybe helped out with a move here or there. But Sean was there from the beginning and had his hand in everything we created, from our personas to our wardrobe to our staging. He even contributed to the songs.

Bill's contributions also get minimized in Gene and Paul's revisionist KISStory. Bill helped us actualize the Beatles concept of four superstars that we instinctively knew we should go for. He treated each one of us as special and gave each one of us his undivided attention.

Bill thought that each of us in the band should get an equal share of the proceeds, no matter who was writing what, unlike the Beatles. We were all onstage for two hours a night and I was beating my drums like a motherfucker and you're playing your bass, and then when we change back into our clothes, you put on a Rolex from Tiffany's and I got a fucking Seiko? I don't think so. He knew that an unequal division of the money would just lead to chaos, especially when you're a band that comes up together from scratch, comes up with the original ideas and concepts and battles through all the shit that's in your way. You needed some semblance of equality, and Bill knew it would be through an equal distribution of the monies.

I was totally happy about this arrangement. It was all great. We were having a good time together—we were four brothers in a band. I wanted nothing more than that feeling of unity, being part of a band. I didn't want to run the band. I just wanted to be an equal cog.

I remember one night, Gene was getting on me in his usual patronizing way about something and we started arguing forcefully and I turned to him and said, "Here's the irony. You went to college, you broke your ass in school, then you taught school. You have all this knowledge. And I never finished high school, I grew up in the streets, yet with all your vast knowledge, tonight when we get paid, I'm making the same as you. So go fuck yourself." He shut right up: There was nothing he could say after that. That was the beauty of Bill's vision.

In his own way, Bill also propelled our self-esteem to the stratosphere. He encouraged us to express our feelings and he never made us feel small or stupid for sharing them. He was a great role model for us, me especially. Sometimes he'd take us up to his place in the country and he'd whip up his famous Aucoin breakfast—scrambled eggs with vanilla extract and other exotic spices. It tasted like shit, but I ate it: I didn't want to hurt his feelings. Who had a manager who cooked for them?

Bill was a mentor to me. He helped to turn me into a gentleman. He taught me etiquette. He'd make me get dressed up and then take me to a really fine restaurant and show me which cutlery to use, which wine to order, which food went with what wine. Then we'd go shopping and he tried to turn me on to Gucci loafers and expensive watches, but I'd never wear Gucci. Bill knew how insecure I was and that soon I would be in front of the eyes of the world. He wanted me to be comfortable in that role.

Bill saw that Gene and Paul would pick on me because I wasn't as schooled as they were and that it hurt my heart, so he would help me with my vocabulary. Bill knew that my reacting like a tough guy to Gene and Paul was all a front. Deep down he knew I had a heart of gold and that I was really a good kid. I think that he really loved me. I know I loved him.

Just like Sean, Bill was so positive and so shrewd. He did nothing on a whim, like I would. Everything he thought up was bigger and better than what any other band would do. He wouldn't shoot down any ideas. "You want to fly over the audience? Why not? Be Mary Poppins." It was never "No, you can't." There was nothing we couldn't try or do in Bill Aucoin's brain. So Bill and Sean added great finishing touches to the pretty crude canvas that they were presented with. And they both did it with class, style, and panache.

On top of that, we had the craziest record-company president around. Neil Bogart was the last Barnum and Bailey of rock 'n' roll. He thrived on the spectacular and would spend a hundred dollars to make one dollar. Neil was a showman. You just had to look at what he went on to do. Besides signing us, he shepherded the Village People, Parliament/Funkadelic, and Donna Summer to superstardom.

Neil was a very hands-on guy, and he immediately came up with ideas to help us refine our stage show. He was a big fan of magic, so he brought a magician up to the office one day to see what magic effects we could incorporate into the show. The magician went through his bag of tricks, and we were nixing everything until he got to fire breathing. Immediately, Ace, Paul, and I refused.

"I'll try that," Gene said.

The fire-breathing effect was done by keeping a small amount of fuel, like kerosene, in your mouth and then blowing it into an open flame on your torch. The first time Gene tried it, he almost burned down the office. Then it became a staple in our live act.

I was once talking with Neil and half-jokingly said that it would be cool if the drums could levitate right off the stage. We started discussing it, and we came up with the idea of using a pulley to get me into the air. We devised a drum riser that would levitate eight feet into the air using a very unreliable chain-link setup. They bolted chains to each corner of the platform, bolted the drums to the platform, and then connected the chains in each corner to a big hook that was attached to another chain. Then they got four big roadies to pull me up on pulleys.

It was always an adventure. Some nights, some of the crew were shit-faced and they didn't pull up evenly, so the drums would go sliding off to one side. Many nights the chain would drop slack and the whole kit would drop down two or three feet. It was enough of a jolt to knock the drums over and almost knock me off the platform. I was petrified every time they cranked me up. My life was literally in those guys' hands until we had enough money to come up with a hydraulic lift system to get me airborne. But that was the beauty of Neil. He was as much of a dreamer and a showman as we were, and he had the balls to take everything to the next level.

Eventually Joyce married Neil, Bill bought out her share of the management company, and Joyce and Neil went on to have a beautiful marriage.

With such a great team surrounding us, we were firing on all cylinders. And we were all happy. We were all looking out for each other in whatever way we could. Gene used his book smarts to make sure that all the business dealings were on the up and up. I handled the physical. If you dared to touch Gene or Paul or Ace, I'd kick your ass. I loved those three guys and they were as close to me as family, maybe even closer. I was easily the most dangerous of the four of us, so if we got in a situation where we were threatened by tough guys from other bands or their crew, I was immediately right in the front going, "Oh, really, you're going to what?" And the situation would suddenly change, because you really didn't want to go up against a twenty-eight-year-old Peter Criss. I always loved the adrenaline and I loved the battle.

In those early days, Paul likened KISS to a car with four wheels. It was true: We needed each other to move on smoothly. And at the beginning we did move smoothly. We were true brothers in arms, brothers onstage, brothers in the darkness. All for one and one for all.

If any of us ever deviated from this team effort and began to get a swelled head, we had a very simple reality check. Maybe it came from putting on our makeup so much. But if someone got off by putting other people down, one of us would say, "You're going to talk about so-and-so? Look in the mirror and then say that again."

On October 10, 1973, we went into Bell Sound Studios to record our first album. We had hired Kenny Kerner and Richie Wise as producers, which to me was baffling. We had done a dynamite demo with Eddie Kramer, why weren't we using him? I didn't know it at the time, but Kerner and Wise went back a long way with Bill and Neil. They were in a group that recorded for Neil and they went on to produce for him. So they got the gig. I really liked Kenny, but Richie and I didn't get along at all. To me, Wise was the best ass-kisser I'd ever seen. "You're right, Gene." "You're right, Paul." It was nauseating.

I put my whole heart and soul into everything I played on those sessions. Warren Dewey, the engineer, and I went through hundreds of snare drums to try to get a really big drum sound. When I was finished laying down the drum tracks, I left—my part was done, unless I had to sing a song or do harmonies. But when I came in for the listening session, I was dumbfounded. Kerner and Wise's job was to capture the energy of the live show on vinyl, but it wasn't there. There were no balls between those grooves. I guess it was unrealistic to expect otherwise, because Kerner and Wise were too old-school. They were making us sound like a pop band. I hated the way they mixed the drums. To my taste, they had great, great songs—masterpieces, even—and they made them sound pedestrian. The strength and the energy and the power of our band had been blunted. We were all really let down.

But 1973 had been quite a monumental year for us. And we were going to ring it out with the first gig of our new era. We were booked to do the New Year's Eve show at the Academy of Music, opening for Blue Oyster Cult, Teenage Lust, and Iggy and the Stooges. In the dressing room, Gene set the tone.

"Let's kill them tonight," he said in his deep monotone. "Once we're done, nobody's going to want to see these other guys."

That was our beautiful arrogance. We were the opening act, but the other acts went crazy when they came to the venue and saw a ten-by-four-foot neon sign that lit up and said KISS. The sign was a surprise from Bill to us. I'll never forget sitting in the back of the theater before the doors opened and just staring at that sign. I knew we were destined for stardom after seeing that.

But our rise to the top could have easily been derailed that night. Gene lit some flash paper and threw it into the crowd and, unfortunately, it hit a kid in the eye. This was a major lawsuit waiting to happen, and Bill could have lost his whole business. But we were such innovative con artists. Bill ushered the kid backstage after the show and we had him pose with us for a photo and then Bill gave him a lifetime pass to the Academy of Music.

That kid wasn't the only thing Gene burned that night. During "Firehouse," Gene unveiled his fire breathing for the first time in public. He spit out the kerosene and the flames went spiking into the darkness, but when he tried to put the lit torch down it accidentally caught his hair on fire. But Sean was quick to the rescue. He came running out onstage like a hero and, ta-da, he dramatically threw his leather jacket over Gene's head, patting out the fire. Then Sean just as dramatically pulled his jacket off Gene's hair and ran off the stage. That drama queen deserved an Oscar for that performance. Afterward, the other bands came up to us and said, "Wow, you guys burn yourselves, huh? That's pretty heavy. You do that every night?" We had to tell them it wasn't really part of the show.

As great as that first show was, we topped it the next time we played. On January 8, 1974, we played a press-preview show at the Fillmore East. This was my dream come true. The Fillmore had been closed for a while, and I couldn't believe that Neil had talked them into letting us rent it for a week for this gig.

The Fillmore had been the cathedral of my youth. I had been in that audience countless times watching the Doors, Hendrix, the Airplane, and the Who. Now I was going to share the same stage with all those icons.

I definitely felt ghosts in that place. We were rehearsing there for about a week and sometimes I'd come in early and go upstairs and sit in the balcony and close my eyes and I could feel all the people, the changes, the shit that went on there. The dressing room itself was heaven. The walls were completely filled with the scrawled autographs of every superstar who had played there. I really wanted to cut a piece of the wall off and take it with me.

The night of the press party came and we had about three hundred invited press, friends, and family in the audience. Before we went on, I looked in the dressing-room mirror. I was wearing a brand-new full-leather jumpsuit with silver studs going up the sides. Sean had put us through incredible paces, and I felt like Tyson going into the ring. I looked around at the other three guys. We were all greased, oiled, and we looked badass.

Our big gimmick then was a big black candelabra onstage that held thirteen candles. One of the roadies would come out while the house was still dark and light each candle, one by one. When the last candle was lit, the house lights suddenly came up and there we were, onstage and blasting away. I looked out from my perch behind the drums and I saw Lydia and my mother and my brother and sisters all crying. I just hit those skins harder and looked up into the empty balcony and knew that we were heading straight for the top.

CHAPTER SIX

I *don't know why, but Paul and I suddenly decided to take off all our* clothes and go naked. This might not have been the smartest thing to do in the backseat of a station wagon hurtling through the backwoods of Tennessee to our next gig, but that's what the road will do to you. We were on our first tour of America, and this was our first exposure to the Deep South.

I couldn't care less where I was, I'd get naked at the drop of a hat—whether it was in a hotel lobby, on a plane, anywhere. The guys called me Nature Boy. I'd run naked down the hallways of the hotel, streak the people in the lobby, then run through a restaurant. I was wild. The staff at the Sunset Marquis in Hollywood to this day tell stories about how I used to dive from the balcony of our room naked into the pool.

But this was different. This was the Deep South. We had just finished watching the movie *Deliverance,* and I was scared shitless that I was going to get fucked in the ass. Even Gene and Ace were uptight and made us put our clothes back on. So we decided to start fucking with Sean. We loved to make him crazy. Paul and Ace and I, in the backseat, started tearing cotton balls apart and gently placing the pieces in Sean's hair. By the time he pulled over to a gas station to fill up, he looked like he was wearing Marie Antoinette's wig.

The gas-station attendant ambled over to the car. I could make out a huge revolver on his hip under his jacket. He took one look at Sean and his face soured.

"Whaddya want?" he barked.

Then he looked into the car and saw Gene wearing leather with studs. We were all dressed in our leather and platform shoes, and we all had tinted blue-black hair. Not particularly his kind of people.

"We need some gas," Sean said. We all started laughing hysterically. Sean was getting angry now, thinking that we were trying to piss this hillbilly off, but we were really laughing at the white mound of shredded cotton atop his head. We didn't let on, but after we gassed up and he drove away, he looked in the rearview mirror, saw what we did to him, and frantically pawed at his hair to get it out.

We drove deeper and deeper into what we thought were the back-woods. I was really starting to get paranoid, and my fear was contagious. Sean missed a turn and he slowed down to get his bearings.

"Don't stop, Sean. Keep driving," Ace said.

"Get us out of here. Quick," I poked Sean in the back of his head. Sean was beginning to steam because he never liked it when we treated him like one of the crew. He was a great singer-songwriter, and he always saw himself as our equal.

All of a sudden, the car started to jog violently.

"Oh, God, the car," Sean said as he pulled to the side of the road. The wagon sputtered to a stop. We were on some forsaken country road, nowhere near civilization, we thought.

Sean turned to me.

"We're out of gas and I don't know where we are," he said. "I don't know what to tell you, but we may have to walk."

Walk? More like run, I thought. And in seven-inch platform shoes.

"You got to be fucking kidding me, right?" I screamed. "We can't get out of this fucking car. We're gonna get fucked in the ass."

By then it was getting dark. The heat became oppressive.

"Get in the back of the wagon and lay down," Sean said. "I'm going to go look for some help." He covered us up with a blanket, rolled up all the windows and locked the doors, and took off.

It was hot as hell under that blanket and we were sweating like pigs, but at the same time we were shivering from fear. We would find out later that Sean had staged the whole thing because he was pissed at our attitude. He had cut off the ignition, flooded the engine, surreptitiously grabbed a six-pack, walked around the curve, and sat down and downed the beer. We weren't even in the backwoods. We were driving through a new planned community.

When Sean came back what seemed like an eternity later, he said that it was the funniest thing to see all four of us lying in the back of the wagon covered by the blanket, with nothing but our teased hair protruding from one end and our platform boots from the other. He began to laugh hysterically and one by one, our heads emerged from under the blanket.

"How do you like it, you fucking bastards? How does it feel to get fucked with?" he said.

Gene and Paul and Ace were cursing Sean out as he revealed his prank and got back behind the wheel and drove off. But I didn't curse him. I was so pissed I didn't speak to him for two weeks.

But we were thrilled to be on the road. We had just finished our first album, and it was time to put our show together. We loved playing live and getting that instant feedback from the audience. So we were primed to get out there and conquer the world. We had started our first tour a few weeks earlier in Canada. Bill thought that Canada would be the ideal place to work out the kinks and get tight before we came to America. But Canada wasn't quite ready for us then.

Our first gigs there were mostly college dates, and the audiences were predominantly hippies who were confused by us. In Calgary we did an interview with the local radio station and went to the studio in full makeup. The receptionist took one look at us and ran out screaming. When we came out onstage, I'd look at the audience's faces and it looked like they were in shock, that they didn't believe what they were seeing. Or hearing. Our objective was to be loud, and then even louder. We kept our amps up to ten. Eventually we'd fill the whole back of the stage with these great big Marshall amps stacked up, all lit up. What the audience didn't know was that most of those Marshalls were just dummy cabinets with no speakers inside. But it looked great.

Some of the Canadian audiences got it and were appreciative. Other nights we'd get booed and they'd throw bottles at us. But nothing deterred us. If they didn't like us, we'd go, "Fuck 'em. We'll blow their minds next show."

A few nights into the tour, we got a chance to pull our first prank. Gene had picked up a chick and they were in his room. I was rooming with Gene then, so I went to Paul and Ace's room.

"Let's bust Gene's balls. He's got a chick in the room," I said. "I'm going to get naked and tie a red ribbon around my neck and my cock and put my balls in a champagne glass and serve it to them."

To my surprise, Paul wanted to join me. And he had a set of balls like a fucking elephant's. So we tied the ribbons and put our balls in two champagne glasses and I slowly opened the door to the room. Gene quickly turned on the lamp, and there was Paul and me with our balls in the champagne glasses.

"Would you or your girl care for a drink?" I said.

Gene looked us over and then pushed us out and slammed the door behind us.

After playing three shows in Canada, we went to L.A. in February to play at a huge party Neil was throwing to celebrate the start of Casablanca Records. He took over the ballroom of the L.A. Century Plaza hotel and transformed it into Rick's Café from the movie *Casablanca,* complete with all the gambling tables. Neil even borrowed Bogart's actual white tux from the movie and wore it that night. The invitation to the party was in the shape of a vinyl single that said, "You must remember this, a Kiss is just a Kiss."

Everybody who was anybody in L.A. came out that night. Rod Stewart was there, Alice Cooper, all these industry bigwigs. Again, we played so loud that most of the people didn't know what to think of us. But Alice dug us. He came over to congratulate us after we played and then joked to the press, "What these guys need is a gimmick."

Thanks to Neil's contacts, we did Dick Clark's *In Concert* TV show and followed it with an appearance on *The Mike Douglas Show*. Douglas had a daytime talk show that was for the housewife set, but we were excited to get the exposure. There was no MTV, no videos then, so you took what you could get. Johnny Carson wouldn't have us on—he hated rock 'n' roll

Right from the beginning, KISS was very polarizing: You either loved us fanatically or hated us to death. I adored the fanatics, but the rebel in me didn't mind being hated. I felt we must have been doing something well to be that despised.

So we were in the dressing room getting ready, and one of Mike's producers came in and asked who from the band would come out to panel with Mike and his guests before we played. Of course it wouldn't be me, because I was the Guinea from Brooklyn who talked like "dis" and "dat." Plus I was too insecure to go out and talk then. Ace, forget about it: He didn't talk much, and when he did, it was mostly squawking sounds that nobody could comprehend. Paul didn't want to do it either. He felt that he was the star, and he didn't want to lose his mystique.

So that left Gene. He always loved to pontificate to anybody who was around him, let alone to millions of people watching on TV. He jumped at the chance. He got introduced and walked onto the set in full makeup with his evil satanic winged costume on. Mike Douglas was flabbergasted.

"Are you a bat?" he asked.

"Actually, what I am is evil incarnate," Gene said.

One of the other panelists was Totie Fields, an old Jewish comedienne, who was looking at Gene and just shaking her head.

"You know, Mike, your audience looks really appetizing. Some of those cheeks and necks look really good," Gene said, licking his lips.

Douglas was just baffled. He didn't know what had hit him.

"Wouldn't it be funny if underneath this he was just a nice Jewish boy?" Totie suddenly said.

"You should only know," Gene said.

"I do!" Totie countered. "You can't hide the hook."

We proceeded to play, and I kept looking over at Mike Douglas, who was sitting there watching with his hands on his head, like he was thinking, What a fucking mistake.

In retrospect, we may have created a monster, letting the monster do the talking that day. When the show was over, we reprimanded Gene for his interview.

"If you're going to talk, it's not about being a monster," Paul said. "We're not a fucking horror band, we're a rock 'n' roll band. You gotta say the record's coming out and we're on tour."

I think that Paul got jealous when Gene began to dominate the interviews. To be honest, sometimes I loved watching Gene hang himself with his babble. But Gene loved that role because he thought that it gave him more power and stature, and that was what was most important to him.

After that show, we went back on the road and toured the South. We had a little crew with a U-Haul truck drive ahead of us, and we would drive in the station wagon with Sean. Those were such great times. We'd stop at Howard Johnson's because their clam chowder was to die for. We stayed at Motel 6s and tiny Holiday Inns. I'll never forget rolling along the highway with Sean leading us in a sing-along of "Ninety-nine Bottles of Beer on the Wall."

We didn't have enough money then to have our own rooms, so at first I roomed with Gene. But he was boring. All he would do is bring home women, and I'd be in the next bed and have to listen to their grunting and moaning all night.

Even worse, Gene was a pig. I liked a clean, orderly room—my pajamas in the drawer, my fruit on the table, my medicine by the nightstand. Gene's shit was all over the place. And his leather outfit just stank to dear hell. We even started calling him Stinky because he'd never dry his leather. After a show, he'd never shower. He'd wear that stinky outfit back to the Holiday Inn and chicks would freak out when they saw that monster walking down the hallway.

Gene was really delusional. He would always tell us that he could look in the mirror and believe he was better-looking than he really was. When Gene and Paul first met, Paul didn't like him: He thought Gene was abrasive. Maybe that arrogance came from his mother always telling him that he was better than anyone else. That was one way to cope with the fact that he was getting the shit kicked out of him every day on the streets of Brooklyn.

I gave Gene the nickname Professor Dope because he'd talk to you as if you were a child in his sixth-grade class.

"Uh, Peter, you know, you have to lift your fork with your left hand," he'd lecture me. Everything he knew he knew from reading it in a book—he had book smarts, but no street smarts. I'd tell him to take that fucking book and shove it up his ass.

Eventually I couldn't take Stinky anymore and began rooming with Paul. When we started up the band, I felt incredibly close to Paul. We would talk for hours on the phone, like chicks, sharing our dreams and plotting out how we were going to make it to the top. Unlike Gene, Paul seemed to be a really sensitive guy, and I related to that.

I began to think that I was going to find another Jerry Nolan in Paul. But it seemed that as we got closer, he started to back away. I began to realize that we didn't have that much in common. I would want to go out and grab a few cocktails, and Paul would be much happier going shopping and looking at drapes or, later, as we made more money, Oriental rugs. Nothing really traumatic happened between us, we just sort of drifted apart.

Paul always had to be the center of attention. He could be incredibly cocky, especially for a kid who came right out of his mommy and daddy's apartment into the band. I had paid fifteen years of dues: That's probably one of the reasons why I was so insecure and driven to make this band a success. I was twenty-nine years old and married. If this ended, what the fuck would I do? Paulie could have gone to college and moved back in with his parents.

Later on, Paul would say that I was volatile and insecure. Of course I was. Name me one rock star who isn't insecure. Bill realized what a tough time I had growing up being abused by the nuns in Catholic school. We would talk about that. But if I was insecure, Paul was a thousand times worse. Since I'd known him, he had been seeing a shrink. Once we went on the road, Paul would call the shrink every night. He wouldn't make a move without that guy.

Maybe some of what they talked about in their sessions was Paul's gender orientation. I've been asked many times, "Is Paul Stanley gay or bisexual?" I would routinely answer, "No, not that I know." But deep down I feel the man had issues. Ace and I would always goof on Paul's femininity. We even dubbed him the He/She. And Gene would egg us on when we made fun of Paul, but he wouldn't say anything to Paul's face, the coward. There was plenty to pick on. Paul would keep his fingernails immaculate. He'd go to women's boutiques to buy frilly blouses that he would wear offstage. He loved dressing up.

But Paul was a great front man. He and Gene were always in competition for the stage, but Paul had the unique ability to get an audience up and keep them up until we left the stage. He worked his ass off onstage. I don't know if anybody could imagine what it was like to wear those seven-inch platform shoes and jump into the air, land on your feet, and fly down those steps we used to have. He had that pizzazz onstage, and today I see many lead singers who are just slavishly copying Paul.

During the course of those early tours, I began to gravitate toward Ace. Gene and Paul were too tame, but Ace was trouble. There was drinking, carrying on, and pussy with Ace. Early in our touring we had a rare day off and Ace and I went to see *The Texas Chainsaw Massacre*. Ace smuggled in a six-pack of beer and I brought a bottle of wine. The movie theater was empty, and by the time the opening credits were rolling, Ace had knocked off half of the six-pack. It was a scary movie. Ace was screaming and holding on to my arm, and we were both soused and laughing hysterically. That was a great experience, and I wound up falling in love with Ace. We became inseparable and started sharing a room and sharing girls. He was just so much fun to be around.

Ace and I were simpatico musically, too. I was a street kid from Brooklyn and I took those streets with me onstage. Was I coarse? Absolutely. Was I uneducated? Sure, in a lot of ways. But nobody ever played any more from the heart on those drums than I did. Some nights I just felt so much spirit, I was so overwhelmed by the audience, that I would literally wreck my drums, smashing my cymbals and throwing the drums over.

Gene and Paul would recoil at some of the things that Ace and I did because they had lived sheltered lives and they had never encountered street kids like us. But wasn't rock 'n' roll all about being a rebel and breaking all the rules? Didn't rock stars wreck hotels and smash up cars and generally act belligerent?

Ace was as passionate about the music as I was. If his fingers weren't bleeding, if he wasn't playing at top volume, he wasn't playing. We were a completely different species from Gene and Paul. But Sean loved us to death, and so did Bill. They knew that we might be sitting in our hotel room drinking and we might look around and say, "Fuck it," and then the TV was going out the window. We thought that was hilarious. We didn't even consider that we might kill someone walking outside the hotel.

But there was an arrogance about Ace that I didn't like. He'd yell at waiters and call them idiots. When we built up a fan base, he didn't really like to stop and interact with our fans in the lobby. He was also a pig. When I started rooming with him, he'd drive me crazy. We wouldn't be in the room for five minutes and there'd be wires, guitars, books, filthy underwear, and socks strewn all around the room.

One of the reasons Ace and I really bonded was that we had a serious fistfight one day during a show in Canada. It was in the middle of the summer, there was no air-conditioning, and we were wearing all that leather. I couldn't get enough towels to soak up all my sweat. Gene was running around, Paul was running around: They were hardworking guys and they were sweating like pigs too. Then all of a sudden Ace decided he was too hot and he sat down on the stage while he played. I was irate.

We finished the set and went into the dressing room to wait for the encore. Ace was sitting down and I confronted him.

"You lazy son of a bitch, how dare you sit down while I'm banging my brains out there with two little fans on me? You better go out this encore and kick ass. You've been lazy the whole time we've been together. You never loaded the fucking equipment—"

All of a sudden, my speech was interrupted by a large bottle of orange juice that whizzed past my head and shattered against the wall.

"You motherfucker!" I screamed, and punched him in the face and knocked him out cold.

Now we had a problem. The fans were screaming for an encore. So we revived Ace and we went out and did the encore. After we got our makeup off, Ace came up to me.

"You want to ride with me in my car?" he said.

"Yeah, I'll go back with you," I said.

Of course, Ace had made sure the promoter loaded the car with champagne. He popped a cork.

"Let's call a truce," Ace said. "You're a fucking hell of a man, Peter, I like that."

"You are too, Ace," I said. "But if you would have hit me with that bottle, you could have killed me."

"You almost broke my jaw, but I love you, man."

And he gave me a big hug and we started crying like chicks. We became inseparable after that.

You could imagine what a hard job it was to literally babysit these four egotistical maniacs. That's what the job of the road manager was. He had to wake us up, make sure there was food at the gig, make sure we'd get in the car or, later, the plane. He'd be your mother, father, shrink, doctor, lover, all wrapped into one. We used to go through road managers like candy. One guy lasted just a day, I think. But Sean was our first road manager, and he was a doozy. First of all, he was as crazy as we were. He was totally hyperactive, with tons and tons of energy. He didn't need coke: He was naturally wired. We tried to give him many nervous breakdowns, but we couldn't succeed, so he was with us for a long time.

Sean would totally obsess over us "babies," as he called us. I never had a woman as crazy about me as Sean was. For some reason, Sean thought that if we got laid, we'd do a bad show because it would weaken our knees. Even if Lydia was on the road with me, Sean would bang on the door and yell, "Remember, nobody gets laid."

"Get the fuck out of here," I'd yell back through the door. "Nothing is going to weaken my knees, you fucking fag."

He was delusional if he thought that he could keep the four of us from getting laid. When we'd bring groupies into the rooms, Sean would storm in there, screaming, "These guys need their sleep," and grab them by the hair and drag them out. We would warn the chicks and tell them that if he came in and threw them out, they should go sit in the lobby for an hour and then come back up again. Sometimes we'd try to hide the girls in the room, in the shower, under the bed, under the covers, under us, whatever, but Sean would throw the lights on and check every inch of the room. He was the pussy gestapo.

Besides a crazy road manager, we had a crew that would kill for us. Our original crew was Chris Griffin and Peter Moose, along with Sean. As we went along, we added Mick Campise, Paul Chavarria, Mike McGurl, Rick Monroe, and J.R. Smalling as the tour manager. J.R. was the man. He was a six-foot-four, two-hundred-something-pound black guy from Brooklyn who wore a motorcycle jacket, blue jeans, motorcycle boots, and a gray bebop hat tilted to the side. You wouldn't want to fuck with J.R., but underneath that Marlon Brando exterior was a sweet, gentle man.

When we arrived at the venue, J.R. would walk into the promoter's office and the first words out of his mouth were, "Hey, man. How's the drug situation? How's the women situation?" He loved his pot. You'd go to his room and get a contact high. After a gig he'd light up a doobie and down a bottle of Nyquil and lapse into a coma. Then we could do whatever we wanted because he'd be out for twelve hours.

One time on the first tour we opened for Argent. They had a little Pakistani road manager who was a tight-ass. He wouldn't let us sound check, and then he tried to pull the plug on our encore. J.R. just went over to this tiny guy, picked him up, locked him in an equipment case, and we finished our song. Of course, we also got booted off the Argent tour.

What was great about J.R. was that he had the same attitude as we did. We were headliners even if we were the opening act. When J.R. walked into a room, people jumped. If there was a problem, J.R. would find a solution. Every place we played, there was a local fire chief on hand because of all our pyro. And if the chief needed to get greased so we could blow our shit up, that would happen.

We had a biker gang from Detroit named the Renegades who drove our trailers. Guys like Hot Sand, Football, Muskrat, and Cheeseburger. They were hardcore bikers, guys with shotguns who did damaging things to people who crossed them. No one fucked with us when they were around. It was more like, KISS is coming to town, hide your daughters.

We never had to worry about our backs with guys like this around. But we did worry about playing. Each one of us would get nervous before a show, but we'd each let it out in different ways. Gene would yell at everybody. Paul would stretch and run around in the dressing room. Ace might have a beer and tell some jokes, but he was nervous too. I would pace the dressing room.

Putting on our makeup was a laborious task. It took a good hour to get it right. There would be days when we'd get up in a hotel, have breakfast sent up, put on the makeup, get in costume, go to a photo session or a radio interview, go back to the hotel, take all that shit off, do a sound check, go back to the hotel, try to get some rest, then go back to the venue and put the makeup and costumes back on. We would do that day after day after day.

But I loved that hour. Putting on the makeup was therapeutic. No one was allowed in the room when we applied the makeup, and the room would get quiet and we would morph into our characters.

After we had our makeup and costumes on, we might mingle with guests, but we always had a five-minute rule. Five minutes before show-time, Bill or Sean would clear out the dressing room and we'd spend the time together, just the four of us, to clear our minds. Being the oldest, sometimes I might start acting silly, making up words, acting spastic, whatever it took to diffuse the tension. Then we'd high-five each other and say, "Let's beat the fucking shit out of them tonight," and we'd charge out there and kick ass.

From the very first tour, the press would always go after us. I used to go back to my room after a show and think, Wait a minute, we just did a sold-out show and the people went absolutely wild for us. So why was I reading, "KISS just might be the worst band on the planet. The only good thing you can say about them is they are loud. I would never buy one of their records"? Where's the mention that the audience didn't sit down once, they stood up from beginning to the wild, orgasmic end of the show?

We'd moan and bitch about the press and Bill would try to mollify us. "Any write-up is good," he'd tell us. "Who cares what the critic says? Your name is in the paper." We also had to contend with not getting any radio airplay. So that meant just hitting the road and building up a fan base.

Most of the time we would blow away the headliners, and sometimes the reaction was so great that we'd get booted from the tour. Aerosmith booted us after two dates. Argent got rid of us. We opened for Foghat, ZZ Top, and REO Speedwagon, and they were all threatened by the reception we got from the crowd. It helped that the four of us had that swagger. When you believe that much in yourselves, you can't lose.

It also helped that we had a great front man, a guy spitting fire and drooling blood, a guitar player shooting off rockets, a drummer who levitated, and tons and tons of flash pots. Try to top that.

On June 14, 1974, we played with the New York Dolls, and it was a watershed show for me. Gene told me that we were going to open for them.

"We're going to blow them off the fucking stage, I don't give a fuck whether it's your friend or not," he warned.

I agreed. And we were even more motivated when the Dolls treated us like shit and made us change in the toilet. We came on like a bat out of hell and the crowd went crazy.

I made plans to hang with Jerry later that night. I hadn't seen him for a long time because we were both working round the clock to be famous. We got together in a room in the hotel and I had a gram of coke I figured we could share.

"Uh, coke's not my cup of tea anymore," Jerry said. "How about I take it and trade it for a little heroin for us?"

I didn't like that idea. I had done heroin, but it seemed a little too down and dirty for that time in my life. Still, I didn't want to ruin our reunion.

"All right, if it'll make you happy, I'll do a few lines with you."

Jerry went out to score, and I waited and waited and he never came back. The next day I saw him on the plane.

"What happened, man?"

"Ah, I met somebody and . . ." he trailed off.

I felt like I was back on the streets of Brooklyn hearing those junkie lies again.

I wanted to call him out on it, but I was too hurt. The guy sitting next to me was not the Jerry Nolan I grew up with and loved. He had totally changed, thanks to junk. I just sat there waiting to get off that plane. We finally landed and said our good-byes and I never talked to Jerry again. Eighteen years later, I got word that Jerry caught meningitis from shooting up and died. I didn't go to his funeral. It would have killed me, but to this day, he's still in my prayers.

The shows were great, but we just couldn't get any radio airplay, so we had no choice but to keep scheduling dates and playing live. The road was grueling, especially with the show we were doing. It was scary being away from home in Brooklyn, so every night I would write postcards to Lydia, my mother, and my uncle George. Things like "Hey Ma, I'm in Duluth, Minnesota. Holy mackerel! There's some strange people here, but I'm having a great time," or "Unc, played last night and I did a drum solo and everybody went crazy. We're still kind of struggling, and we'll be in another Holiday Inn tomorrow. Love you." My family kept those post-cards in a special box all through the years.

We were opening for Rory Gallagher in the Midwest, and Casablanca sent a few execs out to check out our show. They were in the audience with Neil and Joyce, and after we left the stage the crowd was going wild, screaming for an encore. But we didn't come out. Neil sent Joyce back to see what was going on and she got backstage and saw that the back doors of the venue were open and I was on the ground, with J.R. standing over me, trying to revive me. There was a low ceiling in the club, and when they levitated me during "Black Diamond," I started breathing in all the smoke from the flash pots that had risen to the ceiling and I passed out and fell backward ten feet. Lucky for me, J.R. was there to catch me.

On June 22, we were playing the final night of a four-night stand at a club in Atlanta when Paul collapsed and we had to rush him out of the venue and end the show. Well, that's what it looked like to the audience. The truth was that we were on our third encore and had run out of songs to perform. We were in the dressing room, racking our brains to come up with another song, but we couldn't.

"I got it—I'll faint," Paul suggested.

We looked at him like he was crazy.

"You can pull that off?" I said.

"No problem," Paul said.

We didn't even tell our roadies because as great as they were, they all had big mouths and would have told the whole place, "Paulie's going to faint." So we kept it quiet.

We went out for another encore and I sat behind the drums. We went into "Deuce" for the second time, and I was just waiting for Paul to faint. Sure enough, he swooned and fell to the stage. Within seconds, J.R. was knocking people out of the way, rushing to the stage.

Meanwhile Paul was lying there, clutching his head in an Oscar-worthy performance. J.R. and Mick Campise carried Paul off to the dressing room, and the show was over. We laughed for hours after that one.

Touring nonstop was dangerous for me because the Catman lived a very wild life. He did a lot of drugs, drank a lot of booze, got a lot of pussy. I actually wanted to get rid of him now and then and just be Peter Criscuola again. The Catman was killing me.

But Gene and Paul loved the road. They would be happy to be out there 365 days a year. Once Ace said, "You guys don't care, because no one gives a fuck about you two. You have no friends, so you don't really want to stay home, because you won't know what to fucking do with yourself."

Ace was right. Gene and Paul were workaholics. I don't put that down. But Peter Criscuola believed there was time for family, there was time for God, and time to give the fucking brain time off from this fake world we were living in.

So we made a deal with Gene and Paul that first year out. We would always be home for Christmas. We'd play Thanksgiving, we'd play New Year's Eve. But not Christmas. I needed to see a Christmas tree. I wanted to go home and smell the holly, get drunk with friends in a local bar. We wanted one week a year to be with our families.

We learned a lot on that first tour, a lot about ourselves and a lot about our audience. At first our audience was almost 100 percent male. We used to joke, "Where the fuck are the girls?"

But we were getting a very interesting segment of the male population. We were drawing the metalheads, the renegades, the fat kid who sat in the back of the class, along with the skinny kid who got picked on. Our fans were the underdogs, the ones who didn't belong.

They were all, in their own way, outcasts. But when they went home and put on our makeup and put on a KISS album and practiced their stage moves in front of the mirror, they would become Gene Simmons or Paul Stanley or Ace Frehley or Peter Criss. They would escape into KISS-world, and that was a very sacred place for them.

Sure enough, they started wearing their makeup and costumes to the shows and you could see many Peter Crisses out in the audience, many Gene Simmonses and Paul Stanleys and Ace Frehleys.

We embraced these underdogs and gave them a home. I'll never forget the first time I saw a fan come backstage dressed in full Catman costume and makeup. He came up to me, asked for an autograph, and then he said, "Hey Peter, how do I look?"

"You look cool as fucking hell, man," I replied.

CHAPTER SEVEN

When I came to after I blacked out, I didn't know where I was for a few seconds. All I knew was that a naked woman who had been wearing a ram's head was giving me head while I was slumped in a huge chair fit for a king. I looked over to a corner of the room and a guy was fucking a chick doggy-style and her titties were bouncing in joyous unison. Next to them, two guys were sucking each other off. Was I tripping on acid? I felt like I was in a weird movie, a cross between *A Midsummer Night's Dream* and *Satyricon*. When I looked the other way, I felt some relief to recognize Ace, who was banging some chick in the corner. Then I remembered. We were shooting the cover for our second album with the great photographer Norman Seeff. Seeff had hired twenty women and twenty men to surround us in some elaborate medieval Gothic tableau. To lubricate the scene, the set was stocked with plenty of champagne, scotch, whiskey, rum, you name it. It might have been the scotch that gave me that temporary amnesia. It was certainly all that liquor that fueled what became more an of orgy than a photo shoot.

But as drunk as I was, Paul was even more sloshed, which was a rarity for a guy who was so concerned with losing his cool. He was lying half naked on a velvet bed, offering no resistance at all to the half dozen girls and guys who were buzzing around him like bees drawn to honey. That's why Gene made his move. If one dick had gone into Paul's defenseless mouth or up his ass, there would have been seven more dicks a-swarming.

So Gene swooped in and grabbed Paul and carried him out of Dante's *Inferno*. He deposited him in the backseat of our rental car and locked the doors. Welcome to L.A.

We had come out West to record our second album just a stone's throw from the offices of Casablanca Records. We were thrilled to be out in Hollywood. What was not to like? We were used to an asphalt jungle with towering buildings. Here we saw beautifully landscaped houses where movie stars lived. The weather was nice every day. Oh, and there were girls, an endless, endless array of beautiful girls.

We were working with Kenny Kerner and Richie Wise again, and the studio was beautiful and the vibes seemed great, but Gene especially just couldn't deal with the laid-back L.A. attitude. If we needed something in the studio fixed, we wanted it fixed immediately. Gene thought everyone in L.A. was a moron. "They stay out in the sun too long," he used to scoff. We were a bunch of hyper New York workaholics who just wanted to capture our sound and then get back on the road. Besides, there were just too many temptations for Ace and me in L.A.

I thought we had a bunch of real good songs, but again the sound just wasn't being captured. The sessions seemed stale. It was the same old same old with these guys, only in a different room on a different coast.

I didn't really push to get any of my songs on the album. I knew they weren't going to do any of them: They just weren't the kind of songs we were doing. But I did push to sing on the record. Paul had written a song, "Mainline," that was perfect for me, but recording it was torturous. Paul would literally stand in front of my fucking face, making me sing it word for word and note for note the way he wanted it, which puts a bit of a damper on your creativity. In his best days he couldn't outsing me. He had no soul.

Ace had written two songs for the album, but he didn't have the confidence to sing either of them. Gene and Paul could be quite intimidating, and Ace told me many times that they made him feel inadequate. But Ace would always push for me to sing his songs so that I could get a little bit of the spotlight. So I sang "Strange Ways." I also thought that an extended drum solo was just the thing for that song. Of course, Gene and Paul wouldn't hear that.

"Why are you guys always right and I'm always wrong?" I protested. "Why can't I do a solo there?"

"Well, it's pretty obvious that we . . ." they would mumble.

"Yeah, you, but the fans may like it," I said.

I was a solo guy. I loved doing them, and "Strange Ways" was the perfect vehicle for one. So I fought back the only way I knew how.

"If the solo goes, I quit the band," I threatened. Of course I was crying wolf: I just wanted some input into the process.

I recorded a really good solo. But after my drum tracks were done, I never stayed around the studio, so, of course, they just cut the solo out. And I didn't quit.

In fact, I was relatively happy. We were staying at the Sunset Marquis, a real rock 'n' roll hotel in West Hollywood. When the recording was done, Paul and I jumped from our second-story balcony into the pool. Even Gene jumped in, wearing his huge monster boots and heavy leather. Ace didn't partake. He was recovering from getting pissed one night and driving around the same block in the Hollywood Hills, faster and faster, until he wrapped his rental car around a telephone pole.

I remember sitting up on my balcony at the hotel and playing the tape of *Hotter Than Hell* over and over. It felt so great to have two albums under our belts. And despite our occasional differences, it was still fun to be around each other. We would make each other laugh for hours and hours. We were all such different people, but we were united in one goal.

We toured behind the album from October 1974 until February 1975. We were still working on our live show, and sometimes there would be bumps in the road. One of our signature moves then was to have my drumsticks explode. Neil was a big magic fan and he loved flash paper, so we devised special sticks that were hollow and made out of white copper. We packed the sticks with flash paper and put in an ignite switch so I'd have a nice finale at the end of show, blasting balls of fire out over the audience.

Other than the exploding drumsticks, though, we didn't have much firepower at that point in our career. Sean had rigged up a couple of flash pots, but that was about it. Eventually we had enough shit to blow a stadium up. If you stepped in the wrong place on that stage on the wrong night, you were dead. I never trusted that shit. All those pyro guys were nuts. They'd be handling the dynamite and they'd have a lit cigarette dangling out of their mouths.

I found it hard enough to control my little drumsticks. Sometimes one would go off and the other wouldn't. Sometimes they'd just peter out and hit the front of the stage. Other times, they'd misfire and go backward.

We had a much worse accident a few weeks later. We were in Springfield, Illinois, playing a National Guard armory of all places. Our roadie Moosey, a really nice, big Italian kid, was responsible for loading up my exploding sticks. We were in the dressing room putting on our makeup when all of a sudden we heard a loud "BOOM!"

"What the fuck was that?" I said.

Suddenly Moosey came running into the room with half of his hand hanging off. There was blood shooting everywhere and there was white, briny stuff leaking out. It looked like a Quentin Tarantino movie. We found out later that unused powder had accumulated in one of the sticks and he was using a screwdriver to scrape it away when it ignited and blew his hand up. I grabbed a towel and wrapped it around his hand.

"We gotta cancel the show. I have to go to the hospital with Moosey," I said.

The rest of the guys talked me out of it. They were right. It was a sold-out show and we couldn't let those fans down. I couldn't wait for the show to end so I could check on Moosey. He underwent emergency surgery and they were able to save his hand, but it never functioned properly again. We paid for his bills and Bill threw him a few bucks and made him sign a waiver so we couldn't get sued.

On that tour we wound up playing in Detroit on my birthday. After the show, they threw me a nice party that seemed to have a drug theme. I got all this drug paraphernalia like coke spoons and vials and hash pipes. And our great road crew, the Renegade bikers, cooked some Alice B. Toklas brownies that were made with hash and grass. The road crew knew this, Paul and Ace and I knew this, but Gene had no idea. This was a man who had never gotten high once in his life. But he loved sweets! So Gene wolfed down about six brownies and left the party with a female rock journalist.

Later that night, the phone in my room rang.

"Peter, this is Gene. I don't know what's happening to me. My hands are shrinking and my face won't fit in the mirror."

Gene was freaking out so he called me up. I was the guy who knew all about drugs, right? I had to keep from laughing.

"Gene, did you eat any of those brownies at the party?"

"Yes, I had about six of them," he said.

"Well, they were dosed with pot," I told him. "You're just high. You got that girl with you. Get into some sex with her and you'll forget all about the size of your head."

A few minutes later the phone rang again.

"It's not wearing off. It's getting worse," Gene worried.

I didn't have the heart to tell him that the high from eating pot lasts a lot longer than from smoking it.

"You're fighting it. Stop fighting and just enjoy the high," I said.

"Oh, God, I'm going to overdose."

"You won't overdose. You're not going to die. Just have fun with that chick."

"But her face is starting to melt."

I guess it wore off, because he didn't call again that night. I saw him in the lobby the next morning and he looked shaky.

"I will never eat another brownie in my life," he said.

Meanwhile *Hotter Than Hell* had been released, but it tanked. Our live shows were dynamite, but we still hadn't figured out how to capture that sound on vinyl. And I still hadn't figured out why we were using lame producers like Kerner and Wise when we could have used Eddie Kramer. But that soon became a moot point. Casablanca hadn't been paying us any royalties at all, and Bill was basically financing our touring with his American Express card.

After *Hotter Than Hell* disappeared, we had a meeting with Kerner and Wise, the band, and Bill and Joyce. Kerner and Wise told us that they had a major offer from another label to take the band with them as producers to do our next album. It's likely that they didn't know that Joyce was seeing Neil, so the next day, Neil got wind of this, fired Kerner and Wise, and decided that he was going to produce the next album. Nobody had been able to capture our sound, but the great Bogart would.

Now, I love Neil, but he had never produced anything in his life. He had one minor hit as a singer when he was young, but that doesn't make you a producer. Still, he was the head of the record company and he decided we needed to go back to our roots and record not only in New York City but at Electric Lady, so I was pretty jazzed.

We went into the studio the first week of February 1975. The first executive decision Neil made as producer was to bring along a pound of weed. You couldn't walk into that room without getting a contact high. I was dizzy 24/7 during those sessions. Gene and Paul didn't even realize that they were high. Gene would order four dozen donuts and chow down on them constantly.

You don't really want to record an entire album stoned on pot. All of us, especially Neil, were hearing things that just didn't fucking exist on the tape. I distinctly remember playing on a few cuts and thinking to myself, "Jesus, I am fucked up." But there was nothing we could have done about it. What were we going to do, tell the president of our record company to stop smoking his joints?

Once again I thought the songs were good. I figured as long as the material was up to par, everything would come out okay, but it didn't. It came out like shit. But opinions of music are very subjective. A lot of our fans would later tell me that *Dressed to Kill* was our best album. It certainly had one of our best-ever songs on it. Neil was urging us to write an anthem, and Paul came up with "Rock and Roll All Nite." You can hear it today at just about any sporting event in the world. I got to sing an Ace song, "Getaway," because Ace was still too shy to sing. And I was still a little gun-shy to push my songs on the other guys.

Although we seemed to be attracting a very devoted fan base, we still were scuffling as an opening act. In May we played on the campus of Ohio Northern University, and after the show a faculty member saw us walking around the campus. She figured we were typically broke college students, so she gave all of us lunch passes. The student council didn't even have money for us to get a hotel room, so we slept in the dorms that night. I stayed with two crazy science majors who were synthesizing their own LSD. They wanted me to trip, but they settled for staying up all night and smoking pot with me.

In the middle of May we decided to record our live show. We picked Cobo Hall, a venue in Detroit. We had played Cobo before and it was a great hall, plus the promoter was very generous with his blow. Detroit was a lot like New York City in a way. They either loved you or they totally hated you. If they hated you, you were dead meat. They'd hit you with lettuce, tomatoes, eggs, whatever. But Detroit loved KISS and they took us under their wing, especially the females. It was the ideal place to record live, and we sold the joint out and the crowd went crazy. In a lot of ways, Detroit turned a bunch of green kids into men, and we'll always be indebted to that town.

By June we were back out on the West Coast. After playing one show with Billy Preston and trashing his stage with blood and debris, we were thrown off his tour. The problem was Bill had almost maxed out his credit card, so he couldn't afford to get us back to New York. So the plan was for us to check into a cheap hotel in the Bay Area and regroup, then get on another tour. We wound up at the Vagabond Inn, which was smack in the middle of the gayest section of San Francisco.

We were totally depressed. We actually began to think that this circus was over and we'd just hang out there until we could go back to New York with our tails between our legs. I figured that this was the time to get strong. I clicked into survivor mode. If it was going to be over, then let's go out with a smile. It was ironic that I of all people, the one who was usually the most depressed of the depressed, took it upon myself to cheer up the band.

Ace and Gene had a room on the second floor and Paul and I shared a room downstairs. Each room had a kitchen in it. That first night I said to Paul, "Let's do something cool. Let's open up a restaurant. We can call it the Gay Kitchen, and we'll be the gay chefs and cook up a meal and invite the guys down for dinner."

"That's great, man," Paul said. "I'll do the menu."

And he drew up this beautiful menu, full of gay double entendres, with each item on the menu corresponding to a different guy in the band or in the crew. There was:

Tall Paul's Big Ball Scallops
Slick Mick's Big Dick Special

The Spoiler Omelets

And for the Ace in the hole, why not try the Closet Burger?

Soul food anyone? Try Junior's Black Oak in the Can—you'll like it.

Italian food? Get Gino's bloody but hearty pizza. It's not big, but it's filling.

The above items come with the cook of the day: You can't beat that one, kids. Prices according to size.

I had to give it to Paul. We were always busting his chops about his femininity, but here he was camping it up with me and creating this little bit of theater.

We were broke but my grandfather George, the cocksman, lived nearby and he was eager to help us out. He and his seventh wife brought us shopping bags stocked with hot dogs, eggs, beans, Rice-A-Roni, and mac and cheese. So we whipped that up, and then I went up to Ace and Gene's room.

"Dinner will be served at six P.M. sharp downstairs in the gay kitchen," I lisped.

They loved it. The two of them combed their hair, put on nice button-down shirts, and came down. I greeted them at the door, had them sit down at a table that we covered with a checkered cloth, and gave them the hand-drawn menus.

When we served the food and sat down to eat with them, we never broke character. Gene and Ace laughed their balls off. We kept the Gay Kitchen open for the six days that we were stranded there, and by then Bill had booked us to open for another headliner and we were back on the road.

But we were still dirt-poor. Gene stole a fake leather bedspread from our hotel in Vegas and used it at each hotel we'd check in to. Paul was worse. He routinely stole and stockpiled toilet paper and brought it home when the tour was over. He even brought his dirty clothes along at the beginning of a tour so we would pay for his laundering. I wasn't innocent, either. I made sure there would be extra scotch on the band's rider, and by the end of the tour I'd have about seven bottles of Johnnie Walker to take home with me. I also had my little eccentricities when it came to sleeping. I had to have my own pillows, so Lydia made a special duffel bag to carry them in. And my mom embroidered Mickey and Minnie Mouse on the pillowcases.

But I had nothing on Ace when it came to being eccentric. At one point, Ace began to recite jokes into a small tape recorder. Then he would come up to me, say, "Hey Cat, listen to this," play back the joke while he lip-synched to it, and then burst out laughing. He graduated from that to a little laugh box. We'd be on a plane or in a car and suddenly you'd hear this hysterical laughing coming from the box and Ace would join right in.

Before he would eat anything, Ace would have to smell it to make sure he wouldn't get food poisoning. Gene even nicknamed him the Chef. I remember one time Lydia asked him about that and pointed out that we never smelled our food before we ate and we never got food poisoning.

"Blame it on the bossa nova," Ace just shrugged.

He would always come up with these non sequiturs like "thirteen for a dozen." Half the time you had no idea what the fuck Ace was saying. Later on, when we were raking in a lot more money, Ace began to shoot home movies. By this time we had taken on a lawyer and business managers who were all Jewish. Ace would invite all of us up to his house for a party and then screen these home videos that he and his pal Bobby made. We'd sit around the TV and, all of a sudden, Ace would walk into the room wearing a full SS uniform complete with red swastika, hat, and a Luger.

"You vill watch my movie," he'd say, and then he'd show these movies with Ace and his friends in Nazi uniforms torturing other friends who were dressed like the Jewish in a concentration camp.

I'd be watching and then I'd look over at our managers and Paul Marshall, our lawyer, and they'd just look appalled.

And everybody put up with it. By then he was making so much money for them, what were they going to say?

In September of 1975, our lives were forever changed. That was when our live album *Alive* was finally released. It was a crazy time for us. We had tried and failed three times to capture the vibrancy and immediacy of the band on record. We were a huge-sounding heavy metal band on the road, but on the albums we sounded so small. So when Eddie Kramer agreed to come out on tour with two trucks to record us, we were ecstatic.

There had been financial considerations, too. It was a lot cheaper to record a live album than a new studio one. We were still waiting on our royalty statements from Casablanca. Neil had mortgaged his house to keep his company afloat because he had severed his distribution ties with Warner Bros. Records. Our lawyers had sued Neil for the back royalties, and it was getting ugly. It got so bad that back in New York, Bill was relying on friends who were taking turns to take him out to dinner.

Alive would change all that. Although it was crafted to sound like it was recorded in one night at Cobo Hall in Detroit, we actually recorded a bunch of shows. Then Kramer went back to New York and began culling the best performances. Picking out the best drum tracks was the first step. Once you had the drum track, then you could sweeten everything else. If you had to throw on a new lead, you could. Throw on some bass, add some rhythm guitar, all possible. In the end we wound up keeping only my drum tracks, my vocals, and Paul's between-song raps. Everything else was re-created in the studio.

Re-recording was a necessity, not any kind of subterfuge. Every band that's ever put out a live album does it. When you record live, there's always leakage, unless you get lucky. Sometimes guitars would go out of tune or you'd sing out of key. I would always go up an octave when I was singing "Black Diamond" live because I'd get so excited.

Finally, I got to hear one of my drum solos on a record. My solo on "100,000 Years" was scary, if I say so myself. It's probably the best drum solo that I've ever done. I used mallets and flangers to give it a cooler, different, deeper, almost outer-space sound.

We hit the road as soon as *Alive* came out. About a month into the tour, we scored one of the greatest publicity coups of all time. It all went back a year in time. In 1974, the Cadillac Vikings, the football team of Cadillac High School in Cadillac, Michigan, lost their first two games of the season. The head coach decided to play rock music before the game to pump up the players. The assistant coach, Jim Neff, chose to play our albums. Naturally, the team went on to win seven straight games. Neff got in touch with Alan Miller, who worked for Bill, and after a year of back and forth, we agreed to make Cadillac a stop on our tour and play the homecoming concert in the school's gym.

We couldn't believe our eyes when we got to Cadillac that day. It was like living in KISSworld. Everybody was in our makeup—even the politicians and the people who worked behind the counters at the local McDonald's. We rode on a big float in the homecoming parade down a street that had been renamed KISS Boulevard. The mayor gave us the key to the city. We took pictures with the football team. During halftime, I got on the football field and played along with the drum corps on "Rock and Roll All Nite." We had a ball. And we carried along a sizable number of press people who broke it into an international story.

Because Bill knew this story had major legs, he lectured us before we left. I had the feeling he was mainly talking to Gene.

"Be really cool when you're there," he counseled. "Don't sleep with the mayor's wife, don't sleep with his daughter. Stay away from the chief of police's daughter." I still think Gene fucked someone, but he was very discreet.

After two days, we left on an army helicopter from the stadium and dropped thousands of leaflets on the football field that read KISS LOVES YOU. Of course, the Vikings won that homecoming game.

About a month after Cadillac, we presided over the official inauguration of the KISS Army, which would become the greatest fan club in rock 'n' roll history. The whole concept for the KISS Army was formed at the beginning of 1975 when two teenagers from Terre Haute, Indiana, Bill Starkey and Jay Evans, began haranguing the program director of WVTS, a local radio station, to play KISS music. The program director blew them off again and again, telling them that KISS was a "fag band," until the two kids started sending letters threatening to blow up the station and actually picketed the station, claiming to be representing the KISS Army. By July, WVTS had added KISS to its playlist and kept referring to the KISS Army for requesting it. Somehow Alan Miller, whom we nicknamed "Little Bill" because he dressed identically to Bill Aucoin, got wind of this, and with his genius flair for publicity decided we should go to Terre Haute and give Starkey, who was the self-proclaimed General of the KISS Army, a plaque onstage. He also coordinated preshow publicity, and Starkey and his pal

Evans called into WVTS nightly to hype the show. And thanks to these two kids, we managed to sell out a new twenty-one-thousand-seat arena, something that even Aerosmith couldn't do.

So when we got to Terre Haute, we were treated like visiting dignitaries. The local Army base provided a Jeep escort for us from the airport to downtown, where they had a huge parade: the KISS Army meets the U.S. army. Again, Aucoin was way ahead of us on this. "You're the generals, and your army needs you," he lectured us. "You have to go out there and show the kids that you really love them, that you believe in what they believe."

From these humble origins, the KISS Army spread like wildfire. Which just goes to show the devotion of our fans. A KISS Army. Who ever heard of a Led Zeppelin Army or a Rolling Stones Army? This was some serious adulation. And the timing was right. We had just given them a national anthem with "Rock and Roll All Nite." We began to close with that song and drop thousands of pounds of confetti and balloons all over the audience. We had turned our show into a magnificently chaotic party.

Soon we couldn't stay at a hotel without the KISS Army invading it. They would storm the hotel en masse in their homemade costumes and makeup and sit in the lobby and chant song names over and over again: "Firehouse! Firehouse!" "Black Diamond! Black Diamond!" Then they'd start chanting our individual names. Of course the hotel management didn't take too kindly to this, and the police were called every night. After a few minutes, the cops would disperse the crowd and the staff would stick us with the cleanup bill.

I could feel the tide turning. I remember one night we were opening for Dr. John. We were waiting to go on when Mac—that's his real name— came into our dressing room. He had just gone through a bunch of shit: One of his buses got into a pileup and some of his wardrobe got messed up.

"Hey, lookit," he said in his deep New Orleans patois. "You guys don't have to open for me. I'll go on first because I'll tell you what, I ain't an idiot. Those people ain't here to see me. This ain't no blues audience, they got war paint on their faces. So let me get my boys out there now and we'll do our thing. Good luck."

And he reversed the order and went on first and then left. He was truly a cool cat.

Gene had become the de facto leader of the group because he would do most of the interviews. With his blood spitting and fire eating, he became the visual focal point of the group and was the most photographed. All of us, especially Paul, were beginning to resent Gene's dominance. They even met with Bill about it, and Gene calmly told Paul that Paul should be more assertive, not that Gene should tone anything down. Gene was right, but then Paul began to step in front of Gene routinely onstage. Once he did that, Gene would fade. Paul could steal the spotlight from him like that.

As we got more popular, a new monster was created. Paul always had a problem with carving out his own identity. Whatever someone else had, whether it was a car or, ultimately, a house, Paul would buy the same thing for himself. But now that we were drawing bigger audiences and Paul was moving out front more, he became the focal point. He'd get more letters from chicks. More people started wearing his makeup. And it built to a point where he just fell in love with himself.

But Paul would never blatantly assert his authority. He was a major game player, a puppet master. He would let Gene verbalize his feelings and desires. Suddenly it became whatever Paul wanted, Paul got. He was a master at mind games. I guess that's what four hours a day of talking to your shrink will do for you.

The worst, though, was when Gene and Paul worked in tandem to assert their authority over me and Ace. They always claim that they encouraged Ace and me to contribute songs or to sing, but they made it clear that there was a true pecking order in the band: Paul was the lead singer, Gene was the second lead, and they would write most of the material. After a while, they threw us a bone and we'd each get a song on an album. But Gene to this day asserts that the doors were always open for Ace and me but we just didn't deliver. We delivered—they just didn't accept. I was still writing with Stan Penridge, but no matter what I brought to them, it wasn't right for that particular record.

Even their collaborations eventually came to an end. I always found that writing with a partner was the best way to write. And Gene and Paul's early KISS stuff was fantastic. But then the egos set in and they separated as writers, and the songs just weren't as good. Paul started collaborating with other writers like Desmond Child, and he flat-out wrote better songs than Gene. As a drummer, I had a lot more fun playing Paul's songs than Gene's.

The songwriting and song selection were just one manifestation of the power that Gene and Paul always seemed to want to wield. As their power grew, their egos grew correspondingly. Their egos compelled them to make sure that they were in total control of themselves. That's why the two of them really never got high. Gene was frightened that he would lose control and do something embarrassing. Paul smoked some pot early on and took a few white crosses, which he used to sneak onto the road, but he also didn't want to blow his cool.

They'd laugh at Ace and me all the time and look down on us. Ace was just a clown, a space cadet, and I was the hard-edged Italian illiterate. They would have spelling contests—to while away the time, they said, but they knew it irritated me because I wasn't as literate as they were. We all knew it, so why do it if you're going to hurt one of your buddies, one of your band members? Gene would say, "Ace, spell *predicament*." Ace would reply, "Fuck you, you spell *predicament*." Then Paul would go, "Peter?" And I'd say, "You know I can't spell well, so you have to remind me of that? You don't think that hurts, motherfuckers?" And they'd go, "Peter, it's only a game." It was a game. The let's-fuck-with-Peter's-brain game.

The only way I knew how to respond to them was to be brutal. And my own monster would come out and I'd threaten to hurt them. That's all I had in my arsenal. I didn't have the words to put them down. I didn't have the education to stand up to them. But I knew how to kick ass.

They were master manipulators. Ace and I weren't. Gene admits now that if he and Paul wanted to do something and Ace and I didn't, they would "emotionally batter" us. So we were emotional wrecks, too unstable to help make decisions that affected our lives, and their gestapo tactics were justified to bring us in line with what they thought was right for the group.

When Gene was nice to me and treated me as an equal, there was nothing that I wouldn't do for him. There was a sweet side to Gene. Lydia used to pack Ring Dings, Twinkies, and Devil Dogs for me to take on the road. And Gene has a huge sweet tooth. Many times after a show, I'd invite Gene to my room and we'd sit there with a quart of milk and some Twinkies or Ring Dings and we'd watch cartoons together. He was the only other guy I knew who drank his milk with ice cubes in it!

But when he started that fucking power-tripping, game-playing shit with Paul, I had to resort to my street bravado. If they tried to bulldoze me or push me around, I'd go Peter Criscuola on them.

"Do that again and I'll break the table over your fucking head," I'd threaten.

I put up a tough front, but deep down I was a softie. It's easy to hurt me if you know how, and I usually let people know how—that was always my problem. When I do let someone get close to me, I'll tell them all of my business, all my problems, my whole life story. And it is definitely bad to open yourself up to people who are Machiavellian enough to use that information against you and push your buttons. So whenever I showed my sensitive side, Gene and Paul were there to jab at the heart I had just exposed.

Underneath the makeup, we all really knew each other. But somewhere along the line, as we got more popular, we lost our compasses. The magnificent journey became just a job—and then a nightmare for both Ace and me.

The myth of early KISS was that there were two groups within the group. There was the Gene and Paul group: the sane, straight, levelheaded members who shunned booze and drugs and who propelled the band forward with their business acumen. Then there was the Peter and Ace group, the wild and crazy musically creative guys.

We would have business meetings and I would, in my usually crude way, seek to debunk that myth. I would actually be sober at these meetings and proceed to explain that the emperors had no clothes.

"I drink and drug, Ace drinks and drugs, Bill drinks and drugs, Sean drinks and drugs, so naturally Gene and Paul's way is the right way? One of these fuckfaces is sitting here throughout the whole meeting drawing huge, anatomically correct dicks. This other fuckface, all he can think about is getting the fuck out of here and getting laid. And their way is the highway that we all should travel on? Like we didn't get on this road because Ace and I were bad boys? I'm so fed up with you hypocritical motherfuckers."

So this was the state of our union when *Alive* went gold, and then platinum, and propelled us to stardom. Once we finally put out an album that truly reflected the majesty of our live shows, the walls came tumbling down and the stadiums opened up for us. For good reason. As far as I was concerned, we were the best show on the fucking planet. My band would give you every last penny's worth of your ticket price. We had a guy eating fire, a guy levitating into the air, a guitar that shot rockets, and a front man as good as the best of them. It was literally a rock 'n' roll circus. And who could resist a circus?

Halfway through the *Alive* tour, we were informed that we would be rich beyond our dreams. All I ever wanted was a gold record on my wall and a nice living. Maybe sign a couple of autographs when I went out to eat with Lydia. I had no idea that we would become bigger than life itself.

I was thrilled for Bill. We signed a new deal with Casablanca and we got a lump-sum payment as an advance. Bill had invested so much time and effort, maxing out his Amex card to make us stars, that he couldn't pay his rent and had to rely on friends to eat. And now he was sitting in his office, staring at a check from Neil for $2 million. One of the first things Bill did was move out of the offices he had shared with some business part-ners for years and rent a magnificent new office for seventy K a month.

Then he told Lydia and me to move to Manhattan. Our dream had always been to live in a brownstone in the city, so Sean took Lydia out in a limo one day and they found a cute little brownstone on Thirtieth Street, complete with a spiral staircase and a fireplace. We put that first gold album over the fireplace in the living room. Then I went out and bought myself a chocolate-brown Camaro.

For her part, Lydia was ecstatic. She had paid her dues, too, working all those years at Abercrombie & Fitch, paying all the bills. Now she could quit her job. KISSmania was just starting. We had our first smash single off *Alive*, "Rock and Roll All Nite." We did rock and roll all night and party every day for many, many years to follow. And it almost killed me.

CHAPTER EIGHT

We found out from day one that sex was a major part of rock 'n' roll.
Sometimes we didn't even have to do anything to enjoy those privileges. We got booked into the Sahara Hotel in Vegas, opening for the Jefferson Starship. When we got to the gig, the manager of the place pulled us aside and asked us if we wanted any girls. How could you say no? So he took us to one of the shows in the hotel and we sat in the audience. There must have been at least twenty-five beautiful showgirls on the stage.

I was like a kid in a candy shop. "How many can we get?" I asked.

"As many as you want," he replied.

"And they'll come to my room?" I asked.

"Delivered right to your door." He smiled.

At that point one seemed like enough for me, so I picked out a cute redhead. Gene went for a blonde who went on to become a *Playboy* centerfold. Years later, I saw her naked in a hotel hallway, riding Gene on her back while he slapped her ass.

I spent a wonderful night with my redhead. So nice that many, many years later, when we were back in Vegas, I asked about her. A bartender told me that she jumped out of one of the top floors of a hotel because she had been so depressed with the Vegas lifestyle. I thought to myself, No kidding. You're up there trying to make a buck dancing and there's some asshole in the audience pointing and saying, "I want to fuck that one." And this poor girl gets off work and some guy goes, "You can't leave. You have to go up to room 675 and suck that guy's dick." I'd kill myself, too.

But we didn't even have to go through such an elaborate procedure to get chicks. Early on after we started hitting the road, we realized that no matter what town we played, even in middle America, there would always be a large group of girls who dreamt of fucking a rock star. The promoter would usually let ten of them in, because he knew them anyway, and he'd put them right in the front of the stage and you could feel the vibes: You just knew they wanted you so damn bad.

There's something very primal about the sound of drums. Whenever I went into an extended drum solo, you could just see the chicks dancing hypnotically to those rhythms, losing all abandon. It's also a power thing. Women react to men who are up on a stage, commanding the entire room. We didn't even have to be present to elicit that response. We would routinely get mail in the office from girls who sent their pussy hairs taped to a picture of them lying spread-eagle and naked. "I hope you like the smell of this. Call me when you come to Cleveland and you can experience it firsthand."

Many a night I'd be playing and I'd see a chick in the audience and somehow, with all these thousands of people, we'd connect with each other. I'd say to my roadie, "There's a chick in the tenth row, fifth from the aisle. Go get her for me." I'd be playing and I'd watch as he'd walk out, talk to her, and turn around and give me the high sign.

We all used our bodyguards to go out into the audience like predators for what we wanted. I would check five or six girls that I fancied, and Gene would say to his guy, "Get those ten." Ace would say, "Get those three."

It really was a surreal world out on the road. You walked into the lobby of the hotel and there were twenty girls waiting. Before you even put your makeup on, you could grab a chick and take her up to the dressing room and get laid. One time I had four naked women in my room. I didn't know where to put my hands and face anymore—there were just so many tits all over the place. Gene was this Jewish kid who never had so much pussy in his life—why would he want to go home to an empty apartment and not be told how great he is? And even though I was the only one who was married, I didn't want to go home, either. I liked this kind of room service.

In retrospect, I realize that's where a lot of the bending started, because we were being pushed into the world of never leaving the road, which was Aerosmith's problem. I find anything in excess is dangerous. Staying on the road forever and being told every day how great you look, how cool you are, and how much you are the greatest thing on the planet is dangerous shit. That is a drug in itself, I believe. And my guys were all addicted to that drug.

Even though we were getting all the girls we wanted, none of us really wanted them to stay all night all the time. Sometimes I just wanted to fuck and then get them out. I didn't want them sleeping in with me; I wanted to wake up alone in the morning. The phone could ring, it could be my wife, or she could just come through the door any minute: It could have happened lots of times. Sometimes when I let a girl stay over, I'd wake up in the morning and go, "Holy shit! Oh, God, what was I thinking about?" and I'd call my bodyguard and I'd say, "Listen, come in here and get rid of this fucking broad." So there would be a bang on the door and she'd jump up and I'd open the door and it would be Rosie or Big John and they'd go, "What the fuck is going on in here?" I'd go, "I don't know, man, I just woke up." John would say, "Any chicks in here?" and I'd go, "Yeah." Then John would scream, "Get your fucking clothes on and get the fuck out of here, we've got a plane to catch." I'd apologize, "Hey, what can I tell you? He's the man, when he says go, you gotta go."

Sometimes they just didn't want to go. Once we were partying in a hotel room and we told this girl that she had to get out. She agreed, but she asked to use the bathroom. Next thing we knew, she was in there for ten minutes. I was hoping that she didn't OD. After an hour, John broke the door down and she was handcuffed to the fucking toilet.

"I'm not leaving," she said defiantly.

"Oh yeah? You *are* leaving," he said, and he started pulling her arm so hard that I thought he was going to break it off.

"John, we're going to get arrested for abusing this girl," I said. "She's got to let herself out of those."

But she wouldn't, so we called the cops and they came and used a master key and unlocked the cuffs and arrested her. Then they used the same cuffs to handcuff her and they took her out.

About three years into touring, we were bringing so many girls back to the hotel after a gig that we got wise and rented a huge room at the hotel for them. We called it the Chicken Coop, and we would fill it with the willing "chickens." We knew that when we got back to the hotel after the gig there would be a whole room waiting for us, with sometimes fifty girls there. I knew which girls I had picked, but a lot of times Gene's picks would be better than my picks, or I might like one of Ace's picks better. They were all shareable, no matter how many you got.

We'd rush back from the show, take off the makeup, and jump into the shower, except for Gene. He just put his clothes on over the filth. Half of his makeup was still on; he couldn't wait to run to the room. After my shower, I'd get in some cool rock clothes: At least I thought they were cool, satin shirts with big balloon sleeves and some bell-bottoms, the bigger the bells the better. I'd tease my hair, put on my shades, and go straight to the Chicken Coop. Of course, Gene was the first one there. He was still somewhat in character and his eyes would dart around the room and he'd lick his lips and go, "I need a hot meal."

I'd look around, grab a couple, and take them to my room. Maybe later on I would go back, maybe not. Sure enough, though, I'd look down the hall and Gene would be going in again, then coming out with two more. Fucking five in the morning, I'd hear somebody in the hall again, and I'd look out and Gene's going in again, then coming out again. What a business, rock 'n' roll.

But even a room full of fifty girls got boring after a while, so we came up with some stupid games that we'd play. When we first started headlining, we toured with Rush. Gene and Paul were more standoffish, but Ace and I really became good friends with them. They were good old Canadian boys who liked to smoke pot and drink scotch, really down-to-earth guys. And they came up with a character that they called the Bag. One of them would put a large brown paper bag over his head. Then they drew a face on the bag and they cut out eye holes so that, if whoever was under the bag was smoking a cigarette, smoke would come out one of the eyes. It looked very creepy. The Bag was very rude and nasty to women. So we'd invite him to the party just to cause chaos and anarchy. He'd come in and start insulting the women who were there, calling them whores and sluts. Then I came up with a countervailing character named the Pink Fairy. Lydia had sent me a pair of pink Dr. Denton pajamas, the kind that covered your feet and had a flap in the back over your ass. I would get into them and put on a pink beret and crazy makeup and act gay.

The Bag would go around the room insulting the girls, and the Pink Fairy would prance up and say things like, "Oh, for goodness' sake, this one's not so bad. Look at her tits." And I'd rip her blouse open.

"I don't know. They're not that big," the Bag would say. "Let's see a bigger pair." So I'd get a girl with even bigger tits, take them out, and go, "What about these over here?" And I'd throw the chick on the Bag and he'd grope the girl and say, "Nah, she's not good," and throw her on the floor. We'd play these sick insidious games for no reason other than that we could.

One night we were in some hotel in Georgia and Ace and I got one girl really smashed and then we covered her with mayonnaise and ketchup and mustard that was left over from the hospitality table. We threw cold cuts in her hair and dragged her out into the hall naked, pressed for the elevator, threw her in it, and sent her down to the lobby. There was a huge commotion when she arrived. People were going crazy to see this naked girl in the lobby with tuna fish smeared on her body, egg salad hanging off her face, ketchup on one tit, onion dip on the other.

I guess I had the most orgies with Ace. Ace was just wild. He definitely went both ways up and down the street. He would bring his best friend, Bobby, on the road and he'd always be making out with him, kissing him on the lips, and they'd be grabbing each other's cocks. I wondered whether they ever went all the way.

One night I was with Sweet Connie from Little Rock, who was a legendary groupie, the best blowjob dispenser in the world. Every musician knew about Sweet Connie. Grand Funk Railroad even put her in their most famous song, "We're an American Band." She would do the whole crew and then the band. She had the sucking power of an industrial vacuum cleaner. She was so good that when she was finished with you, your legs would be shaking.

So one night she was under the covers of my bed, plying her trade on me, when Ace came running into my room. Ace had gotten bored and had literally wrecked his entire room. The hotel management found out about it, so he hid in my room while our road manager Frankie "confessed" to the hotel manager that Ace had destroyed the room because he had just gotten news that his wife had died. Frankie was totally apologetic and offered to pay for the damages, and they bought the story. The worst part was that we had to flush all our drugs down the toilet. Then we were out of drugs.

So Ace was in my room and he dove under the covers with Connie. What he did down there, I don't know and I don't care, but eventually he came up for air. "You are one sick motherfucker," I said, and Ace just shrugged. He wasn't really a bisexual looking for some hot thrills—he obviously preferred chicks over guys—but to him it wasn't a big deal. If a guy got in there, he didn't back away from it.

We had so many orgies together. One time we were in a room with ten naked women. I didn't know who was doing what to whom. All I remember is that Ace and I wound up lying on the bathroom floor next to each other, sharing a cigarette, while our dicks were being sucked by five pairs of girls, who each took their turn.

Despite all this action, Ace also liked to jerk off. He loved binoculars and telescopes. He said on a good night, he was able to see his home planet, Jandel, using a telescope. But binoculars were great to use if you lived in the city. You could catch something really hot looking through other people's windows, and you could jerk off to that. What made it particularly exciting was that they didn't know you were watching them.

"You fucking get the greatest orgasm," he swore to me.

Ace always brought his binoculars with him on the road. He would go up to the roofs of the hotels where we stayed and peer around and try to find things to jerk off to. One time he went a week without a catch and it was making him crazy, so he was going through an old *Playboy* and found a centerfold where this hot chick was sitting on a windowsill. She had great big old boobs and her legs were parted enough so you could just see the fringe of her pussy hair. Ace thought it looked so real that he took the centerfold out and stuck it on the far wall of his hotel room. Then he went to the other end of the room, looked at it through his binoculars, and jerked off. He told me that centerfold was good for a solid week of jerking.

But of all the guys in the band, Gene had to be the most sex-crazed. He was an equal-opportunity pussy hound. On one tour, he actually fucked our sixty-year-old limo driver. He fucked two sisters. In Atlanta, he fucked a female cop. I went into his room to get something and it was dark and I felt a gun hanging off the back of the bed.

"Peter?" Gene said.

"Yes," I answered.

"I have someone very important here in bed with me. I would leave the room if I was you."

I did.

Gene would invite me up to his room and I couldn't believe what dogs he had up there. But he'd walk around like he was Valentino, with a white robe and a white face towel around his neck as if it were an ascot. He'd have half his makeup still on and he stunk because he still hadn't showered after the show and he'd offer me some dessert. He'd order up four trays of every dessert the hotel had.

"Let Peter see your pussy."

"I don't want to see her pussy," I'd protest. "I just want the fucking dessert."

You could just smell the sex in the room, some of those pussies smelled so bad, but he loved it. "Mmmmm, a hot meal tonight," he'd smile. I'd leave and think, What ever happened to that nice Jewish boy I first met? What made this man snap? Pussy was Gene's heroin.

"I don't care if it smells, I don't care if it's bloody, I don't care if it has pimples on it, I don't care if there's things hanging off it, as long as it's wet and I can come." That was his mantra.

Unlike Ace, Gene never jerked off. In fact, he told me that he never masturbated once in his whole life, that it was an absolute disgrace if you had to jerk off when there were women in the world.

Early on, we were in the Deep South, moaning about the absence of attractive women. We had made plans to have lunch together and Ace, Paul, and I were going downstairs when Gene's door opened and he walked out with a three-hundred-pound farm girl dressed in coveralls. You could smell her down the hall, she stank so badly from manure. But Gene was grinning from ear to ear like he had Marilyn Monroe on his arm.

Gene was so consumed with getting pussy that he documented every one of his conquests on Polaroids. Then he'd carefully paste them into bound volumes, each dated. You opened it up and all you saw was snatch, snatch, snatch. Two chicks doing each other. Sometimes just the vagina. Sometimes just the ass. Sometimes the whole body, if the girl was a real babe.

It wasn't just the band getting all the action. When Sean was our road manager, we were in a hotel in Detroit and he had left his door ajar. I walked by and peered in and he had at least five naked guys dancing and jumping up and down on his bed. Oh, God. I just kept going: I didn't even want to imagine what was going on in there.

If we partied hard, the crew, especially when they were made up of the biker gang the Renegades, made us look like nothing. I went to their room at the Holiday Inn one night and I was shocked. Biker boys don't party like rock boys do. They were really hardcore, fucking the chicks up the ass with champagne bottles, shackling them to the bed with handcuffs. One big guy was jerking off on a girl's face. I saw a girl bleeding from the nose and I started screaming that we had to get a doctor. But one of the guys just shrugged and said that he had laid out a line of Bab-O cleanser and had her snort it.

"What? You could kill her!" I protested. "She's bleeding from the nose, we could get arrested."

"Ah, I'll fucking throw her on the side of the road. What does it matter?" He shrugged. Some of those guys were really crazy. But I loved them.

But it was equally hard to believe how dirty and nasty these girls were. You'd go to any town in the country, meet a girl for a one-nighter, and she'd do everything you always wanted to do in your life. I'd tie women up, blindfold them, put bananas in them. No big deal. One girl flipped me out because she told me she was going to get married that week, but she wanted to experience a rock star before she made the plunge. She brought a girlfriend along and we pulled her out of the Chicken Coop.

"I really want to sleep with you," she told me. "I've been looking at your picture for the last couple of years and I think you're really cute and I just had this desire to sleep with you before I get married."

She was much wilder than I thought she'd be. She just couldn't stop, every position. She wanted to get it all in so that she could hold on to that night forever. Any time the shit hit the fan with her guy, she could always remember the time with me. I've met a lot of girls who were fulfilling dreams or fantasies with us, and I could understand that. It was exactly how I felt about *Playboy* Playmates. But when she left that night, I felt that even though she hadn't gotten married yet, I had somehow violated the sanctity of marriage and that what I did was wrong.

The weirdest chicks were the ones who wanted to fuck me with my makeup on. Gene had no problem accommodating them, but then again, I wouldn't want to sleep with him unless he had his makeup on, either. But I never really wanted to do it as the Catman. I've met a lot of chicks who were wearing my makeup who wanted me to fuck them. One night I was with a beautiful nineteen-year-old girl who was in my makeup. Her mother had helped make her an outfit just like mine, with the spandex. She even had her hair fixed like mine. She said, "I've always fantasized about you. You could put your makeup on, and we'd be two cats doing it." I said, "No, no, you leave it on and I'll take care of every-thing."

I laid her on the bed and my face was staring back at me, except she was naked. Beautiful body. She'd even had my cuff links on, and the leather gloves that I wore. I was looking at her and I got weirded out, so I asked her to turn over.

"Oh, you want to do it from the back?" she asked.

She got on all fours and I banged her from the rear, and I was looking at the mirror watching me fuck myself. How sick was that? I came and pulled out and I told her that I had a headache. So she got dressed and I threw her out.

You have to understand what an unreal world we were living in. There were no boundaries anywhere, especially after we started to make it big. No one ever said no. It was more like, "Here. How much you want? How much you need? Need women? We'll have six come over tonight, no problem. Whatever you want. You want a beautiful Ferrari?

We'll have it parked in front of the hotel tomorrow." It was too much for me, I'll be the first to admit it. Too intoxicating. In time I realized that I was a commodity, making millions of dollars for other people, so it was important to keep me happy and give me everything I wanted. I just lost my mind behind it, and I lost my self-respect. That wasn't who I really was.

I should have known better. I was the only one who had a wife back home. But I was cheating on Lydia before and after we were married. Where I grew up, everybody had girlfriends on the side. My grandfather was a huge womanizer. It must have been in my DNA. But I know Lydia never realized the extent of the decadence on the road.

Another reason I was never satisfied sexually with Lydia was because of the sexual education I had enjoyed on the road. I wasn't the most knowledgeable guy when it came to sex. Then we went on the road and I started meeting worldly women who knew what they were doing. When we finally toured Europe, it was a sexual smorgasbord. I was fucking a French woman one night, a German the next, an Italian girl the next week, then a Swede after her. So when I came home, sex with Lydia wasn't good enough. How could she compare?

I might go months without seeing Lydia. I'd start to miss her, and I did love her very much, so I'd bring her out on the road if we had a couple of days off. She'd come out and we'd have a ball, but she would never know anything about my other exploits. What happens on the road stays on the road. The other guys and the crew always covered my ass. After three days I'd tell her that we had some heavy gigs coming up and she should go home, and she was fine with that. Later on, when we started doing cooler places like Europe and Tokyo, she wanted to come out more, and I was cool with that because I wasn't as sex-obsessed as Gene. If I got sex, great, but it wasn't priority number one. The music always had priority. Ace and Paul felt that way too. Gene could have all he wanted after the show, but nothing was going to get in the way of the music.

Once the show was over, the party would resume. Throughout all that insanity and depravity, somehow I held on to my religion. Every night on the road, before I would go to sleep, I prayed. Amid all that dirt and decadence, I always had that little moment before I closed my eyes. My religion was really important to me because I knew the foundation of it was good, the words were good, the rules were good.

I needed that grip on things because the other three guys were crazy, the road manager was crazy, our manager was crazy, the record-company owner was crazy. Who could I talk to about my real feelings and my spirituality? None of them were religious at all. I couldn't sit down with any of them and say, "I think I'm a little out of control with the booze and the drugs and the chicks. Can you help me with this?" There was no place to fill that yearning during the day, so I would wait until I was in bed and the lights were out. Even if I had two or three chicks next to me in bed, I would do an act of contrition. But I still felt bad. So I'd call my mother. It might be two A.M. back in Brooklyn, but she answered.

"Ma. It's me. I'm not doing so good. I'm doing bad things, sleeping with a lot of women," I'd say.

"Are you praying to God?" she'd ask.

"Yeah, but I don't know if it's working," I'd say.

"Try to be a good boy, Georgie," she'd plead.

I felt like I was falling into a snake pit. But just hearing her voice would ground me and make me feel normal again. I was Georgie Criscuola again, at least for a little while.

CHAPTER NINE

We were in one of the studios at the Record Plant in New York, arguing over something stupid, as we often did, when out of nowhere Bob Ezrin, our producer, came running into the room. He was wearing a T-shirt that read TIME IS MONEY and he had a crazed look in his eyes. Plus he was carrying a metal fire extinguisher.

"You cocksuckers are going to learn what this means," he said, referring to the slogan on his shirt. "You are not going to waste the fucking time that we're paying for arguing over what you're going to eat or when you're going to get some pussy or whatever the fuck your problems are, because you can't even tune your own instruments. I'm going to show you the value of time."

He proceeded to start spraying the contents of that fire extinguisher all over the studio floor, all over the wall, all over our instruments, all over our amps, even all over us. We were shocked and ran out of the studio and into the console room as we watched him maniacally spray down the room. Then he marched back into the console room and sat behind the big board, which had his name engraved on a metal plate that was attached to it. He was that powerful a producer.

"Now who's wasting money and time?" he asked.

Ezrin seemed out of his mind. Maybe the huge mound of cocaine piled up like a small mountain on the board had something to do with this outburst.

"How long is it going to take us to get back into the studio?" Gene asked.

"I don't really care," Ezrin answered.

That was the first day of working with the Boy Wonder, Bob Ezrin. And it wasn't even the worst one.

Coming off our breakthrough *Alive* album, we finally decided to listen to the people who kept telling us that our music should be more sophisticated, more like the Who and Led Zeppelin. I always thought that our strength was in our rawness and balls-to-the-wall energy. KISS was always a great three-chord jerk-off band, the best three-chord band in history. I could understand the desire for change: I was getting pretty bored playing the same boom-ba boom-boom-ba, boom-ba boom-boom-ba beat song after song. But as Gene loved to say, "If it ain't broke, don't fix it." Yet now we were about to fix it after we had achieved our first major success.

We were all excited about working with Bob Ezrin, though. He had produced all the classic Alice Cooper albums and had done a groundbreaking record with Lou Reed. He was, from all accounts, a musical genius. He was also a major coke addict at the time. I had never seen that much coke in one place. I'm not talking about grams—it was more like bags full of blow that would be laid out in pyramids on the mixing board.

It was interesting that Gene and Paul didn't say a word about Bob's drug problem. They were both majorly antidrug, and if Ace or I would get fucked up on drugs, all hell would break loose. In Gene's memoir, he claims that when he saw all that coke on the console, he thought it was Sweet'N Low and put it in his coffee, but he didn't drink it. He must have thought the razor blade was a stirrer and the mirror was to admire himself in.

Paul immediately had his nose up Ezrin's ass, and before we knew it Bob was at Paul's house writing songs with him. The songs themselves were actually quite great, songs like "God of Thunder" and "Flaming Youth." What I didn't like was that they'd come into the studio and tell me how to play the song. It wasn't a suggestion and it wasn't a collaboration, it was "This is the way you do it." Of course I rebelled. Then Ezrin would pour out a mound of coke and use it to reward me for doing it his way.

So if the coke was to be our common ground, I wanted to get up on his level and do the same amount as he did, but it was impossible. Ezrin had a nose like an aardvark and I could never keep up no matter how hard I tried.

Ezrin really took us all to school. One time he was listening to us play and walked into the studio from the console room.

"What the fuck are you doing?" he screamed at Gene.

"I'm playing," Gene said.

"You're not even in fucking tune. Don't you know how to tune your guitar?"

He proceeded to show Gene how to perfectly tune the bass. Gene was a large, intimidating man, but I saw Bob ream him out and carve him a new asshole. And Gene just took it.

Bob did the same thing with me. I was trying to play a song and Bob blew up.

"You can't play this beat?" he screamed. "Give me the fucking sticks." He sat down behind my drums and played the beat and once he showed me and I understood the theory of it, it wasn't hard. But he had to make me look like a jerk to teach it to me.

We all learned an enormous amount from him. It was like being in a musical summer camp. He brought a blackboard in and he wore a little cap and he had a whistle around his neck that he would blow when we fucked up.

"All right, campers, put your instruments down, we're going to school." And he'd write on the blackboard and teach us the fundamentals of music theory. All while he was smashed out of his gourd on coke.

Working with Ezrin was the hardest experience of my life. For me, music is all about emotion and attitude. When you pick up those sticks, you have to feel it or else you're just tick and tocking—you're a mechanical clock. Most of the greats didn't play by the book, they played from the heart. But this was different. Ezrin actually wrote out every drum part for me and came up with some very intricate drumming that wasn't even in my musical style. I was a meat-and-potatoes Charlie Watts, Motown type of guy. Ezrin demanded complexity, so I got frustrated very fast that I wasn't giving Bob what he wanted.

Plus I was cutting my own throat snorting Bob's blow. I guess I could have just said, "Bob, I don't want to do no blow. I'm fucking up here." But I thought I could do the blow and cut it on the drums. I couldn't. My timing was all over the place. After Bob shoved a bunch of blow up his nose, it probably sounded even worse than it actually was.

So Bob rigged up a click-track box for me that he called the Cat Box. He wrapped it with silver metallic tape and drew my face with my makeup on it, and he'd take a drumstick and hit the box to keep me on the beat. I'd hear his click box through my headphones while I was recording. I'd be playing along with it, but all of the sudden I'd hear an extra beat and I'd get thrown off and I'd stop the recording.

"Wait a minute. You just switched up the beat," I'd say. "There's something wrong with that box."

"Nah, there's nothing wrong with the box," I'd hear him say from the console room. There wasn't. He was just fucking with me, playing mind games. As if this wasn't hard enough to do on its own. I started to really hate Bob at that point. But, as with most of the stuff that Bob did, he had a hidden agenda. After a while, Ezrin realized that I had a trigger temper, and he began to push me just far enough so I would begin to take out my anger on the drums. I would see him laughing hysterically and I would hit those drums harder than I ever hit them in my life. I just envisioned Ezrin's face on those drums and I hit them so hard it sounded nasty and evil, which was what he was going for all the time.

It was excruciatingly painful, but the outcome was genius. You listen to those songs on *Destroyer* and you go, "Holy fuck, those drums are amazing." But to get there, I went through hell and so did everyone else. Like Gene used to say, "If Peter isn't having a good day, nobody's having a good day."

As painful as these sessions were for me, they were doubly hard on Ace. Ace didn't respond well to Bob's tough love. Once you get the drums down and add the bass and the rhythm guitar, it's up to the lead guitarist to complete the picture. And then you're up there naked, you're on your own. Ace, like me, loved to play by feel. Ace's brother was a classically trained guitarist, but Ace hated his studied playing. Ace loved spontaneity, but Ezrin had other plans for him.

I didn't get to witness Ace's arguments with Ezrin because the minute my drum tracks were done, I was out of there. Why would I want to stay around to listen to Ace getting reamed out for the next five hours when I could go home and have fun or go to a club?

Ace was drinking and partying with his friends a lot, and he started missing sessions. One time he actually told Ezrin that he couldn't record because he had a previous engagement to play cards with his pals. Ezrin didn't take too kindly to that and called one of his own ace session guys, Dick Wagner, who came in, nailed the songs, and left. The consummate pro. Wagner never got the credit, but it's him playing on songs like "Beth" and "Sweet Pain." Ace was furious he had been replaced and felt that Gene and Paul were traitors.

When Ezrin started working with us, one of his criticisms was that all of our songs were about sex. He felt that to get to the next level, we had to expand our palette a little bit and try to reach a broader audience than the fifteen-year-old boys who were our fan base. Ezrin found that vehicle in a song I had written with Stan Penridge.

Back in the Chelsea days, Stan and I had written a joke song to knock our bandmate Mike Brand's wife, Becky. She would always call him during rehearsals wondering when he was coming home. So the song originally went, "Beck, I hear you callin', but I can't come home right now / Me and the boys are playin', and we just can't find the sound." So we were knocking this guy's wife: Shut the fuck up, quit calling.

I wanted to get a song on *Destroyer,* so one day Gene and I were in a limo and I started singing "Beck" to him. I knew that both he and Paul would never go for a ballad, so I sang him a faster version of the song and he seemed to dig it and suggested I play it for Ezrin. But when I sat down with Ezrin, he immediately understood it for what it was.

"This is a ballad. I hear it on the baby grand. This is going to be a hit record," Bob enthused. "I'm going to get the New York Philharmonic to play on this."

"Yeah, right. In my fucking dreams," I said.

Ezrin just smiled.

"This little song says so much in so few words. 'I wish I was home, but I can't be,'" Bob said. "Everyone will relate to that—businessmen, doctors. It's a universal theme."

He wanted to make one lyrical change, though. He thought we should change the name from Beck to Beth. I was fine with that. Ezrin's man Dick Wagner, who played acoustic on the track because Ace was out in space somewhere, loved the song, too, and immediately thought it could be a hit.

But Gene and Paul kept resisting it. They didn't want a ballad on the record. That's when Bill stepped in. He had heard the basic track, and he thought "Beth" was a hit. So when Ezrin hired the New York Philharmonic and we went down to record the session, Bill suggested that everyone in the orchestra should wear those fake tuxedo T-shirts and that I should go down in full makeup and take photos with the orchestra.

"I know you've been going through hell with them over your song, but I love it to death," Bill told me. "So let me make you feel good."

Bob was in full tails and a top hat and played the baby grand piano. We must have had more than twenty-five pieces in the orchestra. And when they finished the track, I was crying my eyes out, it was so beautiful. And the orchestra was clicking their bows and Bob stood up and called me up to take a bow as the writer. When I was bowing to the room, I never felt so proud in my life.

With the track completed, we then had to go in and record the vocal. I went into the studio and Bob lowered the lights to get me in the mood. Just then, in walked Gene and Paul, and they sat down on the couch in front of the board. I was shitting a brick, all alone in there, about to sing KISS's first ballad. Meanwhile, those two fuckfaces were sitting in the booth stone-faced like they were at the zoo watching an animal through the glass.

"Okay, take one," Ezrin said.

All of a sudden, my legs began shaking. I was so scared I thought that my voice was vibrating when I began to sing. I looked and saw that Gene and Paul were grinning because I was really struggling.

"What's the matter, Peter?" Bob said.

"I can't sing like this," I said. "These two cocksuckers are sitting there laughing—"

"Hey, assholes, get your fucking asses out of the room," Bob screamed at them.

They left, and Bob closed the door. Then he sat down behind the console again.

"Okay, Peter, let's do this. Sing it for me."

We did a couple of takes and Bob suggested I go up a little higher. I did, and it was beautiful.

"I love it, I fucking love it," he said, and called me into the console room to listen to the playback. He had the engineer make a quick mix, and then he called Gene and Paul back into the room.

"Listen to this," he said.

We listened and they had no reaction. No "Wow," no "Hmmm," no "Holy shit," not even a "This stinks." But I was ecstatic. Ezrin had taken Stan and my little song and had turned it into a masterpiece. Now I really understood why he was considered such a stone cold genius.

Not everybody shared those sentiments. When *Destroyer* was first released, we got a strong backlash from our hardcore fans. After six months, the album was dead in the water. The critics didn't think much of it, either. Ezrin had even received a threat from a guy who said he was going to go up to Toronto and punch him in the nose for all the KISS fans.

It was time to release another single from the album to stoke up sales, and I pushed for "Beth." Gene and Paul agreed, but made sure that it wound up on the B-side of the single, with "Detroit Rock City," one of Paul's songs, featured on the A-side. But Scott Shannon, who was working in the promotion department of Casablanca (and who would go on to become a famous disc jockey), loved the song and urged a deejay in Atlanta to flip the single over and play "Beth." The reaction was immediate and overwhelming. "Beth" became our highest-charting single ever. It revived the album's sales and it won many awards, including a People's Choice award. It even got played on easy-listening stations. One day I was channel surfing and "Beth" was playing on three different stations simultaneously.

I was on cloud nine. Not just for the personal accomplishment, but because my song propelled the album back onto the charts. *Destroyer* was our *White Album*, the best album we ever did in our lives, and it was nice to see Bob Ezrin get the credit he richly deserved. He may have been a harsh taskmaster, but the end result was more than worth it. When "Beth" hit the charts, Bill Aucoin came over to our brownstone with a big bottle of Dom Pérignon champagne and we made a little fire and toasted our good fortune.

"The irony is that you saved the album, Peter," he said. "But they're going to hate you for it."

Even though "Beth" had revived the album, Gene and Paul didn't want me to play it live. When we started rehearsing for our next tour, Bill told us that we had to put "Beth" in the show by popular demand. Gene and Paul immediately said that it wouldn't work.

"We'll make it work," Bill told us. "We have new fans who are coming to see us because of that song." So they finally agreed. But when we started trying to play it, it was a fucking nightmare. None of them had played on the original track. Ace had no idea how to play an acoustic guitar.

Then Sean and Bill came up with a brilliant idea. We would play a recording of the musical track and I would come out from behind my drums to the front of the stage, where I'd sit on a drum case and, with a single spotlight on me, sing the song live.

"Fuck you," I told Sean. "I'm not leaving my drums."

Frankly, I was petrified by the idea.

"When you get a taste of what that's like to walk out there and sing your song, I'll have to be dragging you off the stage," Sean predicted.

He was right. When we first rehearsed it, they put my drum seat out front and I sat on it and sang the song. Of course, Gene and Paul went out front and made fun of me. But when we finally did it live onstage, the fucking house came down and I realized that I finally had an ace in the hole no matter what Gene and Paul would try to do to me. I had tears running down my face that first time we did it. Sean was right. From that night on, I couldn't wait to get out and do that song.

You would think that after all my years of struggling, our newfound success would have made me feel more comfortable and secure. In fact, the opposite turned out to be true. While we were in the studio recording *Destroyer*, I got really depressed. Perhaps it was because I was burning my brain to a crisp with the massive amount of coke I was doing, or maybe it had something to do with getting beat up on a daily basis by Bob, but I was on the verge of a nervous breakdown. I went to management, and

Alan Miller recommended a psychiatrist he had seen named Daniel Casriel. He was pioneering a new type of therapy called primal screaming,
and I was gung ho to see him because I had heard that John Lennon had
also undergone primal therapy.

Casriel had a beautiful brownstone on East Fifty-first. We did a con-
sultation and I told him I was miserable. I was always on the road or else
in the studio. I couldn't enjoy my life. I didn't even feel like playing then.
By the end of that session, we determined that my major issue was that I
felt that I didn't deserve to be famous.

"Bullshit, you do deserve it," Dr. Casriel told me. "And eventually
you're going to scream, 'I deserve to be famous' to me."

He had me attend a group session a few days later. There were six
people to a group, and each of us would sit on a mat with Dr. Casriel in
the center of the circle. After a few minutes, I realized that next to these
other people, my problems seemed a little puny. One guy believed that he
had a hole in his head. The woman next to me was one of the most beautiful women I had ever seen, a fifteen on a scale of one to ten. You couldn't
keep your eyes off her, but she thought she was ugly. There was a pilot who
had a problem with flying.

Each patient would get a personalized mantra from Dr. Casriel. The
woman's was "I am gorgeous. I have everything going for me." And he
would make you repeat it over and over again, louder and louder. My
mantra was "I do deserve to be famous. I do deserve to be a winner."
He had me screaming that over and over, louder and louder, until it was
almost like an out-of-body experience or an exorcism. I was rolling around
on the ground, tears coming out of my eyes, screaming, "I do deserve to
be famous." And thanks to my singing, I knew how to scream. I could
shatter glass with my screaming. So all the other people were hugging me
and consoling me and saying, "You do deserve to be famous."

When that session was over, I felt reborn. After a few more sessions, I
had never felt more relaxed. The stress was gone. No more panic attacks.
I had even cleaned up and stopped doing coke and drinking. I felt that
Peter Criscuola had reemerged and that that lunatic Catman had receded
into the background.

New Year's Eve 1976 was a good measure of our dizzying success. Three years earlier, we had opened for Blue Oyster Cult and played to thirty-five hundred people. Now Blue Oyster Cult was opening for us and we had sold out the Nassau Coliseum, all thirteen-thousand-plus seats. When we went onstage, we were treated like conquering heroes. Backstage there were people who wanted to have their picture taken with me, have me kiss their babies. It was frightening to have all these people touching me and grabbing at me. One girl pulled my brother and me aside and pulled up her dress to show us a huge KISS logo tattooed on her ass. If I wanted to, I could have gotten blowjobs onstage, offstage, in-between stage, backstage, under the stage. It was wild.

Onstage, we always felt as if we were looking into some bizarre mirror. Thousands of people in the audience were wearing our makeup. We were on the front covers of all the big industry magazines—*Cashbox, Record World, Billboard.*

Ironically, the one thing that really bugged us was that offstage we would never be recognized without our makeup on. Bill would always lecture us: "Don't ever get caught without your makeup. When you're out, wear big dark glasses that look mysterious." At first that was fun, but after a while it began to bother us. I remember walking into the China Club in New York City one night and telling the host I was Peter Criss from KISS.

"Yeah, and I'm fucking Mick Jagger," he said, and turned away. I had to take out my license and show it to him before I could get a table. I couldn't believe that we'd finish a huge tour, the world would go crazy, and then we'd go home and walk the streets of New York and no one would recognize me.

After *Destroyer* came out, I slipped and fell back into doing cocaine again. It would be glib to say that after working with Gene and Paul, anybody could become a drug addict. The truth was coke was everywhere. The promoters would always have some for you, the radio-station guys would turn you on. Back at the office, Bill was doing it. I'd go to Studio 54 and I'd sit with Halston and Liza Minnelli and Bianca Jagger and Steve Rubell, and everyone was doing blow.

When we'd be in L.A., Ace and I would get a hospitality gift from Casablanca sent to our rooms. It would contain a basket of fruit, an incredibly good bottle of wine, a couple of grams of coke, and some quaaludes along with a card reading, WELCOME TO L.A. LOVE YOU, NEIL. CASABLANCA RECORDS. We'd go out to Le Dome, and half the staff at Casablanca would pull out their little bottles with the spoon on a chain. If you got a job at Casablanca you'd immediately get a Mercedes, and every afternoon a guy would go door to door and take orders for coke and quaaludes, which were put on your expense account. It was insane. We were too naïve to understand the dangers of coke. We figured that if a genius like Ezrin could do it and still produce critically acclaimed platinum albums, what was the downside?

The party scene in New York was just as crazy. There were great clubs like Tracks, JP's, and Ashley's. I would frequent Plato's Retreat a lot because it was a sex club that had terrific orgies. My favorite place was Studio 54. Where else could a kid from Brooklyn hobnob with Warhol and Truman Capote? I would go upstairs onto the balcony and lean over with a drink in one hand while a broad was sucking my cock. Later I'd go downstairs and screw a model in one of the bathrooms.

Even my role model Bill Aucoin wasn't strong enough to resist the temptations of wealth. As we got richer, he got crazier and crazier. He had a beautiful pad in Olympic Towers, one of the ritziest buildings in the city. He began to throw coke-fueled parties where he'd surround himself with nubile young boys, and his apartment turned into Dante's *Inferno*. I remember many nights of partying at Bill's when it would get to be around six in the morning and you'd get that electric feeling from doing too much blow, and the sun was coming up and you'd open the drapes and see the huge 666 sign on the neighboring building on Fifth Avenue. That was a wake-up call right there.

Slowly but surely, I became addicted to cocaine. I got crazier and crazier. I capitalized on the fact that I was in the hottest band in the world and I could get away with anything. I acted out, in part, because I was beginning to feel so alienated from Gene and Paul that I just didn't want to be around them anymore. The joy of making music with them was gone.

There was always a lag between our successes and the fruits of those successes. The money was going to come to us, but it hadn't come in vast quantities yet. So I began to deal coke to our crew. I'd cop a quarter of an ounce from Bob Ezrin's dealer and then Lydia would cut it with baby laxative and sell it as grams. Bill and Sean would score from us. On the road, I was supplying all the roadies and our truck drivers. Gene and Paul never knew this or they would have gone crazy. But it was hard to miss. The crew would literally be lined up in front of my hotel-room door after a show. I charged them sixty bucks a gram, which was a reasonable price, and that way Lydia and I got to snort coke for free.

But after a couple of months dealing coke, it got too risky. All of a sudden I was getting knocks at my hotel-room door at five in the morning.

"Get the fuck out of here!" I'd scream, and throw a shoe at the door. I figured that sooner or later I'd get busted.

But just because I stopped dealing didn't mean I stopped using. I was born hyper. I'd been on medication since I was a kid to keep me calm. So imagine what I was like on blow. Like all coke addicts, I could never have enough. I would stay up for days on end. One time I stayed up for seven straight days. Eventually I started hallucinating. I thought the police were surrounding our brownstone, so I got my gun and made a barricade by the upstairs window. Lydia called Sean, and he rushed over with a handful of ludes. He promised that if I took them he would come back later that night with some really good blow, so I downed them and went to sleep.

Around this time I befriended somebody who could snort me under the table. John Belushi was one of the biggest comedy stars at that time. We met at JP's and hit it off immediately. He was a huge KISS fan. After we hung out awhile, John did a skit on *Saturday Night Live* in which he played a backstage bouncer who wouldn't let people in to see us. John wanted me to come on the show to do a cameo, but Bill didn't think it would be such a good idea to do it without the band, so it never happened.

I think one of the reasons John loved hanging out with me was because he wanted to be a rock star. We met right before he did the Blues Brothers with Dan Aykroyd. When they performed a live show at Radio City as the Blues Brothers, John invited me down. They were so happy to be up there singing the blues with real players like Duck Dunn. John felt he had been a clownlike cliché on *Saturday Night Live.* Music really spoke much more to his soul.

One of the first times we hung together was at a *Saturday Night Live* after-party the week the Stones were on the show. They hosted it at an old bar that John and Dan had bought for their private use. When I got there, we immediately went to the bathroom and did some coke. John's energy was so overwhelming, he lured you right into his insanity. Even the way he did blow was special. He had no time for tiny vials or little coke spoons. He carried a baggie full of coke, and he would scoop some up in his palm and literally shove it up your nose.

We had a great time that night. He introduced me to Steve Martin, who was an up-and-coming comic then. I believe Steve was also wired on coke, because he never stopped talking. But he seemed brilliant, and I just knew he was destined for stardom. The night was magic until some guy started fucking with Keith Richards and Keith drew a derringer on him.

"Keith's a crazy guy," John confided to me, which was saying a lot.

One night I was hanging at John's place in the Village. He had sound-proofed a room in his pad and he would crank up his stereo and blast the Allman Brothers. We had been partying all night, and the sun was coming up when he came up with an idea.

"Let's go to Grand Central Station," he said.

That sounded like a horrible idea.

"John, it's going to be rush hour. I'm too wired to handle that shit," I said.

He smiled his famous innocent smile. "Trust me, you're gonna like this."

Before we left, he called up Aykroyd to tell him to meet us there. I could hear Dan through the phone. He was humming the theme from *The Twilight Zone.*

"Witness: Two morons walking through the early-morning streets of Manhattan doomed to die," he said in his best Rod Sterling voice. "Now I'm going back to bed."

And he hung up.

"Fuck him," John said, and we grabbed a cab to Grand Central. We went to one of the main waiting rooms, and John instructed me to go over to one corner of the room and face the wall. Then he marched over to the opposite corner and did the same. By then the room was filled with the noise of the morning rush-hour commute.

"Peter, Peter, it's me," I heard a voice as clear as a bell coming from the wall. Somehow John knew that the acoustics at Grand Central were such that you could communicate across the room if you faced the wall. So we were talking and talking. I can only imagine what the passing commuters thought as they saw John and me both standing alone on either side of the room and talking to the wall.

Destroyer was released in March of 1976. In May we left for our first tour of Europe. We had conquered our homeland, but Europe was a different matter. We started off in England. Except for the Hammersmith Odeon in London, we played filthy half-filled shitholes that the Beatles had played coming up. How cool was that!

France was a little better. Our promoters gave us a royal welcome, sending hookers over in a Mercedes. They'd pick us up, drive us around, and we'd get serviced in any way we wanted. One night I got so drunk on brandy, I couldn't get it up. She didn't give a shit—she still got paid.

We had a problem with the language barrier in Paris. One day we wanted to go sightseeing, so Gene asked Susan Meneo, one of the girls who worked at Casablanca, if she could speak French. She said she could, so we all piled into a cab. The cabdriver asked us where we wanted to go in French. And Susan said, "Can yooo take uz to zee Champs Eleeezay?" with a heavy French accent. We laughed so hard we almost pissed our pants.

We played two shows in Paris at the Olympia Theater opening for Jerry Lewis, of all people. He was pretty funny when he began his show. "I don't believe what I just saw. That's gotta be the worst or the best thing I've ever seen."

Germany was a strange place. Everybody there tried to act like Hitler had never existed and there wasn't a Second World War. But I rubbed it in their faces one night in Offenbach. We were staying at an old-style hotel and it was the night of Muhammad Ali's big comeback fight versus a German guy named Richard Dunn. While we were watching the fight, I decided to try Jägermeister. I was downing it with beer chasers, and that shit will fuck you up. Our roadie Fritz noticed that the Cat had gone crazy. I was threatening to jump out the window, tear the place up, whatever. So Fritz and J.R. and Campise decided to lock me inside the huge, beautiful antique armoire in my room. They threw me in it and locked the doors.

That gave me flashbacks of being locked in the closet in Catholic school. I started screaming and making growling noises and banging on the doors. Campise told me later that you could literally see both sides of the armoire bust out, the front doors fall off, and the whole thing collapse as I broke my way out. Then I ripped all my clothes off and jumped out the window. There was a two-foot-wide ledge that ran all the way around the hotel. I started scampering around the ledge to the front of the hotel, where there were two huge gargoyles on either side of the main entrance.

I climbed up on the back of the one of the gargoyles, buck naked, screaming, "Muhammad Ali! Muhammad Ali rules, you fucking bastards!"

The police came in two minutes flat. They threw a blanket over me and dragged me off the gargoyle and back into the hotel room. They told Bill that we'd better be out of Germany in the morning, which was okay since we were scheduled to play Sweden the next day. But we had to pay the hotel $10,000 in damages before we could leave.

A few days later we were in Sweden and it was Ace's turn to stir up some shit. We were eating in a restaurant with a unique theme. Everybody sat around a big pool, each table would get a remote-controlled boat, and you'd sail your boat across the pool to the chef, who would load your boat up with the specialty of the house, shrimp. Then you'd navigate your loaded boat back to your side of the pool and have your dinner.

Ace and I were pounding down the drinks when Ace suddenly entered the Forget It Zone. Ace turned to me and said, "Peter, I'm fucking Godzilla."

"Yeah?"

"I'm fucking Godzilla and I'm going to destroy all those boats."

"Go right ahead," I said.

So Ace got up and jumped over the barrier into the pool, fully clothed. He started beating his chest and belting out "ARRRRGGGHH!" and then he began to slap at the boats as they drove past him. Nobody could believe what they were seeing, and the next thing I knew, boom, I passed out face-first right into my salad. But I'm told that Ace picked up a boat and went "ARRRRGGGHH!," and ate the shrimp, then threw the boat across the pool. Then he splashed around some more, knocking the boats around. All the other patrons were freaking out. Shrimp were floating in the pool, the water cascading over the sides. Our group was in hysterics, even Gene and Paul, but everyone else was totally pissed off. One woman was screaming that her dress had been ruined.

Of course we got thrown out. I was still comatose, so Big John had to pick me up and carry me out on his back. The next day he came by and said that Ace's Godzilla routine was the biggest expense of the tour.

But touring wasn't just fun and games. Most of the time, touring was monotonous and lonely. You spent most of your time just waiting for the hour and a half you'd be onstage. And after touring nonstop for so many years, my body was beginning to break down. I couldn't even lift my arms after a while, so J.R. took me to a local doctor to get some shots. He shot me up with a horse needle. He went right to the bone and then moved the needle around so that the liquid soaked the bone down and the joint could move. Do you know how fucking painful that is? But after I got one, I could finish the show. What I didn't know was that they were shooting me up with cortisone. And when that shit wore off later that night, I would be in excruciating pain. I was tearing the ligaments in my arms even more by playing. With the cortisone, I just didn't feel the damage that was being done.

When I found out I was getting cortisone, I flipped out. Meanwhile I was taking coke and every other drug under the sun, but to me cortisone was a no-no. It affected me in weird ways. My attitude got shittier, I was totally miserable, and I was affecting everyone around me. One night the pain got so bad that when we were driving back from a gig, I couldn't even lift my arms. I was sitting in the back of the limo with Paul and I turned to him.

"Paul, if you ever did any decent thing in your life, please cancel this

tour for me. I can't play anymore, I can't even lift my arms, I'm in excruciating pain. I know I cry wolf, but I'm not fucking around this time."

Then I laid my head on his shoulder and I started crying like a baby.

When we got back to the hotel, Paul went right to Gene and told him
we had to cancel the rest of the tour. They called Bill and he canceled the
remaining dates. For once Paul had done the right thing, and I was truly
grateful.

CHAPTER TEN

I knew that things were changing when I set eyes on our new set after we returned from Europe in June of 1976. The money was flowing in, and Bill was funneling some of it right back into the show. I have to admit that I loved the two huge emerald-eyed cats that sat on either side of my drums. But the rest of the staging was a mess. They built a gothic castle for Gene to be a monster in. The Spaceman got his own lunar landscape. There was a modified Tesla coil that was supposed to shoot out electricity during "God of Thunder," but it seldom worked. Neither did the tentacle tree that was supposed to undulate its branches.

"This fucking set looks like a fruit salad," Ace said. I thought it was more like Disneyland. We wound up getting rid of half of it.

Just as the set had changed, so did the people who were responsible for the show itself. The changes started at the top. Bill was seldom out on the road with us. When he did come out, he'd take us all to dinner and then stand on the side of the stage and gloat over us. We felt like kids showing off for their dad. But those visits were so far and few between that we began calling him Good Gig Gui (Gui was his nickname) because he had a tendency to only show up to the larger, most prestigious gigs.

Bill decided that we needed our own business managers. He reached out to Howard Marks and Carl Glickman. Marks had worked with Bill for years and had an active hand in mediating the royalty disputes with

Neil Bogart. Glickman was a real estate mogul from Cleveland who had experience in turning around companies on the verge of bankruptcy. He also seemed to have friends who were "connected": One of those guys was rumored to have acquired a small percentage of ownership in KISS, since he had provided Bill with a bridge loan to keep him afloat before all the royalties from the *Alive* album kicked in.

Then Marks and Glickman began flexing their own muscle. Most of our original crew got eighty-sixed. J.R., Moosey, Munroe, all gone, all replaced by Marks and Glickman's people. Overnight, we weren't a rock 'n' roll band anymore. We had become a big business. All the heart and soul and spontaneity had gone out the door when Marks and Glickman took over.

I loved Bill to death and I never want to badmouth him in any way, but I think a lot of the problems we were facing were due to the coke clouding his judgment. Bill had been the hands-on arbiter of any disputes in the band in the early days.

"At the end of every week, I want all four of you to sit in one room and hash out whatever is bothering you," Bill would tell us. And we did that for quite a while. Each guy would bring up what was bugging him about the others and we'd discuss it and say we'd change and then we'd all shake on it.

But we got away from that. Now there were all these new people around us, and they weren't loyal people who had been through wars with us. Howard Marks didn't know a fucking thing about running a band. All these guys were businessmen. Bill knew us backward and forward, but the coke was making him paranoid.

The only upside to the personnel changes was that we hired the greatest road manager we would ever have. Frankie Scinlaro was an incredibly endearing Italian, a roly-poly guy around five foot six inches with a beard and a razor cut haircut. He was a veteran of the road, having taken Alice Cooper out for years.

Frankie was tougher than any one of us, for sure. He had a way with words that was unrivaled, so it was never a good idea to try to outjab him. He was the "why" man. He'd preface all his comments with Why? If Paul had been giving him a hard time, he'd zero in. "Why, you don't wish you could grow a pussy overnight, next to your cock? Why, we don't make little titties when we go in the shower?"

"Fuck you, fat Frankie," Paul would counter.

"I may be fat, but I please all the girls. My dick's not big, but I can make it spin. Can you?"

Frankie gave all of us nicknames. He thought Paul's nickname, He/She, was perfect, so he didn't change that. Ace was High Octane because he was bombed most of the time. Or Scraps, because he ate whatever was left over on everybody's plates. He called me either Peter Loooong, because I would complain all the time, or the Ayatollah Criscuola because of my imperious attitude. Gene was Gene the Nazarene because he thought he was God's gift to the world.

Frankie's greatest salvos were always aimed at Gene. Gene actually had the balls to ask all of us to refer to him as God. He was dead serious. If I said something as mundane as "Gee, it's a beautiful day today," Gene would say, "Yes, I think I'll leave it that way."

So Frankie would go up to Gene and say, "I'm going to sit next to God. Is it okay for me to be near your presence, Sir Gene?"

Gene would say yes.

"Oh, thank you so much for talking to me," Frankie would say, actually bowing and scraping. "I feel so honored, I can't wait to be like you when I grow up." How could you not love a guy like that who has the balls to put you in your rightful place? He made a jerk out of me many, many times, but I loved him. We all loved him. He would always say, "Why? Who's better than us?"

Frankie would always scam the promoters. Every place we played, he would tell them that it was one of our birthdays that night.

"Hey, it's Peter's birthday tonight. Can you make something happen? You know, some women, some champagne?" Sure enough, after the show I'd walk into the dressing room and all these people would be singing "Happy Birthday" and I'd look all surprised.

Frankie worked the hotel managers as well. One time Ace and I tore a hotel-room door off its hinges. When the angry manager came up to complain, Frankie got irate, blamed it on crazy fans who found out our room numbers, and castigated the hotel security. One time Ace destroyed his room and the cops were on their way over, so Frankie had Ace lie under the covers and told the cops that Ace had passed out and that it angered the people he was partying with so much that they threw all his furniture out the window.

I think Bill got a little jealous of Frankie. By then we had started chartering our own little private planes. One day Gene told me that Frankie was getting fired for taking kickbacks on the plane fees. I didn't buy that at all. I think he was set up and they got rid of him because he got too close to the band. I got together with Frankie quite a few times after he got canned. We'd go for drinks and he'd say, "Peter, I never stole any of your money. I loved you guys. I gave you everything I had. Those guys were full of shit." I believed him. Frankie died years after that. I cried in my room when I heard the news.

We hit the road with our new show on July 3 in Norfolk, Virginia. It didn't take two dates before we had our first crisis. On July 8 in Richmond, a fan threw a live M-80 firecracker that landed on my drum riser and exploded with such force that it literally blew me off my drums. My drum tech had to cushion my fall and we both went down. Then I couldn't hear a thing. They stopped the show and threw me into an ambulance and checked me out. We came right back to the venue, but I was reluctant to finish the show.

Sean would have none of that.

"You fucking go out there and you tell them, 'Fuck this, the Cat has nine motherfucking lives,' and then go right into a drum solo."

I did just what Sean said, and the crowd went crazy. The noise was so deafening it felt like the walls of the coliseum would come tumbling down. The guys joined me at the end of the solo, and it was such a rush.

Two days later, we were back in the metropolitan area. We were playing Roosevelt Stadium in Jersey City. It was a real shithole. But we did have a great after-show party, and Linda Lovelace of *Deep Throat* fame showed up. Of course everyone wanted a blowjob from her, but it never happened.

This was the show where we met our new business manager's tour liaison, Chris Lendt. Chris was a recent business-school graduate, a real clean-cut straight guy. It didn't take us long to corrupt him. Chris and I got along real well. One of the first things I had him do was go with me to Woodlawn Cemetery in the Bronx. That's where my grandmother Clara was resting. Clara had been my second mother. I had undying love for her. She worked her ass off at three jobs to help support my family, all the time keeping the house where she and I lived clean and hospitable. She was my hero. One Sunday night when I came home from a date, she was watching Lawrence Welk as usual, but she was having a little scotch. She never drank scotch before—she was a beer drinker—but her doctor told her that she should switch to scotch now and then since she was a diabetic and there was no sugar in scotch. Now you know why I hated doctors then.

I went to my room that night and lay in the bed, and then I heard a thumping noise. I went into the living room and she was on the floor, unable to get up. I thought she had died and I ran to my mom's house and she came back and we called an ambulance. Clara had taken a diabetic stroke. She couldn't talk after that, she couldn't walk. So my parents took her in and they had to feed her and wash her and give her her insulin injections.

It killed me to see her like that. She was such a strong woman. She was indestructible in my eyes. This was the woman who raised me, put the coats on my back, and helped me through school. But seeing her like that was too much and I just ran, right into Lydia's arms and into our marriage. When my grandmother died, they put her to rest in the Bronx, where her parents and her twin sister, who had died at birth, were already interred. But there was no headstone for her. There was no indication that Clara was there with them. My parents didn't have the money to get her a proper headstone.

But now I did. Chris and I went out and bought a marble headstone for my grandmother's grave site. I think that little trip made a big impression on him. All the other guys were buying expensive clothes and fancy cars with their newfound wealth, and I was buying a gravestone.

After a few weeks with us, Chris Lendt was amazed by our appeal. It was like we had hypnotized the audience, he'd say. "You can go out there and say, 'We're going to lift the whole building up,' and these fans would go and do it." It's true, we did have an unreal amount of control over the fans. It bordered on mania. After a concert in the Midwest, we discovered that someone had broken into our dressing room and stolen my entire outfit. My boots, my costume, my gloves, all gone. The cops thought they might have a lead, so they tracked this guy to his home. Outside his door, the cops heard "Black Diamond" blasting from his stereo. He didn't answer their knocks, so they busted the door down and there he was, sitting in a big chair, dressed in my costume and makeup, downing a beer and watching KISS videos on his TV.

Around the same time, people started coming backstage with their sick kids in wheelchairs. These kids would be dying of cancer or other diseases and their parents somehow thought that we were superheroes and we could cure them by laying hands on them. So we'd hug them and sign autographs and pose for pictures. The next time we hit town they'd show up again, but one or two of them would be missing—they didn't make it. It would break my heart. I would go into the bathroom and cry my fucking eyes out. Eventually I told Bill, "You've got to stop this. I'm not God. It's much too draining for me to do this."

Just being on the road constantly took its toll. I couldn't handle the constant moving around and the loneliness. So one way to combat that was to destroy shit. It's a rock 'n' roll cliché, but it's true. We started out doing simple stuff, like attaching hundreds of feet of cable to our room TVs and throwing them off the roof of the Continental Hyatt House on the Sunset Strip in L.A.

Our techs had a lot of tools with them on the road and we put them to good use. One time Ace and I were next door to each other and we wanted to be able to go back and forth between rooms, so we took a sledgehammer and broke through the wall and created our own connecting door.

At one point I got so crazy on the road that I thought I was a Green Beret and that people were out to get me, so I started wearing camouflage outfits and carrying a cool sawed-off BB shotgun. We were at the Peach Tree hotel in Atlanta with those huge curved glass windows. I was shooting all kinds of stuff around the room with my BBs, but then I shot at the window and the whole thing exploded. It was like a bomb had gone off in the room. They actually had to close the floor down.

To top me, I guess, Ace brought a crossbow on tour. Around that time I began to make a game out of stealing huge paintings from the hotel lobby. I'd wait for the manager or the desk clerks to walk away and then one of the crew guys and I would heist the painting, rush it out of the lobby, and throw it into one of our trucks. Ace didn't even bother stealing the artwork. He'd walk through the lobby, pull out an arrow, and shoot it right through the paintings on the wall. He got so out of control with that crossbow, eventually we had to take it away from him.

It was always fun to bust Chris Lendt's balls. One time we were staying in a hotel with a beautiful golf course behind it. Ace and I got drunk with Eddie Balandas, one of our bodyguards, and we decided to fuck with Chris. So we broke into his rental car, released the brake, and rolled it down the hill onto the golf course. That sucker destroyed greens, knocked down trees, did every kind of damage that could be done to a golf course. That night we stayed in the room and laughed all night long. When the sun came out, the cops found the car, saw that it had been rented to a Chris Lendt, and we had to pay the damages.

Eventually we got such a bad rep that Chris was forced to put down a $10,000 deposit against any damages that we might incur. A lot of that was because of the shit that Ace and I and Eddie would pull. We had heard legendary stories of Keith Moon's pranks and we were striving to top him. We began by simply flooding the toilets and sinks so that the water would cascade down to the lower floors. Then we graduated to cherry bombs and M-80s. Eddie somehow figured out how to hook them up so that you could light the fuse and throw them down the toilet. He'd rig up three cherry bombs with extra long fuses, and by the time we got to our car, they had exploded, destroyed the pipes, and flooded the hotel.

Our all-time greatest prank was pulled on Gene. I came up with the idea and enlisted the whole band, even Bill. The idea was to have Fritz—who was then serving as my drum tech and whom Gene always tormented—get dressed up in one of Gene's old costumes and makeup. Near the end of our last number, I was going to switch places with Fritz and I'd wait backstage as Fritz took up the drumming. It could work because Fritz was a good drummer and he knew all our songs. Plus Fritz would be sixty feet in the air, and through all the fireworks, Gene would never realize that it was Fritz in his costume.

So near the end of "Black Diamond," we made the switch. Fritz threw in an extra beat and Gene looked up at the drums and just stared at Fritz with his mouth open. It was like he saw his doppelgänger. I was backstage, pissing my pants. Gene then looked away and shook his head as if to say, "Did I just see that?" Then he looked over to Paul and Ace, and they both looked noncommittal. When Gene looked back up at Fritz, I told Fritz to start giving him the tongue move. Now Gene was flipping out. Meanwhile, Ace and Paul were playing like there was nothing wrong. We ended the song and Gene looked up at Fritz one last time, dropped his bass, and almost fell off the stage. They had to catch him. Then I rushed up and put my arm around him.

"Great fucking show, man," I smiled.

We took our bows and Gene was still in total shock.

"I think I'm losing my mind," he said. "I saw myself on the drums."

"How can that be?" I said innocently. "I was up there."

"I have to talk to Gui about this," he said, and got into the limo with Bill.

We were playing in Providence, so they had a long ride back to the city. About halfway home, Gene was so freaked out that Bill had to spill the beans and tell Gene about the prank. I don't think Gene spoke to anybody for a week.

On September 25 we began recording *Rock and Roll Over*, our followup to *Destroyer*, at the Nanuet Star Theater in Rockland County, an old theater that had been shuttered. I had gone on an all-night coke binge the night before so for the first time in my career I missed a session, which didn't go down well with everyone else.

Eddie Kramer was back producing, and I told him that we should record my drums in the upstairs bathroom to get a better sound. We could put a video feed up there so I could communicate with the control room. Of course, having a camera up there was going to interfere with me doing lines, so whenever I wanted to do a bump, I moved the camera away and pretended we were having technical difficulties. Then I'd shake it, and miraculously it would work again.

I sang two songs on the album. One night, Paul played "Hard Luck Woman" for me when we were standing around the pool table on a break.

"I love that fucking song," I said. "I'd do anything to sing that."

"Well, I was thinking of Rod Stewart," Paul said.

"Fuck Rod," I fumed. "Don't I have a raspy voice? Come on."

Paul gave me the song, but while I was recording it he stood in the studio next to Kramer from the beginning to the end, constantly talking to me over the intercom. "No, more raspy." "Speed it up there." I wanted to stab him in the forehead with a knife. Toward the end of the song, I broke away from Paul's direction and did some free-flowing soul stuff, and I think that's the best part of the song.

I must have done something right. The song was released as our first single off that album, and it went to number fifteen. Years later, Garth Brooks covered it.

Gene and Paul let me contribute one song to the album. But even then, they fucked around with it. My original version of "Baby Driver," a song I had written with Stan Penridge, was very cool. But these pricks had to go in and change it around. I never fucked with their original songs. They were like two gestapo agents, always exerting their will. Later they even had the balls to say that they rearranged the song but didn't take credit for it so that the fans would think that everybody in the band was as creative as everybody else.

With the album completed, we got ready to go back out on the road, naturally. But first we flew out to L.A. to tape Paul Lynde's Halloween TV special. My mother was thrilled. Paul Lynde was her favorite comedian. My mother loved gay people, and she thought he was the funniest. We were a little out of place on the show, with guests like Margaret Hamilton, Tim Conway, Florence Henderson, Betty White, and Donny and Marie Osmond, but it should have been a wake-up call. We were rapidly leaving the rock 'n' roll rebel label behind us and winding up as Hollywood pablum.

We were back on the road by the end of November, a tour that would last until April of 1977. There's just no way to overstate what a bizarre circus a KISS tour was. We were staying at a fancy hotel in Ontario once when Billy Miller, one of our road managers, got a dispatch on his walkie-talkie from Big John, one of our security guys.

"Ace is small," Big John said.

That was the road crew's code for Ace is drunk. It seemed that Ace got smashed and was convinced that tiny green men had entered his brain and made him small.

They put Ace to bed, but a few minutes later they heard a German shepherd barking its head off. Then there was the sound of glass breaking. By then everyone on the floor had woken up. Suddenly, Ace's door flew open and Ace ran out of his room in his underwear screaming, "He's getting me! He's shooting me!" It turned out that Ace had put on a sound-effects record before he had passed out, and when the guns started firing, he thought they were real.

Does this sound like a madhouse or what? We were all crazy in our own way, but that didn't stop our juggernaut. From 1976 to 1978 we made more than $17 million from record sales alone, and more than $7 million from touring, not counting merchandise.

Suddenly we were getting awards, too. In 1976 and 1977 I won the *Circus* magazine Drummer of the Year award. The first year I gave my award to Lydia. The next year Belushi got it. But the award that was dearest to my heart was the People's Choice Award for "Beth." Of course, we were touring at the time, but the guys let Lydia fly out to L.A. and accept it for us on the telecast. They had hooked up a satellite link to where we were, and even though we knew we had won, Bill told us to act surprised. After we waved at the camera, Lydia was brought onstage in L.A. and she picked up the actual hardware.

Halfway into the tour we finally realized our long-sought-after dream. On February 17, 1977, we played the mecca of our dreams, Madison Square Garden. As soon as I got the tour schedule, I called my mother to tell her that we were going to be at MSG. The day of the show, all four of us were scared shitless. It hit us when we walked backstage and saw all those photos of Sinatra and Ali. This was the world's greatest arena. I think I threw up twice before the show. Paul was climbing the walls. You could cut the energy with a knife. Bill was trying to keep people away from our dressing rooms. He was a nervous wreck, too.

Part of the reason we were nervous was that the sound sucked at the Garden. We were disappointed at sound check because the room was so dead. It wasn't made for concerts—you either get nothing back, or the sound bounced off that back wall and came right back at you. And the

Teamsters were a nightmare. My crew hated them. You couldn't even take a pen up on that stage, they had to carry it up for you. My drum tech told me that it was taking them hours to set up because they'd carry one cymbal at a time. Who's going to tell the Teamsters what the fuck to do, though?

Before the show, I put one single red rose in each of the other guys' rooms, from me to them. The note said, LET'S HAVE A GREAT SHOW. I LOVE YOU, PETER. Right before we put on our makeup, I went to see Gene.

"We're going out to play the Garden," I said.

"Son of a bitch, man, you said it so many times," he chuckled.

When I got up behind the drums, I scanned the audience and I found my folks. We started to play and tears were streaming down my mom's face. Even my dad was all teared up. This was the one thing that I wanted more than anything else in the world—to be on that stage and see my mom and dad watch me play. I started bawling and my makeup started to run down the sides of my face.

It's funny: No matter what age you reach, you're always still trying to please your parents. We never had money, but they let me pursue my dream. This was something I could give back to them, to make them feel that all that sacrifice was worth it. My mother was always so proud of me. She would actually go up to Gene after a show and say, "You know if my son leaves the band, there will be no band. He makes the band great. Without a great drummer, there's no great band."

Gene would say, "I guess you're right, Mrs. Criscuola," but he'd look like he wanted to choke her. But Bill would always take it up for her.

"You are absolutely right, Mrs. Criscuola," he'd tell her. "Your son is the heartbeat of the band." Then he'd give her a hug.

Three days after the Garden show, we came back down to reality. We were finishing our show at the Nassau Coliseum on Long Island when it was time for me to levitate. By then we were using a scissors lift to get me up. Those things were not balanced, so sure enough the platform tilted to the left and half of my drums were hanging off it.

"We just played the Garden, and now we look like idiots," I fumed afterward. I was pissed. That night I went to Ashley's to chill and I hung out with Boz Scaggs until closing time. I got home at daybreak, drunk and wired, and I wanted to have sex with Lydia but she refused. So I grabbed the keys and stormed out of the house and went to the garage down the street where I kept my Camaro. The attendant brought me my car and then turned around to take care of other business. I was so fucked up that I got into the car and accidentally floored it and smashed into the wall of the garage. Then I put it into reverse and floored it again and hit the rear wall. I kept repeating this until the car caught on fire. Lucky for me, one of my neighbors was getting his car and he pulled me out. By then the attendant had called the cops. I was sitting on a bench with my nose broken, bleeding profusely, and I hadn't even left the garage yet. Somehow I was conscious enough to tell the attendant to call Bill and have him to rush over to the garage.

The cop arrived just before Bill.

"Peter Criss from KISS!" the cop said. "What the hell did you do?"

He looked into the car with his flashlight and he saw my .38, my drugs, and a switchblade. Just then Bill came. Bill took the cop to the side, but I could hear them talking.

"There's a gun in the car. Some drugs too. But since he didn't hurt nobody but himself, get this stuff out of here in five minutes and I didn't see anything. But you owe me," the cop told Bill.

Bill promised him lifetime passes to any KISS show. I had to go to the hospital, so Bill called Lydia and asked her to clean out the car while we went to Bellevue. By the time Lydia arrived at the hospital, I was lying on a gurney in the hallway with two black eyes and a busted nose. They put a bandage on my broken nose and sent me home with a big bottle of Percodan. I had never taken Percodan before, but they were a revelation. A couple of them with champagne was a killer high. But I'm getting ahead of myself. It took Belushi to introduce me to the pleasures of Percodan.

I was back at the brownstone, healing in bed, when John came over to visit.

"How you feeling, Peter?" he said softly.

"Oh, Johnny, I can't breathe. I'm fucked up," I said.

He was anxious to hear the blow-by-blow account of the accident, and as I related it to him, his eyes wandered to my nightstand.

"So what did the doctor give you?" he asked.

"I don't know what they're called. Some pills for the pain."

He picked up the bottle.

"Wow, Percodan!" His eyes lit up. "These fucking things are dynamite. Do you mind?"

"No, take what you want—" I didn't even finish the sentence and John had emptied the rest of the bottle into his mouth.

"Whaddya got to drink?" he mumbled.

I motioned toward the bar and he grabbed a bottle of tequila and guzzled it down with those pills. In seconds he was flying on top of the buzz he had when he came over. After a few minutes, John said he had to leave to meet Dan.

"John, you're really fucked up," I said. "Why don't you hang out a little longer, and I'll get out of bed and we'll watch a little TV?"

"Ah, stay in bed, I'll be fine."

We said good-bye and watched him stumble out of the room. But he couldn't deal with our spiral staircase. Seconds later, we heard, boom, boom, boom, boom. I jumped out of bed.

Lydia yelled down the stairs, "Are you all right, John?"

"Yeah, I'm fine," he mumbled back. Then we heard the front door slam and we could hear him screaming for a cab in the street.

If Belushi likes these things so much, they must be cool, I thought as I went back to bed. The next day I called my doctor and got the prescription refilled. Before I knew it, I was addicted to them.

CHAPTER ELEVEN

"KISS go home! KISS go home! KISS go home!"

We could hear the chants from the hotel room where we were all huddled together. Outside, a mob was picketing, holding up handwritten placards that read KISS—KNIGHTS IN SATAN'S SERVICE and HIDE YOUR DAUGHTERS—KISS IS COMING TO TOWN. Some creative types had even dressed up a few dummies in our makeup and costume. When they began burning us in effigy, we knew that it was getting serious.

"You're all going to spend the night in this one room," Bill was lecturing us. "After I leave, I want you to double-lock the door and then put the dresser in front of it. These people are irrational. There's no telling what they might do."

We had just played a show in Asheville, North Carolina, under some duress. It seemed that one of the national evangelical Christian TV shows had decided that KISS stood for Knights in Satan's Service and that we were all agents of the devil. That was news to this Catholic boy, but you don't argue with Bill when you're in a town where every few miles you can see a huge billboard of a man in a white sheet, riding a white horse and carrying a cross, that reads, SUPPORT YOUR LOCAL KLAN.

"Oh, and Gene," Bill hesitated before he left the room. "Don't you dare stick your dick in anyone down here. We have to get safely out of this town tomorrow."

I was scared shitless. The Ku Klux Klan doesn't fuck around. I surely didn't want my skinny ass dragged outside and hung from a tree. I was so scared that I actually called my mother from the room.

"Ma, I'm barricaded in a room in North Carolina. The KKK is picketing us." I was being a little dramatic, but that's me.

"What's he talking about?" I heard my dad ask in the background. My mother made me promise that I'd call her first thing in the morning and let her know I was okay.

We managed to leave town intact, but there was one irony. During our show that night, a bunch of girls showed up in leather masks and dominatrix-style bondage gear, and while we were playing, the crew got to fuck them. That's how strange America was back in 1977.

It was a lot stranger, though, in Japan. In March of that year, we made our first foray over to the Land of the Rising Sun. We flew over on a huge 747 that we called "the Kiss Clipper." It even had the KISS logo on its tail. Besides the band, we were carrying about forty press people on an all-expenses-paid junket.

We exited the plane, in full makeup, to the most ecstatic reception I'd ever seen. It was Beatlemania, only much more high-pitched. Thousands and thousands of fans had swarmed the airport and were screaming their heads off. The terminal was actually shaking from the press of people. We jumped into a limo, but so many girls were hanging off the hood and banging on the windows that we had to jump out and get into a bigger van to escape the airport.

It was no better when we tried to walk in the streets. Hundreds of screaming fans followed us everywhere we went. As loud as the fans were on the street, they were quiet and docile during the shows. We didn't realize it was a cultural thing to listen to a song in silence, a way of showing respect. But when the song was over, they'd cheer and go crazy like any other audience.

I had brought Lydia with me, so I missed out on the highlight of everyone else's trip. The promoter, Mr. Udo, took the other guys (except for Ace, who had his wife there, too) to a traditional bathhouse where you'd lie on a rubber sheet, have hot oils massaged all over your body, and get an unbelievable happy ending. According to Paul and Chris Lendt, the handjob was so good it was almost heart-stopping.

I had to content myself with going to Kiddy Land, the most over-the-top toy store I'd ever seen. I bought lasers, iron dragons, pistols, and pellet guns. Most of us bought the pellet guns, so the next morning at five A.M. we had a shoot-out in our hallway. Sean was nursing his welts for days after that shoot-out.

We had some other fights that weren't as much fun. We would always argue over song selection, but one night in Japan the argument escalated to the point that the dressing-room door was locked. But we went out and tore through a killer two-hour show for the fans.

We were really on a roll. We were voted the number-one rock band for three years straight, 1977 to 1979, in the prestigious Gallup Poll. And we were spewing out product like crazy. In June of 1977 we released our sixth album, *Love Gun*. I always liked working with Eddie Kramer, but this wasn't really a band effort. Except for "Love Gun," which I loved to play, I thought the songs were pretty mediocre. My song "Hooligan" was butchered. Ace's song "Shock Me," which was inspired by his near elec-trocution onstage one night, featured his first lead vocal as a member of KISS. I was very happy that he was finally getting a chance to sing, but let's face it, Ace might just have the worst voice in the world. I thought the best thing about the album was the cardboard gun that came inside. But it didn't seem to matter, the album went platinum just weeks after it was released. We could do no wrong.

In fact, we were doing so well, our business managers told us to go out and buy houses. Lydia and I took a ride out to Greenwich, Connecticut, with Chris Lendt one day in May of 1977. We drove down one road and it kept winding and winding around and all of a sudden, there was our dream house. It was a European-style chalet with stone floors, beamed ceilings, window boxes, balconies, a big medieval front door, and an eight-foot fireplace. I thought Lydia was going to faint.

The owners were Scandinavians, and they had these gorgeous blond kids running around with a whole new litter of sheepdogs. It was like a movie set. Chris and I told Lydia not to act too excited in front of the owners, and we started negotiating. They were asking $375,000, which was a steal. We told them that we'd make an offer, and then we went for a bite to eat and to look over some other properties, even though we knew this was the one.

At the restaurant, I looked across the street and saw a Mercedes dealership.

"Hey, Chris, can I get a Mercedes too?" I asked.

"Sure, why not?" he said.

I marched over there and picked out a chocolate-brown 450SL with a camel interior.

"How does it feel?" Chris asked me on the ride home. It felt like an epiphany. All those times that I didn't go out and play ball with the kids, all those hours of practicing on the drums, had finally paid off. With a mini-mansion and a Mercedes, both bought on the same day, I had more than I had ever dreamed of.

The *Love Gun* tour started up in Canada in July. We had rented a twin-prop army-transport jet that had been converted and outfitted with beds so we could get laid. Gene was a horrible air traveler.

After a few flights, we all developed a fear of flying because our pilots turned out to be party animals. At first all we knew was that we would hear them fighting in the cockpit. Then we started landing at the wrong airports and almost hitting the guardrails on the landing strips. Eventually someone told us that our pilots had been at every after-party, drinking champagne and doing blow. Great, now our lives were in the hands of two coked-out pilots.

The more successful we got, the more fragile the bonds between us became. In September we went into the studio to sweeten a few new live songs for our second live album, but Ace rarely bothered to show up, he was so fucked up. Bob Kulick had to replicate all of Ace's leads.

Even Gene and Paul were fighting by then, mostly over the covers of the magazines that always seemed to feature Gene in a prominent position and relegated the rest of us to the sidelines. This was especially true in Japanese music magazines because Gene wore his hair in that samurai bun.

Jealousy pervaded everything we did. Gene came up with a great description of it. Whenever we found out about a new status symbol, whether it was a car, a toy, a television, or a house, Gene would tell Bill, "Buy four." It was especially true for Paul, because he really was a chameleon. I was the first to get a Rolex in the band. Next thing you know, Paul's got the Presidential Rolex. And that still wasn't good enough, so he got the Presidential with all the diamonds around it.

Here we were, four guys who started out putting shoe polish on our faces and dying our hair in a bathtub in the Village, and now we're vying for the most expensive watch. It was sad to see how greed and pride and ego were suffocating the band.

We were making so much money we didn't know what to do with it all. In November, Howard Marks showed up to a show in San Antonio with papers for all of us to sign. We were investing in coal mines and oil rigs as tax shelters, moves that would later bite us in the ass.

In 1977 alone, our gross income was over $10 million. So Bill started thinking really big. He wanted to break us out of having to tour all the time by making a movie. Then he thought we should each do a solo album to reinforce the idea that we were four larger-than-life superstars. Of course, Gene and Paul were all for these grandiose ideas. Ace and I weren't so sure.

Alive II was released on October 24. Bill was pushing for another live album for a pragmatic reason. "The idea of not having to be in the studio together for all those hours made sense to everyone," he diplomatically told one journalist.

The *Alive II* tour was actually fun, mostly thanks to Fritz Postlethwaite. He had worked his way up from being a monitor man who was routinely spit on by Gene to being the top banana. He deserved it. Fritz was a short blond Eastern European brainiac. His big round glasses earned him the nickname Poindexter after that cartoon character. Every day he would come around with a chart of everyone's biorhythms. He was as crazy as we were. After some time with us, he bought a mini chainsaw and he'd chainsaw the hotel furniture when he got frustrated.

We got home in time to celebrate Christmas in our new home. On Christmas Eve I really got into the Christmas spirit. I had Nat King Cole on the stereo; I was drinking a scotch and wearing my Santa Claus pajamas. *It's a Wonderful Life* was playing silently on the TV. Of course, we had some blow and Lydia was snorting it and talking on the phone to her annoying cousin Phyllis. With every line, Lydia stayed on the phone for another half hour talking about bullshit. Soon the movie was over, I was on to my fourth scotch, and that much scotch would make me crazy. Lydia was still yapping away on the phone in the other room. And I hate phones.

Is this what it's all about? I thought to myself. Is this what I broke my ass on the road for? To sit here on Christmas Eve listening to Nat King Cole by my fucking self, looking at the fucking tree? Whoop-de-fucking-do. She could be talking to her fucking cousin any fucking day of the year. I got champagne on ice and we're alone on Christmas and she's talking for three hours about a fucking dress? This is fucking bullshit.

I opened the drawer next to the couch and pulled out my nickel-plated .38 snub-nose.

"Fuck this!" I screamed, and I shot the Christmas tree two times.

"Merry motherfucking Christmas," I said, and then I put the gun back in the drawer. Lydia came running into the room.

"Oh, you're off the phone now? Now can we enjoy Christmas?"

We were back on the road in January when we got the official word that we were all millionaires. We learned that from watching an Edwin Newman special on NBC called *The Land of Hype and Glory*. We had been interviewed for that show, and Bill was adamant that Gene do the talking because Newman was a "genius" and Bill didn't want us to look stupid or crazy or drugged out. On the show they were talking about these four crazy kids from Queens and Brooklyn and the Bronx. "You may think they're clowns and we may laugh at them, but they're all millionaires."

I looked over at Lydia. "Wow, I'm a millionaire."

That was the first time we had official confirmation. We had been told in one of our meetings with Marks and Glickman that we would be "rich beyond our dreams," but this put the icing on the cake.

It's not like we had time to enjoy being millionaires. In March the tour went back to Japan, where we would spend the entire eight days in Tokyo. That gave Ace enough time to dig up some authentic Nazi SS uniforms complete with armbands, medals, boots, and Lugers. Ace, Paul, and I put them on and posed for pictures. We got fucked up on sake and then Ace and I paraded down the hallway, banging on the crew's doors, yelling, "We demand to see your papers!" Then Ace and I did something really wrong, even for us.

We knocked on Gene's door. Gene opened the door.

"You vill give us your name, rank, and serial number, or ve vill throw your Jewish ass into the ovens!" we said, and we cracked up like two kids.

Gene's expression didn't change. He didn't smile, he didn't yell, he just stared at us with a look that could kill. We knew we crossed the line, and we went back to Ace's room.

We were taking off the uniforms when Paul came in.

"What the fuck were you thinking? Don't you know that Gene's grandmother died in the fucking ovens?" Paul said. He told us that Gene's mother was a beautician in the camps who did hair for the Nazis' wives, and they made her watch while they put her mother in a gas chamber.

We were devastated. Why didn't that prick tell us that before? We marched right back to Gene's room to apologize.

While we were in Tokyo, we spent a lot of time shopping for all those great toys that you could only get in Japan. But Gene hardly came out of his room at all. He was too busy talking on the phone with his new love, Cher. Gene had met Cher because Chastity was a big KISS fan. From the first time we met Cher, everyone loved her. She was sensitive and smart and she really treated Gene well. Cher taught Gene how to relate to a woman for the first time in his life.

Cher was totally into Gene. One night, months later, we were sitting in her room on the road somewhere and she said, "You know, Petey, I would marry Genie, I love him that much. But I don't think that's going to happen." She was right on that count.

Despite what the press said, everybody in the band loved Cher. Paul, the chameleon that he was, loved her so much that he started dating her sister. The only thing that bugged me was that Gene was getting tons of press because he was going out with a major star like Cher. Every time I picked up a paper, you'd see a picture of Cher and a picture of Gene trying to hide his face. So I must admit, I got jealous.

Eventually Gene moved to California to live with Cher. Again the press made it sound like we were all pissed off by that decision. But I didn't feel threatened by Gene leaving New York. I was personally happy he was gone.

Around this time, we put out our first greatest-hits album, *Double Plat-*

inum. The ironic thing was that we had nothing to do with it. Sean had gone into a studio for a couple of weeks and remixed all our hits. It was just as well: By then we couldn't stand being in the same studio together for that much time. Bill thought that we needed to get some product out because we were about to embark on two of Bill's grandiose ideas—the TV movie and the four solo albums that would all be released on the same day.

I had no idea that going to Rod Stewart's party in Hollywood would forever change my life, but it did. It's funny because I almost passed on the party. We were taking the noon flight to L.A. to begin preparations for our first movie, *KISS Meets the Phantom of the Park*. Alison Steele, a popular New York disc jockey, was on board and had organized a card game. She took me for a couple of grand and I was tired and jet-lagged, so I checked into my suite at L'Ermitage Hotel in Beverly Hills and went straight to my room to get some room service and a good night's sleep. Then I heard the knock.

"Hey, Petey," Ace said. "Come to Rod Stewart's party. There's gonna be prime chicks there."

Alison Steele had invited all of us to this party while we were playing cards.

"I don't know," I said. Then Paul swung by.

"You know that you're going to regret not going when we come back and tell you how great it was. You're going to hate us," he said.

He was right. So I took a quick shower, put on a really cool velvet jacket and velvet pants, and teased my hair up to look like Rod's. I had rented a white Rolls for the time we were in L.A., so me and Rosie, my bodyguard, made a bit of an entrance. We walked past a huge gate and I immediately thought, This is what a Hollywood party should look like. There were all these people hanging around the big pool, drinking, snorting blow, falling into the pool. We started roaming around and Alison introduced us to Rod, like he gave a fuck. Then I met Ronnie Wood, and he was pretty nice to me. There were so many stars roaming around, you couldn't even count them.

At one point I looked over and saw Hugh Hefner surrounded by ten knockout girls, each one better than the other.

Just then, I looked out on the dance floor and there were two of Hef's girls dancing very sensuously with each other. They both were terrific-looking, but I fixated on the blonde and suddenly my libido was just blasting through my pants.

"Go get her for me," I instructed Rosie. I was half in the bag by then.

"I'm not going to do that," he said. Rosie was an ex–Hell's Angel, so I decided not to push it. By then the blonde and I were making eye contact, so I figured that sometimes you had to do things for yourself.

I went right onto the dance floor, grabbed her hand, and pulled her away.

"I gotta get to know you," I said. "I've never seen such a beautiful woman in my life."

We started talking. She said her name was Debra Jensen and that she was a *Playboy* centerfold and a lingerie model. I didn't even comprehend half the things she was saying. I just felt like a little kid, drinking in her face. I had never met anyone that gorgeous.

Of course, I told her I was the drummer for KISS.

"I hate that band," Debra said. "They wear makeup and look like maniacs."

I was really bummed out.

"But I think you're cute," she said.

Whew, I still had a chance. At one point she had to pee and the bathrooms were all occupied, so we went outside the house and she peed in the bushes.

When she came back, I was determined not to lose this chick, so I invited her back to the hotel. She hemmed and hawed and told me she was there with all these other girls; she even brought me over to meet Hef. But I was persistent. I gave her a few lines of coke and then I slipped her a quaalude. It was like leading a donkey to water. Once she got into that white Rolls, there were no complaints.

When we got to my suite, I put on a show for her. I donned this tacky red designer robe and I strutted in like I was Errol Flynn.

"How do you like the robe?" I said, trying to be suave. "It's an Yves Saint Laurent."

Later she told me that was one of the funniest things she'd ever seen. Here was a girl who knew her fashion. She was into the top tier of designers, like Halston. But she didn't want to hurt my feelings.

"It's a really nice robe."

We fucked nine times that night, my all-time record. We fucked everywhere and anywhere we could in that suite. We even used the bidet. I had no idea what a bidet was.

I was totally in love. I just wanted to give this girl the fucking world: Nobody had ever fucked me like that. I was smitten. I couldn't believe I was with a Playboy Playmate! Suddenly Lydia felt like a high school sweetheart to me. This was not true love. My dick was in love, not my heart, and drugs didn't help. I didn't want to stop touching her or kissing her. I couldn't stand the thought of her leaving.

The next day she got up to leave and put her phone number on the back of an eight-by-ten photo of herself. She signed it TO PETER, LOVE, DEBRA JENSEN, like she was the star. Later she would tell me that she didn't even plan on ever seeing me again. She was moving on. She had just done the January centerfold and she was getting ready to do more covers. But I was convinced that this woman loved me. What a delusional little Brooklyn Guinea asshole I was. Here was this California girl who had slept with Hef, who was way ahead of me. I had been with a lot of chicks on the road, but I had never had Beverly Hills pussy before. And there's a huge difference between Beverly Hills pussy and road pussy. Beverly Hills pussy is about money, road pussy was for free.

Of course I called her that night. She said she was going to Vegas with her girlfriend Patti McGuire, a Playmate of the Year who wound up marrying Jimmy Connors, the tennis player.

I was begging her, "No, you don't want to go to Vegas. I'm starting a movie tomorrow. Come visit me on the set." I figured that would win her over for sure. I was taking no chances. I had finally found one of those centerfold girls that I used to jerk off to hanging on the wall of that butcher shop back in Brooklyn when I was a kid. Pussy could be just as devastating and scary and deep and dark as any other vice. I was about to find out firsthand.

I was going into the shooting of the film with mixed feelings to begin with. I had always wanted to act, but the plot of this film was that we had to use our superpowers to save a California amusement park from destruction at the hands of an evil inventor. It was the lamest thing I could've imagined. When I was told that we had to fight the Wolfman one day and Frankenstein the next, my brain started to hurt. Why should I have powers to levitate things with my hands? What did any of this have to do with rock 'n' roll? Our fans were going to think that we were pansies. I became a drummer in a rock 'n' roll band because I was a rebel, I was fighting the system, fighting the Vietnam War. Now we were just buffoons. What happened to the guys who got up there and did "God of Thunder" and "Black Diamond"? All of a sudden we're doing slapstick? I knew right then that my career as a rock musician was down the toilet.

Before the script was written, we met with the screenwriters so they could get a feel for how we talked. Ace refused to even talk to them. He just mumbled his non sequiturs like "I kills 'em all" or "Thirteen for a dozen" and made his crazy parrot sounds. So when the script came in, Ace had no lines. Once in a while he'd just go, "Arrgghh." He was furious.

On the first day of shooting, our first scene was to be filmed around a pool. I was sitting up in a big lifeguard's chair, wearing a long, crazy robe. I think my line was something like, "Gene was an only child," or maybe it was, "Aye, matey, let's cut her throat." They were both equally stupid. I was ready to deliver the line and I looked over to the side and my heart leaped into my throat. Deb was standing there next to Fritz and Rosie. She had canceled Vegas and come to the set.

She was a vision in a white top with a black skirt and black nylons. Who gave a shit about the movie anymore? I just wanted to get in her pants.

Deb coming to the set spelled doom for the film. I had to be on set every day at six in the morning, and we would stay up all night and fuck and do blow until five when I got the call that the car was outside waiting for me. Deb had just turned twenty, so she could take it, but I was in my thirties. The later we stayed up fucking and drugging, the more I forgot my lines and started slurring my words. And the more I did that and pissed off the director, the more I hated being there.

Ace felt the same contempt for the film. We would visit each other in our trailers and we both stocked our refrigerators with wall-to-wall green bottles of Heineken. We'd drink and snort coke all day while we waited for our calls. That was the worst part of moviemaking, sitting around for sometimes ten hours before they'd be ready for the scene. I wasn't accustomed to that kind of discipline, especially when we were in our full makeup, waiting hours to do a five-minute scene. We'd get so fucked up that when we finally got the call, we'd stumble out of the trailer slurring our words and hitting the walls and knocking props over.

One night the director wanted to meet with me privately and read me the riot act. He was lecturing me, telling me that I had to cool it with the drugs and stop getting high with Ace because we were getting behind on the budget.

"Yeah, fuck you," I said. "I don't care what happens with this fucking movie. I'm a drummer in a rock band and I don't give a shit about you or Hanna-Barbera or the Wolfman and Dracula, you can all go fuck yourselves."

I got up and walked out and left him sitting there.

The next day he came up to me on the set.

"How are you feeling today, Peter?" he asked.

"The same fucking way I felt yesterday," I said.

All I had to look forward to was Deb visiting me. We would screw so much that my trailer was moving up and down constantly.

One day she came over and asked if I would fuck her with my makeup on. We started banging and there was a mirror right near us and I looked at it and saw my face and I freaked out. My makeup was running, my whiskers were all askew, the black and silver had rubbed off on her face, the lipstick was all over the place. I just looked demonic. I realized that I was out of control, that I had lost my fucking mind and that I was fucking up the show. But I didn't care.

After a few weeks of shooting, I had had enough. I walked off the set and went back to the hotel. I sat there and figured that I had a lot of money now. I had a beautiful new girlfriend. I was about to do a solo album. What did I need this shit for? I was a big enough star that I could put together my own band and do well. So I called our lawyer,

Paul Marshall, and told him to fly out to L.A. because I wanted out of the band.

"You're out of your fucking mind, Peter!" he screamed. "We're in the middle of making a movie. You can't just leave this."

Paul and Bill and Howard Marks took the next flight out and we sat down and had a big meeting with everyone. And everyone bullshitted me again. They told me that the film would really take the band to new heights, that it would cost millions if I walked away, that if we could just get through this film we'd do our solo projects and everything would be okay. But it wasn't. It was really over by then. Even Gene and Paul knew it. They had had enough of my and Ace's crap and we certainly had had enough of theirs. We weren't a band anymore.

They kept working on me, and I agreed to finish the movie and then we'd see where we were at. So I went back to the set, and now it was time to shoot the "Beth" scene. It was a love scene, and they were going to let me fake play an acoustic guitar. The original script had me alone singing the song to the leading lady. But I got to the set and the script had changed. All of a sudden Paul was playing the guitar, the band was sitting around the pool, and I was sitting there with my dick in my hand singing the song to her.

"What happened to me with the guitar?"

"Well, everybody knows you can't play," Paul said.

"How the fuck do you know that? You mean everyone on this set knows that because you fucking told them. You're just afraid I'm going to get some camera time . . . ."

That was how the arguments would start.

So Paul got the guitar part, and the next thing I knew, all they needed was the music. They didn't need the vocals. I went ballistic. I threatened to quit again, so they put the scene back, but it wasn't good. KISS doesn't sit around a pool, with me resting my boot on a diving board, singing "Beth" to some chick who wasn't even particularly hot, with Paul and his pouty lips playing acoustic.

My next big scene involved me opening a box to reveal a talisman inside. In the movie, our lair had just been robbed and we were afraid that the talisman had been stolen. I was supposed to say, "Wow, they didn't get the talisman," but I was so loaded it kept on coming out *tal-eeees-man,* like in that Harry Belafonte song "Day-O."

"Peter, it's *tal-is-man,*" the director would say.

"Okay, right," I said, and they'd roll tape again.

"Wow, they didn't get the taleeeesman," I said.

Paul and Gene started dancing and singing, "Hey, Mr. Tally Man, tally me bananas."

I lost it.

"You fucking assholes, how dare you make fun of me!" I screamed, and threw the box against the wall, shattering it. I walked off the set and Ace started going, "Arrggh, arrggh."

"I guess that's a wrap," the director said. "Let's try this again tomorrow."

I had one big action scene where Ace and I were taking on two masked samurai fighters. I was supposed to grab my attacker, flip him around, and give him a couple of punches to the face while I was ducking his sword thrusts. We started shooting and I was ducking the sword and then I swung at him and boom, I broke right through his mask, hit him in the eye, and knocked him to the ground.

"Cut!" the director yelled. Buddy Joe Hooker, the head stuntman, came running up to me.

"Are you crazy? Where the fuck did you get the idea you could punch one of my men?" he said.

"Nobody told me I wasn't supposed to hit him," I said innocently. I really believed that those guys hit each other but they knew how to slide and take a punch.

"My man has a black eye from you," Hooker fumed. "You're lucky I don't punch you out right now. You do that once more, we'll stop this movie."

Not much of a threat, really. I would have gone back and cracked a bottle of champagne and celebrated if they canceled the movie. But I did feel terrible about injuring the guy. I kept apologizing every day, and eventually they made me an honorary stuntman and gave me a plaque.

On May 19 we shot a huge outdoor concert at Magic Mountain, the amusement park where the movie took place. It was a free show and there were KISS banners everywhere. This was to be the climax where we battle the bad guys onstage, knock them out, and the audience would go crazy. At this point I was ready to shoot myself. I would have rather watched Cal Worthington's used-car ads on an endless loop than do this movie.

We got to the last song, "Black Diamond," during which the drums levitated. We shot take after take, and the drums were going up and down and up and down, and I just flipped out.

I took my sticks and threw them into the drums and stormed off in my limo with Rosie. They had to get some middle-aged stagehand to throw on one of my costumes and sit in my seat. They continued filming from different angles, so you couldn't really tell that it wasn't me. By then Ace had also walked and they used a black guy as his double, which seemed to piss him off.

By then Lydia had come out to visit. Of course I kept her and Deb apart at all costs. On May 27 we wrapped the shooting, so we had a party back at L'Ermitage. We were playing a really fun card game called Acey/Deucey and at five in the morning, I had just won a pot that was worth $7,000. I don't know if you've ever seen seven grand in hundreds and fifties and twenties, but it was an impressive sight. When I won that pot, everybody quit for the night. But I was jazzed. And stoned.

It was my last night in L.A.: The next day Lydia and I were supposed to fly back to New York. I was dreading that because I was so in love with Deb that I couldn't bear the thought of leaving. So I decided to get in my leased 928 Porsche and go for a drive. It was Fritz's birthday that night, so he said he wanted to go with me. We got into the car and we started racing around town and I wound up driving over to Deb's house. We walked into her house carrying a half-full magnum of Dom Pérignon. In my pocket I had a bag of ludes and at least an eight ball of coke. I tried to persuade Deb to come out and keep partying, but she was having none of it.

"I think you guys should stay here," she said. "I know your wife is at the hotel, but you can call her. You're really too smashed to get back into that car. That would be a big mistake."

I knew that if I stayed there I would get laid, and then I'd never want to go back to the hotel for the flight to New York, so we decided to leave. Plus Fritz was urging me to go because he didn't really like Deb. His allegiance was to Lydia. He was being responsible. So against my libido's judgment, we left.

On the way back to the car, Fritz asked me if he could drive. Hey, it was his birthday, so I said, "Why not?" He got behind the wheel and put on his seat belt. Me, I didn't buckle up. We started driving. Deb's place was only about five minutes away from the hotel, but we seemed to be driving in circles and it was taking forever to get back. It turned out that we had driven all the way to Marina del Rey. The sun was coming up and Fritz turned onto Sepulveda Boulevard and gunned that car up to ninety miles per hour. I popped an Eagles cassette into the player and "Hotel California" started to play.

The next thing I remember was seeing the white light. But it wasn't just any white light—it was the warmest, deepest, most breathtakingly pure white light I had ever seen in my life. I felt totally comfortable and at peace. And I seemed to be moving toward that light, getting closer and closer, and the thought of that was making me feel better than any drug I had ever taken.

CHAPTER TWELVE

I *was almost totally bathed in that white light when I began to hear* some noises. They seemed indistinct at first, but then I thought that I heard my name being repeated over and over. And in the background, I could hear horrific screaming and the words "Oh, God, help me. Help me. I can't take the pain!"

Finally I opened my eyes and saw four doctors staring into my face. I was really pissed off that they had prevented me from going to heaven.

"Shut the fuck up!" I yelled at the source of that horrible screaming.

"Take it easy, Mr. Criss," one of the doctors said. "You're in a hospital and you're in good hands. But you got a little bent out of shape in that accident."

Then they filled me in. Fritz had been doing ninety miles per hour when he hit two telephone poles, knocked down a mailbox, and side-swiped four cars before ramming into a huge pole that caused the engine to blow up. The explosion threw me through the windshield and fifty feet into the air, at which point I went face-first into a curb in a fetal position. When the cops arrived at the scene, they didn't even know I was there—they thought I was just some debris on the side of the road. When they finally found me, my heart had stopped and they had to revive me on the scene. As it was, I had broken all my ribs and all of my fingers when I went though the windshield, as well as busting my nose and sustaining a concussion.

I was the lucky one. Fritz had been belted in and he got caught in the inferno. He had burns over 70 percent of his body, which was why he was in such agony. He was so badly burnt that they had to give him morphine through the bottom of his feet. Bill Aucoin was one of the first civilians on the scene and he took pictures of the wreck but would never show them to me. They were too horrific.

They wheeled me into a private room and I passed out again. When I came to, the adrenaline had worn off and I was in agony. Lydia moved into a nearby hotel and visited me every day. Unbeknownst to her, Deb drove by the hospital every day and looked up at my room. She was afraid to come in and bump into Lydia, so she sent me a single red rose.

I had so many flowers in that room that it looked like a funeral parlor. But they started getting stinky and making me sick, so I threw all of them out. Except for that single red rose, which by then had withered considerably.

"Why are you keeping that one rose?" Lydia asked one day.

"I don't know," I lied. "There's something about it."

After a few weeks in the hospital, Paul came to visit. He walked in indignantly and looked down at me with disgust.

"Look at you. You really fucked up," he said.

"No shit," I said.

"How long are you going to be here?" he asked.

"I don't know. A while," I said.

"You have to do your solo album. How could you do this? You're really a fucking idiot," he said.

What compassion. What heart.

"Well, I just came to see how you're doing," he said. "You're not going to see me again. Oh, and Gene wanted me to tell you that he thinks you're a loser and a moron and that you deserve everything you got. Good luck on your solo album, but he refuses to set foot in this hospital."

"Really?"

"Yeah, he wanted me to relay that message," Paul said.

"Well, you did, so get the fuck out."

Unlike the other two, Ace was by my side from the get-go. He came in the day after I was admitted.

"Cat! Look at you!" he said.

"I'm in such pain, brother," I complained.

"Fuck this," he said, and stormed out looking for a doctor. Seconds later, he had dragged the doctor into the room.

"You give him something for his fucking pain or I will burn this hospital down. Better yet, I'll buy it and fire every motherfucker in here," Ace said.

A security guard came into the room because he heard all the commotion, but Ace didn't care.

"Bring in more bodyguards. I'll kick their asses, too," he said.

One night I was lying in bed in the hospital when this young nurse came in.

"Hi, Mr. Criss, how are you feeling?"

"I feel like shit," I said. "I need painkillers. I can't sleep."

"Well, I'll take care of you."

She opened up the IV and I got some of that morphine drip.

"Are you feeling better?"

"Yes," I said dreamily.

"I can make you feel even better," she said, and she pulled the blanket down and gave me a blowjob. I couldn't believe it. It was like something you'd read in *Penthouse Forum,* except she wasn't that good-looking. Not that I complained.

When she finished, she smiled.

"I just wanted to be able to say that I gave Peter Criss a blowjob. I'm a big fan of your band."

It was a great blowjob. I was coming and I was in pain and I had a kink in my back all at the same time.

She went and got a basin, wet a facecloth, and washed my dick, washed my balls, and put the blanket back on me.

"Good night, Mr. Criss," she said. I never saw her again.

Fritz had been transferred to a major burn center by then. Eventually he made a full recovery and stayed in the business. When I got out of the hospital, I was still hurting and I wasn't strong enough to go home. But we had to begin work on the solo albums, so I wound up staying in L.A., which was okay by me since that meant I'd see Deb.

I was head over heels in love with Deb. In retrospect, it was more lust. I was so taken by her beauty, but there was no depth to my feelings. No sense of companionship. I just wanted to fuck her every minute of the day. Was that so wrong? I didn't think so.

Lydia had gone back to work on our new house, and the calls became less and less frequent. It wasn't that we had a major falling-out. I was never that happy sexually with Lydia. It was impossible for her to measure up sexually to these girls who would do anything to boast that they slept with a rock star.

Deb could, though. She was a total party animal who could drink and snort as much as me. Plus she had a voracious sexual appetite. She was bisexual, which was really exciting since I had never had a girlfriend who went both ways. Later I found out that it was an asset in Hef's world. His favorite thing was having three chicks at a time. He loved to watch and he liked to use elephant-sized vibrators. Deb once took me to a part of the Playboy Mansion where they had twenty-five vibrators and two-way dildos hanging on the wall. I liked Hef. He was a real role model for men: Who wouldn't want to walk around in a bathrobe and get laid 24/7?

So all that hot sex had turned my head around. I convinced myself that I had fallen out of love with Lydia. I felt bad about cheating on her with Deb, but I couldn't help myself. My dick was thinking, not my brain. When I decided that I was going to stay in L.A. to do my album, I went out with Chris Lendt and rented Vincent Price's thirty-seven-room house in Holmby Hills, a stone's throw from Hef's mansion. I moved in with my bodyguard, Rosie. A few days later, I had him contact the Playboy Mansion and find Deb. He got her on the phone.

"Peter's going to do his album in L.A., and he'd love to see you for dinner," Rosie told her.

We went out to Chasen's and she looked gorgeous. I brought her back to my place and we fucked all night and she moved in.

In retrospect, doing the solo albums probably put the final nail in the coffin of the band. From the start, Sean was against it. He thought there would be winners and losers, and that would be the demise of KISS. Sean's idea was that we should each back the others on their solo albums.

But we got sucked into Bill and Neil's grandiose schemes. We would make KISStory by releasing four solo albums on the same day. No band had ever done that before, and no band has done it since.

When it was time to break away and do the albums, Sean got depressed because he found out that he wasn't going to produce mine. I had gotten together with Stan Penridge and worked on some new songs for the album. Stan and I would often get together and write when we were on breaks from touring. I decided that I wanted Giorgio Moroder to produce me. He had done a lot of work with Casablanca at the time and he would go on to do the music for *Scarface*. He turned me down because he didn't like the demos that Stan and I had done, so then I tried Tom Dowd, who was Rod Stewart's producer. Tom was in Mexico at the time, and the message he got was that a "Mr. Christ" wanted to talk to him about producing his album. By the time he cleared up the confusion and got back to me, it was too late.

So I went back to Sean, but he had already committed to producing Gene's album. So I got pissed off. But Sean went into Electric Lady with me, brought in some great players like Elliott Randall and Paul Shaffer, and wrote and produced two songs, "I Can't Stop the Rain" and "Rock Me, Baby," for me to use as demos to get another producer. They turned out so great that we ultimately used them on the album.

It's a shame Sean and I didn't work together on that album. He had a miserable time working with Gene. Gene was such an asshole then that he wouldn't even call the great musicians Sean had rounded up by their proper names. He'd call them "Hey, lead guitar," or "Hey, drums." It took a revolt where they almost walked out of the sessions to straighten Gene out.

I wound up hiring Vini Poncia to produce me. He had produced Melissa Manchester, but I was more excited because he was Ringo Starr's cowriter. We hit it off immediately. I hadn't completely healed yet, so I played drums with little casts on each finger. It was incredibly painful but I had a goal in mind—to do the best album of the four and leave the band with dignity. If my fingers weren't burning, my neck was in such pain I had to wear a brace. And when I really belted out a song, my ribs felt like I had just gotten stabbed. Vini was really impressed with my dedication.

I couldn't wait to get to the studio every day we recorded. There were never any arguments, no fights in the room, no egos, unlike my other recording experiences. I treated the musicians as if they were my real band, as if we had been together forever. When we recorded "Rock Me, Baby," I had three black backup singers and we all got loaded on champagne and put our arms around each other and sang our hearts out. This was the way an album should be made, having great fun working with a great producer and great people.

People often ask me how I come up with my lyrics and ideas for songs. Well, take "That's the Kind of Sugar Papa Likes," a song on the album that I cowrote with Stan. I was at the house one night watching Humphrey Bogart in *The Treasure of the Sierra Madre,* and in one scene he finds out he has a winning ticket and he's going to get two hundred pesos. He says, "That's the kind of sugar Papa likes." Of course, we changed the sugar reference from money to sex.

How I ever completed an album while I was living in Vincent Price's house is beyond me. I really went into total Elvis mode. If Deb wasn't enough of a distraction, I decided to fly in Stan, my old partner in crime. He cowrote a lot of the songs and he was a collaborator in all my drug experimentation. We'd do a session and then come back to the house and shoot some pool in the huge billiard room. If we got bored, we'd watch a movie in the theater that was almost the size of a small art-house cinema. Vincent Price had a huge vault for storing mink coats, so we kept our champagne chilled in there. He was a gourmet cook and he had a kitchen the size of an average apartment in New York. Rosie tried to follow Price's recipe cards but half the time he almost burned down the kitchen, so for the most part we were living on Entenmann's chocolate donuts, champagne, and cocaine.

While in L.A., Rosie had met a doctor who he thought was a pushover.

"It'd be a piece of cake to get some drugs from him."

"You think so?" I was suddenly fully interested.

"He told me he loves you. He'd be happy to give you whatever you needed."

I made a list. Fifty quaaludes, thirty Percodans, forty Valiums, thirty Seconals.

I didn't think it was real, but sure enough, like clockwork every two weeks there'd be a big bag dropped off at the back kitchen door. Rosie would bring it in.

"Hey, boss, we got partying," he'd grin.

I would throw these wild parties and invite a hundred people. I wouldn't even necessarily show up at them because you could watch what was going on in the pool from a window in the basement. They couldn't see you, but you could see them. So Deb and I would go downstairs with some champagne and a few ludes and watch everybody fucking, jerking each other off, guys finger-fucking chicks, and we'd fuck on the couch, watching them. After a while, I'd call upstairs, "Rosie, get the car." We'd leave the party and go hang out at the Rainbow on the Sunset Strip.

We had been partying for five straight weeks when Lydia decided to come back out West. On July 3, I had sent her three dozen yellow roses to commemorate the day we met, but I kept dodging her phone calls. When I finally spoke to her, I told her that Rosie and I had spent the Fourth of July weekend in Malibu. I didn't tell her that Deb was with us and that we had been at a great spa/resort that Deb knew about.

When Lydia arrived, I barely gave her a peck on the cheek. I was just not in love with her anymore. I told her that we shouldn't have sex because I had gotten herpes from a blood transfusion at the hospital. I was fishing now. I told her that I wrote a song for her on the album called "You Matter to Me," but that was a lie. Vini had written that song with John Vastano and Michael Morgan. I had to tell her something.

While Lydia was there, I went through my pockets and found all the credit-card receipts for that July Fourth weekend that Deb and I had in Malibu. I threw them into the wastepaper basket in my office and covered them with the other trash. I figured I'd dump it all when I got back from the studio that night. We left Lydia in the house, and while I was in the studio she turned everything upside down and found all the receipts. I couldn't believe it. Of course, I insisted Rosie was my date. But I had a hard time explaining the receipt for two bracelets from Simon's Jewelers.

Lydia hung around L.A. for a few more days and then went home. In August, Lydia got a call from Bill's office. Sean got on the phone and told Lydia that it would be a shame if that bitch wound up with all Peter's money. When I found out about all this, I was furious.

I confronted Sean. "How could you have loyalty for Lydia and not me?"

"I don't like who you're with," Sean said. "This chick is gonna kill you. She is the worst fucking thing ever to happen in your life. Can't you see that?"

I couldn't.

"Fuck Lydia. Fuck Greenwich. I'm moving to L.A. Look what I have here," I said.

Sean didn't say a thing. He gave up on me and went to Lydia's side from that day on.

But I was conflicted myself. About a week after Lydia found out about Deb from Sean, I decided to move back to New York and give my marriage another go. My record was finished and there was no excuse for me to stay out in L.A.

I sat down with Deb.

"I gotta go home," I told her.

"Are you going to stay there?" she wondered.

"You know, Deb, I don't know. I think I'm going to try and see what happens with me and Lydia."

"I understand," she said. "I love you but I'm not in love with you like I'm sure Lydia is. I've had the greatest four months of my life with you, but if you don't come back, I get it."

It was time to leave my mansion. I had ordered two limos, and we came to a fork in the road off Beverly Hills Drive. I was going one way, and Deb was going the other. I looked out the window at her and she turned back and looked at me. I threw her a kiss, she waved back, the cars split away, and I sat back and thought, Oh, my God, I can't believe I'm losing the most beautiful woman in the world.

So I went back to Connecticut and I tried, but I just couldn't get Deb off my mind. Even our dream house in Greenwich didn't look as good to me now as when we had bought it. Lydia and I fell into our old routine and started doing a lot of blow again, and eventually we fucked, but I think she could tell I wasn't into it.

On September 18, record-industry history was made when all four of our solo albums were released on the same day. They were a mixed bag for sure. My album reflected my musical tastes—Motown-inspired R&B with horns and black backup singers. Paul's was more the English Zeppelin sound that he liked. Ace's was his typical Hendrixy thing, and Gene's was the most bizarre, almost a pop album. He later wrote that his intent was to piss off KISS fans and push it in their faces that their musical tastes were one-dimensional and his weren't. That's how crazy we all were then.

To placate our egos, Neil had shipped each of the albums platinum. But collectively the albums sold what one KISS album would have, so the resulting returns destroyed Casablanca's bottom line. Two years later, Neil was forced to sell the company.

On the heels of that disaster, our movie finally aired on October 28, 1978. We were incensed that the movie ads all featured Gene with the rest of us in the background. That was just a symptom of the state of the band. Five years in, we were blowing things out of proportion. We were fried and miserable from all the albums, all the touring, all the things we had been through.

All of us were ultimately embarrassed by doing that movie. The reviews were uniformly horrible. The *L.A. Times* called it "a four-star abomination. A five-minute idea for a cartoon, disguised as a two-hour movie." We actually got a lot of hate mail from fans after that movie. Maybe my feelings about the movie weren't so crazy after all?

What had happened to the tough New York City kids who had clawed their way to the top? Now we were on the cover of *16* magazine. Gene had totally gone Hollywood. He was dating Cher, and then he dumped her for her best friend, Diana Ross. Paul was still searching for Paul, so he was just buying bigger and bigger apartments in New York and decorating them.

I just didn't want to do this anymore. We had become a fucking Barbie doll–selling lowlife piece-of-shit merchandise band. We didn't even play our instruments well anymore. We'd just go out there with our makeup on and act like fucking clowns and rake in the money. Everything became money, money, money. Who doesn't want to get rich? Especially when you get there making music, doing something that's fun. But the fun was gone. Now it was just putting out product and touring all the time and not even being able to enjoy the fortune we were making.

A lot of this was Bill's fault. He owned the merchandising company that handled all our products, and he was getting 50 percent of the proceeds from the merch. It's one thing to sell T-shirts: Every rock band did that. But lunch boxes? Dolls? It always amazed me that our songs were so filthy, all about sex and partying, and now we were selling stuff to children. Even Paul couldn't understand why we were selling kids' lunch boxes. He had a lot of disagreements with Gene over the merch. Bill and Gene would get together and the next thing we knew we were selling KISS My Ass toilet paper. People weren't coming to see our music anymore. It was more like a trip to see some Disney act.

Between 1977 and 1979, we grossed over $100 million from the merch alone. No wonder Bill was able to get an apartment in the Olympic Towers. We had two whole floors in our office building on Madison Avenue, one floor devoted to cranking out KISS product. I'm sure some people would say, "You're a fucking asshole. I would cut my balls off to be a comic-book hero." But I really wanted to stay true to my rock 'n' roll rebel roots. I always thought of us as the Stones or the Beatles. Not the Monkees.

As confused as I was by the band's direction, I was equally confused in my personal life. Deb had left L.A. to go to Paris to do some modeling. I called her in Paris and she said she missed me, but I could tell that she wanted to just get off the phone and that bothered the hell out of me. One day I was hanging out with Lydia in our house and we were doing coke and ludes and I finally came clean about my affair with Deb. I don't think this was a revelation to Lydia. She knew.

The real revelation was about to be mine.

"I've been having an affair," Lydia admitted.

I was shocked. Apparently Sean had introduced her to a guy named Mickey, the bass player of a band called Angel, which had a contract with Casablanca. Sean had let them conduct their affair over at his apartment.

I wanted to kill Sean. This was his way of getting back at me because he didn't like Deb and he was close to Lydia. But to set her up with a guy in a shit band like Angel? I could understand if he was in Zeppelin, but she was fucking someone beneath my status to make me look like a jerk.

A few days later I called Deb and asked her if she would like me to come out to Paris. She thought that would be great. I didn't know it then, but Deb had been fucking some rich guy from Germany whom her aunt had set her up with. He had just dumped her and bought her an expensive Rolex as a good-bye present. Schmuck that I was, I went to Tiffany's with Chris Lendt and bought her a nice wedding ring that she could wear so we would feel married.

Chris was not so keen to see me go to Paris. But when I was insistent, he decided to go with me. I was happy to have him watch over me: I really liked Chris. Casablanca had an arrangement with a Parisian record label, and whenever we went over there they had the local guy hook us up with drugs. I guess the guy confused blow with heroin, and instead of getting a package with some blow, they delivered some pure China White from Marseilles to my hotel. How cool was this going to be, doing China White in Paris? I never expected to do heroin again, but I wasn't going to pass up a chance to do some legendary China White direct from Marseilles! Being the lunatic that I am, instead of doing matchsticks I started snorting whole lines. All of a sudden I got incredibly high and incredibly sick at the same time. I threw up a number of times, and then I started scratching all over.

Deb came back from her photo shoot.

"What the fuck are you high on?" she asked.

"Blow," I lied.

"You're not acting like you're on blow. You're nodding out."

"I got a little heroin," I admitted.

"I hate that shit. Please dump it down the toilet."

Hey, I paid five grand for that shit. It wasn't going down the toilet. I promised to only do a few hits every now and then. Bullshit. I did it every chance I had. It was the greatest high ever.

We had a great time in Paris. Deb was working most days and I had nothing to do so I just roamed the streets, stopping at small cafés to drink wine. At night we'd party and hit the discos. On her days off, we'd go shopping for clothes.

Chris left to go back after a couple of weeks and we moved from the hotel to an apartment that the modeling agency had. It was in a pretty seedy neighborhood. Next thing I knew, I was running around with underground Parisian guys. Between these guys that I met at a drug bar and the two musicians who lived above us, I started doing dope with all these wild guys. We'd drink brandy and snort heroin and then go out to seedy jazz clubs and listen to music.

When Deb's job finished, we flew back to New York. I had called Gene from Paris and asked him if I could crash at his Central Park pad since he was in L.A. with Cher. Gene said, "Abso-fucking-lutely. Stay as long as you want." Despite being an egotistic Machiavellian control freak and sex maniac, he really could be nice when he wanted to. At one point of my life I really loved Gene, a lot more than I ever loved Paul or Ace. Underneath everything, I really felt then that Gene had a heart, and that one thing I could always count on was Gene telling me the truth right to my face. Little did I know.

So we moved into his penthouse that overlooked the Tavern on the Green in Central Park. One night Stan and his wife came over to visit. We were all snorting and drinking and carrying on, of course, and while I was talking to Stan, Deb and his wife were watching Gene's huge Advent projection-screen TV. There was a movie playing and Warren Beatty was up on the screen and I overhead Deb telling Stan's wife that she had slept with Beatty at Hefner's mansion. I was told that Beatty had a cannon between his legs—that was one of the reasons why every woman in L.A. wanted to sleep with him. I looked over and Deb had her hands about a foot apart and it was obvious she was demonstrating how hung Warren was.

I went over to my bag, picked up my trusty nickel-plated .38, and walked back over to them.

"That was your boyfriend?" I asked, nodding toward Beatty on the screen.

"No, no," Deb lied.

"I heard what the fuck you said."

I fired the gun and the bullet went right through Beatty's head on the screen, through the screen, and into the wall. Now there was a huge tear in Gene's projection screen. I bought a brand-new screen and had the office send people over to switch them out, plus I had a guy come over, remove the bullet, and patch up the wall.

On January 3, 1979, my attorney served Lydia with divorce papers. By then Deb and I had moved into an apartment in the Claridge House. We had just begun to decorate this empty apartment when Deb started missing home. She hadn't been home since Paris and she wanted to see her parents. So she left me with all the clothes I had bought her in Paris and went home. I was in that empty apartment all alone, doing coke, and I began to get paranoid. It seemed that the calls from Deb were getting fewer and farther between.

One night I got really wasted and I called Lydia. "Can I come up?" I asked. She said, "Sure." I was mad that I hadn't heard from Deb for a couple of weeks. So I drove to Greenwich and one thing led to another and we started having sex. She gave me a blowjob like she never had in the past. Someone once told me, "Lend your wife out and you'll get her back better." There must be something to this, because Lydia was not the same woman in bed.

I spent the night there and I started thinking, You're gonna give this up? But I was still crazy about Deb. When I got back to the city, I tracked her down at the Playboy Mansion and then I found out that she was staying at Dave Mason's mother's house. When I met Deb, she had just broken up with Dave Mason. In fact, he had written his hit song "We Just Disagree" about her. She told me that she was madly in love with him.

I put two and two together and realized that she was seeing him again. Finally she called me and asked me to send her stuff back to L.A.

"Why, you're not coming back?" I asked.

She hedged. "Yeah, I'm coming back, but I'd like to have my clothes while I'm out here."

One night I got whacked out and I called her.

"I'm gonna send your clothes back—my way. I'm going to throw them out the fucking window. They should make quite a splash falling twenty-five floors, especially all those nice shoes you got in Paris."

She went ballistic. "Don't you fucking dare do that!"

"You want to get this stuff, you get on a plane and come here and get your stuff. I'll send you a ticket." She flew back and we patched things up, but it was never easy.

While all this was going on, KISS was in the studio making another

album. I had told Bill that I would quit the band unless Vini Poncia produced the next KISS album. I was excited to work with Vini again, but
Paul immediately went to work on Vini. They started hanging out, Vini
moved into Paul's apartment, and Paul poisoned Vini against me.

Vini had snorted up a storm of blow while I was doing my solo album,
but now he claimed to have turned into a saint. "I don't do drugs," he said.
I began to hate him because he had turned against me. Or maybe the coke
just made me think he had turned against me. I felt that I had fought to
get Vini this gig, and now I was getting thrown under the bus.

I hardly contributed to *Dynasty* at all. We recorded "Dirty Living," a
song that Stan and I wrote about the drug scene in New York in the seventies, and that was the only cut I played drums on. They got Anton Fig to
play on the rest of the album, but I didn't feel betrayed; I was happy they
got him. I didn't really want to play with them anymore.

The feeling was mutual. Paul started auditioning other drummers to
take my place on the tour. Kenny Aronoff came down and played with
them, and he later told me that it was maddening to work with Gene and
Paul. Carmine Appice, Tico Torres: They jammed with a few really great
drummers, but no one could take their Machiavellian tactics.

The cruelest blow of all was Paul's attempt to write a contemporary hit
for *Dynasty*. He came up with "I Was Made for Lovin' You," KISS's first
out-and-out disco track. What little credibility we had left was flushed
down the toilet when we did that. Ace was totally incensed. "What's with
this fucking disco shit?" he asked me. "We're a fucking heavy metal band.
Why, because it's in now, we gotta do disco?" That song has since been
cited by MTV and VH1 as the worst thing that KISS ever did.

The *Dynasty* tour began in June and ended in December of 1979. By
then the cancer of our four solo albums had even infected the song selection for our concerts. I went ballistic when we started incorporating songs
from the solo albums and not one of mine was picked. I threw a shit fit,
so they tried to work out "Tossing and Turning," but can you imagine
musicians like Gene and Paul trying to play that? They had no funk, no
soul. We actually tried it live twice and it was horrible. They put no effort
into it at all.

Ticket sales for the tour started very soft. We had new costumes now, studded with rhinestones. We were a caricature of ourselves. Someone should have taken us in the back like dogs, made us get on our knees, and put a bullet in each of our heads. We had gone totally Vegas. I looked like a trapeze star in my fucking new outfit. Gene began to believe his own hype. He gave an interview and said, "KISS has become rock 'n' roll circus entertainment for the whole family. Rock 'n' roll tried to create a generation gap, and KISS is bridging it. If the parents could swallow KISS, every other rock 'n' roll band will be much more palatable. The rules of rock 'n' roll no longer work with us, we're a band unto itself." He was out of his mind.

Hearing shit like that just solidified my resolve to escape the madness. I was burnt out on KISS. I was sick of playing disco songs and selling Barbie dolls. Between the drugs and my marriage dissolving, I was a wreck. Ace was almost as bad with his drinking. Gene and Paul's egos were cascading out of control. I don't know how I made it through some of the shows on that tour with all the blow I was doing. I really believe that I had two angels looking over me, one on each arm—Double Deckers, I called them—to help me make it through the night. I'd be the first to admit that I played like shit that tour. How couldn't I? I play from the heart. If I can't pick up those sticks and play with feeling, then I can't play with you. I didn't have any feelings then, I was so anesthetized with coke. But even if I hadn't been high, I still didn't want to be involved with them anymore and my playing would have suffered.

It was no secret that both Ace and I wanted to go out and have solo careers at that point. That was one end product of the solo KISS albums. Winning that People's Choice award for "Beth" had definitely blown my head up a bit. I was delusional behind the coke and thought that I could start emulating Sinatra. Hey, he was a much better role model than some disco diva!

We were spending money like water on the show. We had five elevators onstage, the highest riser I'd ever used, fog machines, the works. Paul shot a laser beam out of his eye. My drum riser had the capacity to turn in all directions. Ace's guitar would emit blasts that would shoot down elevated speaker cabinets. Gene was able to fly around the stage. We had really begun to believe our own hype.

That balloon was punctured when shows started getting canceled due to poor ticket sales. When all these high-tech tricks began to break down, I saw it as a metaphor for the state of the band. In Lakeland, the first night, my riser wouldn't go back so Gene, Paul, and Ace had to push it back.

One night Gene's flying contraption broke and he started being dragged back and forth along the stage like a rag doll. We all laughed so hard we pissed our pants. Gene was trying to stay in character and made his growling monster noises and flicked his tongue in and out, but it was clear that he was a puppet on a string. One night he got stuck way up in the air and we started calling him Mary Poppins.

By the middle of July, Marks and Glickman called an emergency meeting of the band and management. We met at Carl's office in Cleveland on a day off during the tour. Carl opened the meeting by informing us that we were losing a ton of money on the tour. To counter that, a plan was proposed that there be two shows. The A show would play in all the major markets. But a scaled-down version of the show, the B show, would play the secondary markets. This way we could save money. But the band thought that the idea of a B show was heresy. Bill backed us—he didn't want to dilute the show at all.

We compromised on costs by cutting Ace's champagne. By then he was traveling with his own custom-made steel traveling bar, stocked with Taittinger. Ace agreed to pick up his own bar tab. But we wouldn't think of changing to regular rooms instead of suites. And we wouldn't touch the twenty-four-hour limos we all had. We were spoiled rotten.

On September 13, my divorce was finalized. Lydia got a lump-sum payment of $1 million. She got the house in Greenwich, all the new furnishings, the stereo, the Mercedes. I left everything behind, even all my personal photos. I knew I was wrong for what I'd done to her, and the least I could do was to let her have everything to help assuage the pain. Little did I know that years later she would cause me so much hurt by publishing a coffee-table book full of the photos and personal items.

That same month, Bill's contract with the group was expiring. Marks and Glickman were egging on Gene and Paul to get rid of Bill. Bill had let KISS's success go to his head and he expanded his business, signing lots of new clients. We were jealous that he was spending a lot of time with his other clients, especially since we were probably the only ones to generate income for him then. I also think that the coke was making him paranoid, so he didn't want to be around us.

Marks and Glickman arranged for a showdown with Bill in Fort Wayne. They all flew in along with our lawyer, Paul Marshall. We booked the conference room at the Holiday Inn. We all sat around and listened to a litany of things that Bill was doing poorly. All these Judases like Howard Marks, who Bill brought in, and Paul Marshall, who was originally Bill's lawyer—everyone was reaming him, and Bill just sat there and took it.

Of course, Gene and Paul realized that Bill was being hung, so they jumped in and made sure the rope got pulled extra hard. They started in with how much more Bill was making than us, how Bill was going to have to give it up or get out, how Gene and Paul agreed with Marks and Glickman and Marshall. Ace and I were quiet, but I couldn't keep still any longer.

"I don't agree at fucking all," I piped up. "Maybe some of this is true, but how can all of you forget how we got here in the first place? You forget whose credit card we lived off. Boy, it's easy to forget now that we're all sitting here nice and fat and rich."

I looked over to Glickman and Marks.

"Life is nice, huh, that we made you motherfuckers so wealthy and now you're telling the guy who started all this which way the door is? If he goes out that door, I'm fucking right behind him because I'll quit this band. If Bill goes, I go." This time I really meant it.

Bill looked at me and smiled. What did I care? I was dying to leave the band. I figured that if I went with him, he'd manage me and get me a band. Regardless, he deserved my loyalty.

Then Ace said pretty much the same thing. He suggested that we renegotiate some of Bill's fees and percentages, and Bill agreed to do that.

Marks and the others had probably planned for this all along, because they opened up a new book and started reeling off proposed changes to Bill's contract. It was sad because now they were dictating to Bill what his job would be.

We resumed the tour, and it was torture. Every night, despite my drug abuse, despite my desire to be anywhere else than on that stage, the high point of the show was my drum solo. I'd go crazy, taking out all my frustrations on those skins, and I'd end up hitting a huge Chinese gong. The audiences would go wild. But during the solo, the other three would take a break in a special dressing room constructed under the stage and laugh and make fun of my solo. They wouldn't acknowledge, "Wow, our drummer is kicking ass." It was more like, "What the fuck is he doing up there?" Once in a while Ace would compliment me on my solos, but never once did those other two fucks say, "You were really hot tonight." But why should I expect them to give me a compliment when they never had in the past?

I was out of control. So I began to sabotage the show. I was wrong. I was an asshole. Cocaine does not allow you to make good decisions. I certainly should never have taken my troubles out on the fans, I know that now. But cocaine is an evil drug. I wouldn't dream of staying at a Four Seasons hotel now and throwing the TV through the window. I couldn't fathom picking up a lamp in the room and smashing it into the mirror. When you're addicted to drugs, you do bad things.

In retrospect, bringing Deb on tour was a big mistake. By then we were fighting. In the middle of the night you'd hear glass breaking and furniture being overturned. She was a drama queen, so she'd rush out into the hallway half naked and everyone would come out to get a look, of course.

"He's going to kill me," she'd scream, and look for a shoulder to lean on. Usually it was George Sewitt, the tour manager. I started calling him Mr. Shoulder. It was always drama: the Playmate and the Rock Star.

As far as Gene and Paul were concerned, all they had to do was control Ace's and my craziness and the band would continue to rake in the money. It was all about control. And in October, Gene and Paul learned, on national television, that Ace and I would no longer be controllable.

We took a break from the tour to fly to New York to tape *The Tomorrow Show with Tom Snyder*. Doing shows like this usually intimidated Ace, so he started drinking champagne hours before the show.

"Hey, Cat, you want a little champagnio?" He had his own name for everything. So we both started drinking water glasses full of bubbly. We emptied a bottle and Ace opened another one.

Meanwhile, we were putting on our makeup. Paul was in front of his mirror, fluffing up his hair. He must have used at least five cans of Aqua Net, the cheapest hair spray, before every show. I'm convinced that Paul alone is responsible for global warming.

On the other side of the room, Gene was finishing his makeup and starting to make monster noises. He'd stare at himself in the mirror and Ace and I would look at each other and say, "Gene's going away." That's what we called his transformation.

In the middle of this madness, Bill came in with a bottle of vodka. So Ace started gulping vodka along with the champagne. You can't mix vodka and champagne. By the time we walked out on that set, we were wobbly as hell.

But we loved Tom Snyder. We felt like this was the ultimate—he was even cooler than Carson. So he started to ask us questions, and Ace all of a sudden picked up Tom's teddy bear that he kept on the set and started customizing it with his wristbands.

"What are you doing to that teddy bear?" Tom asked.

"It's a space bear now!" Ace proclaimed.

Tom was astonished that Ace was so lively: His producer had told him that he'd be lucky to get Ace to open his even mouth once. But Ace was drunk off his ass and he was hilarious, and Gene was getting more and more pissed off. At one point Tom asked us who our audience was, and Paul answered that he once looked out his hotel window and saw parents with kids and twenty-year-olds and older people, all in line for our show.

"And if you saw our show in Bombay, you'd see cows in line too," Ace cracked.

The more Ace and I cut up, the more Gene was fuming. Every time Ace mentioned drugs, Gene quickly cut in, "He's kidding." Paul seemed really pissed off too.

When Tom asked me what my hobbies were, I said that I had a gun collection.

"Toy guns," Gene interjected.

"No, I collect guns. I shoot them at a range, I'd never shoot an animal," I said.

Then I said that gangsters fascinated me, and if I could go back in time I'd love to be Dillinger or Baby Face Nelson.

"In the movies," Gene cut in. He was so concerned about one of us saying something real, something he couldn't control.

Even Tom picked up on it. He turned to Gene.

"So you're the guy who keeps it all straight?"

"He's the mother," I said.

"He's the mother superior," Ace added, and we all cracked up. Except for Gene and Paul, who were fuming.

"Everybody's got a fantasy and we're all good guys. You know what I mean?" Gene had to have the last word.

"Tell me what you were doing at four this morning," Tom suddenly asked Ace.

"No. I don't want to be arrested," he said, and we all cracked up. Except for Gene and Paul, of course.

For the first time in KISStory, Ace and I had hijacked an interview from Gene and Paul, and the result was hilarious. When the show was over, Tom came back to our dressing room, but Ace had passed out on the couch.

"Great show, guys," he said. "Everybody on the staff is still laughing." He shook our hands. "And tell Ace when he wakes up that I love him. He was great."

Maybe the Tom Snyder appearance emboldened me, I don't know. But I certainly wasn't going to take the same shit I had taken for years from Gene and Paul. On December 8 in Shreveport, Paul humiliated me in front of the audience in the same way he had done many times before. That night, in front of a packed house, Paul turned toward me in the middle of a song and he lifted his arm in an exaggerated gesture to tell me to slow the tempo down. What that says to everybody in the arena is that I'm the one fucking up the band.

He may have had a point. My coke dealer was at the show that night, and we were doing blow in my room before the show. So maybe he was right. I was a little edgy and probably playing a little too fast. But his exaggerated gesture was a slap in the face. And now he was waving with both hands, gesturing to slow it down.

"You want it slow, you'll get it slow, motherfucker," I said to myself, and I slowed the song down to a crawl. When I started slowing real down, he turned around again and faced me and gestured wildly with both arms: "Up, up, up."

I'm like, "*Make up your motherfucking mind!*" People in the audience could hear me screaming that at him. I just stopped playing. I didn't care anymore, and Paul said, "We're out of here, good night." We went back in the room and yelled back and forth for a few minutes and then I think we went back out and did two numbers and left without a real encore. I was finished. Ace suggested we end the tour and go home. I refused to commit to any more shows until I talked to my lawyer. Then I told Paul that if he ever did that again, I would throw a drumstick at him so hard that it would go through the back of his fucking head and come out one of his eyes.

The other guys were angry with me, but they both agreed that Paul was wrong, too.

"Peter's got a point," Ace said. "You can't blame him in front of the whole audience."

I shouldn't have sabotaged that song but Paul could have easily waited, finished the show, and talked to me about it in the dressing room. I would have taken that fine. But the way he did it was so girly. He had to have everyone looking at him admonishing me.

Two nights later, at the next gig in Jackson, Mississippi, I stopped playing during "Move On" and walked off the stage. I was just so fed up with them. The other three finished the song, and then we went back-stage. When we went back onstage fifteen minutes later, Paul made up some story that I had been hit in the eye with a fragment from a broken drumstick. Later that same show, after I finished singing "Beth," I threw the mike on the floor and stormed offstage again.

Things were just escalating. They reached a breaking point the next night in Biloxi. For years, when Gene or Paul would try to upstage me and stand in front of the drums and obscure me from the audience, I would throw a drumstick and hit them in the head. And they got the message and moved away. But I also used to throw sticks out to the audience as souvenirs.

That night in Biloxi, I was throwing sticks out to the audience during our last song before the encores and, on a whim, I decided to hit Gene with one. I didn't mean to hit him hard, but the thick end of the stick whacked him. He turned around and glared at me, but I just figured he was in his demonic state. When I got downstairs after the song and we were waiting to go back on, Gene came into the room and walked up to me and kicked me in the shin. And it hurt with those gigantic boots. I was in pain.

"You son of a bitch!" I screamed. "What was that all about?"

"Don't ever throw a drumstick at me," Gene said.

"Gene, it was an accident, man. I didn't mean it," I fudged. I certainly didn't mean to hurt him.

We went back on for the encore and my shin was throbbing. I got furious. I was plotting during the song how I was going to get back at Gene. Should I whack him immediately or hit him in the back when we were going back for the second encore?

When the song was finished, I jumped off the drums and was the first one back into the room. I found one of Ace's empty champagne bottles and broke it against the table. As soon as Gene walked into that room, I went after him with the broken bottle, but some of the crew intervened and dragged me away.

We managed to go back out and do the last encore. When we went back in the room after that song, Gene and I were glowering at each other.

"This is great," Paul said. "Gene Simmons kicks the drummer of KISS. Peter Criss kills Gene Simmons. Band over with, no more KISS." We begrudgingly shook each other's hands, but I knew that was it. We had broken another cardinal rule of KISS: You never hit each other. Sean had told us years ago that once you put your hands on one of your band members and physically attack him, it's over. Ace and I had done that years before when we were just starting out, and we bonded and became closer after that incident. But now, with so many years between us, this was different, and there was no turning back. We finished the final two shows of the *Dynasty* tour without incident. But KISS, as the world knew it, was over.

CHAPTER THIRTEEN

It should have been a tip-off, but I was too stoned on coke to realize it. Along with two hundred other guests, I was waiting for Deb to come to L'Orange, one of the most exclusive and expensive restaurants in L.A., so we could make our wedding vows and then party all night. I started getting nervous when she was half an hour late.

"Where the fuck is she?" I mumbled to Neil Bogart. "Maybe she's not gonna come."

This conversation was taking place in the bathroom.

"Here, this will help you out," Neil said, and passed me a vial of coke.

That conversation was repeated with Larry Harris, another Casablanca executive, and a few of my other friends. Each time I got the consolation prize of a vial. And each time I had to chase that electric feeling with a nice scotch.

After two hours, Deb finally showed up. By then I was pie-eyed, but so was she. Her pupils were totally dilated and she was half in the bag.

"Where were you?"

"I was with Eileen back at the bungalow," she said. I had rented a nice bungalow for us at the Beverly Hills Hotel.

"We opened a bottle of champagne and we found your blow so we started doing it," she said. Three bottles and a few grams later, it finally crossed their minds that Deb had a wedding to attend.

I wasn't going to let a little tardiness spoil my big day. We had gone all-out for this wedding. Chris Lendt, who loved to do stuff like this, made all the arrangements, including getting a custom-made cake from one of the best patisseries in town. We began the festivities with a black-tie prewedding dinner for two hundred people at Regine's in New York City. Once we got to L.A., I passed on a bachelor party and instead had a dinner a few nights before the wedding at Chasen's, the legendary Hollywood restaurant. Chasen's was my ultimate spot, because Humphrey Bogart used to be a regular there. At one point in the evening I decided to do my Fred Astaire impression, so I took off my jacket and leaped up onto the table and danced. The food went everywhere, but I didn't care. I was living my Hollywood dream.

The wedding itself was marred by an ugly incident involving my parents. I had seated my parents at a prime table in the front of the room. Deb and I were up on the dais. Between the salad and the main course, Deb's mother and her aunt, who had married a very prominent Beverly Hills dentist to the stars, came up and sat down with us. They were both pretty bombed and just stayed there drinking and bullshitting. Somehow this bothered my mother.

"How the fuck can they go sit up there and we can't?" she fumed to my father.

I could see that she was upset, so I went over to their table.

"What's the matter, Ma?"

"This is bullshit. We're leaving," she said.

"Where are you going?" I was in shock.

I'd done everything to make my parents feel proud and special. I had put them up in the Beverly Hills Hotel in a nice suite. I wanted my folks to have fun, but fancy-schmantzy places like L'Orange made my mom nervous. She had bad teeth, so she always covered her mouth when she talked to "important" people. She and my dad were simple Brooklyn people. They felt out of place in this glitzy L.A. world.

"We're leaving. You're not going to insult me like this. Come on, Joe," she said, and got up. My father and grandfather and his wife sheepishly followed her out. My mother didn't talk to me for a year after that incident.

This was probably my mother's way of not approving of the marriage.

God knows, many of the people closest to me were horrified that I was marrying Deb. I should have realized that our relationship was incendiary from the start. We fought like cats and dogs. She would pull stunts like hanging naked from the balcony of my suite at L'Ermitage, drunk and coked out of her mind. I told my dad that story. "What are you getting into? A naked woman hanging from a balcony? What's going to happen in the future?" he warned.

But pussy is like heroin. I couldn't stop. And the makeup sex was extremely hot.

The more I found out about Deb's abusive childhood, the more I should have understood. Bill Aucoin used to say to me, "The whole picture is right in front of you. Look at her family. This isn't Lydia, this is a whole different animal." Sean was just as dramatic. "Peter, she is a cancer that is going to kill you."

"Yeah, but what a wonderful way to go," I'd smile.

Gene and Paul and Ace all attended my wedding. But when it was time to go back into the studio to record the next KISS album, *Unmasked,* I was absent. I just had no desire to play with them. I was tired of the makeup, tired of playing the same old fucking songs. On top of that, now they were actually telling me how to play the songs. They brought in Anton Fig to drum again. The group was so fractured by then that Ace wouldn't let Gene play on his songs. He played the bass himself.

Now that my problem couldn't be contained, it became an issue for the organization. Peter needed help. Where had they been five years earlier? Paul Marshall sent me to see a Dr. Feelgood, a psychiatrist whom his wife was seeing. All I got out of these visits was quaaludes, Valium, chloral hydrate, and Seconal. Not quite a recipe for the road to Wellville.

I did take a first step toward confronting my problem when I was on my honeymoon in Rio. One day I said to Deb, "Maybe they're right. I was a fucking jerk that last tour. I should get off this shit and straighten up and go back and give those guys another try." So I stopped doing blow and I cut way back on the pills. I even started taking drum lessons with Jim Chapin, Harry Chapin's dad. The more I thought about it, the more I thought that maybe things could work out.

A few weeks after I got back from my honeymoon, I got a call to come to the office because the guys had something important to discuss. I got there and the whole fourteenth floor was empty. It was like a ghost town. That was odd: It was usually a madhouse up there. I walked past the vacant desks and looked into Bill's office, and it was empty. I got to our conference room, which had a nice bar and a huge round table and all our gold records on the walls. There they were.

"Where is everybody?" I asked.

"Ah, this is between us," one of them said.

They cut to the chase. They didn't want me in the band anymore. I was too out of control. I had lost my chops.

"So you're firing me?" Here I was about to tell them that I had cleaned up. I'd been straight for a month. I was taking lessons. I was really motivated. It's not easy for Mr. Tough Guy to confess his feelings, but I was about to eat crow and ask to come back to the band.

"Yup," they said.

"Well, I fucking quit!" I yelled. Now I was really hurt. I looked over at Ace, and he couldn't look me in the face. Paul and Gene actually looked like they were gloating. I was furious. They got up to leave, and Ace was the last to exit.

"Hey, Cat, I'm not happy about this, man, but you were out of control," Ace said. This was the pot calling the kettle black.

"I'm not crazy now," I said.

"I get it," he said, and left.

I was so stunned I couldn't move. Then I just broke down and cried.

"Where the fuck is Bill?" I said out loud. He was the best man at my wedding. I had saved his ass when he was getting canned. Where was Sean? If anyone loved me and eased any blows, it was them. Now, when I needed them, they weren't here, and I hated them. They had betrayed me.

I went straight home to the Claridge and I dialed my dealer's number.

"Bring me a couple of grams," I said.

Deb looked at me like "Oh, no!"

I hung up, cracked open a nice bottle of scotch, poured a drink, drained it, and poured another. I was right back in it.

"Hey, you wrote 'Beth,' you could get another band together," Deb said, trying to cheer me up. "You're still a star, it shouldn't be difficult."

She was clueless how hard it was to make it to the top of the ladder. But I knew. With each sip and each snort, I felt my world collapsing around me. Then I just started crying again. I had never felt so hurt in my whole life.

A few weeks after that, Ace came by my penthouse.

"Cat, I really can't go on without you, it's going to be a nightmare with these two guys," he began. "Look, they're willing to give you another rehearsal. If it goes great, you're back in the band."

I knew that Bill had been pressuring them to give me another chance. The *Unmasked* tour was about to begin, and the last thing they needed was to find a new drummer.

"Ace, I don't want to play with the band no more," I said. "I'm burnt out. I love you, but I can't be with them anymore. I'm going to get my own band. You should do the same, you're miserable."

"I'm telling you, Cat, I can talk them into it."

"Don't talk them into anything. I don't want to have anything to do with them anymore."

But I had to admit I kind of liked the idea of going to rehearse with them again. I really wanted to get back at them for all the times that they'd put me and my music down. I had learned some new stuff from Chapin and I wanted to shove it down their throats.

The day of the rehearsal, I arrived at the SIR studio carrying an attaché case and a music stand. I was going to play this out to the max. Instead of the fun-loving, clothes-shedding Catman, they were going to see a new, improved, serious Peter Criss. I set down the attaché case, opened it up, and took out some pieces of sheet music. Then I set up the stand and put the sheets on it.

Before I left my house, I decided that I wouldn't show any emotion, any vulnerability to them again. I wouldn't lose my temper, I wouldn't scream, I wouldn't crack jokes. I had never been so serious my whole life, and it really freaked them out. I was extremely locked into myself from the blow. They didn't know what to make of me.

"Okay, should we proceed?" I said, and I began to sabotage that rehearsal for spite. I really think that they were sincere about giving me another chance. If I would have played well, I'm sure they would have said, "Let's go for it again." They didn't really want to lose me and all that money that was lined up. Maybe they thought by firing me, they were scaring me straight. I don't know. But I did know that I hated them even more after they fired me.

The music stand and the sheet music were props to bust their balls. I couldn't read music that well yet. I had only been studying for three months. But Chapin had taught me how to play some really hard beats that were jazz-oriented, so I broke them out. They tried to join in but they were lost.

"Can't you follow me, you assholes?" I said.

I'm surprised that they played with me as long as they did. I was expecting them to say, "Hey, you fucking bastard. You want to be crazy, we're leaving." But they stayed there for an hour or so, until they were finally fed up and left. At the time it felt like I was throwing my life out the window, but who's kidding who? It really had been over for a long time already.

So I was out of the band. We began a series of negotiations, and I wound up retaining my 25 percent interest in the band. It was a really great deal for me, and I imagine it must have driven Gene and Paul crazy to have to share that money with me. Although I was no longer officially in the band, we kept up the pretense that I was still a member and I was listed on *Unmasked* as the drummer. I remember that Chris also had me come to a big meeting with PolyGram, the company that had acquired Casablanca, where I had to pretend that I was still the drummer for KISS.

The reality of my departure finally hit me the day that we shot a video for "Shandi," a song on the new album. When I sat down at that mirror and started applying the makeup, it struck me that it would be the last time that I would be the Catman. Even though I had prayed to get out of that situation, it still hurt. There's a scene in that video where we're walking with our heads down and it reminded me of the Beatles during *Let It Be*. They knew it was over when they were filming that, and so did we. There was a really strange vibe on the set that day. Everyone seemed so down. When we finished, they rushed to the dressing room and took their makeup off in record time. Ace and Paul walked out without even saying good-bye to me. Gene was still in the room when I sat down in front of the mirror.

As Gene was getting ready to leave, I saw that his bass guitar was propped up against the wall.

"Hey, Gene, can I have your bass? I'd like to have something to remember the band with," I said.

"You really want it?" he said.

I nodded yes.

"Yeah, you can have it," he said softly.

After he left, I sat alone in front of my mirror. Random thoughts started racing through my head. Where did all the years go? Am I making the right decision? Can I ever make it big again like this? And then I just felt so bad that they had left me sitting here alone, like a piece of dirt. My three brothers in arms. I cried so hard that all my makeup washed off my face. For the last time.

When the organization finally acknowledged that I was no longer a member of the group, they used the stock excuses: creative differences, desire for a solo career, et cetera. You never read, "We threw Peter out of the band because he was a mad drug addict and he fucked up." That would come later.

But at the time, PolyGram was fine with me leaving the group, and they gave me a contract for a solo album. They had also bought out Neil and owned Casablanca, so Marks was able to negotiate a very lucrative new contract for KISS. All this meant that I wasn't hurting for money. I had no idea how much I was worth, but it was more than $10 million for sure. I remember that Deb and I went out to the Four Seasons with Marks one night and he made the huge mistake of bragging to her about how well-off we were.

"Your husband is richer than God," he told her. "You guys will never be broke." He was drunk.

This was not the right thing to tell a woman who spent money like she could. I never had the head for business and money management, and Lydia had taken care of our finances since we'd first been together. So I made the mistake of putting a twenty-year-old girl who graduated from the Hugh Hefner School for Wayward Women in charge of our fortune. And Deb had graduated with honors. This was a woman who was into Charles Jourdan shoes. I never imagined that there were women paying

$2,000 and up for a pair of shoes that consisted of a piece of lace and a heel. Deb introduced me to the world of Rolex and Cartier and Halston couture. I spent a ton of money on a custom-made white lynx coat for her. I would never do that now, because I'm not into hurting animals, but I thought it was cool at the time. I had her wear it to visit my parents in Brooklyn on Christmas Eve one year, and my mother hated it.

"What are you, movie stars?"

By then my mother was talking to me again. Well, yelling at me.

"This is Brooklyn. You got a Mercedes outside, your wife is wearing a white fur coat. What's happened to you?"

I began working on *Out of Control,* my first post-KISS album, even before the announcement had been made that I had left KISS. After years of hearing Glickman and Marks constantly telling me I was out of control, I thought I'd give them a sly shout-out. Stan Penridge, my longtime musical partner, came up to my place at the Claridge House, and we wrote all day. We'd get a bottle of red wine, roll a couple of joints, and go to work. Sometimes we'd write for fifteen hours straight. And the time that we weren't writing, we'd sing Lennon-McCartney harmonies for the hell of it. It was incredibly liberating to make my kind of music again.

When we had a bunch of songs, I was ready to record with Vini Poncia again, but something came up and Vini couldn't do it. He suggested I use a friend of his named David Wolfen, who had worked with Stevie Wonder and Barbra Streisand and had produced Dusty Springfield and Paul Anka. He wasn't exactly chopped liver.

The songs were heavier than the stuff I had done on my KISS solo album. It was like going back to my roots and pulling out Nautilus and the Sounds of Soul and adding some British metal to it. I thought the fans would love it.

We went up to RCA Studios on Forty-eighth Street, where Elvis had recorded a lot of his early stuff. Imagine how excited I was to record in that same big room where Elvis had done his classic tracks. Stan and I put together a great street-sounding band with a Young Rascals–New York sound. They were all white Italian kids, but their harmonies sounded soulful. I was so in love with them I was going to take them out on tour.

David Wolfen had come up with a song for me called "By Myself," which really was about me starting all over. "For once in my life I got a chance, I'll take it / I've waited so long, and baby this time I can make it by myself / Starting over again." We were going down that road looking for another "Beth." Who wouldn't want another People's Choice?

The sessions went well, and it was time to come up with an album cover. Originally I wanted to put my face on the cover, since nobody had seen it all those years in KISS, but Bill and Howard Marks thought it was too soon to expose my face. So I wound up designing a cover that featured a jukebox blowing up and shooting out all these 45s, and one of them was "Out of Control." I also had an artist draw Deb, and we put her in the lower left-hand side of the frame, running from the exploding jukebox. It had a real pop-art Warholian feel to it, and Deb looked great.

We could have put an actual photo of Deb naked on the cover and the album wouldn't have sold. I could have written contemporary versions of "Yesterday" and "Eight Days a Week," and it wouldn't have mattered because the record company buried the album. After four months the record had gone nowhere, and I went up to Bill's office.

"Come on, Bill. What did I do wrong?" I asked.

He got up and closed the door.

"I don't want anyone to hear this, this is heavy," he said. "They black-balled you. The record isn't going anywhere, and they made sure of that. God forbid you should come out with your first record and it was a hit. They actually threatened to take a hike if your record did well. So the record company buried it." *Out of Control* was released in Europe, but you could hardly find it at all in the States.

By this time I was licking my wounds in my new mansion in Darien, Connecticut. Deb had gotten pregnant in the summer of 1980, and I didn't want to raise my kid in the city. My mom was thrilled. I was going to settle down and live the suburban dream again. I wanted to move back to Greenwich. Greenwich was filled with artists, producers, directors, all the cool people.

"Nah, you lived in Greenwich already," Chris Lendt told me. "You should get something grander. I see you in a big mansion in Darien."

Let me tell you something about Darien. Darien was a place where Jewish weren't allowed. They even made a movie about anti-Semitism in

Darien called *Gentleman's Agreement* starring Gregory Peck as a journalist who passes as Jewish to experience prejudice firsthand. And if you were black, forget about it. No chance. Darien was the ultimate in Waspiness.

But Chris found us a beautiful hundred-year-old colonial house with more rooms than I could count and a guesthouse on four acres. It cost plenty, but that was no problem then. We moved in, and a few months later Deb went into labor.

"I'm ready. Get the car, I'll just throw on some clothes," Deb said. I grabbed her suitcase, threw it into the car, closed the door, and ran around and got behind the wheel. And started driving. I was five minutes away from the house when I looked over and realized that I had forgotten Deb. So I raced back and she was standing in front of the house, stomach out to here.

"Get out of the car," she barked. "I'm driving."

I dropped her off at the hospital and went to park the car. Then it was time to wait. Each minute seemed like an eternity. Deb and I had taken Lamaze courses, so I was in the delivery room, breathing right alongside her. She hadn't touched a cigarette or done any drugs while she was pregnant, so that helped me get clean too. So I was totally clearheaded when I saw the miracle of that little head pop out. They cut the umbilical cord and handed her over to me. I was thrilled. I had desperately wanted a girl. The nurse was cleaning her while I held her, and we put her in a nice swaddling blanket and put the little pink hat on her. I still have the little bracelet made of dice that spelled out her name. After a while Deb told me she was tired and that I should go home.

When I got home, I cracked open a bottle of Johnnie Walker Black and started calling all these people to tell them that we had a daughter. By the time I got to the fifteenth person on the list, I was ossified.

"*Weee jusssst haaaad a babbbby girrrrlll,*" I said, and passed out.

When I came to, it all hit me. I was a father. This was even better than playing the Garden. I had a healthy baby girl with an absolutely drop-dead gorgeous woman. Life was good.

But having a kid didn't derail our partying. After a while, someone brought over a gram of coke and we did it and before we knew it we were back to our stupid drug ways. We'd put the kid to bed and break out the blow and champagne. During the week I'd drive in and hang out at the

KISS offices. Hey, it was still one-quarter my office, and Bill was managing my solo career. "Here comes the country squire," people would say when they saw me in the halls. I'd hang around the office for a while, then go out for a martini and have lunch at the Four Seasons or the Palm. Deb would drive in with me and she'd shop and then lunch at the Copacabana. We were both living in a bubble: Rock star/Playmate. We had a part-time nanny and nothing else to do but shop, drink, get high, and throw parties. By then we had converted a dance room into a rec room with a beautiful 1920 nine-foot Medalist pool table, complete with leather pockets. We filled that room with all my gold and platinum albums, a nice wet bar, and mirrored walls.

I never thought of the guys, I never missed the makeup, I never missed the touring. I felt like I had escaped from some prison.

We traveled a lot, even when Jenilee was an infant. When she was only a few months old we took her and the nanny to Barbados. One day I went out on a Jet Ski and lost control. It was dragging me all around the ocean. Eventually I felt somebody pull me out of the water and bring me back to shore. When I got the sand out of my eyes and got acclimated, I realized that Paul McCartney had saved me! He and his wife owned a house right around the bend from where we were staying. It turned out that Linda and I had a common friend in Eddy Kramer. The McCartneys were wonderful, down-to-earth people. Paul even did a little tap dance in the sand for Deb.

I saw a lot of Ace in those days. He lived in Connecticut too, and he'd come over for marathon pool games. Or we'd go fishing. If he didn't catch something, he'd get bored and pull out an Uzi and shoot the fucking fish. Around that time I met a man who would become my best friend for life, Eddie Mulvihill. We came together in the most unusual way.

While living in Darien, I found a local YMCA that was like a freaking country club. It had an Olympic-sized pool, beautiful racquetball courts, the works. Ace and I were really into racquetball, so we joined up. We were gung ho at first, but then it got a little boring, although we still played so we could stop at a neighborhood bar. The owner always had coke and he was happy to share it with us so we'd go down to his office, lock the door, and snort away.

One day Ace showed up at the Y for our game and pulled a huge bag of quaaludes out of his gym bag.

"I got a great idea. Why don't we play on ludes?" he asked.

"Ace, do you know how fast that ball goes? We're going to be playing in slow motion," I said.

He thought it would be great, so I caved and we both took two ludes. We entered the court, started volleying, and in no time the pills starting kicking in. I served the ball and it looked like it was going in slow motion. *Boom . . . shing . . .* Ace was waiting for the ball and it darted right by him and he swung about three seconds too late. Then the ball rebounded and hit him in the back of the head.

Ace rubbed his head and picked up the ball. He started bouncing it and the movement fascinated him. He just watched the ball bounce and bounce and bounce until it finally stopped. Eventually we played while we were both lying down on the court. We looked like two big fish out of water, slowly swinging away as the ball rushed by us. Thank God nobody had cell-phone cameras then because if they did, we'd be all over YouTube. We were both wearing headbands and wristbands and we had on those high-cut pants with tank tops. Finally we just gave up the pretense of even playing the game. We were both lying facedown on the court.

"Ace, did you hit the ball?" I slurred.

"Fuck the ball," Ace said.

We were just about to pass out when I rallied.

"Ace, we've got to get up. They're going to find us in here and revoke our memberships."

"You're right, Cat," he said.

Somehow we made it back to the locker room.

"Let's take a sauna," Ace suggested.

"I'm not going into the sauna on two quaaludes," I protested. "I'll die in there." It was true. Ace used to go into the sauna straight and he'd conk out from the heat. We'd be in the sauna and he'd pass out. His towel would fall off his body and he'd be naked with his big schlong hanging down. His big balls would be sweating and his mouth would be open. He looked like a giant dead tuna. People would come into the sauna looking like, "What the fuck is that?" and they'd look at me and I'd shrug and they'd storm out of there.

"Come on, you fuck, let's get out of here," I'd say.

"Throw some more water on the coals," he'd stutter.

I'd drag his lifeless body out of the sauna and into the showers and blast him with cold water and he'd wake up.

One day we went to my bar after the Y at about three o'clock in the afternoon and we sat and drank and snorted until closing time. When it was time to close, the owner locked the front door and me and Ace and a couple of other people who were in the bar kept drinking. Finally we heard a *boom* and looked over and Ace had passed out cold onto the bar.

"What do you want me to do with him?" the owner asked.

"I don't know—put him in a booth. I'm not driving all the way to Wilton at this hour," I said.

All of a sudden, a guy who was sitting at the end of the bar piped up.

"I'll take him home," he volunteered.

"Who's this guy?" I asked the owner.

"That's Eddie. Eddie Mulvihill. Great guy. Ace will be in good hands," the owner said.

"I'll get your boy home safe and then I'll come back and let you know he got home okay," he said.

Sure enough, he drove Ace back to his house. He rang the doorbell, Ace's wife Jeannette answered it, and Eddie had Ace over his shoulder.

"My name is Edward and I'm a friend of Peter's and they were drinking together and Peter asked me to take Ace home. Where do you want him?"

"Put him on the couch," Jeannette shrugged. He dropped Ace on the couch and walked back to the door.

"Nice meeting you," he said.

"Nice meeting you," Jeannette answered, and closed the door.

Eddie came back to the bar. By then it was snowing outside and he was all bundled up.

"Your buddy is safe," he reported.

That was the beginning of a beautiful friendship between two very different guys. Edward's father was an Irish merchant who married a Spanish aristocrat. He grew up on a plantation in Spain, pampered by many servants. I brought out the bad boy in him and he showed me real friendship. We had a ball together.

I was getting a little bored from all this fun, so I decided to go back into the studio and do another solo album. This time I made sure that Vini Poncia was available to produce. I couldn't have been happier working with Vini again. We met and discussed ideas for the album.

"I want you to sing the best you're ever sung in your life," he told me. "I don't want you to worry about the arrangements, I don't want you to worry about drumming, I just want you to worry about how you're going to walk into the studio and blow me away with your voice and sing these songs like they've never been sung."

I could dig that, especially when I saw the material that Vini was suggesting I do. We did a great Russ Ballard tune, "Let Me Rock You," that was the title song of the album. We did a cover of the great John Lennon song "Jealous Guy." Vini even persuaded me to do a song by Gene, "Some Kind of Hurricane," that had been a KISS outtake. After hours of debate, Vini promised me that he'd do a dynamite arrangement complete with great female backup singers and he was right, it was a monster.

We recorded the instrumental tracks in L.A. then went back to New York City to lay down the vocals. One night it started snowing heavily and Big John, who was my bodyguard again, told me that there was a kid who had been waiting outside the studio for hours to get my autograph.

"I told him to go home but he won't," John said. "He says he's been following you guys since '72. He used to stalk you when you were living in the Claridge House. He and his pal would wait outside for hours until you came down to walk your sheepdog."

"Get the fuck out of here," I said.

"I'm telling you, Peter, this guy is crazy."

I had to see this guy for myself. I went down and saw this big chubby kid shivering in the cold.

"Hey, how you doin'?" I greeted him.

"Oh my God, oh my God, it's Peter Criss," the kid said. We started talking for a bit and he told me that he lived in Long Island in Brentwood with his parents and his name was Vinny Gonzales. Then he told me that his mother was 100 percent Italian.

"I'll tell you what," I said. "You know who Steve Stevens is, right? We're going to do a song that Steve wrote for me tomorrow night. If you bring two trays of lasagna and one tray of meatballs and sausage with spaghetti, I'll let you upstairs to hear the session."

Vinny rushed home and had his mother, Nancy, cooking all night. The next day I got to the studio at five P.M. and Vinny was standing there with four big shopping bags full of food.

I was a man of my word, so I let Vinny up into the studio. Steve Stevens, the lead guitarist of Billy Idol's band, had written a great song called "First Day in the Rain" and played on the track. Vinny was thrilled to be there to witness it, and Vinny and I developed a relationship. Deb and I visited his house. Another time I brought my parents to his house and his mother, who is the sweetest lady I know, cooked us a killer meal. That night, Vinny had the whole neighborhood waiting outside for our limo to pull up. He took us downstairs to his basement, where he had erected an altar to KISS. He had every merch item we'd ever put out, he had my cymbals, he had drumsticks, he even had our underwear. Vinny is one of a kind, but he is emblematic of all the KISS fans, the greatest fans in the world.

Vini Ponzia had gotten an all-star cast to play on the album. I spent some time with a vocal coach and it really showed in the grooves. I was proud of *Let Me Rock You*. It was probably the best I had ever sung in my life. The songs were all classy. They were made for me. Each one was better than the next.

And at last, they were going to put my face on the cover. We got our lawyer Paul Marshall's wife to take the photo, and I loved it. Bill even hired a press agent to make me feel good. But it was all a charade. This time the record company didn't even release the album in the U.S. Again, I was blackballed.

The year 1982 was horrible for me. It was a crushing blow that my two albums had failed. Deb's favorite aunt died of cancer. I delved deeper and deeper into cocaine addiction. I was depressed and getting bloated. On top of all that, I was popping pills by the handful. I could have put a group together and toured, but I didn't have the incentive. Touring crappy shit-holes after selling out stadiums would have just made me more depressed.

So I put my drums in storage in the attic and I decided that I was going to be the best father that a daughter could have. I didn't want to leave Jenilee's side in her formative years, so I hung up the bad-boy leather and became Mr. Mom.

What a stupid fucking idea. I should never have put my drums away, but I wasn't making rational decisions. There was nobody in my life to tell me, "Don't do that, you'll kill yourself with those drugs," or, "Stop playing with those guns," or, "Stop buying your wife lynx coats. You're going to run out of money soon." I really needed my grandmother or my uncle George to slap the shit out of me, smack me back to reality. I loved my family, but I was never close to my siblings. It was as if they were living in another world. I felt like a total loser, sitting out in the richest county in the country, surrounded by fucking Wasps who despised me and everything I stood for. I had a huge house with big black custom-made wrought-iron gates to keep the world out. It worked. Nobody was coming to see me.

The cocaine had completely changed my personality. I didn't want to go out anymore. I was starting to get paranoid, convinced that there were people outside watching the house. I believed my phone was bugged. I started carrying a gun 24/7. And then I got a phone call from Sean Delaney.

Sean had broken up with Bill Aucoin and was living in San Francisco. He had just written a rock opera called *Spotlights and Lonely Nights,* and he wanted me to sing on it. So he sent me a tape and I listened to it and it was brilliant. I played it for my mother and she cried like a baby.

"You can't let this one go by," she urged me. "This is a piece of genius."

The lyrics were sensational. "Spotlights and lonely nights, I guess that's the game I'm in." The song was all about groping for stardom and then getting distracted by drugs. I called Sean to tell him how much I loved the song.

"We need to do this together," Sean said. "Remember the old days?"

Both of us were misfits at this stage of our lives, both estranged from KISS. So I told him to come out and stay with us. He flew out and we got down to work. Every day, Sean taught me how to sing the song operatically, like Freddie Mercury would. After a few weeks of really working hard, Sean said, "I need a little break. Would you mind if I flew in my lover from San Francisco?"

So the boyfriend came out, and he brought a ton of blow. Instead of working, it became party central. And when Deb and Sean were stoned on coke, it was like dealing with a gargoyle with two heads. They'd go crazy. I got into a huge argument with Sean about how his lover was distracting us from working, so the boyfriend got irate and went home.

Sean started pouting. He was really busting my chops, and I was on coke and booze and Valiums, so I was in no mood to take his shit. I went upstairs and grabbed a .357 Magnum. When I came back downstairs, Deb and Sean were playing with Jenilee in the kitchen while the nanny cleaned up.

I confronted Sean. "The only way I can think of getting you to shut the fuck up is to shoot you and bury you in the fucking bushes out there," I said. With that, I let one off aimed at the ceiling and there was a huge *boom*. Smoke poured out of the sides of the barrel.

Sean screamed like a chick and went running out of the kitchen. Meanwhile, the nanny was in shock—she'd never seen anything like this. Deb was holding on to Jenilee for dear life, looking horrified. I started chasing Sean through the house, but somehow he found the doorway that led to a side door out of the house. He started tearing ass down the gravel path and I was running behind him, but I couldn't catch up to him.

Sean ran two miles into town and went into the local police station. He told them that I had gone mad and I was holding my wife and our nanny at bay with a machine gun and grenades. Now the cops were in fear of their lives if they responded, so sure enough they dispatched six cars, filled with SWAT teams, all in total riot gear. They were ready for war.

I came back inside the house and Deb and the nanny and Jenilee were huddled under the kitchen table. I had a feeling that Sean was going to the cops, so I grabbed a few more guns and went out the back of the house and over to the guesthouse, which was a converted carriage house. It had a nice loft that overlooked the property. In my delusional state, I thought that was the best place to hold the cops off. So I laid out my guns in front of me like I was James Cagney.

Suddenly I heard what sounded like a squadron of cars rushing onto the gravel road. Sure enough, it was Sean and the cops. One by one the policemen poured out of their cars and took up formation circling the carriage house. Then the top cop stepped out with a megaphone.

"Mr. Criss, your house is surrounded. We'd like you to throw your weapon out and come out with your hands up."

"Fuck you!" I screamed.

In the background I heard Sean sobbing, "He's gone crazy. Don't shoot him. Don't smoke my baby." Deb and the nanny had come out, and I saw lights coming on in the nearby houses and cars pulling up on the side of the road looking in.

Well, if I was going to go out, I'd go out in a blaze of glory. This is how out of my mind I was. I hadn't slept for days, I was totally coked up, and now I was going to go out in a blaze of glory? I'm a fucking musician, I'm not Public Enemy Number One. Peter Criscuola, where are you? I can't shoot it out with the cops, I'd get killed. There was probably a police sniper with a bead on my fucking stupid face ready to blow me to kingdom come.

"We really don't want to hurt you, Mr. Criss," the head cop said. "Please throw out your weapon and come out of there with your hands up. We're here to help you."

"All right," I said, and I threw one gun out and slowly walked out with my hands up. Then, like in the movies, they put me up against the car and patted me down, but they were really being gentle about it.

Meanwhile, they sent a guy into the carriage house and he came out with my arsenal.

"Jesus, was this guy expecting a war to break out?" he said. They grabbed the guns and put them in another car and then Sean got into one of the cars and we all drove back to the station.

At the station, they sat me down behind an interrogation desk and a senior officer pulled up a chair.

"You want some coffee, Peter?" he said amiably.

"I don't want no fucking coffee," I spat back.

"Come on, be nice. Let us give you a cup of coffee. You'll feel better."

So I drank the coffee.

Nanny and me with Aunt Rosie's cat, Devil.

Nanny and me at my confirmation.

Uncle George and Aunt Rosie.

My first communion at my school, Transfiguration.

My first set of drums. I would have slept with them if I could.

My grandfather, Peter Criscuola.

Mom and Dad. God, I miss them every day of my life.

The Kings Lounge in Brooklyn, where it all started.

In the King's Lounge with The Barracudas, singing "In My Life" by the Beatles.

The Barracudas

Joe

Tommy

Angelo

Jack

Pepe

Pete

The Sounds of Soul

Nautilus

Chelsea

Jerry Nolan, Gene Krupa, and me. It doesn't get better than this.

My family with Lydia and me at our wedding, 1970.

Sgt. Pepper's era.

Our Canarsie apartment. I painted the mural on the wall.

Check out my Beatles boots, mid-1960s.

My first KISS costume. My mom helped me make it in 1972.

Grandpa George and Stepgrandma Pauline, ready for a KISS show in San Francisco, 1979.

Big John and me in our early desperado days.

My personal bodyguard, Rosie Licata, who has the heart of a child.

Debra and me on our wedding day, 1979.

First European tour for KISS, in England. Cool car, right?

The Tomorrow Show with Tom Snyder; Ace and I took over for the first time.

First tour of Japan, 1977.

The day we recorded "Beth."

Promo photo for the
Peter Criss Alliance.

The great Jim Chapin, my drum teacher, 1980.

My daughter, Jenilee, 1981.

Sean Delany, his boyfriend, and me.

Mark St. John and a band we were trying to start.

On the Charles Bridge in Prague, early '90s.

The band Criss. I would do anything for Mark and Angel.

The wardrobe room on the Farewell Tour.

The famous Superman drape for our dressing room. You walk in one way, and you come out a superhero.

Edward Mulvihill III and me backstage at MSG, July 1996. He was my greatest friend, and I will never have another like him.

Reunion tour. Dave the Hairdresser and I loved to joke around (having fun).

Having fun after a Jones Beach show, taking off my makeup in the limo, 2000.

With Bill Aucoin, backstage in Palm Beach, Florida, 2003.

Steven Tyler with a little Peter Criss.

My fifty-eighth birthday, and my last show with my band KISS, December 20, 2004.

The TV show *Millennium*. Ace and me as cops.

Rush. We became really good friends from the early days.

HBO's *Oz*. Tommy Waites about to kill me.

Gigi and me at our wedding, 1998.

Tim Sullivan, Sam Huntington, and me on the set of *Detroit Rock City*.

With Tom Fontana. He gave me a chance to really act, and I will hold on to that moment forever.

Jenilee and me at Lake Tahoe, having a ball, 1988.

With my dear friend Dr. Terry Hammer.

My cat, Fanny.

With John Good of DW. I love him to death.

My acting coach John Eyd, his wife, Anita, and me.

George Marino and me.

Vinny Gonzales and KISS fans meeting me as I came out of a studio in NYC.

Helping to raise money for the victims of 9/11 with Josselyne Herman-Saccio and friends.

Me with the love of my life, Gigi.

With Dr. Alex Swistel. This man, along with God, helped save my life.

Ribbon-cutting for the breast cancer walk.

"This is a very conservative community . . ." he began.

"That's why I live here," I interrupted.

"I respect that," he said. "But this kind of activity can't be tolerated here."

"That fucking guy drove me crazy," I said. If I was going down, I was taking Sean with me. "He came to my home to visit and he brought drugs and he got me all fucked up on them. I don't even know what he gave me. Some sort of powder."

I heard Sean in the next room, with his high-pitched voice, "Oh, he's lying. He's lying."

"Search him if you don't believe me," I said, and sure enough they searched Sean and found some blow, but they didn't arrest him. They gave him twelve hours to get on a plane back to San Francisco. Then they turned their attention back to me.

"You know we can't let you go home, okay?"

"What! I'm going to jail?" I protested.

"No, we're going to put you up tonight in a suite at the Marriott down the road. You'll spend the night there and when things are right again between you and your wife, we'll give you back your guns. But right now, your wife doesn't want you back in the house. Maybe she'll change her mind tomorrow."

This was Darien-style justice.

So I went to the hotel and got my first good sleep in days. The next day I woke up and thought, Oh, God, what the fuck did I do?

I went home, but Deb was still furious with me.

"I'm leaving, this is it," she told me. "I've had it with you. You're out of your mind. I'm taking the baby and going to California."

They left. And I started partying. I went into the city and picked up two eight balls of coke and some pills. For weeks I was drinking and drugging by myself, distraught over losing Deb and the baby. It got worse and worse and lonelier and lonelier, but I couldn't reach out to anybody. By then I had gotten the guns back from the police and I would roam around the house aimlessly with a gun strapped to me, totally paranoid. My nose would be bleeding because I couldn't get any more coke up it.

One night I was sitting at the kitchen table with a loaded .357 Magnum, an ounce of blow, and a huge jar filled with uppers and downers. It was a scene straight out of *Scarface*. I was mumbling, "So this is it? This is it? I've got a huge house, three cars, millions of dollars, and I'm miserable and I got nobody. For what?" I picked up the gun and walked down the steps into the cellar. I figured that if I would shoot at the walls, which were composed of big gray stones, the bullet might ricochet and hit me in the head and that would spare me from having to kill myself. So I aimed the gun at the far wall and *boom,* I fired the gun and I heard a couple of pings and that was it.

I fired the gun again.

Ping, ping, I heard.

This was bullshit. I was going to try it one more time. I shot again, and this time the bullet hit a pipe and it blew up and water started pouring out of the pipe. I didn't even give a shit. I went back up the stairs and went up to my bedroom and passed out. The next morning I woke up in a daze and remembered that I hit the pipe. I went to walk down to the cellar and the water was almost up to the top of the stairs. So I grabbed a phonebook and called the first plumber I found. He went down there, and hours later he came up grinning and handed me an elbow section of pipe with a huge bullet hole in it.

"Me and the guys were down there last night and I guess we got a little wild," I said.

He just smiled and said he wouldn't mention it to anyone, but that was bullshit. In Darien, everyone talks about everyone else. He gave me a bill that totaled in the thousands of dollars and I signed for it and gave him a credit card. Then he left and I just sat there, looking at the elbow.

I picked up the phone and called Tex, who had been Ace's guitar tech for years. He came over with a gal named Mary Joy, who used to dress us on the road. Tex took one look at me and shook his head.

"Catman, you look like you're going to die," he said.

"I feel like I'm going to die, man. I'm at the end of my rope. I'm really scared and lonely, man."

So we sat around that table for days. I still had some of my coke left. And we had every colored pill in the world on the table. We played pool and we talked about getting better. But most important, he was there for me, and I bless him and Mary Joy today for that.

Then Tex and Mary Joy left and I picked up the phone again. This time I called Chris Lendt.

"I can't control this anymore," I told him. "Get over here right now. I want to be put away."

CHAPTER FOURTEEN

Chris rushed over and spotted the gun, the mound of cocaine, and the empty magnums of champagne.

"I think I need help," I told him. "I don't want to do this shit anymore but I can't stop."

Chris immediately started making phone calls. This was early in the game, and there weren't that many rehab places that knew how to deal with coke addiction. Finally, after about ten calls, he found a place in Long Island called South Oaks Hospital.

"They'll take you, but we gotta go now."

"Right now?" I said.

"I thought you wanted to go," he said.

I tried to stall. "Let me just do a few more lines and a little more champagne," I said.

"Now," he insisted.

I did as much blow as I could anyway, and I backed it with some champagne and a few quaaludes for good measure.

"Okay, let's fucking go," I said.

Chris called for a limo and I started loading it up. I packed two suits, some silk shirts, a couple of pairs of nice boots, a killer pair of rock 'n' roll leather pants. I brought a snare drum with sticks and a stand so I could practice in there. I had four *Playboy* magazines and a couple of paperback books to read. An acoustic guitar. I was packing like I was going to a resort where I'd have my own room where I could play my guitar, read, chill out.

The ride there was pretty quiet. I was whacked out from partying with Tex. It was at least four or five days since I had slept, so I looked really bad. As we got closer to the place, I started having second thoughts.

"This is going to be good," Chris said. "You ain't getting Deb back unless you straighten out."

"I don't want to lose her and Jenilee," I admitted. I loved them to death.

We pulled in to the grounds and I was impressed. Lots of land, nice foliage, the buildings looked nice. If you're going to have to be put away somewhere, this didn't seem so bad. We drove around to the back of a building where it said ADMISSIONS and it looked like you were checking in to a resort. Later I found out they don't take you through the front because the sign there says SOUTH OAKS PSYCHIATRIC INSTITUTE. I would have flipped out if I thought I was going to a nuthouse. But that was where I belonged.

We went in and were directed to a room where I did my intake interview. My doctor was a five-foot-two Indian named Dr. Rai.

"So tell me your problems," he said in his thick Indian accent.

I went into my history and this brown man started turning white. I told him about stuff on the road, I told him about the SWAT team episode; I was totally honest.

Dr. Rai excused himself for a moment to confer with some of the other people there. Then he came back into the room with an admission slip.

"The first step to recovery is admitting that you have this problem. You should be very proud that you've taken that first step."

In truth, I should have been there long before. I signed the paper and I looked up and a nurse had come into the room accompanied by two giant guys in white shirts and pants and shoes. I started to get a little uncomfortable.

"Mr. Criss, we're here to take you to your room," one of them said.

"Okay, is all my stuff that was in the limo up there already?" I asked.

"What's up there will be what we put up there," Dr. Rai said. "But there's certain things that you can't bring in here. We cannot have any musical instruments. And there's no place for dirty magazines here. We will give you hospital clothes to wear so your friend can take your suits and such back. None of that is coming into my hospital. Don't worry, we will take care of you. We are going to take you off the bad drugs that you're on and give you drugs that are necessary for you, like antiseizure medication."

It suddenly hit me that this was not going to be a vacation. I was numb when Chris came over and gave me a good-bye hug, but I thought this was a good move. I really trusted Chris.

Then the two huge orderlies escorted me out of the building and we crammed into a small compact car. The nurse got behind the wheel and started off toward a nearby building. I was still stoned out of my mind, so I started rapping and telling them that I was Peter Criss, founding member of KISS. They were agreeing with everything I said but it dawned on me later that they would have agreed if I had told them I was Napoleon. I had no idea that they were taking me to a mental ward.

We got to the other building and climbed out of the car. One of the orderlies took out a huge loop of dozens of keys and started opening the doors. As we went past a door, he turned around and locked it again. The whole time, the other orderly was holding my arm. We couldn't even get on the elevator without using a key.

We finally got to my ward and they checked me in and took me to my room. It wasn't the Four Seasons, but at least it was private. But I noticed there was no lock on the door. As I was settling in, the nurse brought me some meds. A Valium, a painkiller, and an antiseizure pill. Hey, I never turned down a pill, so I took them and then walked out onto the floor of the ward. I took one look around and I thought I was in the film *One Flew Over the Cuckoo's Nest*. There were all these people just shuffling around with vacant looks on their faces. I later found out that they were all on Thorazine, a powerful antipsychotic, and the slow, deliberate way they walked was called the Thorazine shuffle. One black guy came up to me and dropped a lot of money in front of me, saying that he didn't need it because his family was wealthy. Another guy was sitting in the corner of the room telling jokes and laughing to himself. One older woman suddenly went into a rage and they threw her into a straitjacket and carried her off. A few hours later, she came back a vegetable. I was in the middle of all this and I was scared. I thought, "What am I doing in this hell? I didn't come here for this—I just came here to kick the fucking drugs." I felt so bad for the people who were truly mentally disturbed, but at the same time it was frightening to be up there with them.

When it was time for dinner, they served roast beef. But they wouldn't give us knives to eat it with. Do you know what it's like to eat roast beef with a plastic spoon?

I didn't sleep well that first night. But I was stuck there because I had voluntarily signed in, so I figured I'd better make the best of it. Out of the twenty-five or so patients on this ward, four of us were kicking alcohol, two of us were in for coke, and maybe a couple were kicking heroin. The rest of the people were mental patients. The ward was nicknamed the Flight Deck because it was where you took off from. But from the looks of most of the people there, they weren't getting very far.

I got incredibly lonely my second night there. I hated sleeping alone. I missed the camaraderie of being out on the road with an army of guys. I started thinking about Deb and her seeing me in a place like this. Then I thought about letting my parents and all our fans down. I felt so guilty for getting so out of control, for not being able to handle the drugs, Mr. Cool Tough Italian Kid from the streets of Brooklyn. I found out later that it was actually normal to feel this way, it was part of the therapeutic process, but right then I just felt like such a loser.

I was lying in bed and these thoughts were just flooding my head. I saw Jenilee and then I saw myself as a little boy and it was Christmas and we were bringing a tree home in the snow. I started crying uncontrollably and I couldn't stop. Just then, a young male nurse walked into my room and sat down on my bed. He was around five foot ten, probably weighed around 170 pounds, dark hair, a really nice-looking man. He had pens and pencils in his perfectly white starched jacket.

"We're going to get you through this, Peter. It's tough tonight, I know, but don't worry," he said. Then he told me that he saw me perform once at Madison Square Garden and that I was terrific. Now I felt even guiltier, a fan seeing me like this. It killed me. But he couldn't have been any sweeter, and we talked for hours on that bed. He made me feel good about myself.

His visit got me through that horrible night. The next morning, I asked the head nurse at the desk if I could see him again.

"Uh, Mr. Criss, we don't have any male nurses on the night shift. This is a lockdown ward. There was no male nurse on."

"Bullshit. He came into my room and told me everything was going to be cool."

"I'm sorry, but there was no male nurse on duty last night."

I thought to myself, "Holy shit, you idiot. Either you hallucinated that whole scene or you had an angel come into that room." Deep down I knew he was an angel. And right then I decided that I was going to stick this out and get better.

One morning I went to the breakfast table and there was a beautiful girl sitting across from me. I looked at her—I couldn't help it, she was so pretty—and I noticed that there were burns on her arms, and her wrists had scars on them, and her throat had been cut in three different places. I couldn't believe that a girl that pretty didn't want to live.

I spent a week on that ward. I didn't like it; it wasn't easy to see people getting put into straitjackets and shuffling around and staring vacantly at the big TV. On Saturday night they had a big party and we could all stay up late, watching TV and eating potato chips and pretzels and drinking soda. It wasn't like drinking champagne and snorting coke and getting in a hot tub with some naked women, but it had to do.

After a week, Dr. Rai asked me if I wanted to stay.

"You can legally leave now, but I wouldn't recommend it," he said. "The full program is nine weeks, and if you did that I would be very proud of you."

I thought about Jenilee and how much I didn't want to lose her. I was worried about Deb, but I was more worried about my daughter. So I thought, I can do nine weeks.

After a week on the Flight Deck, they moved me to a ward that had only alcoholic men. The place smelled like a fucking drunk tank and it was impossible to sleep with all their snoring. I would sit up all night and bullshit with the head nurse because I didn't want to lie down with all these drunks. Deep down I felt really bad for those guys. I spent a week on that ward and finally they transferred me to a much nicer unit.

Now I was on a ward with my own people—the cokeheads and junkies. Finally I could sit and eat with people who didn't want to shoot themselves or cut their wrists. It was just a bunch of guys relating war stories: "Yeah, I started with a line and next thing you know I was shooting coke . . ." It was funny, I had been such a rebel my whole life, but in here I never broke the rules. I did everything I was told. I never once caused a fight or gave the nurses a bad time. I was never confined to my room. I was a model patient because I really wanted help.

I was also learning major lessons in humility. I couldn't just go out and have a steak at Peter Luger's. I had to eat whatever they were putting on the plates that night. They had a chapel there, and I went to it every day and got a lot closer to God. I did so much praying, I should have been a priest. I started realizing that the drugs had changed my personality, and after a few weeks I felt like I didn't have that monkey on my back anymore. But still I would beat myself up and wonder, "How the fuck did you let yourself get to a point where you needed to be here? How could Peter Criss do this to himself?"

Whenever I got on that guilt trip and felt like such a failure, Dr. Rai was there to lift me up.

"You did nothing wrong," he'd say. "You're just like every other Tom, Dick, or Harry. People fall into the trap. People get addicted. You're not above all that. I hate to tell you that even though people tell you you're a big star, you're not that unique."

I felt comfortable in this new unit. They woke us up at five in the morning for breakfast and then I'd see Dr. Rai for an hour. Then we had group therapy and then a class about the chemical impact drugs had on the body. After lunch we saw another therapist and then had a few other classes. You'd see your doctor again for a brief time after dinner, and then we had another group session before lights out at ten o'clock.

I would lie in bed all night thinking about how I wound up in this place. I realized just how much pain I had to endure to do my job. I'd tear ligaments all the time, in both of my shoulders, just like a professional athlete. But we were in the middle of a tour so we couldn't stop. We had to think about our careers. So I'd see a succession of doctors to get those huge cortisone shots to alleviate the pain. The injections themselves were extremely painful, but I took them because I wanted to play. I remembered when we had to stop that European tour and I had to be taken off the plane in a wheelchair because I was in so much pain. I had to lie on my couch in my brownstone for weeks and just rest. If I had continued, I wouldn't have been able to play again for the rest of my life, the docs told me.

I remembered getting a shot from a quack doctor at the L.A. Forum just so the show could go on. I had to play that show—we were taping it for *Alive II*. By then my right hand had been broken a few times. I had been partying with Ace the night before the show. It was getting to the point that we were getting so big and people were screaming so loud no matter what we did that the success almost got depressing. We were doing the same songs night after night after night. I needed an out from all that, and the drugs were it. Right before that show I remember putting half of my makeup on, looking over at Ace, and saying, "Ace, I can't go on, I think I'm going to die."

I felt the room was closing in and my breathing became erratic. Sean and Bill conferred and Sean ran out and found that fugazi doctor who gave me the shot. I felt like I was playing on another planet that night.

Eventually our road managers would travel with a footlocker filled with sleeping pills, pain pills, muscle relaxants. The show must go on. Just keep me going, and they'd worry about it afterward. It got to a point where I wouldn't go on unless I had coke. And the promoters would supply the coke. Everyone had coke: The roadies had it, the truckers had it, the groupies had it. I'd lie in bed in rehab and think about all the insane events that had conspired to get me there.

Our little group got tight. There were two pilots who flew for Pan Am who were coke addicts. They told me that they used to steal the whiskey from the hotel minibars and stuff them into their pockets so they could take the edge off the coke when they were landing.

"I could have been on one of your planes and you could have killed me," I protested.

"Yup, that's why we're here," one of them said.

There was a nurse, there was a plumber, there was an electrician getting help. I got friendly with a reporter named Tommy who worked for a big newspaper. And a motorcycle cop named Tim who was in there for alcohol addiction.

My story was just like any of the others'. I was addicted and I wanted to stop. I was doing five grams of coke a day. If my nose was bleeding too much to snort the coke, I'd take a cold capsule, empty the little beads out, fill it with coke, and take it orally, just to get high. My habit ran into thousands of bucks a week.

I was really shut off from the outside world. Deb and my parents didn't even know I was in the hospital. After four weeks they allowed me to have visitors, and Chris started coming by every weekend. He'd bring me a couple cartons of cigarettes, which I didn't need to smoke anymore since I wasn't doing blow, so I passed them out to the other patients. He'd also bring me candy and magazines and fill me in on what was happening at the office.

The band sent me one fucking card the whole time I was there. GOOD LUCK. GLAD YOU ARE THERE. FUCK YOU. GENE, PAUL, ACE. I guess they thought they were being funny. Other than Chris, I had no contact with anybody else in the office.

Right after my fourth week, the doctor told me that he wanted to bring my parents up.

"No way," I said. "I don't want them to see me here."

"You've got to have them come up," Doctor Ray said. "It's part of the treatment."

The day they visited was the worst day of my life. My mother came in and shot me a look that was just crippling. I'll never forget it until the day I die. It was like she was saying, "How did you get here, after all that work, all those hours of practicing, all those years of suffering? You finally became what you wanted, you married a gorgeous woman, you have a beautiful daughter and a beautiful house, and now you're in a nuthouse." I could just hear that internal monologue.

Ironically enough, it was my father who cried like a baby, the guy who could never show any emotion to me at all.

So I started crying, too.

"I wish I could help you," he said.

"Me too, Dad."

He must have gone through three hankies. My mother later told me that he cried all the way home to Brooklyn.

"I told you that woman you married was crazy. Now look where you are," he said.

"Don't talk like that," Dr. Rai said. "You have to be positive."

"What positive?" my father said. "He wouldn't be here if it wasn't for that crazy girl he married. And where's your big-shot band? And your manager? Where's all the people who said they loved you to death? They got rich, and you got addicted and put in the nuthouse."

The session had become a nightmare. Dr. Rai told them that I was a cocaine addict and I didn't have any control over it and they were going to clean me up and put me back into society so I could go back to my music. But until then, I was staying right there and he would like it if my parents could come up and visit me more.

"You'll never see me here again," my mother said, and they left. I went back to my room and cried my eyes out. I felt like a pile of shit. My own mother was refusing to come back because she was so hurt. She loved me so much that this was all too much for her.

Now it was time to deal with my wife. I had tried to write Deb a few letters the first few weeks I was in there, but Dr. Rai wouldn't let me send them. He told me they were a little too emotional, but I think, in retrospect, that he was worried Deb would leave me. And that was the last thing I needed at that point. I later found out that Deb had actually written a letter to me after Chris told her that I was in rehab. It was a very heavy good-bye, adiós, it's-all-over letter. She told him to bring me the letter, but Chris never did. He held on to it and eventually tore it up because he knew that if I read it, I would have broken out of that place and flown to California.

But Dr. Rai was preparing me for the worst.

"You know you may go home and she may not want you still," he told me. "You may straighten yourself up and feel great about yourself and you may still go home to an empty house and a divorce. We hope that's not the case, but I want you to prepare yourself for that, if it happens."

So he felt it was too early for me to see Deb and the kid.

I had to be content with seeing Chris. But there was something strange going on there, too. One time Chris came up with some long legal documents concerning KISS that he wanted me to sign.

"You cannot do this," Dr. Rai said. "He is in no state to sign such documents while he is in treatment here." So Chris finagled them into allowing me out for a walk on the grounds. We walked out to a large field and sat down on a bench and Chris opened up his attaché case and took out some documents. He had me sign them and then he quickly put them back in his attaché, as if he was afraid of getting caught. I didn't even know what the fuck I was signing. To this day I don't know what those papers were about.

Finally, Dr. Rai told me it was time to contact Deb. He brought me to his office and, with my counselor there, we got Deb on the phone. It was bizarre. This was the first time I was speaking to her totally sober. I was crying like a child, expecting her to tell me to fuck off, that she would never see me again, but she didn't do that. She said she'd come back East and see me. I felt reborn after that call.

A week later, Deb came to visit me. I felt great. I was really going to fight and win this. It was a weekend, and Deb pulled up to the place in my Datsun tenth-anniversary gold-and-black Z. She brought Jenilee, who was still too young to know what any of this stuff was. Everyone's families were visiting, and I had bragged to everyone about my beautiful model wife who had been in a big Coppertone ad. She was on billboards all over the country in a bikini showing her wonderful Coppertone tan lines.

She walked in looking like a million bucks, like a class act from Beverly Hills. But when we started our session, I couldn't believe my ears. Everything was on me. "He beats me up, he goes crazy when he's on drugs," she told Dr. Rai. It was like she had never snorted a line in her life. I felt like Mike Tyson on Barbara Walters listening to Robin Givens. "He's intolerable. He's an absolute maniac when he starts with the blow. He wrecks things." I was dying to butt in and say, "She's just as fucking bad," but I thought if I started squealing on her, there was no way of getting her back.

I was tearing up and she was going, "Oh, Peter, look at you. Look what you got yourself into. It's breaking my heart." I was thinking, "You fucking bitch. You were the one who was two hours late to our wedding because you were snorting up a storm." Instead I was reduced to saying,

"I'm so sorry, come back to me. I'm a changed man. Ask Dr. Rai, I'm the best patient here."

We sat down alone later in the little cafeteria and we talked. It was almost like we were strangers. I asked her if she would stay with me and she said, "Let's see how it goes." She was adamant about me sticking it out for the full nine weeks.

It was a hard day. When she and Jenilee left, I was up all night in bed crying. I felt ashamed that after all we had been through and been blessed with, she had to see me here in this place.

She came back the next weekend. I counted the days until Saturday came around. The next time she came I was so horny I was beside myself. I knew it was totally against the rules to have sex in the hospital, but I didn't care. We got someone to watch Jenilee and we snuck upstairs to one of the rooms and she lifted her dress up and we did it. It lasted maybe a few seconds, I was so horny. We were both giggling, hoping not to get caught. The next weekend, I got a pass to go home for the weekend. We could have proper sex, but it was weird. It wasn't hot and wild like it used to be because I was sober. I didn't even know what to do straight. I was worried about everything I did, everything I said. I was walking on eggshells.

With Deb and Jenilee back, I was feeling a lot better. I began taking over the whole ward, and we actually started having fun there. I made up CLASS OF '82 T-shirts for everyone. By then Thanksgiving had rolled around, but they wouldn't let me take the whole four days off. They let me go home for dinner, but I had to be back that night. My pal Tim, the cop, had a friend who had a private plane and he dropped me off at the airport near Darien. I was sitting there with my little bag waiting for Deb to pick me up. Deb drove up and we went home and the house smelled wonderful from all the great stuff she was cooking.

She had invited the Kellys, the family who had sold us the house and who lived in a smaller house nearby. The husband, Joe Kelly, was a hell of a drinker, complete with one of those big bulbous red Irish noses. We sat down for dinner and I could see in their eyes that they were uncomfortable because they couldn't even have a glass of wine in front of me. It was silly. My problem was never alcohol, it was cocaine and pills.

After dinner, we went to the billiard room and shot some pool. Just

months before, I had been sitting in this room, up all night, shooting bil-
liards and betting a thousand dollars a shot. Now I looked in the mirror
and a drug-free guy was looking back. Soon it was time to leave and Deb
fixed me a turkey sandwich to take back. Joe drove me back to the hospital in my Datsun Z. Back on the ward, everyone was so depressed, sitting
around with their turkey leftovers and little slices of pumpkin pie.

My nine weeks were almost up. Christmas was coming up, my favorite
time of the year, and we all got in the spirit and decorated the ward. We
were all excited about the prospect of going home. Before you "graduated," as they called it, you had to have an exit interview with your family
and a panel of doctors and nurses and counselors.

"You know this will be no picnic for you, Peter," Dr. Rai told me.
"You'll have many temptations in the business you're in. Nothing has
changed with respect to that." He was right on the dime. What changed
was me, and hopefully I had the tools to deal with the outside world.

That day, after the interviews, everyone went to the chapel and every
patient gave a little farewell speech. When it was my turn, I thanked Deb
for standing by me and I thanked my doctor and the nurses and the counselors and my fellow class of '82. I had ordered up a special stretch limo for
the day and we loaded my stuff into it and I shook hands with everyone
and hugged and thanked Dr. Rai. He was such a cool man.

I remember looking out the back window as we drove off the grounds,
vowing never to come back to a place like that. Then I looked at Deb
and said, "I'm so sorry," and we kissed and hugged like little kids in the
backseat.

We had a quiet Christmas Eve. We put up a tree and exchanged gifts.
I wasn't putting any medals on myself, but I was proud that I had made
it through. I was so confident in myself that I had a couple of beers on
Christmas Eve and nothing happened.

But I was facing big changes in the new year. KISS was in turmoil.
Ace had been miserable in the band after I left because he was on his own.
"They were fucking animals," he told me one day. "They ganged up on me
morning, noon, and night. I lost every vote." When we hung out together
in Connecticut, he was always threatening to leave the band. He finally
did in 1982.

There were other changes, too. The album sales had declined and the tours were losing money. Howard Marks had promised my wife that we would never have to worry about money, but now management was singing a different tune. I was told that my house in Darien was costing too much and that I should sell it and move to a cheaper place. They also told me that they could no longer afford to pay the rent on my parents' new apartment in Queens. That really upset me. All of a sudden there wasn't enough money to pay for a little apartment in Queens? My parents had never had nice things in their life. Getting them that little apartment made me feel so good. Now it was going to be taken away. I always felt guilty that I hadn't done more for them. They had it so hard. But it wasn't my fault they were losing that apartment.

All I could think of was getting revenge on Marks and Glickman, who, in my mind, were fucking me. I was still raw from rehab and I wasn't exactly making the best decisions. So I reached out to a kid I had met in rehab. Let's call him Tony Vinzini. Tony and his older brother Christopher were at South Oaks for cocaine addiction. Tony was a little skinny guy, but Christopher was 250 pounds at least. He was in rehab for beating up a couple of cops and smashing their patrol-car window in. No jail: They put him in rehab. I told Tony who I was and he went crazy: "Oh my God, KISS!" One weekend he said, "My family is coming and we'd like to take you to dinner." I went and met the mom. She had all the diamond rings, the leather skin from too much time down in the Miami sun, the bleached blonde hair. A million gold bracelets, a gold Rolex, and diamonds the size of your head. There was no father. They told me that he been involved in an accident in which he fell in front of a train and died.

Their older brother, Louie, was running the family business now, some sort of waste-management operation. So we got friendlier. After I got out of rehab, they invited Deb and me out to their house. We got there and I was in shock. There was a guy standing guard at the front door with a shotgun. They lived on the water in Long Island, and there were speedboats docked in front of the house. There were a ton of expensive cars parked in front. In the backyard they had a huge swimming pool surrounded by statues of lions and horses and Zeus. It was like Disneyland meets the Parthenon.

The clues were obvious, but I was clueless then. I was vulnerable. Obviously the older brother, Louie, picked up on that. I was such a mark.

So I told Tony I was having a problem with my management and he set up a meeting with his older brother. Louie struck me as a very scary individual, but I was so consumed with revenge that I didn't care. At dinner, I started telling Louie my tale of woe. I was in this huge band, they stole my money, they're telling me I have to sell my house, blah, blah, blah.

"Lookit, I'll get your money back," he said with great bravado. "We'll straighten this shit out with these guys who ripped you off. You got books? Why don't you bring me your books?" he said.

I went to my safe-deposit box and I took all the financials that Marks and Glickman had given me over the years. I had never looked at them once. I brought the books over to Louie and he went through the documents, and then he knew more about my finances than I did. This had to be the craziest thing I've ever done, and I've done some pretty crazy things.

Next I set up a meeting with Howard Marks and Louie. I wanted Howard to know that Louie was now representing my interests. We walked into the office and Louie started asking Howard questions that made it clear he had read our financials. I could see that Howard was freaking out. He was shooting me looks like he wanted to kill me. Louie started demanding some exorbitant amounts of money that he claimed Howard owed me.

"He already has a deal in place," Howard said. "What are you talking about?"

"Well, it seems to me that you owe him a lot more money," Louie said.

"He's got twenty-five percent of the band and he's not even in it anymore. What more does he want?" Howard fumed. What I didn't understand was why my parents' rent couldn't be paid anymore.

They agreed to meet again to resolve the differences. I walked out of there content that I had some muscle behind me to get back at these guys. By then I had realized how connected Louie and his family were.

The KISS office cut me off from any money, since Louie was disputing their figures. He had predicted that, so I was impressed. He convinced Deb and me to take twenty-five grand out of the bank so he could invest it: We would quadruple our money. Deb was so excited about this that she added ten grand of her own money. We handed over the money and Louie gave us promissory notes that looked as though they were drawn up by a sixth grader. Somehow he convinced me to have him hold my beautiful set of black-and-silver-striped drums, worth a good $15,000. One day a truck came up to my warehouse and they went into the truck, never to be seen again.

He even worked on Deb and told her that he had good contacts in the modeling business and he could get her a gig with Jordache Jeans. Next thing, Deb was handing her valuable portfolio of all her work over to him.

I turned my attention to selling the house. Deb was pushing for us to move to California, but that seemed too radical a step for me then. In the interim, I decided that we'd sell the house and put our stuff in storage and rent a house nearby. I wanted to turn the house over quickly. Louie decided that he was going to help me sell it. That's when I knew something was wrong with the picture. I had a little voice telling me that maybe I shouldn't give him the twenty-five grand, but Deb was confident he'd make us money. But the voice was getting louder. And it was saying, "Don't do it, Peter."

We listed the house with a broker and soon enough, a couple from Texas was interested in it. But Deb made the mistake of telling Louie that we were about to sell the house to a really wealthy Texas family. A week later, the Texan came by our house. Apparently Louie had somehow tracked him down and threatened him if he went ahead with the purchase. Then he told the guy that if he did buy it, he'd have to pay Louie 10 percent of the sale because he was my attorney.

"Who is this Louie guy?" the Texan asked me. "He's following me around, threatening me."

I sat him down and explained the whole story. When I was finished, he just shook his head.

"That's crazy shit," he drawled. "In Texas we'd kill someone for doing that."

"This ain't Texas," I said.

A few days later I called Howard. "I invited the Mob in and I'm really sorry about it. We really should talk." He suggested we meet in a tiny, low-profile bar near his office. He was waiting at the bar when I walked in but then, out of the corner of my eye, I saw Louie and four guys follow me into the bar. Howard and I both turned white.

Louie walked right up to me.

"What are you doing here?" he asked threateningly.

"What do you mean? I'm having a drink," I said.

"What's Howard doing here?" He nodded in Howard's direction.

"We're, uh, having a drink together."

"I don't understand something. One minute you hate the guy, he stole from you, you want to get rid of him, and now you're having a sociable drink with him? What shit are you guys talking about behind my back?" he fumed.

"What I don't understand is what you're doing here," I said.

"Let's just say a little birdie told me there might be something going on," he said.

"There ain't nothing going on," I lied.

I walked over to the bar where Howard had been watching all this.

"Hi, Peter," he said.

"Hi, Howard."

"You told me you were going to meet me here alone," Howard said.

"Well, that's a fucking dream," Louie said. "That ain't gonna happen. Whatever you guys need to talk about, you can talk about it in front of me."

"I have nothing to say. I'm leaving," Howard said, and he paid for his drink and walked out the door.

I didn't know what to do.

"I'm going home," I blurted out.

"Yeah, I think you should do that," Louie said.

A week later I was sitting in the house, having a couple of beers with my racquetball partner Don. Deb came into the room.

"Louie is coming over, he wants to talk to you."

"I'm not talking to him. I thought we got rid of him," I said.

"He sounded scary and he said he was going to be right over," she reported.

I grabbed Don and we went out the back entrance of the house. There was a thick wooded spot not too far from the house and I led him there.

"What's going on? Why are we hiding in your own bushes?" he asked.

"Look, I got involved with some bad guys and they want payback or something, so just be quiet. I don't want them shooting us," I said.

"Are you kidding me?" This situation was just not computing with his Darien mentality. He shut up. After a few seconds, I heard a car come up and then the muffled sounds of a conversation.

"I'm telling you he's not here," Deb said.

"Bullshit." I recognized Louie's voice. "I know he's here, and we're going to find him."

I saw flashlights illuminating the backyard. Don and I were crouching in the brush like two little mice, not making a sound.

They looked around the perimeter of the house, then they went back in. Soon after, I heard their car leave. We came out of the bushes and went back inside. Don looked like he was in shock.

"They're fucking crazy," Deb said. "Should I call the police?"

"No! Whatever you do, don't call the police," I said.

That was the last I saw of Louie. But I still wanted my money and my shit back, so I hired a big-shot attorney who had been involved in the Agent Orange litigation. He reviewed the case and wrote a letter to Louie's attorney, but then he called me into his office.

"Peter, if all you've lost is twenty-five thousand dollars and your wife's portfolio and you can still walk, I would do just that. You say you might move to California? I couldn't think of a better time. You don't want to mess with these people."

I got the message. I dropped the suit.

In retrospect, I think that Howard got these guys off my back. He was pretty connected himself to a couple of well-connected guys, and someone probably made a phone call and the trouble went away. Louie probably thought Howard was a piece of cake, a rube waiting to be taken. All I know is that Louie didn't make any more trouble for any of us.

But new trouble was lurking just around the corner. By then we had sold the house to the Texans and were living in a small house on a lake in New Canaan. The Texans were throwing a big housewarming party, and they invited us. It was a little weird, I thought, going back to my old house when someone else owned it, but Deb convinced me to go. We weren't there five minutes before a guest came up to us and offered us some blow

I went up to the bathroom with her and Deb, and I didn't take any, but she and Deb did a few lines and they got whacked out.

We went back downstairs and Deb started dancing with Joe Kelly's attractive wife, who was equally drunk. They were both so out of it that they fell on the floor at one point. Deb went to the bathroom, probably to do some blow, and Kelly's wife came over to me.

"Do you know that your wife is fucking my husband?" she said out of nowhere.

"What?"

"My husband is fucking your wife," she said.

"I don't know anything about that," I said.

"Well, I do," she said, and walked away.

My mind started reeling. I remembered that they had taken Deb with them on a vacation to Jamaica about a year ago. The three of them were probably fucking each other in Jamaica. I stayed home with Jenilee, and when I picked Deb up at the airport she came off the plane looking like Bo Derek. Her hair was all in braids, she was stopping traffic, and there was her schleppy husband with the kid. It didn't even cross my mind that she had been cheating on me.

I was so in love with Deb, and this love was certainly blind. Ace had tried to hip me to the situation. One day he came over after I had gotten out of rehab and we were in the back, fixing the mopeds. Joe Kelly came over and he was in the house with Deb for hours.

"What's this fucking guy doing in your house for two hours?" Ace asked me.

"He's a friend of ours," I said. "When I was in the hospital, he helped out."

"Yeah, I'm sure he helped himself to a lot of things, including your wife's pussy," Ace said.

So when we got home from the Texans' party, I told Deb what Joe Kelly's wife had said to me.

"Are you fucking this guy?" I asked her point-blank.

"No. She's drunk, she's out of her mind," Deb said.

"Why would she say you fucked her husband?"

I was so confused. I didn't want to acknowledge the truth. But it hit me over the head when I went into a bar in New Canaan one night to get a drink. By then we had left the lake house and moved to a townhouse near the bar. I walked in and Joe Kelly was in there drinking. He saw me and he turned white as a ghost. He lived ten miles away in Darien. Why would he be at this little pub around the corner from my place in New Canaan?

Deb kept putting the pressure on me to make the move to California. She and Sean had really worked on me that time Sean had come out to stay with us before I went to rehab.

They both got me going, saying that my solo records had failed, that I was going nowhere here. Living full-time in California never appealed to me. I almost died in a car crash there. But the two of them were like stereo magpies in my ears.

"You can work at A&M, you love that studio," Sean said. He knew just what buttons to push. "Your grandfather is up in San Francisco, you can see him more often."

They convinced me one night. But then I went to rehab. Shortly after I got back from rehab, my grandfather George died of cancer and I was devastated. California seemed distant after that. But we had sold the house and had some money. Besides, who wanted to live in a townhouse in New Canaan anyway?

Deb started working on me again.

"I think I'd like to go back home," she said one night. "We can get a place in L.A. You're straight now—you can make a fresh start. All the record companies are out there. You know everybody."

"All right, let's do it," I said.

Someone should have walked into my house and shot me the minute those words left my lips. I should have been put out of my misery and spared the consequences of making that move.

CHAPTER FIFTEEN

I'm sitting here and the view of the Pacific is just spectacular. We're hundreds of feet above sea level and I only wish you can hear what I'm hearing now. It's a coast guard helicopter patrolling the shoreline. I live in a very beautiful town, Palos Verdes, and I'm sitting here in my very special place that I don't share with anybody. It's a cliff that I drive to and park and sit on the edge and look for whales and check out the sailboats and watch these helicopters go by. I can even see Catalina from here. It's just beautiful, man, totally beautiful.

—Peter Criss dictation, 1984

I didn't know California then. All I knew was the Sunset Strip and Hollywood Boulevard. Deb went out to California a month before we moved out and found a place to rent, with an option to buy. It was up on a cliff in Palos Verdes. We had a ginormous living room with a spectacular view of the ocean. There was a small two-seater balcony off the living room. Both our bedroom and the kitchen also overlooked the ocean. If you went up one flight, there was Jenilee's room, a guest room where I was going to set up my drums, and a large room for the pool table and all my gold and platinum albums. If you went out the sliding doors, there was a huge deck with a large swimming pool overlooking the ocean. Above us were just cliffs and rocks. This was like a movie star's house. And it was costing us a movie star's salary. We even had an elevator.

Other than the occasional king snake in the swimming pool, it was paradise. Eventually I thought I'd start a band and write my book, but first I just wanted to enjoy California, get a tan, sweat, swim in the ocean. For the first year there, I fucked off. We'd go to Deb's parents' house every Sunday for a big family dinner.

After a few months out there, I felt like a different man. I was actually mellower. I felt good about Deb—I didn't fear that she was sneaking off and fucking Joe Kelly. We were a tight-knit little family. On Friday afternoons, I'd take my sports car down the hill and rent four or five movies and bring back a couple of shopping bags filled with Chinese food. I didn't miss playing at all. I was a man of leisure. I woke up and went to sleep with Jenilee. In between we'd watch TV. During the commercials, I'd go to the kitchen for a snack and grab Deb's ass. Life was pretty comfortable then.

Deb and I didn't have that much in common, so I made an effort to try to get into some of the things that she enjoyed. Deb liked golf, so I started playing. I was a natural at it, and it was something we could do together. I had a funny incident happen to me playing golf. I was in the men's locker room and these black guys came in to play a round. They took one look at my long hair and one guy said, "Shoot, I didn't know they allowed women in the men's room."

"Yeah, we've all come a long way, brother," I said.

When Deb and I got into drinking together, it never worked out so well. We just didn't get along when we got drunk. Even when we were sober, we'd still fight. Not the knock-down, drag-out, bruising and battling fights of our earlier days, but enough to keep you on your toes.

After about a year or so of fucking off, I began to get the music itch again. It started when I took Jenilee to A&M Studios to visit. They all knew me there and they would let us come in and they would show her all the consoles. By the spring of 1986 I was ready to make a move. I had heard that the group Steppenwolf was looking for a drummer, so I met with their manager, Ron Rainey. It seemed like a good fit for me. They played real steady-Eddie beats, straight-ahead rock 'n' roll.

"I'm impressed that the drummer of KISS would come down for a job with Steppenwolf," Ron said. "But I'll tell you right off the bat, John Kay is no way going to have a drummer bigger than him in the band. He'd go crazy."

Apparently Kay was a control freak. Everything was business first, and they toured in a Winnebago that Kay had designed, playing the same reliable places every year.

But Ron had gotten a tape from a new group that featured a chick singer named Jane Booke. Her husband was in the band, too, and they wrote the songs together. He told me they were looking for a drummer. I went down and listened to them and I thought they were pretty good. Jane was just adorable. She was around five foot six with unbelievably beautiful legs, the greatest ass, and big pouty lips accentuated by her flaming-red lipstick and framed by long, curly black hair that gave her a gypsy look. She'd have a guitar hanging off her—she couldn't play it for shit, but it looked cool.

The husband played bass and he was good-looking, and they had this guitarist who was trying to stop drinking so he would smoke all the time, but Jane wouldn't let him smoke in the loft they rented so he was going crazy. He could play, though.

We started playing together, and we sounded great. They had never played with a hard drummer like me, so their light-poppish sound became heavier. Jane sounded like Chrissie Hynde and did all those Chrissie moves, and I liked that since I had a great view of her little ass in front of me all night.

Ron got some money for us to do a demo at A&M, and it was like a homecoming for me. The demo came out okay and Ron started shopping it around. They had come up with a name by then, Balls of Fire, which I hated. We kept rehearsing all the time at their downtown loft. It took me an hour and a half to get there from Palos Verdes: That's how dedicated I was to making this thing work.

Jane kept telling me that she didn't know who KISS was, so I invited her and her husband to my house. I showed them all the gold and platinum and they were in shock.

"Wow, you guys sold a lot of records," she said.

"Yeah, we were a pretty big band," I admitted.

"Were you bigger than the Bay City Rollers?" she asked.

I wanted to take a straight razor and cut my wrists. How could she be that stupid? Now I was pissed.

We went into the kitchen and I was feeling disrespected.

"By the way, if we get a record deal, I want fifty percent of everything. We'll get a deal because of my name, so I want the lion's share," I said.

They went crazy and told me they wouldn't give me any percentage of the band. I told them I would quit. We finally decided to let Ron figure it out.

By then Ron had sent Atlantic the demo and they liked it. So he set up a showcase for us at the Whisky A Go Go where all the Atlantic execs could come down and hear us live. I couldn't believe that I was doing the Whisky after headlining Madison Square Garden, but I thought, "What the fuck. The Doors played there."

That night, the whole place filled up with KISS fans wearing either black KISS T-shirts or Peter Criss T-shirts. We were in the dressing room, oblivious to all this, when Ron came in.

"The Atlantic guys are all out there," he reported. "Plus a lot of KISS fans."

"How many of them?" Jane asked.

"Pretty much the whole audience is KISS fans," he admitted.

"Are you kidding me?" she moaned.

"It doesn't matter," her husband said. "When we go out there, they'll go crazy."

"Absolutely. For me," I said. "See, that's why I want fifty percent."

"*Whateverrrr*," she said.

Finally it was time to play. We walked out there and the audience started chanting, "PETER! PETER! PETER!"

She started counting off the count but none of us could hear it, the crowd was making so much noise. We started the song and she was standing right in front of me and someone yelled out, "Get the fuck out of the way! We can't see Peter!" Then the audience started chanting, "GET OUT OF THE WAY! GET OUT OF THE WAY! WE WANT PETER! WE WANT PETER!"

Jane went ballistic.

"If you fucking want to see him, here he is," she screamed, and she smashed her guitar on the stage and walked off.

"Get the fuck off!" someone screamed back, and then everyone started requesting the songs I sang in KISS. Her husband dropped his head, put his bass down, and left the stage, followed by the guitarist. I came around from the back of the drums to the front of the stage, blew some kisses, and then I left too. The guys from Atlantic walked out, and that was the end of Balls of Fire.

I enjoyed being onstage again, however short-lived it was. And it was time to start making some money. We were living off the proceeds of the sale of the house because KISS had stopped paying me. When I relinquished my 25 percent share of the partnership assets, I never realized that the character and makeup I created was part of that agreement. Later, this would become a bone of contention. So that was the end of the revenue stream from KISS. Still, I never paid attention to my finances. Deb had total charge of that. My best friend, Eddie Mulvihill, was always telling me that he was convinced that Deb was siphoning off my money, especially after we got taken for that twenty-five grand by Louie. Eddie always had my back. He was my rottweiler, just like Sean Delaney used to be. Eddie worried more about my money than I did. He told me that they would do blow together and she'd bitch and bitch about losing ten grand of her own money in that deal.

"That cocksucker idiot," he told me she said. "I lost my own personal money. I should start opening up my own bank account."

I never thought too much of it until I saw that she started getting statements from a bank that wasn't our neighborhood bank.

I could never know if Deb was ripping me off. When we needed money back in New York, we'd just go to the office and ask for some and they'd open up a big leather bag, give you three or five or ten grand, and make you sign a receipt for it. She could have easily done that and stashed some of it away. One thing I did know: We weren't going to be able to keep on paying an exorbitant rent if we didn't start making some money.

You know sometimes you can get real scared, you think you're lost and you think it's over, man, and you figure the glory days are gone. And now I face the pressures of everyday living that I never knew about. Being in KISS, it was always taken care of for me. Now that I'm a parent of a five-year-old girl, I find that the stress is enormous. Sometimes I freak out at night and go out on my balcony, look out over the ocean, and say, "Man, is it over? Do I still have it? Am I too old?" I guess every man must ask himself these questions when he's struggling to get back on top of something he succeeded at. I want to make money and enjoy playing music at the same time. I get scared, man, I think maybe it's not going to happen for me again. I've got a young wife, I know she loves me, but . . .

I just get scared. All I know about is drums, man, that's all I've ever known and that's what I do the best. You know in sports when you're a young, tough jock, you can do a lot of moves. When you get older, you can't do those moves. That's what happens to us in music too, especially drummers, it's such a physical instrument. But I am a survivor. I am a survivor.

—Peter Criss dictation, 1986

After the Balls of Fire fiasco, I couldn't get anything going for the next two years. In 1987 I did get a chance to play with my old pal Ace, though. By then I had really assimilated into California and I had grown my hair long and dyed it blond. I don't know why Deb hadn't intervened and said, "You're Italian, are you out of your mind? There are no blond Italians." I actually thought I looked great. Don't forget—it was the '80s, the Hair Band days.

Ace called me up and told me that he was going to play in L.A. with his group Frehley's Comet, and he wanted me to come down and jam. I brought Jenilee with me and we had a great time.

Ace's band played a great set and on the final encore, he announced, "I have a really good friend who I called up and he said he'd love to come down and he's here tonight. Peter Criss."

I came out and the audience went crazy. I walked out with my blond hair and a black tank top, tight black leather pants, and my high tops.

I waved and then got behind the drums and we played "Deuce." It was a home run.

Playing with Ace whetted my appetite. In 1989 I hooked up with a guitar player named Mark St. John. Mark had a short tenure in KISS, but they had crippled him to the point where he couldn't play anymore. He had played on *Animalize,* and by then Gene and Paul weren't talking to each other. So Gene had booked studio time in one studio and Paul was recording his songs at another place. Paul would call Mark to come by to record and he'd get there and Paul would be there with the producer and the engineer. Paul would tell him what to play and Mark would go into his Eddie Van Halen shit because that's how Mark played, much too busy. He'd work with Paul for six hours. Then Gene would call and have him come to his studio, where he'd work him for another six hours. Mark told me that he would have to go home and put his hands in ice because he couldn't move his fingers. When they went on tour, his hands failed him during the first show and they fired him. He went to a doctor and the doctor said that he had worn out his cartilage.

I thought working with the former guitarist of KISS would surely make Gene and Paul crazy, but it made *me* crazy. I'd go to his house to rehearse and half the time he'd have overslept. One time the door to his room was open and I found kiddie-porn magazines from Germany all over the floor. It was really sick shit. This wasn't Ace jerking off to a poster—this was way, way beyond that. When we recorded some demos with a singer we'd picked up, Mark came to my hotel room the night before at three A.M. with a cheap hooker and asked me to hold his eight ball of coke. After he left, I flushed the coke down the toilet. I was furious. It cost me thousands of dollars to pay for the demos and they were a disaster. We never came close to getting a deal.

Around the same time, I decided I wanted to write my memoir. I hooked up with some publishing company on Sunset Boulevard near A&M Studios. I told the head honcho there my tales of woe and all the crazy KISS stories and he thought it would make a great book. They kept sending ghostwriters over to my house to work with me and that was a disaster, too. So I drove down to Big Bear and got a cabin and started dictating my story. I'd give them the tapes and the writers would come back with something that had nothing to do with what I said. I'm a Brooklyn kid, I talk with a certain syntax, and these guys were just fabricating a different Peter Criss. So I dropped that idea.

By the end of the eighties, Deb and I had to downsize once again. One day Deb came to me and told me that the realtor said it was insane that we were paying so much in rent and that it would be prudent to buy something. So we put down a chunk of money and bought a brand-new townhouse in Redondo Beach.

It was spacious enough to house my pool table and all my records, and we had a nice private backyard. We had a big sundeck and a storage area that I converted into a makeshift studio. But it was Redondo Beach. It wasn't Palos Verdes, it wasn't Beverly Hills, it wasn't even Manhattan Beach, which was much more expensive.

One good thing about being in Redondo was that I got totally into biking. I had dabbled with it in Palos Verdes, but now I got serious. I bought a custom-made bike and I'd get up at four A.M. and ride along the coast from Redondo all the way to Malibu and back. I was never in better shape; my leg muscles were like steel. Riding was a great natural high and it was always fun to ride past all those beautiful California girls in their skimpy little bikinis. I'd come home really horny after a ride and jump on Deb.

I figured I'd get a band together, and Deb thought about going back to modeling, doing some catalog work. That was the plan. Deb tried to get bookings but it wasn't happening, so she started a gourmet-basket business out of our garage. She'd take imported salamis and cheeses and mustards and spruce them up in a nice basket and sell them. That should have been my tip-off that money was running out.

My relationship with Deb was as flat as my career at that point. I really loved her, but I didn't think she really loved me. Sure, she loved me when we were living in a mansion and we had money up the ass. But now she was pushing thirty and she realized the party might be over. We never had a deep relationship. We never made a spiritual connection. We never talked about our feelings. But we still were able to regularly push each other's buttons and fight. I remember we were sitting in the car one night. Nothing seemed to be going on musically for me, and she turned on the little light over the dashboard and said, "That's the last fucking spotlight you'll ever have." I was just crushed.

That only made me double my efforts to get a band together. A guitarist friend of mine put me in touch with a Canadian songwriter named Phil Naro. I got his demo and it blew my socks off. He was a great writer, and he hit the notes with the kind of clarity Steve Perry had. Phil told me that Gene and Paul were hip to him and Paul wanted to write with him. I convinced him to come down to Redondo and write with me instead. When he got there, I think he was a little bit uncomfortable with me smoking the occasional joint. He was a born-again Christian and he didn't do any drugs at all. I don't think he liked being away from his wife and newborn kid because he was calling her all the time.

But I started cracking the whip, and we wrote every day. It was like having Stan Penridge around again, but better. This guy could sing like an angel. Now I didn't have to be the lead singer. I could still do "Hard Luck Woman" and "Beth" and "Black Diamond," but he could sing the new songs we were writing.

Part of my urgency to write stuff and get the band together was thanks to a little letter we had received from the IRS. Apparently some of the tax shelters that Marks and Glickman put us in when I was with KISS were bogus, and now we were all on the line for a million dollars in back taxes. Of course I didn't have nearly enough money to pay it off, so we decided to find a tax attorney who could represent us.

Deb had met this fat woman named Maureen, whose kid went to the same school as Jenilee. Maureen's kid was a troublemaker and was always getting Jenilee into trouble. I guess the apple didn't fall far from the tree: Maureen's husband was in prison. Maureen worked at a big law firm that did a lot of environmental work, and she recommended that we go see a guy named Bob "Mac" McMurray.

We met with Mac in his office in Santa Monica. He was a typical lawyer: tall, blue eyes, dressed suave, a lot of confidence. He promised to refer us to a tax guy, and he also said he could help me with my music career.

With the IRS hanging over our heads, Deb got a job as a perfume girl at Nordstrom. The gourmet-basket business had gone to hell and she was getting nervous about our money situation. Eventually she worked her way up to salesperson, but it was still a far cry from being a lady of leisure in Darien.

As if things couldn't get any worse, I found out that my mother was sick. I flew back to New York and went with her to see her doctor the next day. After her examination, I asked if I could see the doctor in private. My mother was furious. We went into a nearby room and the doctor broke the news to me that my mother had cancer. It had started as lung cancer, but it had progressed to her bones. Now they wanted her to do chemotherapy.

I came back out shaken. On the way home, my mother gave it to me.

"You son of a bitch, what was that about? Now you're Mr. Big Shot, you've got to talk to the doctor alone and find out what's wrong with me? I know what's wrong with me—I have cancer and it's a reality and I'm not happy about it."

She had really changed. She was angry and bitter about her fate. She was only sixty-two but she had smoked Pall Malls all her life and never really followed through on follow-up visits to doctors. But now she was going to get chemotherapy, so I went back to California. I called home every so often and my sisters would tell me that Mom was doing okay, so I thought things were under control.

Then, on New Year's Day 1991, I got a call from my brother.

"You better come home, Ma's dying."

I was devastated. I hung up and called a travel agent. I had to take three planes to get to New York. I drank all the bars out on each flight and I still couldn't get drunk, I was so sick to my stomach. Did my wife come with me? No. I took these horrible flights alone, rushing home to see my mother die, because Deb came up with some excuse not to go.

I finally got into the city five hours later than scheduled. I rushed right to the house. They had an apartment at the back of their antiques store. I knocked on the door and my dad opened it. He had his head down and I walked into the room and I looked over and my mother's bed was empty. The sheets were all made up.

I sat down on the bed.

"She passed on five hours ago. There was a blue moon out and it was shining on her face through the window of her room and she looked like an angel," my dad said.

"Maybe you were blessed that you weren't here," my brother, Joey, said. "You wouldn't have recognized her." My mother was a big Irish-German woman, but she was down to sixty pounds when she died. Despite what Joey said, I was crushed that I never got that chance to say goodbye and tell her how much I loved her.

I sat on her bed and felt a huge wave of guilt wash over me. I was too late to hold her hand, too late to kiss her good-bye. Sure, I had been wrapped up in my problems with the IRS and trying to start a band and a rapidly deteriorating relationship with my wife. But now the closest person in my world was gone.

How could I have fucked up like this? I didn't have millions anymore, but I had some money. I should have rented an apartment in the neighborhood or even slept on my parents' couch so I could be there for her. It took me a couple of psychiatrists and a couple of good benders to accept the fact that I didn't fuck up. I should have, could have, would have, but it was too late. So now was I supposed to carry a cross forever? My mother would never have wanted that. She always understood me. She was always my pal.

I stayed in Brooklyn and we made all the arrangements for the funeral. I called Deb and broke the news to her and asked her if she could come out as soon as possible. She gave me some shit about something that she was doing in L.A. When I asked her to bring me a pair of my dress shoes for the funeral, she told me to buy some new ones. And when she finally came out, she was a day late.

We had a three-day wake for my mom. They were three of the worst days you'd ever want to have in your life. I was the oldest son, so I greeted all the people at the door so my dad wouldn't have to. I had to sit there all day looking at my poor mother in the casket. That was the last time that I went to an open-casket funeral.

Deb came on the second day and I felt no sympathy at all from her. It was clear that she wasn't in love with me anymore. Her hugs were fake, her tears were fake: It was all a show.

I hardly made it through the burial. I was in a state of shock the whole week. That was why it barely registered that there were reporters hanging around outside the funeral parlor. When I came in or out, they would ask me crazy questions like, "What's it like to sleep in the toilets of Santa Monica?" I just thought they were there because I had been in KISS. My father even got a call from a journalist who asked him, "Is it true that your son is a bum, sleeping in the streets?" My father went crazy and hung up on the guy.

But when I got back home, I got a very disturbing phone call from John Good, the vice-president of DW, my new drum company. They were just starting out and I was only the third drummer to sign with them, but I really liked them, and John and I had become close friends.

John sounded concerned. "Peter, are you okay?"

"I'm fucking far from being okay, John," I said.

"Well, it's all over all the tabloids," he said.

"What's all over?"

"They say you're totally broke and you're sleeping in the toilets of Santa Monica," he said.

"What are you talking about? You're on the phone with me in Redondo. I just got back from New York, where I buried my mother."

He was confused. He didn't know anything about my mother, he just knew that his office was fielding a ton of calls from fans who were concerned that I was a homeless bum in the streets of Santa Monica because they read about it in *Star* magazine, and then all the other tabloids picked the story up.

"Peter, I'm so sorry. I guess you haven't read the papers. They wrote that you had burned through all your millions and you were homeless now. I would look into it when you're feeling up to it."

I checked it right out and I was blown away. There was a photo of some bum who was claiming to be me lying in the toilets in Santa Monica, and next to it was a photo of me in my KISS makeup. I was furious. But it got worse. Tom Arnold and Roseanne Barr, who were big fans of mine, were scouring the downtown area of Los Angeles, looking for me on skid row.

Deb and I decided we had to sue the tabloid that was putting out this phony story, so we went back to Mac, the lawyer who was helping us out when the IRS got on our case. Mac said he had the perfect lawyers who would sue *Star* magazine and get us a big settlement.

While we were waiting to see the lawyers about suing the tabloids, Mac got a call from *The Phil Donahue Show.* They wanted me to come on and talk about having an imposter pose as me. Mac was convinced that it would be a good thing to show to the world that the story was bogus, so we agreed to do the program.

I had second thoughts. I looked like shit. My hair was still blond, I had put on a few pounds from drinking so much, and I was zoned out on tranquilizers because I was so out of it from losing my mom. I was literally anesthetizing myself morning, noon, and night over it. On top of that, add the IRS problem and the fact that I was getting that vibe from Deb that things weren't really copacetic with us. But Mac was putting the pressure on and Deb wanted to go because it meant first-class everything, so I agreed. I just wanted it all to go away, I was so hurt.

We got to New York and they brought us to the studio. They hid us backstage and put the imposter, a guy named Christopher Dickinson, on first. Phil was asking him how he could run around impersonating me: Didn't he have any remorse for causing me all these problems? The guy was a total alcoholic maniac and he didn't seem to care at all how any of this affected my life. To make matters worse, they had a girl and her mother who had flown this guy out to her house and let him live there for a week, thinking he was me.

Next thing you know Phil said, "Well, we have the real Peter Criss here, and we're going to bring him out now."

I came walking out, and they all looked at me in shock.

"You know, you made my life a living hell," I told the guy. "You made me sick and my mother just passed. How dare you?"

Out of nowhere the chick says that I, the real Peter Criss, screwed her. She said that she had heard that I was homeless and she flew this guy out to her house but that when he got there she realized he wasn't me. But now that I was here, she claimed that she had an affair with me.

I was ready to kill someone at this point.

"My wife is here," I said. "Can my wife stand up for a second?"

Deb stood up. She looked really classy and beautiful.

"Look at her and look at you," I said to the girl. "Do you really think that I would sleep with you after I married someone like that? You're a pig."

The audience went crazy.

Phil started taking live phone calls, and Lydia and my ex–road manager George Sewitt called and both vouched for my character. That was nice of them.

When the taping was over, I went over to Dickinson.

"Are you happy about what you did to my life, you fuck?" I said.

We were backstage in the dressing room getting ready to leave when Donahue came in.

"I feel really bad for this guy," he told me. "Why don't you and I both throw in a grand and we'll give it to him?"

"Fuck you," I told Donahue. "You want me to give him money after he made my life a living hell?"

Donahue left the room. I was infuriated. What a jerk. Later on I found out that this Dickinson guy was crazy. He was going all around L.A. impersonating me—booking time at A&M Studios, ordering limos under my name. But I couldn't even get satisfaction from outing this guy, I was in such profound pain over the loss of my mother. Everything that was said to me I heard three times. It was like I was experiencing life behind a smoky mirror.

Meanwhile we had a lawsuit to pursue. These young lawyers that Mac found for us were great. They arranged for *People* magazine to come to my house and do a photo spread to show I wasn't homeless. We did mock trials: They put together big blowups of photographs of the imposter and me side by side. They were convinced that we would kill *Star* magazine at trial. We never even got into the courtroom. We met their lawyers in the hallway and the two sides talked. My lawyers came back to where we were standing.

"They want to give you a substantial amount of money and we're out of here. Or we could go to court. It might be costly, but I think we'll win. That's why they're making such a generous offer," my lawyer said. He strongly suggested I take the money and run, so I did.

That little bit of good news was overshadowed by the news I got from

Bill Dooley, a nice engineer at the Record Plant who had felt sorry for me and given me free time when Mark St. John was running up my bill in the studio. I invited him and his wife to dinner at our house. We also had Mac, the lawyer, there because he was divorced then and it would be nice for him to have a home-cooked meal. The next day, I saw Dooley in the studio and he looked a little squeamish.

"Can I tell you something, Peter?" he said. "It's really uncomfortable, but I feel close enough to you that we can talk about it."

"What?"

"My wife says that your wife is fucking that lawyer that we had dinner with last night."

"Get the fuck out of here, Bill," I protested.

"I love you, man, and you've been through a lot with your mom and the tabloid shit, but you have to know this. My wife saw them making out in the kitchen while we all were shooting pool."

I didn't want to believe Bill, but deep down I knew he was right. I had felt those vibes for months. It certainly explained why Deb wasn't with me on that flight to see my dying mother. She was too busy back in Redondo fucking Mac.

Now that I was back in L.A., I redoubled my efforts to put together a band. I really wanted to get on the road and escape the hell that my life had turned into. It was really hard on Phil Naro to get comfortable with us and the daily arguments Deb and I were having. Plus he might as well have been a male version of "Beth," calling his wife every fifteen minutes. He stayed with us a little while longer and we wrote a beautiful song about my mother dying called "Blue Moon Over Brooklyn." The demos we did were good, and I wanted to take a band out on the road, but he freaked out. He wanted to get back to his wife and kid. I really liked Phil. He was great but it just didn't work out.

I was getting all these musicians through my friend Bob. I had met Bob when I was still living in Palos Verde. Bob sold the best fucking marijuana in the world out of his small mobile home. We became incredibly close, and Bob wound up just giving me all the pot I needed. In return, I let him hook his camper up to my electricity source. I'm sure the neighbors loved that.

Bob was a real authentic granola-loving hippie who introduced me to a Spanish guitar player named Ray Carrion, who brought in a bass player named Mark Montague. And along with Phil Naro, the first incarnation of Criss was born.

When Phil split, we replaced him with a singer named Phillip Anthony. I rented out a little rehearsal space in Redondo for twenty bucks a day and we rehearsed our asses off. All the guys had day jobs because I didn't have the money to pay them. I was riding on my fame just to convince them to join the band. When it got too rough and someone wanted to quit, Bob would bring them pot, and these guys were just pure weedheads—no coke, no pills—so that convinced them to stick around. They were all hungry to make it.

We did a couple of shows in November of 1991 at the Exposure 54 club in downtown L.A. To me it was atrocious to be back in a club, but these guys were flying on cloud nine because they were onstage with a famous person. They all bought special clothes and made their hair up all chicky and we got a great response. It was enough to make me get an agent and start touring.

But we still couldn't get a record deal. We floated the demo around to Geffen first, but they were like, "No way." Then we took it all around town but we got shot down everywhere. The record industry had jumped on the grunge bandwagon, and that wasn't my kind of music. It wasn't rock 'n' roll. None of the guys could believe that we couldn't get a deal, but it wasn't like KISS was doing so well themselves at this point. They were on the balls of their asses, losing money left and right.

Meanwhile things just seemed to be deteriorating with Deb. I still hadn't confronted her with the news I had heard about Mac. We were fighting a lot about the most trivial things. I noticed that she was a little more cynical and a little more cocky than usual. That was probably because she had a rich lawyer waiting in the wings.

So after one fight, I decided to bluff her.

"I'm going to move out and take my gold records," I told her.

"Fine, take them and go," she said. She was so cold.

We'd say shit like that and then we'd make up. But not this time. We got into another fight, and I repeated my threat. I started taking my records down off the wall, but instead of stopping me, she didn't say a word. In fact, she even took me to Hollywood and helped me pick out a place to live. So all of a sudden, we were getting separated.

"I don't want to live with you anymore," she said. And then she told me all about Mac. I can't remember the exact words, because hearing them was so devastating my brain went blank. But the gist of it was that she was seeing Mac and she wanted a divorce.

I was miserable living alone in Hollywood. My friend Bob the hippie thought that he would cheer me up by setting me up with a skinny little rug-rat blonde who had done some porno films. We talked a few times on the phone, some hot, nasty talk, and then one night I answered the phone and it was her.

"I'm downstairs in front of your place. Why don't you come down and get me?" she said.

I was lonely and I figured I'd check her out at least. She was sitting downstairs, and she actually looked pretty good. So I brought her up to the apartment. Nothing happened that night, we just talked, but I saw her another time and she came to a rehearsal. That day I took her back upstairs and we tried to get it on in bed. We used to do a thing in KISS called the reach-around. When you're making out with a girl, you stick your finger in her pussy, move it around a bit, and then, while you're still in front of her making out, you surreptitiously take a whiff of your finger. If there was no odor, she'd pass the finger test. But if she smelled funky, there was no fucking.

Well, this chick did not pass the test. She was definitely a "Whoa." So we got into bed and started fooling around and I couldn't really get it up. The whole thing was too depressing. But at one point I get semihard and I got as far as putting the head of my dick in her pussy before I freaked out about catching something from her. Later I obsessed about it and felt like my dick needed to have a year of not being touched because I went into the most unholiest hole in L.A.

A few weeks later, I took Deb and Jenilee out for dinner at Benihana. We had a few of those crazy mai tais, so Deb got a bit of a buzz on. I dropped them back at the townhouse in Redondo and I got out of my new Eddie Bauer truck to say good-bye and Deb told me to wait there, she and Jenilee just wanted to get out of their clothes. Well, Jenilee didn't return, but Deb came back in a see-through nightgown. The truck was in a carport and Deb led me to the back of it where nobody could see in and she opened her nightgown and she was naked and she grabbed me and wanted to fuck right there on the truck.

I would have, but it suddenly hit me that I had been with that rug-rat tramp a week before. The last thing I wanted to do was give Deb some disease. I did have class.

"We can't do this. We're separated," I protested, but I didn't tell her the real reason I was holding back.

"Go to hell," she said, and tightened her robe and stormed off. Then my daughter came out and said good night to me. And my shot of ever fucking Deb again was over.

Of course, I had no disease—it was all in my head. I should have thrown her over the truck and given her the fuck of the century, but I didn't.

A week after that, Deb called me and begged me to come over. I got there and I had never seen her so distraught.

"Mac broke up with me," she was crying. "He dumped me and I don't know what I'm going to do. I'm so in love with him."

I was sitting there like, Should I shoot her or just throw her through the window? My heart was breaking and she was going on about this schmuck dumping her. But as much as I was pissed off, if she would have said, "Come back to me," I would have. I was that stupid and still in love with her. Of course, a couple of weeks later they got back together.

It was only a matter of time until I got served papers. Deb's fat friend Maureen, who introduced us to Mac, came by my apartment one day with her kid and Jenilee. I opened the door and she handed me some papers.

"What's this?" I asked.

"Read it," she said, and stood there gloating. I should have punched her right in her fat fucking face.

I didn't look at the papers, but I had an idea.

"No, you've got to read them and see what they are," she said. She just wanted to see my expression.

"I'll read them later."

"No, I have to wait. Debra told me," she said.

So I pulled them out of the envelope and it said, "You are hereby served that Debra Criss is filing for a divorce . . ."

She broke out into a shit-eating grin. I just slammed the door on all three of them.

Then I sat down at my kitchen table and just stared at the papers. This was it. The end of the line. The reality just slapped me in the face. I had always harbored the fantasy that maybe Deb and I would get back together. Sometimes I'd call her mother. Betty, Deb's mom and I got along great. I really felt she loved me. She'd say, "You guys may get back together. She's seeing this guy, but who knows?"

When I got the papers, it was the death knell to that idea. I had put thirteen years of my life into that relationship and now I had nothing. It went further than the money; it was devastation. My family was now officially shattered. The white-picket-fence life was forever over. I sat down at the table at three in the afternoon just staring a hole in those papers, and when I finally looked up at the clock, it was three in the morning. I don't know where all those hours went.

While we figured out the divorce, I got to see Jenilee every weekend and on holidays and birthdays. Saturday morning was like Christmas for me. I'd wake up elated and then pick her up like clockwork and take her to Disneyland or to the park. We'd eat Chinese food and rent spooky movies and then I'd bring her back Sunday night. Driving home alone after dropping Jenilee off was pure hell. I would play sad music and cry all the way home.

By now my settlement with *Star* magazine was finalized. Out of the settlement I had to pay my lawyers and Deb's portion of the IRS bill and then hire a divorce lawyer to represent me. So I wound up with a hundred grand. Oh, and I was also supposed to give Mac a $35,000 finder's fee, but he got nothing. He was fucking my wife and I'm going to give him money too?

By then I had a booking agent and we lined up a tour of Canada. Mark the bass player, whom I nicknamed Tall Man, found us a funky bus and we were off. After a few dates I realized that Ray was driving me crazy. He was a great guitar player, but he was one of those Spanish guys who would preen around with his hair in a net, totally in love with himself. He thought he was running the band, so Mark and I decided it was time for him to go. I like Ray but he just got crazy.

By 1993 I scored a record deal with TNT records, a small label out of L.A. By then the band was me and Mark from the original lineup and a new singer named Mike Stone and a guitar player named Kirk Miller. We had four good original songs and a nice new version of "Beth," so I convinced the label to put out an EP that would only be available to KISS fans. I figured this was a way to say to the fans, "I'm back and I love you and only you the KISS fans can get this—this ain't for the public." It was a way to promote the upcoming CD, and we got a great response.

With the band I was trying to get my mind off the breakup of my marriage, but it didn't really work out that way. When I was on the road I'd desperately miss Jenilee and then all my mixed emotions about Deb would surface. In fact, I hadn't really had another woman since that disastrous encounter with the rug rat. But one night while I was on tour in Canada, I met this chick who was nothing like the type of woman I had ever been with. Her name was Maggie and she was short and heavy with big tits, a big ass, and piano legs, cute but a lot less attractive than most of the women I'd been with. She was only twenty-one, but her sexual experience belied both her years and her appearance.

She came backstage one night and we were making out and I just thought there was something sensuous about this young farm girl with glasses. That night we went back to my hotel and I learned that you can't judge a book by its cover. She was an absolute perfect ten in bed. She was unbelievable. We fucked all night long and—Eureka!—the Spoiler was back. I got on the bus the next morning and I was grinning like a Cheshire cat.

"Good morning, gentlemen," I said.

I'm never like that: I'm a nasty bastard in the morning. But I felt good again. I had finally gotten laid after a year, and it felt great. Maggie made me appreciate sex again.

She showed up at the next venue and the show after that and it was great. Eventually we left Canada and we would call each other on the phone and have hot phone sex. On a hiatus from the tour, she invited me up to her parents' place in Canada. It was summertime, they had a big house on a lake, and I met her parents and I liked them. Canadians are pretty crazy. We just spent the whole day screwing—screwing in the guest-house and screwing in the canoe. This girl couldn't screw enough: She was twenty-one! I was going through a midlife crisis so I wasn't complaining.

Before I knew it, I was asking this young girl to move into my apartment in Hollywood. It wasn't easy. We had to clear a lot of hurdles with immigration, but I moved her in. In retrospect, I probably should have had my head examined for doing this. I liked her at first because she was open and bubbly and wild and I was really, really lonely. But after a few months, whatever we had going on on the road or at that cabin or in that canoe wasn't there anymore. Every night she just wanted sex, sex, sex, sex, and after a while I got burnt out on it. We had nothing else in common; our age difference was too great.

I started going crazy, and I told her that she had to move back home.

"What?"

"You gotta go back. I'll pay for everything, but you gotta get on a plane and go home. I don't want to be with you anymore."

It was horrifying. She cried all the way to the airport, she was hanging on me screaming going through the terminal, and she cried while she was getting on the plane. I felt bad, she was always nice to me, but I just couldn't take living with her any longer.

I was alone again in my shitty little apartment in Hollywood. I briefly had a new girlfriend, but she paled in comparison to my ex. I had hit the road again, but I was playing small clubs instead of huge stadiums. I still hadn't fully gotten over the loss of my mom three years earlier, and my father didn't seem to have the will to continue without his life mate. It was truly the worst of times. And then I felt the tremors and the walls came tumbling down.

CHAPTER SIXTEEN

I *woke up the day after the earthquake in a much better place. I was* in the middle of recording the Criss album, and I did have a record deal and a great bunch of guys who loved me. It's not like I had nothing. That day, I had an appointment for my yearly checkup with my doctor, Terry Hammer, who was also a close friend: I always loved seeing him. He's such a giving human being. I got in my rental car and had to take the local streets to Torrance because the town was a mess and a lot of sections of highway had collapsed.

We talked a little bit about the earthquake, and then I confessed to him how close I had come to committing suicide.

"Really?" he said, concerned. "I think I should give you something for depression. You've been through a lot, Peter. Your mom dying, your marriage dissolving, the earthquake . . ."

"Don't worry," I said. "The thoughts are gone. I'll be fine."

"All right, but call me if you need me," he said. "I'm always here, and I love you."

I went back to the car for the ride back to Hollywood. Before I took off, I checked the trunk of the car. I'd brought the bag with my hundred thousand in cash because I didn't want to leave it back at the apartment. I had heard there was a lot of looting going on post-earthquake. I also had the .357 in the bag, along with a .38. And, just to be safe, I was carrying a tiny .25 automatic in my money pocket. You couldn't be too careful amidst all this chaos. Hey, I was a street kid.

On the way back I got detoured and wound up in a shady part of Venice. I pulled up to a stop sign and there was a six-foot-four-inch black guy who looked really fucked up in the crosswalk. He was taking his sweet time to walk in front of me and I got pissed. I was ready to run him over. When he just about made it past the car, he hit the side of the hood with his fist.

I gave him the finger.

I looked down for a second, and the next thing I knew it felt like my head had shattered. This guy came around to my open window and punched me right in my orbital bone, shattering my cheekbone and part of my jaw. It helped that he was wearing big brass knuckles.

I had never been hit that hard in my life. Not only did I see lights, I saw explosives. I slumped over, I was in another world. Now this guy had the door open and he was tugging at me, trying to get me out of the car. Thank God my seat belt had jammed. I had sort of come around and I saw that he'd gotten frustrated and was walking away.

That's when I thought, "Shoot the motherfucker. Take the .25 and go behind him and shoot him in the head. You won't get arrested. He hit you with brass knuckles, he tried to rob you, you're famous, and you shot him in self-defense."

"But you don't just shoot someone in the back of the head," another part of me argued.

"You were in shock. Any good lawyer can get you off that. Just show the jury your injuries."

I wasn't really rational at this point, but I finally realized that the last thing I needed to do was kill someone. I was bleeding profusely, and the best thing to do was to get home. I got to the apartment and gingerly walked through the rubble to the bathroom. The mirror had shattered, but there was a big enough piece of it to check out the injury.

"Holy fucking shit," I gasped. My face looked as if it had been run over by a truck.

I got really dizzy and I went into the bedroom and fell on the mattress that was on the floor, and passed out. The next morning, I woke up in excruciating pain. I looked down at the mattress and it was literally soaked in blood. I called Michael, my new guitar player, and he came right over. He took one look at me and turned pink, purple, and blue.

"Catman, you're really fucked up," he said. He rushed me down to the car and we drove back to my doctor friend Terry's office.

Terry walked into the room and his face hit the floor.

"Peter, are you all right?"

Before I could even answer, Terry was ordering X-rays and making plans to contact a surgeon.

Just my luck: Dr. Lowe was down the hall, one of the best reconstructive surgeons in L.A. Terry called him and he came in and he took one look and said, "We've got to operate now. I'll call the hospital to have him admitted."

They rushed me into surgery and I was in there for five hours. It was a very painful procedure. They had to go through my mouth to reconstruct the cheekbone. This doctor was pretty rough, and he didn't have the best bedside manner. One thing I learned: Your bones are not meant to be held together by screws. One whole side of my face had this scaffolding device, so I couldn't really move my head. I was in so much pain the whole time I was in the hospital that I kept pressing that button for dope nonstop. I think my morphine bill alone came to ten grand.

I was so excited the day that Deb and my daughter came to visit me. I was still in love with my ex-wife. But she came in and she was as cold as ice. She just stared at me.

"How are you feeling? Are they taking care of you?" she asked in a real off-hand manner.

I could hardly talk because my jaw was wired and my face was all bandaged. But I could feel the iciness filling the room. I could understand that my daughter might be in shock to see her dad fucked up like that, but Deb's aloofness was just reprehensible.

When they left, the room just filled with loneliness. I was lying there wishing that she would just die—that on the way home she'd crash the car and my kid would survive, but she'd be killed. I would never have treated a dog the way she treated me in that hospital room.

When my doctor friend Terry came in that night to check on me, I was beside myself.

"I can't believe she just came here and walked out and she ain't coming back, she told me that," I wailed. "I don't even know if I want to get better." To add insult to injury, Terry confessed that it was his idea for Deb to visit me.

I really felt like I didn't want to live. I just lay there in that bed crying, thinking, How could people be like that? This was a woman whom I had put up on a pedestal, bought her anything she ever wanted. And now my doctor was showing me more love than my ex-wife.

I felt like the world had forgotten Peter Criss, that I was just another casualty of the wars of L.A. after the earthquake. As much of a cocksucker as I may have been in the past toward other people, I could never have pulled off something as heartless and selfish as Deb had. I knew that if it had been Deb in that hospital bed, I would have visited every day even if I didn't love her anymore. The Catholic in me would been there with flowers. She was still the mother of my daughter, and that connection would never fade. But for her to leave me there in that bed like a wounded animal and not show an ounce of compassion was heartbreaking. That was the worst pain someone could experience, much worse than the violence that had put me in the hospital. It was a pain that I carry even today. And I can never forgive her for that. I could forgive her for fucking around behind my back, but this was deeper to me than cheating. I just couldn't comprehend how the mother of my child could be that callous and cold to me.

But my band members dropped by often, and Terry came in every day to check on me. I finally got released and they brought me out in a wheelchair and Michael came to pick me up and he was horrified. My whole face was bandaged up and my eye was sagging off to one side. I looked like a mummy. That day I nicknamed him Angel because he and Tall Man were the only ones who really took care of me. They put my bed back together and cooked me meals, whatever I could eat with a straw. Tall Man even slept on the floor beside my bed because we were still getting some aftershocks.

I had to keep going back for follow-ups to make sure the screws were in place and that I hadn't developed an infection. But I had an album to finish, and the record company kept calling me to see when it would be done. All that was needed to complete the album were my vocals, so I bit the bullet, so to speak, and went back in the studio. I carefully removed the wiring from my jaw, popped a bunch of painkillers and swigged them down with some scotch, and went in and sang. I thought I was being noble and strong and showing the band some real leadership, but I'd go home and cry all night from the pain. When I'd go back to the doctor, he'd explode, "Why are these screws moving? You can't sing right now." But I did. To this day, I still get pain in my face.

When I recovered, the guys urged me to go back out on the road. They were so uplifting and so great to be around. There wasn't the constant game playing that went on with Gene and Paul. These kids adored me; they looked up to me. I was the old-timer, and everything I said was gold. I thank God to this day that they were around at this time when I was getting beat up from all angles.

Deb let me slide on the child-support payments until I had healed. The IRS wasn't so compassionate. Every so often I'd get another bill, and it seemed that the amount I owed was doubling. Not that I could pay anything anyway. Or even knew how to. I had been married most of my life and I always had my wives or people like Chris Lendt taking care of things. So I never even knew what to do with a bill. When I moved into my apartment, I started getting gas and electric bills. I called Tall Man.

"What the fuck is this?"

"Those are bills, dude," he explained. He literally took me to a bank and opened up a checking account for me and showed me how to make out the checks and keep a record of them. I was forty-seven years old and learning how to write a fucking check. When you're living in that fame bubble, you don't have to worry about anything but playing. It took me a long time to adjust to real life.

Now I had to go out looking like a mummy, and it wasn't pleasant. The last thing I expected was to find a girlfriend in this state, but somehow I did. On the ground floor of my building there was a big health-food store with spectacular food, and being a bachelor and recovering from my surgery I wanted to eat right and regain my strength for the tour.

I was shopping there one night and I saw a cute little redhead approaching me in the aisle. She was in her thirties and she was wearing a white shirt and black tie like waitresses wear, and that impressed me. We started talking and she didn't seem to be at all taken aback by the bandages on my face, which impressed me even more. She had a majorly cool personality and we started talking about food and she told me she worked at a Japanese restaurant.

I got her phone number, I called her, and we went out for some high-end Chinese food on Beverly Boulevard and we had a great time. The next time Lynn and I went out, I brought her back to my apartment and one thing led to another and we screwed all night. She was really hot and she had nice perky natural boobs, which you don't often see in L.A. Lynn was a real exotic knockout, a half-Swedish, half-Hawaiian mix. I was not the most handsome man at that point, especially with my eye hanging down like Igor's, but that didn't seem to bother her. I was just beat up in general—from my divorce, from the loss of my fortune, from all the drugs I had taken—and here was this girl who looked right past that, so I was truly grateful.

The Criss album, *Cat #1,* came out in August of 1994. I learned first-hand what it was like to be on a chintzy label like TNT. They had no real distribution, so when Tall Man and I went to their office in the Valley, I saw boxes and boxes of the record stacked up in a supply room.

"What's going on with the record?" I'd ask.

"Oh, it's going good. We got orders," they'd say.

But there were no promo people pushing it, nobody out there hawking it. One day they got the bright idea that if I did a bunch of interviews, it would sell some discs. So I sat there from nine in the morning until ten at night, doing the same interview over and over again. It didn't make an impact. I was furious that I had signed such a bad deal. My only hope was to hit the road, play in a city, do an in-store signing, and move some records.

Meanwhile, my relationship with Lynn was blossoming. We were seeing each other every weekend and I suggested that we move in together. But I was over Hollywood by then and I told her that I wanted to live near the ocean. She suggested Venice Beach, one of the coolest spots in L.A.

There were bodybuilders there, hippies, skateboarders, beautiful chicks walking by all day half naked. What's not to like?

We found an adorable pink beach house with a big living room, a decent-sized bedroom, and a guest room. It had wood floors and a fireplace and the rent was reasonable, especially since we were going to split it. I was sick of being taken to the cleaners by women. I wanted her to feel that she had to contribute something if we were going to be in a relationship.

Things started out okay. We'd bicycle on the promenade every day until the sun would go down, and then we'd have a margarita at a local joint. It was a really cool life for a while. Then one day she told me that she had lost her job at the Japanese restaurant.

"I'm actually a topless dancer now," she said. I didn't know it then but she always had been.

"I don't really give a shit. I love you—whatever you do is cool with me," I said. But it really wasn't. I settled for it at first. She would get home at three in the morning and I had to get up and rehearse all day with the band for our tour.

I had done a few tours with the band, or at least with Tall Man, who was the only original member left. Those early tours had been brutal. We had a shitty beat-up bus and I'd curse from the first day I got on it. But the guys loved it—they didn't know any better. There were a few nice moments. On our second tour we were driving through Yellowstone in a blizzard on a two-lane melt-top road, and when we got down to the valley floor, a herd of buffalo started running alongside the bus. We opened the door and you could literally touch them, they were so close.

My Smith & Wesson .45 came out a lot on those early tours. Tall Man would open the curtain on his bunk a little bit and he'd see me waving it around. I think I busted a few caps into the pool in Lake Tahoe. Hey, it was boring on the road.

We didn't really know what we were doing those first tours. Hippie Bob was the road manager, and he was in charge of the merch. We found out that he had brought only one box of T-shirts on the tour, and that was the only way we made our extra money, since we didn't have any albums yet back then. He sold out the T-shirts the first night, and that was that. But he did keep the guys in righteous weed. We all made it clear that if there wasn't top-of-the-line smoke, we weren't going out. Bob came through and delivered a nice little package to each guy on the bus.

I had Tall Man handle all the business. He'd get all the shit straightened out and then he'd present me with the options and I'd make the final decision. For doing that, I gave him a percentage of the profits. The agents, the manager, the record company told me I was out of my mind and that I should just pay him one twenty-five per show like the other guys got, but that didn't seem fair. He was taking on a lot of responsibility and he deserved to be rewarded for that.

For the new tour, he found us a great Silver Eagle bus. They were the original rock 'n' roll buses; this one probably had a million miles on it, but it was dynamite inside. It slept twelve and there was a game room in the back with lounge chairs and a big television in the middle. Each bunk had nice curtains and a small TV. There was a nice-sized kitchen and a bathroom. I didn't know how we could afford it, but the guys decided they would rather go in comfort and be safe than have a bigger paycheck.

This was the tour that the Captain emerged. The first day, I walked onto the bus wearing a navy officer's blue coat with the hash marks and gold stripes, and I had on an officer's overcoat with the stars and epaulets. On top of my head was a white admiral's hat with the navy emblem. I looked like a white Michael Jackson. Our bus was going to be called the Enterprise, and I was going to run it like Captain Kirk. Mark, the Tall Man, was my Number One. Angel was Number Two. Whoever was the vocalist, and they changed often, was Number Three.

The driver even got into it.

"Are we ready for warp speed, Captain?" he'd yell back.

"Absolutely, let's leave this shithole," I'd say, and we'd take off.

"Everybody in their quarters?" I'd ask.

"Yes, Captain," I'd hear them all answer.

A lot of that was just bravado to hide my pain. I was still hurting and angry. I was missing Deb: I really loved her still, even though she had run off with my lawyer, and I loved my daughter deeply and I never got to see her enough. The IRS was still up my ass and I was in a band that was playing shitty little bars with pool tables and drunks shouting throughout the whole show, and then I was going to my tiny room at a Motel 6.

Some nights I'd go to the back room on the bus and lock the door, which meant no video games for the boys. I was amazed by how much beer I could drink and not get drunk, I was so depressed. I'd put on the Eagles' "Desperado" and play it over and over and over. Then that feeling of doom would come over me and I'd obsess over what I had lost, especially Jenilee. The pain from the screws would start in my face, and many nights I cried myself to sleep, my face in the pillow so the guys wouldn't hear me like that.

Sometime during that tour in 1995, I got the news that my dad had died. I'm certain it was from a broken heart. He had actually given up on life after my mother passed on in 1991. He was just lost without her. Even though my sisters took care of him, he didn't care about eating or washing or getting out. I had gone to see him before the tour and I stayed with him for two weeks. He had been having some episodes of pleurisy that required constant monitoring and routine treatment, but he just wouldn't cooperate with the doctors. It killed me inside to see him like that. I felt so bad for him. He was such a strong man in his heyday.

Tall Man and I took a plane to New York and made it to the funeral. This was the horror trifecta. My mom had died in '91, my favorite uncle George died two years later, and two years after that, my dad was gone. I went back to the tour and I stayed drunk for a week.

I realized how much I had missed my father and how much I wished we could have communicated better. I was a cocky kid and I would visit them with the Mercedes and the hot blonde, acting like a big shot. I wouldn't do that now. Over the years I began to understand his frustration, his own private suffering. He was totally dependent on my mother, and I think he felt guilty for that. So when she died, he lost the will to live.

Being on that bus with a bunch of kids who had such heart and spirit was what got me through those grueling twelve-hour drives. I saw myself in them, the same gleam in the eye we all had at the beginning of KISS. They were so thrilled to be a part of rock 'n' roll, even at this level. Angel had family in St. Louis, and when we got there, they all came to the show and were so proud of him. He showed off the bus to his parents. I just fed off their youth and their positive outlook and their energy and their joy to be playing with me. That got me through the darkest hours.

I did have my idiosyncrasies, though. I could never really sleep on the·
bus. It was hard for me to sleep anywhere, but I hated sleeping on the bus,
especially after I heard that Gloria Estefan and her group had that horrible
accident when the bus driver fell asleep. I'd think of that and I'd be in my
berth with my eyes wide open, staring at the ceiling all night. Sometimes
I'd get some coffee and sit up front and bullshit with the driver all night.
About an hour before we got into a town, I'd call Tall Man to my quarters.

"Tall Man, just get me to my room at the hotel and then come back
right before showtime. You do the sound check, have my tech sit on the
drums. I don't want to see the place before I have to."

Then I slept for a few hours. Around six the road manager would
knock on my door and bring me food, usually some tacos that tasted like
chicken marinated in sweaty gym socks. I was a picky eater.

"What the fuck is this?" I'd ask the road manager.

"It's a burrito, Captain."

"Do I look like a guy who would eat a burrito?" I'd throw it at the wall
and make him go back and get something else.

Then Tall Man would come in with the scouting report.

"So how's the club?" I'd ask.

"It's not so bad, Captain," he'd fudge.

"How many people are there now?"

"About fifty. But they expect it to be packed at showtime."

"What's the capacity?"

"Two hundred fifty."

"That's about how many people I used to take out partying after a
KISS show," I'd lament. "Tall Man, I can't do this."

"Come on, Captain, we can do it."

So I'd have him get a couple of Rolling Rocks and I'd get ready. I'd put
on some tight jeans with glitter and snakes down the sides and I'd pick
out a killer shirt and vest and a nice scarf. I'd punk my hair up and put on
some eyeliner and good old Number 15, a makeup from the old vaudeville
days that gave you the best complexion a man could have. Then I'd put
a little rouge on my lips and some on my cheeks. I'd look in the mirror,
down another beer, and we'd get back on the bus.

We'd pull up to the dump and they'd always have big banners advertising Budweiser or Jack Daniel's alongside old posters of bands that once played there. There'd be tons of vehicles parked in the lot, mostly pickup trucks. I'd walk in the back entrance and make my way through the kitchen and I'd hear the noise get louder and louder and then we'd enter the main room and take the stage.

I didn't even want to look at the people in the audience, so I'd walk in with my head down, wearing big, round, dark glasses. I'd get behind the drums and when I finally raised my head and looked out, I'd see a sea of KISS fans. And they'd all demand to hear KISS songs. But we played all originals for most of the set until the end, when we'd all come out to the front of the stage with acoustic instruments. I had a really cool percussive box that I'd play. We'd do "Hard Luck Woman," "Nothing to Lose," "Strange Ways," and then we'd end with "Beth." We'd win them over and they'd cheer for an encore.

One night we were playing someplace in Quebec, and when we started into "Beth" there was a wave of energy from the crowd that almost knocked us on our asses. We finished late that night, there was a blizzard, and we had a ten-hour drive back to New Jersey, so we walked right off the stage and onto the bus. It was like, "Let's get out of here, no autographs." But that crowd came out of the club, surrounded the bus, and started rocking it back and forth. "You think you're leaving? You're not going anywhere," they seemed to be saying, so we stayed for a while and signed all their stuff.

We played some great places too. In New York, we did a show at the Limelight, which was an old converted church. We tore the roof down and got great write-ups in the newspapers. But then there were places like the Sandbox. We were wondering about that name when we pulled into Wheeling, West Virginia. I was dropped off at the hotel and slept and ate my meal. Now it was time for Tall Man to report.

"How's the place?" I asked.

"I can't tell you or you won't go. You'll get right back on the bus and drive to the next gig."

I was still wondering about the name when I entered the club through the kitchen. I couldn't believe my eyes. The club was literally a sandbox. They had filled the entire floor with sand and they had tacky paintings of palm trees and the sun on the wall. The stage was made out of plywood and it was so wobbly that Tall Man got hit in the face by his own microphone. After the second number, everyone was up and dancing. The sand and dust was kicked up and permeated the air. I wanted to throw my sticks down and leave. Talk about being humiliated, about feeling like a piece of shit after you'd been in the one of the biggest bands in the world? Now you're playing the Sandbox. And the next gig was at a place called Uncle Tom's Cabin. I was miserable.

Which often times led to what we called the Greyhound Treatment. The Greyhound Treatment was usually reserved for incompetent road managers, sometimes sound guys. We'd instruct the bus driver to find the nearest Greyhound station, have the guy pack his bags, and we'd pull up, open the doors, out he'd go, the doors would close, and we'd move on.

One guy who got Greyhounded was a tour manager with a shaved head whom we nicknamed Fester. We were staying at a hotel in the Midwest that had balconies. I was upstairs and the guys were beneath me. We had finished the gig, there was no food, and I was starved.

"Where's the fucking food?" I yelled down off my balcony at Fester. "Food and sleep. Food and sleep, that's all we want."

It was about two in the morning and Fester went out to get some food. He came back at four and reported to Number One. He had scrounged up two microwave TV dinners.

"You're really going to take that upstairs, man? Are you serious?" Tall Man warned Fester.

Fester brought it up to me, and the next thing Tall Man saw was two microwave TV dinners Frisbeed off my balcony. Fester was on the Greyhound the next morning.

When we toured for *Cat #1,* our lead singer was Mike Stone. He was a great singer. He wore a cool mohawk and always had a cigarette hanging out of his mouth. But he left for a deal that fell through and then he hooked up with Queensryche.

We replaced Stoney with a singer-guitarist named Jason Ebbs. He got the job because we needed to go out and there was nobody else around. Jason would play and sing out of tune, but he was a good-looking guy with dreads, a real chick magnet, so we hired him. One night Jason played the entire set out of key. I kept telling him to check his tuning, but with each song it got worse and worse. When the set was over, he was standing near the stage talking to some chicks and I walked over and hit him in the back of the head.

"You will never play out of tune onstage with me again," I screamed. "You're fired."

We got on the bus that night and there was stone silence. Everybody was tiptoeing around because I had turned into this monster. One by one, the guys came up to me and told me I was being hard on Jason. They were right. I have a big heart, so I kept him on. He never played out of tune again.

There were always groupies around, but I let the boys have them. I really wasn't too sexual at this point. When I was out on the road right after my split with Deb, I hated all women. I had a hard and fast rule: No women on the bus. But sometimes I'd loosen up. After every gig, the girls would line up alongside the bus. Once in a while, I'd pick out about ten of them and bring them onboard. They'd be sitting there giggling and Tall Man would break out the beers and the girls would all get fucked up.

Then we'd say, "We're pulling out tonight for a ten-hour drive. You could come, but I don't know how you'll find your way back." And they'd say they wanted to go, thinking that they were going to have a good time with me. We'd sit there and I'd be grabbing their titties and biting them on the neck and making out with a few of them and getting them all crazy, and then I'd say, "I'm going to bed. I've had it." The girls would be in shock, but then the boys would jump on them. Tall Man was tall and thin, with beautiful blue eyes and long dark hair. Angel was like Robert Plant, with big blond curls and the face of an angel. Our lead singer was always good-looking. So I'd lie back there and hear them fucking all night.

When we were staying in hotels, it was a different story. Tall Man would grab a stack of business cards from the hotel where we were staying and he'd hand them out at the gigs to the best-looking girls. Then I'd make my appearance in my Captain's hat and the girls would all go, "Oooh." Then I'd play around for a while, but I'd go back to my room alone.

We were on hiatus at the beginning of the summer of 1995 when I heard that KISS was doing a convention tour and they were going to be in L.A. For years, fans had been organizing unofficial KISS conventions where they'd meet and sell their KISS collectibles. After a while, Gene and Paul decided that they should be making all that money, so they organized a KISS Konvention tour. For a hundred-dollar admission fee, a fan would get a laminated pass and access to the booths that were selling all the KISS merch. Of course, Gene and Paul would get a cut out of anything sold there. There would also be a two-hour appearance where the band would take requests and play songs and answer questions from the fans. Right away, I realized that the band couldn't be doing well if they had to co-opt the fans' gatherings. Gene and Paul decided to remake all their merch and sell it again. They even had their road manager call me and ask if they could sell Peter Criss drumsticks. I wound up ordering five thousand pairs of drumsticks, and they sold like hotcakes. I was getting checks for a few thousand dollars every month from the conventions. I thought, If I'm making a few thousand on some drumsticks, what are they making?

There was going to be a convention in L.A. on June 17, and I wanted to take Jenilee so she could get a better appreciation for what her dad had done. I asked a journalist to get me in, and he had called Gene, who promptly called me.

"Peter, you don't have to ask somebody else, you're part of the band's history. This should be your place, too. We'll send a limo to pick you up. You'll be treated like a king, because you are. Whatever you want is yours. Why don't we have lunch tomorrow at the Sunset Marquis and discuss it?" Gene could really bullshit you.

I had just come off a Criss tour and I was playing really well and my voice was great. I'd just bought a Mitsubishi 3000 and I was living in Venice with Lynn. I felt good about myself for a change. So I pulled up to the hotel and Paulie was standing there in his leather pants and tight velvet shirt, opened to the waist, and cowboy boots. I think he wanted me to see how good he looked right off the bat.

He was kind of surprised to see me driving such a cool new car, but we exchanged pleasantries and walked into the hotel. Gene ran up to me all dramatic, as if he'd missed me all his life. He picked me up, held me in the air, and hugged me. I was thinking, Fucking bastard, I'd like to stick a knife right in the fucking side of his neck—because I still didn't like them, and I thought they were up to something as they always were.

We ordered lunch and began catching up.

"We think you should sing at the convention," Gene said. "We'll have a great time. And we're actually rehearsing in an hour right around the corner. Why don't you come over?"

Okay, so they wanted to test me. I went along with it. We got to the hall and I said hello to Bruce Kulick and Eric Singer, the latest replacements for Ace and me. Immediately Gene told me that the whole idea of me singing was Eric's. I didn't say anything, but I knew it was bullshit. Eric might have come up with the idea, but knowing them they put it in his head. They're trying to make this schlep look like a hero. Eric started sucking my ass and telling me how much he liked the way I sang, especially on "Hard Luck Woman."

"You want to sing it now?" Gene said.

"No, I forgot the lyrics," I lied.

"We have them right here," one of them said, and sure enough there was a music stand with the lyrics set up on it. They were going all out to see if I could still sing. I had been singing that song with Criss, so I sang the shit out of it and they were blown away.

I drove back thinking, What the fuck was that all about? Then I called Tall Man. "Watch out, Captain, they got a trap for you," he said. "You're going into uncharted territory and those are fucking Vulcans, man."

"I'm well aware of that, Number One," I answered.

We went to the Hilton the day of the convention and it was mobbed because word had gotten out that I was going to be there. I knew that Jenilee didn't understand the extent of my fame, so the minute we arrived in that limo and were met by bodyguards and screaming fans trying to get at me, she was literally in shock. We went up to our room and Paulie came up and introduced me to his then-wife Pam and their newborn baby. The baby was beautiful.

"Wow, you got a kid. Whoever would have thought," I said. It looked like Paul had settled down. He was a family man now, and I liked it. And Gene was now with Shannon Tweed and they had a couple of kids, so I got a good family vibe off this whole thing. Yeah, right.

I went down and peeked out from behind the curtains and the place was packed. I heard Paul address the crowd. "Remember earlier we were saying that without the four original guys, we would never be here today? We were talking about Peter and Ace. Well, I thought it might be something special, something you really deserve. You deserve this and it's gonna be a kick for us. We told Peter to come out and sing a couple of songs with us." And he started a "Pe-ter!" chant. And he goes, "Peter Criss!" and the place exploded. They were crazier than my audiences on the road. I wanted to scoop them up and take them all down to the Sandbox. They never sat down.

When I walked up on that stage and the whole place went absolutely crazy, I felt so good. I looked at Jenilee standing off to the side and she looked so proud of me. I felt like a million bucks, and I just wanted to sing the best I ever did. Gene and Paul probably thought that I would be doing it to impress them, but I was really doing it for my kid.

I hugged Paul and Bruce and then sat down next to Gene to share his microphone.

"You know, originally Peter just wanted to come by and be with you and us. It was actually Eric Singer who said, 'Why don't we get together and play?'" Gene had to get that bullshit in. We went into "Hard Luck Woman" and the place went crazy. I couldn't believe that my daughter was standing to the side seeing all these people screaming for me. It was a real golden moment. We finished the song and I high-fived everyone. I looked over at Gene and he was smiling from ear to ear. I could hear the cash register in his head going *Ca-ching, ca-ching, ca-ching.*

"You wanna hear more? What do you wanna hear?" Gene said. There were a million requests, but we went into "Nothing to Lose." We did a killer version, and then I waved good-bye to the crowd. Paul ran up and put a leather motorcycle jacket on my shoulders. They were selling it there. On the back it said KISS ARMY, and there was a logo of a hand giving the finger. Paul wrapping the jacket around me and giving me a big hug, it just felt like the whole thing was scripted. They knew exactly what they were doing. They always did.

Backstage everyone was hugging me, and Jenilee was blown away. Later I took some questions from the audience and managed to plug my upcoming tour with Ace. Then I went back upstairs and said good-bye to everyone. It had been a special day.

I was about to get together with Ace again. George Sewitt, our old road manager, was now managing Ace and had gotten in touch with us to persuade us to join up with Ace for a tour of Canada. He wanted to call it the Bad Boys Tour, but I wasn't really a bad boy anymore. Still, it meant playing at bigger venues and making more money, so I agreed to do it.

We had trouble right off the bat. Ace refused to open for us, so we went on first. But then we were supposed to come back on after three songs and do three songs together. That first night, Ace was on the sixth song and they hadn't called us up. Tall Man went ballistic on Sewitt's ass. He was screaming at Sewitt and I was standing behind him smiling and saying, "Look what you get, George." From then on, we came on after Ace's third song and did "Hard Luck Woman," "Strange Ways," and then ended with "Rock and Roll All Nite." I hated that idea. Why were we doing Gene and Paul's fucking song? We were that hard up for applause? But Sewitt was smart. Eighty percent of Ace's set was KISS songs. That's what the audience was really there for. We did all originals, so we didn't get the same response.

For the most part, we were playing much better venues. But we did one show in Oklahoma where only ten people showed up. Ace played for three hours that night, almost twenty minutes for each person in the audience.

It was great to be back on the same stage with Ace again, after we'd been through so much together, but I got scared because he seemed to be getting worse with his antics of drinking and drugging. Ace could get away with anything because his band idolized him the way mine idolized me. The audience never knew it, but his roadies would fill up a six-pack of Coke cans with rum and he'd get drunk every night onstage. By the time we did our encores, he could barely see me.

Over the years that Ace and I were touring, both apart and together, we had heard that Gene and Paul would often send spies down to our shows to report back on how we were doing. Sometimes they would actually tell us that Gene and Paul had sent them. I figured they were just interested in seeing if Ace and I were still fucked up so they could gloat. But I think they were really planning a reunion years ahead of our actual reunion.

Why shouldn't they? KISS wasn't exactly on a roll after Ace and I left the group. Between 1979 and 1982, KISS record sales dropped 75 percent. When Gene started dating Hollywood stars, he began thinking he should be a movie star, too. Of course, he wasn't a handsome man, so there was no way he was going to be a leading man. He wound up doing a couple of movies where he was cast as the heavy. You had to strap his fucking head down to contain his ego. He wasn't the sweet Gene, and even the Monster was gone. He just became an egotistical Hollywood madman. He started managing Yvonne De Carlo and he told me that he fucked her. A sixty-three-year-old woman. Then he started a record company, and that failed. He founded a company to book bands, and that failed. Yet in his mind he was the World's Greatest Entrepreneur.

The years that Ace and I were out of the band were easily KISS's leanest years. David, their hairdresser, later told me it got so bad that one night they played for five hundred people! Paul would joke, "Why don't we order two pizzas for the audience?"

When they took off their makeup, Gene was totally lost. They became a hair band, and one thing that hair bands had was young, good-looking guys in them. These guys weren't young anymore. Gene just didn't know how to behave onstage without the Demon persona. Like an old fighter, Gene never shook the habit of stalking the stage, but now when he would stick his tongue out, people would just laugh. It was sad, like watching Godzilla die. Then he started wearing loud, androgynous clothes, but he looked like a football player in a tutu.

Paul was delighted, though. He could come out with pink feathers around his neck. He'd wear skintight pants and orange wristbands and he'd have all these bangles going up his arms in every fucking color in the world. He looked like an old drag queen.

By 1983 KISS fell millions into debt with their record company. They had to sell off land that they owned in Cincinnati. By 1988 they decided to scapegoat Howard Marks and Carl Glickman and they fired them along with Chris Lendt. Eventually they hired Dr. Jesse Hilsen, Paul's shrink, to manage the group. He was a real doozy. Paul Marshall, our lawyer, said that Hilsen used to call up the business office and threaten to let Paul go crazy unless he got paid. Now Hilsen was in charge. He rented a penthouse suite and hired a full staff and began spending money left and right. He didn't last long before he fled the country.

In a way, I was glad they were going through such hard times. I wanted them to learn a life lesson—that they were not the geniuses who created this band, that the success didn't flow only from them but also from me and Ace and Bill and Sean and Chris and all those people who were now gone or fired. If they were so smart, why had they hired a charlatan psychiatrist to run their business affairs?

Gene and Paul invited both Ace and me to do a convention stop in New York City. Neither of us could do it, but then George Sewitt told us that KISS was offered a chance to do *MTV Unplugged,* and they wanted us to do a few songs together. Ace and I immediately told George to tell them to fuck off, but George was persistent.

"This is fucking huge. I don't know if you two guys understand," he told us. "You guys haven't been together in seventeen years. You've got to do this, it's going to help the tour, it's going to help record sales."

Lynn and I flew first-class to New York. I went to rehearsal the next day to make sure my DW drums were set up properly, and the first thing I saw were cameras everywhere. They were documenting everything on video without Ace's and my permission. I walked in and Gene went, "Hey, Peter Criscuola likes Coca-Cola. How you doing?" Then Paul and Eric came over and everyone was hugging and kissing and everything was love and peace and all that bullshit. Of course, Ace came in an hour late. "Aceleh, Aceleh, Aceleh!" they said, and now Ace was getting the love treatment. The whole thing was weird. It just seemed like something underhanded was going on.

Each day the rehearsals got harder, especially for Ace. It took Kulick hours to teach him how to play "Beth" on an acoustic. But we got through them. Come the day of the show we all got nervous, especially Ace. But he wasn't drinking because he didn't want to fuck this up and have to deal with Gene and Paul's wrath. When we got to the studio, there were hundreds of kids lined up around the block.

They did the bulk of the show with their current members. Then Kulick and Singer left the stage.

"We're going to do something special. We got some members of the family here tonight, and we're not talking about Mom and Dad. We're talking about Peter Criss and Ace Frehley," Paul announced. We walked on to a tumultuous ovation. I swear it was like walking onto the Garden stage again, it was like that old feeling never went away. The energy in the room was just insane. And it was historic, too. This was the first time the original band played together without makeup.

"I don't think anybody expected this, did they?" Ace said.

"Oh, it was a secret," Paul said. "Let's see, what could we play?"

"How about something from a couple of old friends of mine, Mick Jagger and Keith Richards?" Ace suggested, and we launched into "2,000 Man." The audience went wild. Then they set up a chair for me up front and I came off the drums and sat between Gene and Paul. Gene started tweaking my ear playfully.

"This is the sensitive stuff," Paul said, and we did "Beth." Ace had mastered the song on acoustic and we sounded dynamite. I looked over at Gene and he had that *ca-ching* gleam in his eyes again. He could just smell that money.

Then Paul said, "We're bringing everybody out," and when Bruce and Eric came back on, a large portion of the audience started booing them.

"C'mon," Ace admonished the crowd. "They're part of the family too."

Frankly, I was astonished. Those guys had been in the band longer than me and Ace, and they're booing them? But the people had spoken. They didn't want them to come back because it was the original band again. We all did "Nothing to Lose" and then finished with "Rock and Roll All Nite."

Years later, Gene wrote about that night in his own book. "Bruce and Eric were kind throughout. In fact, they were so accommodating that they planted the seeds for what would become their worst nightmare. Their kindness enabled Ace and Peter to step in and unfortunately push them out of a job."

What total bullshit! Yeah, the control freak was going to let an emotionally shaky guy—which is how he characterized me—and a drunk push two great musicians out of the way? All of a sudden, it was out of his control? Who does he think he's fooling? As soon as the KISS Army booed Eric and Bruce, Gene realized that a reunion would be massively profitable.

After the *Unplugged* show, Ace and I went on the road again. Shortly after this, George told me that he got a call and KISS wanted to do a reunion. To me that meant millions of dollars, and I wanted it. I sure wasn't going to go on living in Venice Beach with a topless dancer and playing clubs like the Sandbar when I had had a taste of both the good life and the bad life. I preferred the good life.

So I called a band meeting in my quarters on the bus.

"I'm going to leave the band. KISS wants to do a reunion, and I have to do it. I'm too old to ride the Eagle with you guys. I want to get back to stadiums and earn some real money again. I have to think about my retirement someday. I have to get a little selfish here, I hope you guys understand."

Tall Man, who had the most to lose from this, said, "I just want one thing, man. Front-row seats at the shows."

"You got it, man," I said.

Then it was time to deal with Lynn. We hadn't been getting along well for a few months. By the time we got back from the *Unplugged* show, the sex had become much less frequent. I realized that there's something nutty about any woman who goes to dance half naked in her thirties and gets paid for it. I don't want every topless dancer in the world to hate me for this opinion, but I just think there's another way of making a buck at that age. But who am I to talk?

After *Unplugged,* I had to break up with Lynn. When I walked into the Rihga Royal hotel that day in New York, I felt the power again. I was treated like a major star: This wasn't the Criss band on a bus. This was Peter Criss of KISS, a side of me that Lynn had never seen before. I didn't want to be tied down, I wanted to be free and enjoy this ride. I didn't want to have to call and check in every night.

So I told her that when I got back from the Bad Boys tour in December, I wanted her shit out of the house. She did it, but she hated me. She wrote me horrible, angry letters. I remember they said things like, "I'd like to tie you up to a chair and then fuck your brains out and then beat the shit out of you." So that didn't end well at all.

We got back from our tour on December 20. The bus pulled up to my little house in Venice and I unloaded my gear. Tall Man told me I was due about five grand, but I told the boys to keep it and divvy it up as a Christmas present. It was a poignant scene—the Big Eagle parked on that street with all these little houses, me bringing my drums into my now-empty house. We had gone through a lot together. These guys had nursed me back to health when my face was all busted up. I really loved them deeply. I remember holding Tall Man, and he was crying. Then Angel started crying, and so did I. I began to have second thoughts—maybe I shouldn't leave these guys, I'd never be loved like this by bandmates again. The reality was we weren't going anywhere, the TNT deal was over, we didn't have any other prospects on the horizon. But we weren't dealing in reality that night. It was just pure emotion, all these guys hugging me like I was their dad, and they were saying good-bye to the best time of their lives. The bus was about to pull away when I ran inside the house and came back out with a rug. It was the rug on which Tall Man and I had written many of our songs.

"Hey, this is yours, Tall Man," I said, and gave him the magic rug.

He got all choked up and then they all got back on the bus and it pulled around the corner and out of my life.

I walked into the house and closed the door. It was quiet as a mouse inside. I looked around and the closets were empty and all Lynn's stuff was gone. I tried to turn on the TV but she had the cable people take the box away, so I had nothing to watch. But I had a Betamax and a big collection of old movies on video. Suddenly I realized it was my birthday and I should celebrate. "You're going back with your band, you're going to make a lot of money, you can get out from under that IRS debt, maybe you can buy a nice house again and maybe even meet a nice woman." I marched out and bought a nice bottle of Dom Pérignon. Then I went to a cigar store and asked the guy for his best cigar. The guy gave me a quizzical look.

"I don't really smoke cigars, but it's my fiftieth birthday and I want to celebrate."

"Well, this is the best one, kid," he said, handing over a cigar. It cost twenty-five bucks, but I didn't care.

I got back to the house and threw on "Hotel California." I loved that song. I poured myself a glass of champagne, lifted it up, and said, "Happy

Birthday, Peter. This is going to be a good year." I took a sip of the Dom and then lit the cigar. I started puffing away and I was turning green but I didn't care. I just felt good. I looked in the mirror and watched myself puff on that stogie and drink my champagne and I started laughing at myself. "God, look at you, you crazy bastard. You're going to be rich again. Life is good, you fucker."

CHAPTER SEVENTEEN

Once I got the whiteface on, it was smooth sailing. Then I did the outlining and the powdering, a little more coloring, and one eye was done. Next I worked on the nose. It was getting weirder and weirder. I got the black down and added the metallic silver and finally got to the whiskers. Then I finished with the ruby-red lipstick, added some green over my eyes, and sat back and looked into the mirror.

"Holy shit, I haven't seen you in seventeen years, man," I said. Then I put on the boots, stood up, and I was almost seven feet tall! I put my bandoliers on and my belt with the bullets and my leather gloves, and I looked into the mirror again. My face looked like porcelain: There wasn't a line on it. It was like I had gone through a time warp and I was twenty-six years old again. An unbelievable feeling of power surged over me and I knew, deep down, that everything was going to be all right, I wasn't going to die an old, broke, forgotten man with nothing to show for all my work.

I looked around the room in Gene's house and I saw Gene—I mean, the Demon—again, darting his tongue in and out of his mouth. Ace stood up and he had the same weird walk. It was creepy. It was as if nothing had changed in seventeen years. And now that we had donned our costumes and our makeup, we could announce to the world that KISS was back for an epic reunion.

It hadn't gone smoothly, though. Months earlier, George Sewitt brought us to a meeting in the offices of KISS's new lawyer, Bill Randolph. One look at that guy and I hated him. He was the most pompous, arrogant piece of shit I'd ever met, one of those guys who wears a three-thousand-dollar suit and thinks he's God. Yet whenever Gene or Paul ordered him to do something, he got it done like he was a robot. I guess he had to: They were his only client. Gene and Paul were in L.A., so the office rigged up a huge video screen and conferenced them in.

Gene and Paul went into their rap about how they had kept the brand going for years and that Ace and I were coming back again basically as employees. It was like they had practiced their lines for years—they had it down. "We're going to get this, you're going to get that . . ." I'm listening and it boiled down to Gene and Paul dividing 70 percent of the proceeds while Ace would get 20 percent and I would get 10 percent. One of their justifications was that Ace had been named guitarist of the year in *Guitar* magazine. I'm thinking, So what? He didn't write an award-winning song like "Beth."

"You're all out of your fucking minds, I'm not doing this," I finally said. "Over my dead body is Ace getting more money than me. There would be no KISS without us. I was the third member of the band. You forget that? You're telling me you're going to give this fucking guy more money than me?"

Ace and I started bickering, and Randolph tried to calm us down.

"You give me and Ace an even split and I'm aboard," I said.

"Well, this is what we talked about with George," they said. For the first time, I realized that Sewitt was ready to throw me under the bus in a second. Tall Man had warned me that he was a piece of shit. How right he was!

"I'm out of here," I said, and started packing my stuff up.

Randolph was in shock.

"You're going to walk away from a million dollars?" he asked incredulously.

"A million? It better be a fucking hell of a lot more than a million dollars we're talking about, because a million is shit. I can only imagine what your clients are going to make."

"Let's stop this," Ace interjected. "Can I talk to Peter in private?"

Ace, George, and I went into a private room.

"We have to make this work," Ace said. "We can make the same money." So we whittled down George's commission and agreed to make the same percentage. We should have dumped George and taken all the money for ourselves, but we were stupid. We thought we needed him.

We went back into the meeting and announced our decision and everyone was happy. Then George mentioned that Ace had a record deal that was worth a hundred grand, so he wanted that amount from them because he wouldn't be able to do his album. So right away, he was making more money than me anyway. There was no record deal. It was all bullshit.

Gene told us the next step was to come out to L.A. and talk about rehearsals. Then they disappeared from the screen. I left without even shaking Randolph's hand.

We met again a few months later at Gene's house in L.A. Gene and Paul wanted to introduce us to Doc McGhee, KISS's new manager. They made it clear that Doc was managing Gene and Paul, but he would also be doing things that would benefit Ace and me, and we could always go to him if we had any problems.

With that, Doc made his grand entrance into the room. It was like watching Michael Jackson walk in—he was that much of a showman. Doc was a small man, maybe five foot six, but he was built like an ox. You didn't want to fuck with him. He had been a wrestler in school and he could throw you through the fucking wall. He was a nice-looking man and he dressed impeccably and wore a twenty-five-thousand-dollar watch. He looked the part.

He had the stories, the dance, the pizzazz. He had made Jon Bon Jovi huge. He created Motley Crue and put the Scorpions on the map. Now he had a dream for us. Next thing we knew, Ace and I were falling in love with this guy: He was such a great con artist. Of course, he neglected to mention that all those other groups had fired his ass.

"We're going to make a lot more money than you think," Doc said. "I have great ideas. When Gene and Paul came to me with this, I told them I would not touch you guys unless Peter and Ace were on board and you all put the makeup back on. That is the only way we're going to make millions of dollars. We're going to make enough so we can all retire."

That was nice to hear. Gene took the floor again and pulled out a list of conditions: If they weren't met, he could pull the plug on the tour at any time. All band members had to be on time, we had to do interviews, we had to work out to get back in shape. There were to be no drugs, no heavy boozing. I was willing to do all of this anyway, without Hitler's prodding.

By January of 1996, rumors of our reunion began to surface. Gene was doing a radio interview in Chicago when the announcer asked him if a KISS reunion was possible. "Fairy tales can come true, it can happen to you," Gene coyly sang.

We made our first public appearance in makeup at the Grammy Awards on February 28. We were backstage in full makeup and costume, and most of the stars thought that we were a KISS cover band about to perform. In actuality we were going to present a Grammy with Tupac Shakur, the rap artist. Right before we went on, we convened in a little room and Gene and Paul started lecturing me condescendingly on how to speak to Tupac. "Peter, you know that Tupac Shakur is a real gangster. He's been shot a number of times and he's the real deal, so don't rub him the wrong way, don't call him names."

Of course, there was no drama. Tupac was wearing an expensive Versace suit and was a perfect gentleman.

"Let's shock the people," he said, and we ambled out onto the stage. The audience went berserk and gave us a standing ovation, led by Eddie Vedder.

Backstage afterward, all the stars had finally realized that we were the real KISS, and they all applauded us. We were on our way.

Now the hard work began. We each got a personal trainer. Mine was named Gregory and he was a weirdo. He had been Paul's trainer and he belonged to the Hare Krishna cult so he had a shaved head. He took me to his temple one night and we did some chanting together.

Gregory just kicked my ass. He had me drinking power drinks, distilled water, cleaning out my whole system. I'd meet him at Gold's Gym in Venice at nine in the morning and we'd train for two hours straight. We did the treadmill for a half hour and then stretched and lifted weights. He taught me yoga positions. He was literally chiseling my body. I lost more than twenty-five pounds. I was in the best shape of my life.

After the gym session, I'd drive to my drum tutor and drum for an hour. I had to relearn all the old KISS songs. It was humiliating to go meet some punk drummer and copy him playing my old shit because I had forgotten how to do it. At night I would watch VHS after VHS of KISS concerts. My tech and I would study them like football coaches. I had to relearn my body movements, the way I moved my head, the way I spun my sticks. I hated myself because some of that early drumming was pretty intricate.

After working with the drum tutor, I'd spend an hour or two playing with Tommy Thayer, just guitar and drums. He was Gene and Paul's butt boy for everything, but he was a KISS historian who knew the most minute details of every show we ever did. We'd play "Deuce" and "Strutter" and "Detroit Rock City," and it wasn't easy to relearn all these songs I hadn't played for almost twenty years. Then I'd go downtown and rehearse with the band. They rented some cheap crammed little studio. That's the way they wanted it, so no one could fuck up and make a mistake and get away with it. Gene and Paul were right on top of my drums, so I was lucky to be able to breathe. We worked like dogs in that place.

But I didn't mind working hard. I was fifty years old, older than the other guys, but I just thought of it as training for Tyson. You better be in great shape to get in the ring with him. Gene and Paul were workaholics to begin with, so they worked their asses off. But Ace was Ace: He was always lazy. He didn't take too kindly to all this regimentation.

When we thought we had gotten better, we went into a larger rehearsal space, SIR. We set up on a stage with a sound system and we'd mike my drums. Gene and Paul would get there early, just to try to catch us if we were late. I was always on time but Ace never was, and Gene would sit there and look at his watch. I'd get upset with Ace, too, because I was ready to go. So Gene sent a fax to the effect of "If you don't get your shit together, I'm going to pull the plug." It infuriated me. I hadn't missed one second of rehearsal but already he was asserting his power. Gene loved that fax machine. Sometimes he'd send a fax of three words. I went over to his house one time and he had ten broken fax machines lying around. He had worn them all out.

By April we were rehearsing in New York at SIR. And because New York is the media capital of the world, we were forced to go to great lengths not to be seen together. Despite the Grammy appearance, there had been no announcement of a tour yet. That happened on April 16 at a monumental press conference on the USS *Intrepid,* a museum docked on the Hudson River. We got dressed up at our hotel and then drove over to the ship in a van. Every now and then we'd stop at a light and people would see us, go crazy, and charge the van. When we got to the ship, there were hundreds and hundreds of press people there. Doc had the room completely darkened, and then a huge KISS sign lit up and we each walked out with a spotlight on us. It was like the scene from *Close Encounters* when the aliens walk into the light.

The cameras clicked away like crazy. After we posed, we sat down at a table and the questions came from reporters from all over the world. I was so proud to be part of something that was the biggest story on the planet at the time.

The tour dates were announced, and tickets went on sale shortly after that. I was back in L.A., asleep at six in the morning one day, when the phone rang. Groggy, I picked it up.

"Peter, are you sitting, standing, or lying down?" Gene said in his monotone.

"I'm fucking sleeping," I said. "The sun is just coming up."

"We just sold out Tiger Stadium in forty-seven minutes. Forty thousand seats." No enthusiasm, no excitement, no emotion. He was just Joe the Robot. But I jumped out of bed, screaming. And that was the way it went for venue after venue. Two straight years of touring, all around the world, sold out.

Once the tour had been announced, I got paranoid that the IRS was going to garnish my wages. By then my tax bill had mounted to $3 million and I had finally hired Carol White, a tax specialist, to help me. She had me file for bankruptcy, which Ace also did. That was a heavy day for me. Going from millions and millions to filing Chapter 13. By then both Gene and Paul had paid a million each to the IRS. Gene told me that he was sick and throwing up every day for a year after he signed over that million-dollar check to them.

Carol worked it out so that after a certain number of days of my bankruptcy filing, my IRS debt would get wiped out and everything I made after that was mine. My biggest fear was the IRS would get wind of the KISS tour and that I'd be working for them. Those days went by so slow. Every day I dreaded getting that letter in the mail from the IRS. But despite all the publicity, even being on the cover of *Forbes* magazine with an article about how much money this tour would gross, somehow they never came after me. I sweated out the days, and my IRS debt went away.

After a warm-up gig in California, the tour started at Tiger Stadium in Detroit on June 28, 1996. We were all nervous wrecks that day, but we were flying on adrenaline. Everybody got up early and we were in and out of each other's rooms at the hotel. At one point, some groupies had come to my room while I was getting my hair colored. I wound up making out with one of them, but they were kind of funky, so I settled for watching the two of them get it on.

Then I got the call to come down, so I threw them out. And I had a panic attack. I momentarily forgot all the songs, all the arrangements: I didn't even remember the opening song. Everything went blank. But once we got in the car with Doc to go to the stadium, I calmed down. Doc told a million jokes and then regaled us with all these funny backstage rock 'n' roll stories. Gene and Paul were calm and Ace was quiet. I was my usual physical self, talkative, very up. I still had that crazy energy.

When we got to the gig, Gene and I shared one room and Paul and Ace had the other.

"Wow, we're gonna play for forty thousand people," I said in awe. "That's freaking me out."

"I knew this would happen," Gene said coolly. He wouldn't even admit that he was excited. After we all went into the makeup room and put on our faces, we got dressed and they brought us up to the stage in golf carts, two to a cart. My heart started exploding in my chest. I was sitting next to Gene and I started beating out a fill on my leg and then I started playing his leg, just like I used to do for our big shows twenty years earlier.

I finally broke him. He started laughing.

"You Italians, nothing changes, huh?" he said.

"Man, this is going to be good," I said.

"Let's just stick to what we rehearsed. Don't change anything," Gene said.

I agreed. Gene had spent a lot of time helping me with my drum solo. At first I just couldn't get it again, and he stayed late after rehearsals and helped me with it and then it was like riding a bike. I could close my eyes and it would be the same solo I did in 1975.

The cart came up the ramp and the roar got louder and louder and suddenly we were in the stadium and the huge lights illuminated the field and the stands. It was an incredible feeling, like going to a giant church.

They stopped us at the ramp to the stage, and we walked up the steps to our positions. There was a huge black curtain obscuring the stage, but the fans on the sides could see us and they went crazy and then everybody started roaring. By now the house lights had been dimmed and it was pitch-black in the stadium. All you could hear was the enormous hum from the amplifiers, and then purple searchlights started cascading around the stadium.

We looked at each other and gave each other the thumbs-up sign.

"You wanted the best, you got the best . . ." The old familiar intro was back, and then, with the curtain still lowered, we went into the first few bars of "Deuce." Then there was a loud explosion, the curtain dropped, and there we were. It was like going to heaven. I felt like I could do no wrong, we were such a well-oiled machine. We played for over two hours in the sweltering heat but I didn't feel a thing. This was why we had put in all those grueling hours of training. At that moment, every second of that agony was worth it.

When it came time to do "Beth," the next-to-last encore, I walked around from behind the drums and sat on that stool again and I started crying. We always had a special bond with the Detroit fans: They were the ones who embraced us first and put us on the map. I was overwhelmed by the love that was coming toward me, people calling my name and saying they loved me. I hadn't heard that for seventeen years. How could I not cry?

We had a spectacular show, combining elements of all our previous shows. Gene was spitting blood and spewing fire again. During "God of Thunder," he would fly up into the air to a platform where he sang the song. Ace's guitar would shoot rockets that would hit the stage lights and cause them to explode or dangle from a wire. Of course my drum kit levitated high into the air. Doc felt that Paul needed a grand moment too, so later into the tour they devised a rig that enabled Paul to fly over the audience. One night it malfunctioned and people actually hung on Paul's leg as he cruised over the audience. He was really pissed off. But he loved flying. When we played venues where it was impossible to set it up, he'd get furious.

One of the major changes on this tour was the addition of a huge, high-tech video screen.

"Everything you do will be visible to the audience," Doc lectured us. "There isn't anything the fans will miss now."

"Remember to smile, Peter," Doc constantly reminded me.

"Wait a minute, KISS never smiled. Now all of a sudden we're smiling? What's so funny now? We're smiling because we're going to the bank?" I'd ask.

The truth was that just a smile on that big screen would make the audience go bonkers. It was that powerful a tool. A few nights I'd be nursing some wounds from something Gene or Paul might have done and I'd have my head down and be cursing, and the camera would catch me mouthing the words with that nasty face. So I quickly learned to grin and bear it.

But at first everything was wonderful. We were all getting along, and the good vibes were infectious. Paul brought a ghetto blaster into the makeup room and we chose our favorite music to play while we put on our faces. Sometimes we would play golden oldies like the Four Seasons, and Ace would go ballistic. He hated that music. He wanted to hear Hendrix.

There were still women around, but the Chicken Coop had been replaced by the hotel bar. We were staying at Four Seasons hotels and they all had high-class bars, but on the nights we were there, the room was crawling with women, from teenagers to retirees, all wanting us. The guys invited me down a few times, but I was turned off by the scene. I'd be chatting up girls who were barely a few years older than my sixteen-year-old daughter, and I felt like a pervert.

Plus the old gray mare wasn't what she used to be. Those young girls were probably used to guys from the football team who would bang the shit out of them from sunup to sundown. Now, there had been a time when I could've killed them one by one. They could come and go and everybody would get their pants fucked off. But the Spoiler wasn't the Spoiler anymore. I could imagine what they'd say: "What's the whole thing about the Spoiler? Peter fucked me once and fell asleep, whoop-de-do." I just didn't want to put myself in that kind of situation.

Frankly, I didn't want women around at all at that point. Playing drums for KISS was incredibly hard work. I wouldn't have been able to do it if I had been up all night boning a groupie. No band on the planet worked as hard as we did. Mick Jagger can wear some jeans and throw a scarf on, Tyler puts some tight pants and a chick shirt on, but we had the boots and the heavy costumes. Even wearing that makeup for two hours was no picnic. When you started sweating, the sweat had to break through that powder, so you were sweating under the makeup. Then you took it all off and showered and had to get ready to do it all again the next night. So I put the girls on hold, for the most part. I was fifty, not twenty-six. Forget about it.

Gene was the only one of us who still had the roadies or the body-guards out scouring the audience for chicks. Sometimes he'd fool around with them during the show. He had a little station that was curtained off to the side of the stage where he could grab a coffee or some water. I'd be in the middle of my drum solo and I'd look over and he'd have two girls at the station. One of them would be flashing me, and he'd bend the other one over and grope her. I couldn't believe it. He just couldn't get enough sex.

Gene was in the dressing room one day getting dressed and he had a herpes outbreak so bad that it was all over his neck, his chest, down his stomach, down his legs. They had to bring a doctor in to give him an injection. I heard that Shannon got wind of it and Doc had to go out and get her a very expensive rock to calm her down.

Gene was truly a pig when it came to sex. I remember one day early in our career when we were rehearsing and Gene and Paul had to share a microphone and Paul suddenly recoiled as if he had been shot.

"Holy shit, what the fuck did you eat?" Paul said.

"You know what I ate," Gene said. Then he smiled and you could still see the menstrual blood on his teeth.

"I didn't brush my teeth this morning. I want to savor the taste of it all day," Gene said. Paul refused to continue the rehearsal until somebody found a breath mint.

Sometimes on the reunion tour I'd be in my room at night and there'd be a knock at the door. I'd open the door and there would be a chick with fucking gazombas out to here standing there.

"Hi, Mr. Criss."

"What can I do for you?" I'd say.

"Well, there's a lot of things you can do for me."

"Do me a favor. Go over to Gene's room," I'd say, and just then Gene would stick his head out into the hall.

"I just wanted to see if you would take the bait," he'd smile. It was a constant battle between good and evil with Gene.

For the most part, Ace didn't partake of the groupies, because most of the time he brought a mistress on the road with him. All of them were drug addicts or drunks or perverts. All Ace would do was stay in his hotel room, take drugs, and have sex. He'd set up a bunch of computers and there'd be cords and hard drives and outlets all over the place. Ace was not allowed to have a key to the minibar, but he was usually able to sneak some alcohol in.

One time Valerie, one of these girls, knocked on my door.

"What do you want, Valerie," I said with disgust. I just didn't like this chick. She was really crazy and the worst influence on Ace.

"Ace wants a bottle of wine. Actually, two would be good. He'll pay you for them," she said.

"No. Ace is cut off. He can't drink," I said. I was specifically told by Doc not to sell Ace any booze. I was breaking her balls.

"What?" she said. "Ace said I could depend on you, that you're cool."

"I am cool. But I can't sell you the alcohol."

She was dumbfounded.

"But I could give it you. And I don't want to hear a word about this," I said, and handed her a bottle of red and a bottle of white. Her face lit up like a Christmas tree.

Whenever Ace did get a new girl on the road, he'd go into his whole doctor routine with them.

I'd be sitting in the dressing room after a show and I'd hear him talking to our wardrobe girl, whom I had nicknamed Baby Beth.

"Hey, Baby Beth, put some rubber gloves in my bag and make sure there's a big jar of K-Y."

I knew right then it was going to be a sick night.

"You in tonight?" I'd ask him.

"Oh, yeah, I got to operate on a few patients later. Rubber gloves tonight, baby. We're going in deep."

One night I actually heard them from all the way down the hall. His current girlfriend loved anal sex and I heard her screaming like a banshee, "FUCK ME LIKE A TRUCK DRIVER! FUCK ME LIKE A TRUCK DRIVER!" as he banged her in the ass. I could only imagine what the businessman in the room below him was thinking.

We were the hottest act in show business during the reunion tour and, of course, all that attention and adulation just magnified Gene's already Godlike ego. The crew was so pissed at Gene that they made a loop of the scene in one of Gene's movies where Gene's character had a grenade shoved into his mouth and his head got blown off. When they wanted to have fun, they'd smoke a joint, pop open a beer, and watch Gene's head explode over and over and over again.

Gene even tortured poor little Baby Beth. She broke her hump for us night in and night out, but Gene just kept demanding shit from her and heaping abuse on her when she wasn't waiting on him hand and foot. One night she went crying in Doc's arms and told him she wanted to quit. Doc consoled her and then went to see Gene.

"You fucking asshole," Doc reamed him. "We got a long tour ahead of us and nobody can dress you guys like her. Nobody else would put up with your imbecilic shit and your filthy body. Now, I'm going to bring her in here, and you're going to apologize to her and give her a raise."

So Beth came in and Gene said, "Come here, Beth." And he sat her down on his lap.

"You know I'm sorry, Baby Beth. When I put that makeup on I'm just not myself—something happens to me and I become that monster." She was getting a speech instead of an apology. But he gave her a raise and she stayed.

In fact, she turned the tables on him. Doc had instituted a little pre-show ceremony that he had done with some of his other bands. We used to form a circle right before we went on and he'd give us a pep talk like a football coach.

"All right, you fuckers, there's seventeen thousand people out there that paid their hard-earned cash to see you guys because they love you and you're the best band in the world . . ."

After a while we alternated. Me, Tim Rozner, our tour manager, or someone else would give the little speech, and we'd try to crack everybody up and lighten the mood. One night we asked Baby Beth to do the speech and this little four-foot-nine firecracker got in the circle.

"All right, you four lame, old, fat, wig-wearing clowns. Get out there and earn your money! If you can make it up the stairs," she said. We cracked up so hard we could barely get on the stage.

Berating the crew was one thing. But shortly after the tour was under-way, Gene and Paul began to direct their wrath toward me and Ace. They had always wanted the power when we were coming up, but Aucoin had always been there to check their darkest impulses.

I went into the reunion with a positive vibe. I wanted it to work; I wanted to make amends. But every step of the way, they would wield their power. Ace and I were instrumental in creating KISS, and now we were being treated like replaceable sidemen. And the same forces—greed and power—that years earlier had conspired to destroy the band were coming into play again, only now they were magnified because we were playing on such a greater stage.

The way that Gene and Paul would address us was beyond belief. If anyone would ever talk to you with such condescension and contempt, you'd have every right to break their nose.

I lost interest in fighting with them. I was like George Harrison in *Let It Be*: "I'll play whatever you want." Paul was never happy. Was I playing too fast? Too slow? Not slow enough? You couldn't please him. Everything had to be perfect for him, yet here's a guy who was imperfect in his own head. He couldn't even be happy in his own skin, so he strikes out and hurts other people to get his rocks off.

Now that the two of them controlled the band, they could have their way on everything. Ace and I had no votes anymore. Gene was the more vocal of the two with all his dictums. Forget about spontaneity and the joy of creation. We had become a big machine, lumbering our way from city to city. Gene's conception was that the band should be like the Japanese restaurant chain Benihana. "You go to chef school at Benihana and you learn exactly how many peppers to put on the grill, how many shrimp, how much sauce. And it never varies from restaurant to restaurant." Great, now we're the greatest Japanese restaurant chain in the land.

It was disheartening, but I could take the abuse when it hit me directly. When the abuse was being published in articles that my daughter could read, I drew the line. When Ace and I left the band originally, there was no mention at all in the press about drug problems or alcohol abuse. We were leaving because of "creative differences," and we were all still one big happy family. But now Gene and Paul had control and they could redefine the terms.

Now that we were back on top, the press was crazy to get any new angles on us, so they began asking why we had broken up in the first place. Gene had a mouth that matched the size of his fucking ego, so he was only happy to oblige them.

We used to get a folder every morning with clips of all the news articles written about us. One morning I was thumbing through it and I started reading an interview Gene had done with some big-city newspaper. He was quoted talking about my extensive drug use and Ace's alcoholism and how they impaired our ability at the time. I went crazy. I thought, "My daughter is going to read about all my past drug use? She doesn't know anything about this stuff." In fact, hardly anyone knew about it, but now it was in black and white in the Seattle paper and the Washington paper and the Detroit paper and the New York paper that I was a crazed drug addict in the '70s. But this was the '90s.

I walked over to Gene and threw the clippings in his face. Now that he had started mouthing off to the press, all bets were off as far as I was concerned.

"You fucking piece of shit. Why are you saying shit like this?" I yelled. "We're back together and you have to tell people that I was a fucking insane gun-toting drug addict? You don't see me saying you were an ego-maniacal herpes-ridden sex addict."

"Oh, they got it wrong," he hemmed and hawed. "The writer changed my words around. It's not my fault."

"I have a family now. They don't need to know about that shit. Don't you ever open your big fucking mouth again."

Who was fooling who with the drug-addict talk? By then Paul was carrying around a huge Louis Vuitton bag full of enough pills to choke a horse. Paul was a major hypochondriac so he had muscle relaxants, tranquilizers, pills to make you tan, pills to make you lose weight, pills to get you going. He once showed me his phone book and he had at least fifty doctors' names in there. Ace would look longingly at Paul's bag and say, "If we could only rob that bag."

The irony was that I was completely clean now. I was straight, and I enjoyed playing straight. It was such a gas being up on that stage again. We knew that every show was sold out and that the minute the curtain dropped, everyone loved us.

Gene and Paul have largely written the history of KISS, and in their version the rap on me is that I was a complainer. It was true, I was a complainer. But if you analyze what I was complaining about, you'd see that I had every right to bitch and more so. I hadn't taken hard drugs in twenty years, but when Ace continued his drug use, I would always be tarred with the same brush.

I also routinely complained about my compensation—the grossly unequal distribution of monies between Gene and Paul and Ace and myself. Besides the patently unfair terms that we agreed to before the tour started, there were all these other streams of income that those two guys were divvying up and not even telling us about. They'd have meetings with Doc and the accountant and never tell me. I'd walk into the lobby and Gene and Doc would be talking about something, and when I'd come up they'd change the subject abruptly.

And when your bandmate berates you in front of your own child, how could you not complain? I took Jenilee out on some of the dates on the reunion tour and during a sound check while Jenilee was sitting by the stage, Paul turned around to me and said, "What the fuck are you playing?" or "What's with your fucking timing?" They knew how much I loved my daughter; all I talked about was my kid. For them to humiliate me in front of her was so sinister. They were masters at beating you down and pushing your buttons so that you'd ultimately feel like a loser.

Between the two of them, Gene was much more in your face, but Paul was passive-aggressive. When Paul didn't get his way, he'd start getting flustered and pacing the room in circles and you could just feel the bad vibes. Gene would then do whatever it took to placate Paul. Gene might have been a control freak, but Paul usually got whatever he wanted. We couldn't stay at certain hotels because Paul thought they made their pancakes the wrong way. I'd get revised plans under my door all the time because Paul wanted to leave a city and fly to the next town for one petty reason or another. One night we actually left a hotel because it reminded Paul of a funeral parlor. And I was the crazy one?

Paul is much more Machiavellian than Gene. Gene was crass and brutal, but he had a real naïveté about him. But Paul could cut your throat and he'd be out of the room before you even realized you were bleeding. He probably picked up a lot of techniques going to see his shrink all those years.

Gene and Paul really have nothing in common. Gene embarrasses Paul in public with his crude behavior. Paul likes to feel that he's cultured: He dabbles in painting. The only thing they can agree on is the importance of making money. Then they overlook each other's faults and connive together to optimize their earning power.

It was primarily the money issues that divided us on that tour. Having George Sewitt represent Ace and me was a huge mistake in retrospect. George threw a lot of fuel on the fire but when it came to crunch time, he folded like a cheap accordion.

The bickering started when Ace and I got our first paychecks on the tour. The amounts didn't seem right, so Ace and I grabbed George, threw him into the wall, and told him to get us more money.

"I didn't spend thousands of hours in a gym to get this chump change," I protested. "We're on the cover of *Forbes* magazine, we must be earning some serious money."

So George made up a whole list of our demands and vowed to talk to

Gene and Paul. He said Ace and I would get everything we wanted. The day of the meeting came and George actually wore a suit and tie. It was the four of us and George in the room. George started telling them all of our demands. They listened for a little while, and then Gene and Paul just reamed George out.

"Who the fuck do you think you are?" they berated him. "You're not our manager, Doc McGhee is. You're just a guest on this tour." They told him that he wasn't going to come on the tour anymore unless they approved it, and that they didn't give a shit what his concerns were.

George started to melt. I'd never seen a man break down like that. Ace had to step in at one point. "Can you stop this? Enough is enough," he said. They walked out of the room and George was devastated. His excuse was that he had taken a Valium before the meeting and it fogged his brain. Yeah, right. At one time this guy could do more blow than anybody in the room and he falls apart because he took one Valium?

Ace's response to all this misery was to retreat into his own cocoon of drugs and booze. Ace had a very large ego, almost on par with Gene's, so it must have been extremely painful for him to be treated like an employee by those two. But doing coke and designer drugs was not the solution. Even I was lecturing Ace and telling him to straighten up. I would tell him that he couldn't bullshit a bullshitter and I knew when he was fucked up. I'd remind him about his daughter and how'd she react to her father being blotto. But with a girl by his side to enable him, it was an uphill battle.

The only time I got in trouble on that tour was when I had a little too much red wine. We were playing Madison Square Garden for three nights about a month into the tour and after the first show, I took my whole family to some nice Italian restaurant that Doc rented out for me. The bill came to five grand, but I didn't care. They were so happy to have us at that place that they kept plying me with red wine so by the time I got back to the hotel, I was loaded. Red wine always made me romantic, so I started missing Deb. I decided I wanted her there at this glorious moment. I was back on top of the world: We had sold out the Garden for three straight nights. I was going to be rich again, a lot richer than her husband. And that's all she ever wanted, right, the money?

So I called her. It was about two in the morning in L.A. and I woke her up.

"What are you doing?" I said.

"I don't know, I was sleeping."

"Where's Jenilee?"

"She's in her room, sleeping."

"Why don't you get her and get something on and I'll fly you to New York first-class and spend the week with me. I'll wine and dine you and I'll take you out and you can buy anything you want and we'll have a great time." I was drunk out of my mind. She was married to Mac by then, but I didn't care. Just like he didn't care when I was married to her.

"You're crazy."

"Yeah, but so are you. This is a tantalizing proposition, isn't it?"

"Well, it's nice, but I'm married, Peter. I have a son now."

"Bring him, too. I've got a lot of money now, Deb. We could buy a mansion in Hollywood . . ."

"I think you really have to sober up, Peter. I'm sure you'll feel different tomorrow. Jenilee and I can't hop on a plane and see you."

"All right," I said, and hung up. The next morning I woke up with a brutal hangover and I thought, 'What the fuck did you do, you idiot? You're gonna do the same thing you did before, you're that stupid?'"

It was a reality check for me. I was so drunk and delusional that I thought I could do anything.

Now that Deb was definitively out of the question, I went back to keeping my eyes open for girls. I actually had seen one girl backstage that first night before I went out to dinner with my family. I came out of my dressing room after the show and I met my best friend, Eddie, and his wife, Dottie. I was hugging them and I looked down the hallway in the Garden and I saw this tall blonde with black nylons. She was so hot. Plus I was a sucker for long legs. She was walking with this guy with long hair and I could only see his back.

"I've got to have that," I said, and Eddie laughed.

"No, I'm serious. I want to see what she looks like from the front," I told him.

So I hugged them good-bye and I caught up with this woman. The guy she was with was Robbie Affuso, the drummer from Skid Row. He was a real sweetheart.

"Glad you came down," I told Robbie.

"I wouldn't miss it. You guys were so great," he said.

Then Robbie introduced me to the girl, whose name was Gigi. She had a flyer that she'd had signed by Gene and Paul and Ace, and now she asked me to sign it. I did it.

"Is this your girl, Robbie?" I asked. They both answered no simultaneously.

"Oh, that's cool," I said. "You're really beautiful."

They were going to a Ford Modeling Agency party after the show. So I said good-bye but I kept checking out Gigi as they walked away.

On the third night of the shows, I looked out into the audience, and there was Gigi again. I pointed at her with my stick and winked at her. There was a party after the show at the Rihga, where we were staying, and somehow I wound up in Gene's room, where he was entertaining a stewardess and a beautiful girl we had met in Tupelo. Gene wanted to get rid of the young blonde from Tupelo and be with the stewardess, so he suggested that I take her downstairs to the party.

We went downstairs and I felt a little dirty that I was sitting with this corn-fed twenty-one-year-old. I looked over and sure enough, there was Gigi sitting at a table with a bunch of hot girls and Ron Delsener, the legendary promoter. Apparently one of Gigi's friends, who looked kind of trashy to me, wanted to fuck my brains out but didn't have the nerve to approach me, so she had Gigi escort her over.

Now I was sitting at a table with three chicks. Gigi started talking to Tupelo because she wanted to create an opening for her friend. But the whole time that I was talking to her friend, I was staring at Gigi. Before I could make a move, Gigi and her friend got up and circulated. Now I was desperate to get in touch with Gigi, so I left Tupelo for a second and went over to Ron Delsener and asked him to get Gigi's number for me. He said it was no problem and I went back to Tupelo. Then we went upstairs to my room and we were lying on the couch, watching TV, and I started playing with her titties. Then I threw her on the bed but I couldn't get it up. I couldn't handle being with such a young girl. I didn't want to let her down, so I gave her probably the best head she'd ever received. She had a major orgasm and then she was waiting for me to fuck her and I went, "I really don't feel well. I think you'd better leave." She looked at me like I was out of my mind, and I was. So she left and I went to bed.

We had the next day off and I called Delsener and he came through with Gigi's number. So I had a couple of beers and called her at home. She was a little taken aback that I had gotten her number from Ron, but she warmed up a bit and we started yakking for hours. I asked her to come over to the hotel but she told me that she was getting honored with a chip that night for twelve years of sobriety. That was impressive to me. I told her to drop by afterward, and she did.

When she got there, Doc was sitting with Gene at a table by the bar and he told Gigi that I was up in my room and that I was expecting her. Well, that didn't sit too well with Gigi, going up to a stranger's room in a hotel. So she asked Doc if it was safe to go up.

"Absolutely," Doc said. "Of the four of them, Peter is the truest gentleman. He's the oldest and the nicest. He will never, ever step out of line with you. I would bet my career on it."

A nice endorsement.

She came to the door and I was happy to see her. I had ordered crème brûlée earlier and I hadn't touched it, so we split it and then we talked. And talked. And talked. This girl could talk. She was obviously in tune with her emotions and she had hung out with older people so she seemed wise beyond her years. I was thinking that this was the greatest girl I'd ever met.

Suddenly it was four thirty in the morning.

"Why don't you spend the night?" I suggested. "I won't touch you if you don't want me to."

"No, I don't want you to and you're not going to touch me. I'm not that kind of girl."

"What do you think, you got gold between your legs?" I joked.

"Well, yeah, and most men will dig for gold until they get it," Gigi said.

But she agreed to spend the night.

Meanwhile, I was thinking, Yeah, right, you don't want me to touch you, but once your ass is in the bed, it's all over.

I gave her a pair of my boxer shorts to wear and we both got into bed. I put my arm around her.

"Don't even think about it. I just told you," she protested.

So we each slept on our side of the bed. I was intrigued because this was the first chick who had turned me down since I had become a musician.

In the morning we ordered breakfast and Doc came to the door. He suggested that I take Gigi with us to Boston for the next gig. We were flying for the first time in our new jet. Doc cleared it with the other guys, and Gigi agreed to go. She was going in the limo to the private jet. She was going to see the full power of KISS. She's going to drop dead and she's going to fuck me tonight in Boston. No way around that.

We got to the airport and boarded the G-4 and I was floored. None of us had ever seen such luxury in all our lives. Beautiful leather seats, a gorgeous bathroom, great food. It was obvious we were at a whole new level. We went in and everybody grabbed their spots. Doc and Paul sat toward the front of the main compartment. Gene went right to the rear because he hated flying. Ace, Gigi, and I sat in the seats next to the big table in the middle.

Now, I know my boys, and they were all checking out Gigi. Then Gene started showing off and threw Gigi a prototype of the new KISS collectible baseball.

"What do you think of this baseball, Gigi?" he asked her.

She looked it over and saw that there were two pictures of Gene's face on it, one of Ace, and one of Paul. And none of mine.

"Well, it's a nice ball, but where's Peter?" she asked, and threw it back to him.

"You didn't give him permission to use your copyrighted image, Peter?" she asked me.

Gene almost shit himself.

"Yoko Ono," he said with venom.

We got to the hotel and we had a big meeting before the show. I was still hurt by what had happened the last night at the Garden. It was a Saturday night and we were running late and the Teamsters were going to get some outrageous amount of money if we hit overtime, so when we came back after our first encore, Tim suggested we cut "Beth." He didn't know that that was my big moment, especially in the Garden, where I would hand my mother a rose after I sang the song. When we came offstage after "Rock and Roll All Nite," I was in tears and explained to Tim how important "Beth" was for me to perform at the Garden. He had unwittingly taken away my homage to the memory of my mother.

I brought cutting "Beth" up again in the meeting and Gene and Paul just were ruthless, making fun of me and my concerns. I went back to the room where Gigi was and I was literally shaking and sweating.

"What's the matter?" Gigi asked me.

"Could you just do me a favor and hold me?" I asked her. She was probably thinking that I was just conning her to have sex, but we laid down together in the bed and she just held me.

"We just had a meeting and you don't know how horrible these guys are," I said. "Nothing has changed. I thought these guys were different, but they haven't changed at all."

We played that night at the Fleet Center and the show sucked. Ace played especially poorly because Joe Perry and his son were in the audience, and having Perry there would always make Ace choke. That night I tried messing around with Gigi again but she didn't go for it. I realized that this broad was serious. I flew her in on the private jet, had a nice steak dinner, she saw the band perform for free, and she still wasn't putting out. I started thinking that maybe this was just the right type of woman for me. She actually thought for herself, she didn't do drugs, and she was drop-dead gorgeous. Her ass could stop traffic. I wasn't an ass guy, but I became one.

The next day Gigi flew back to New York and we went on to Canada. I began to live on the phone with her. I was falling in love and I couldn't wait to get back to my room after the show and call her up. And I hate the phone. We'd stay on the phone for two or three hours every night and I told her about my youth, my first wife, my second wife, all of my problems.

About two months later we played Philadelphia and Gigi came down to see me. We came back to the room after the gig and I was in full makeup and I leaned over to give her a kiss and she got all freaked out. Maybe it was my lipstick. So after I took off my makeup and stage costume, we sat down on the bed and Gigi suggested that we play cards. I think she said that to divert a sexual encounter, because we still hadn't had sex.

That night, I asked Gigi to go steady with me.

"Like you're my girl and I'm your guy and there's no women for me and no other men for you," I said.

"Yes, Peter, I know what going steady means," Gigi said. And then she said we should give it a try. From that moment on, we each gave 100 percent of ourselves into the relationship.

Which meant that I was finally getting lucky that night. Sort of. The first time we had sex was not great. I felt pressure after all those months of a long-distance courtship and I had a problem getting stiff. The Spoiler was more like a noodle. This was complicated by the fact that Gigi had insisted that I wear a condom. She started lecturing me about AIDS and genital herpes, and since I was a rock star I was a prime candidate for all of that. I hadn't put on a raincoat for what felt like centuries. So we argued about that for a while and I had to call and get one of the roadies to get one.

Now that I had it, I had forgotten how to even put it on. Finally I got some sort of erection and it was getting bigger and I finally got the fucking thing on and it was half on and half off and I was losing it.

"Take your time, I understand," Gigi said.

"There's nothing to understand. It's the fucking Trojan. It's not used to being covered. C'mon, we're not kids."

Finally she rolled over and I put it in from the back and came immediately. I thought, Jesus, mother of God, I waited all these months and it's over already?

So I dozed off for a few minutes and then I woke up and I was feeling horny and thinking I can keep it up so I started poking her in the back to wake her and she said, "You're not going to get it up again."

"How do you know?"

"Because I know, and then you're going to get frustrated and you're going to get angry."

"Well, maybe you should suck it. You don't even know what to do," I said, and we started arguing and she got up crying and put her coat on and walked out. Now I was pissed off and she was crying in the hallway and I felt like shit. I called her back into the room.

"I'm sorry. I guess I'm just accustomed to sex-crazed women that do wild things to arouse me. I'm not used to sleeping with a lady and being gentle. You're like a butterfly, you're really tender, and I'm not used to that. You've got to give me a little time to adjust."

We still had differences in what we enjoyed sexually. But I started weighing it out and I realized that in nine years I was going to hit sixty and it wouldn't be about sleeping with four women or running naked through a hotel lobby. It would be more about really caring for one partner.

Gigi was the first woman I ever met that really loved God, like I do, so there was a spiritual connection there that I had never experienced. All I ever missed about Deb was fucking her. I never missed her company. No marriage will ever last on a foundation of sex alone. Eventually the raging fire will diminish into a pilot light.

When Gigi and I first met, we were sitting there and I said, out of the blue, "The heart is a lonely hunter—"

"Yeah, that hunts on a lonely hill," she said, finishing the poem. She told me that when she was a girl she had found that poem and she loved it so much that she kept it in her wallet. Fireworks went off in my brain. I knew that Gigi and I had to be destiny.

We had a break in touring and I took Gigi to Hawaii and we had a great time. I learned more about romance on that trip. I learned how to be nicer in certain ways, nicer than my usual no-holds-barred attitude about sex. When I left her early that last morning to go to the airport on my way to Japan, it was really emotional.

"I love you. I really think I'm getting this love thing," I said. "I'm still not happy about a lot of things, though."

"Yeah, I know what you're unhappy about," Gigi said. "But I'm sorry. It's just not me. I'm not Deb."

She was right. I had to get over the fact that every woman I got into bed with wasn't Deb or Sweet Connie from Little Rock. It was a hard lesson to learn because I had been around crazy women my whole life.

It was nice to have a two-week break, because every place we went on the reunion tour was total pandemonium. We'd have press following us everywhere we went, motorcycle escorts to the arenas. I used to love going up to the motorcycle cops and hugging them and telling them how much I loved policemen. They got us to the venues in time.

It was the same outside the country. There was always KISSmania in Japan, so that wasn't new. We played the Tokyo Dome and the show was a nightmare. The stadium was so big that they had ramps on either side of the stage that protruded so far sideways into the audience that if you went all the way out on them, you couldn't even see the other guys in the band. And if that was the case, who was going to cue the end of the song? Well, Paul took one look at those things and he immediately went ramp running. He was gone—he wasn't even in the band anymore. Gene saw this and wasn't about to let Paul have all the fun, so he took off—and he was the cue man. So I looked out and all I saw was Ace and a gazillion people. I was playing, and I was hearing Gene and Paul's chords, but they were sloppy because they were out touching girls and throwing kisses. So the whole show went down the shitter. Then Ace disappeared. He wasn't going to be left out. So I was all alone on the stage with all my guys running on the ramps.

Then I got an idea. At the very end of each show, all four of us would come out to the front of the stage and count one, two, three, and we'd all bow in unison. It was bullshit that I wasn't getting noticed like the other three, so right before we lined up for the bows, I ran out on the ramp to the very end and gave a victory salute to the fans, and they went crazy. Then I came back, running right by the guys who were waiting to do the bow, and did the same thing on the other side of the stage. When I ran back and got in line, Gene leaned over to me.

"Are you satisfied?" he said.

"Very," I smiled.

It was a wild trip for those two years we were out on the reunion tour. I was convinced that Doc was in collusion with Gene and Paul, ripping Ace and me off on all sorts of side deals. All I knew was that when the tour was over, Gene and Paul would be building mansions and Ace and I would wind up with a fraction of that kind of money. I wouldn't put it past Doc to get involved in shady dealings. He was arrested in 1988 for helping a drug-smuggling ring—with connections to Panamanian dicta-tor Manuel Noriega—import forty-five thousand pounds of grass from Colombia to North Carolina. He pled guilty to a conspiracy charge but never served time.

Doc had hired this accountant named Paco who had toured with the Who and Led Zeppelin. Paco knew every trick in the book. One day Gigi accidentally walked into the count room, the place where the promoters settled up with the band. She saw two identical suitcases, one black and one brown, both packed to the brim with cash. They banned her from that area for the rest of the tour. When we told Ace that story, he was convinced that they were skimming off money and putting it into a Swiss bank account. Sure enough, we played Zurich and on a day off, Doc and Paco had to go attend to some business. We even told Gene and Paul about our suspicions, but they just chalked it up to Ace's paranoid con-spiracy theories. What else did I expect to hear from them?

I wanted the reunion to make up for certain things. I thought that maybe Gene and Paul had a point: Maybe they weren't as crazy as I thought they were. Well, they were even crazier when we all got back together. I thought some of that old camaraderie would resurface, but in the end it was all about the M-O-N-E-Y. And here I was, trying to make amends for fucking up onstage in a show in 1978. So it was disheartening when I realized that they were taking so much from the party, and I was working so hard for so little. I had been a co-CEO of General Motors and now I was cleaning the latrines at a plant in Detroit.

It was so irritating to hear Gene say, "You're working for me and you'll do what I say or you'll be fired just like any other employee." I wanted to cut his throat from ear to ear. If he had said that to me back in the day, I would have taken a bottle and smashed it right across his forehead. But I had changed, even if they hadn't. They were making more money than they'd ever make again in their lives because of Ace and *me*, the two fuck-ing lunatics. Without us, KISS would have been a boring band. But now we were the second-class citizens of the group. Anything that went wrong, we got the blame for. And if I'd object to any of these inequities, I'd be labeled a complainer.

So I made a strategic withdrawal. I had millions at one point of my life, and it was all gone. So I realized that I had to stick it out for however long we were doing this and make enough money so I wouldn't have to work again. Take it in the ass as long as you can take it, put up with their shit, bite the bullet and just do it, be a man and get that fucking cash and then say, "Good-bye, I don't fucking need you. Take this job and shove it." Music had never been about the money to me but now, at fifty, I'd been to hell and back and I needed it.

I decided not to be part of the boys' club anymore. Doc and Paco were upset that they couldn't drag me into their fold, smoking cigars and drinking. I knew that if I went down to the bar, I wouldn't be able to say no. I'd have a scotch, it'd taste good. I'd see some tits and ass, and they would look better. Doc would buy me another round and everything would look even better yet. And then I'd take someone up to my room and fuck up. And I'd feel and play like shit the next day. That wasn't going to happen.

Who wanted to hang with them anyway? When we finished playing each night, they'd invite me to dinner, but I didn't even want to sit at the same table with those guys. They weren't my people anymore. You had one pompous asshole in Gene, a supreme egotist who would drool over every woman in the restaurant. If the waitress was attractive, he would take her hand and lick it and try to give her his room number. It was so embarrassing. He'd be wearing this stupid KISS baseball cap to cover his balding, weaved hair. He used to have this weave that looked like a Davy Crockett hat. It looked like birds were living on his head. And his stupid cap would sit on top of it because it couldn't fit over that plugged-up monstrosity. Every night he wore the same blue work shirt that said KISS on it, so he stunk to high hell. He still wouldn't shower with us. He'd just take a wet rag and wipe off all the blood he spat during the show: down his chest, on his dick. He'd wipe it off, throw the rag in the corner, and then he'd take a towel so you wouldn't see him naked, slip his underwear on underneath, and then drop the towel. There would still be nasty blood dripping down his legs, nasty spit; his hair had all this stuff in it. He'd just take another towel, wipe it, and put on his blue work shirt and those cheap vinyl pants that were supposed to look like leather. And this prick thought he was handsome!

He'd call the waiter over to the table.

"Mr. Simmons, what's wrong?"

"This is chicken?"

"Yes, sir."

"It looks like the dead carcass of a pig's asshole, you jerk. Go get me something that looks like food, not road kill." As the waiter walked away he'd say, "Waiters. No money, no brains. Morons."

Why didn't I want to eat with them?

Then I'd have the Machiavellian Starchild at the table. Paulie had to have everything perfect. "This food is horrible. This isn't the way it should be made." So the waiter would say, "Well, how would you like it, Mr. Stanley?" And he would say, "I have to tell you how to cook?"

Ace would be slobbering over his food and Doc McGhee would be laughing, drinking: "Let me tell you another story about Michael Jackson. I was in his room once . . ." Blah, blah, blah. It was a circus. I just couldn't sit at this table of fools. As much as they accused me of being a degenerate drug-addict maniac, I had more class in my pinkie than those animals will ever have with all their money.

They would sit there, Doc and Gene and Paul, and they would talk over important band business as if Ace and I didn't even exist. Doc would joke, "So on the Super Bowl show, I have an idea. We get fifty-six naked chicks running around—" And if we chimed in with our opinion, they'd be like, "What did you say?"

"I'm in the band, no?"

"No, you're Ace and Peter. We're KISS. We make the decisions, you guys just play in the band."

They'd say that stuff at the dinner table with the local promoters there and their guests—like I needed to be put in my place in front of strangers?

Gene and Paul would always act superior, make you feel like you were beneath them. You had to constantly be on your best behavior; you couldn't loosen up and be yourself or laugh and have a good time without thinking that they were going to make fun of you or stare weirdly at you. They would just feed on every weakness you had. If you pronounced a word incorrectly, they'd jump on you and correct it in such a condescending way in front of everybody. Ace wasn't like that. He was so dysfunctional himself that he certainly couldn't throw the first stone. Ace wasn't evil, I thought.

I brought Gigi to dinner with them once and she never wanted to go again. She was kicking me under the table, whispering, "Now I know why you don't want to go out with them, they're insane." So we would just go back to the room after the show. That was what that song on my last album "Doesn't Get Better Than This" was about. We'd lock that hotel-room door and Gigi would call up room service. We'd eat something good, order up a movie, make love, go to sleep. So who wanted to go down and have dinner with the fools?

CHAPTER EIGHTEEN

I *was a nervous wreck the whole day, just waiting for the armored car* to arrive. Finally, the doorbell rang in my apartment in Marina del Rey. I rushed to get to the door before Gigi. A man with a gun strapped to his holster gave me a small package. I quickly signed for it, tore the package open, and removed its contents.

"Who's that, hon?" Gigi said from the other room.

I didn't answer. She came into the living room to investigate. And then I got down on one knee, just like I'd seen so many times in the movies.

"I know I've been an asshole lately, but I love you so much and I will take very good care of you and I'll always be there for you and I'll provide a good life for you."

Gigi looked down on a fifty-two-year-old long-haired man with tattoos. Later she would tell me that this wasn't quite what she had envisioned for herself. She thought that she'd be married to a dignified, straight, Waspy guy, someone like Peter Graves. Instead she was getting Peter Criss.

"Will you marry me?" I finally asked her. We had been together for a year and a half by now and I knew Gigi was the right one. She was a sober, clear thinker, a good role model for my daughter. I love being married, so this just seemed right to me.

"Yes," she said. She put that ring on and went out onto the balcony and kept looking at her hand. We celebrated with dinner at the Magic

Castle that night, and then we shot some videos of ourselves kissing and bouncing around the apartment like two little kids.

Meanwhile, Gigi was getting unsolicited advice about our marriage. One night Gigi got a call from Deb, who was obviously drunk.

"You know, Peter's really a son of a bitch in the long run. You better be aware of what you're getting yourself into," she told Gigi.

Gigi got irate.

"Who are you talking to?" she said.

"Well, I'm his ex-wife," Deb said.

"Yeah, ex," Gigi answered. "How dare you talk about Peter like that to me?"

They got into a huge fight and at one point, Deb actually said, "It should be me in that Learjet, not you." When she hung up, Gigi told me that now she understood why I wanted to kill Deb.

We got married on May 3, 1998. I had a traditional big church wedding with Lydia and a posh Beverly Boulevard wedding with Deb, and I thought both of them sucked. So I suggested that we have a quiet wedding, just me and her. We'd fly out her mother. My drum tech could be the best man. Gigi liked David the hairdresser on our tours, so he could give her away. I could tell she wasn't that thrilled about not having any of her friends there, but Gigi agreed.

I loved the Bel-Air hotel. It had a lot of great history: Marilyn stayed there, Gregory Peck stayed there, Jimmy Stewart, Bob Hope. It was really exclusive. We rented a big, beautiful suite.

I didn't invite the band. I didn't want Gene and Paul there for sure, and I certainly didn't want Ace to be there with some crazy chick, stoned and fucked up. It was Gigi's and my day. The guys wound up sending two big diamond watches to show respect. Gigi invited Rachel, one of Gene's longtime girlfriends whom she had gotten close to. I thought that she was just going to spy on us for Gene, but it was Gigi's wedding, too, so she came.

I wanted a priest to officiate but you can't get a Catholic priest if you're divorced, which is bullshit, so we found a great minister through my doctor friend Terry Hammer. Gigi looked absolutely gorgeous in a simple white dress, no big ruffles or flowers. She looked so classy she should have been on the cover of *Bride* magazine.

We exchanged vows and then had a sit-down dinner in a private dining room next to the hotel kitchen. They served a great dinner, soup to nuts, and some good champagne. I swore to Gigi that I wouldn't get high, but I started knocking back that champagne and soon enough my jacket came off and my tie was loose.

That night there was a mix-up, and instead of a nice suite, they put us in a regular room. Normally I would have gone crazy over their screwup but now, all of a sudden, I just froze up, and the magnitude of what had happened just hit me. I went out and sat alone in the garden.

"Is this cool? Should you have gotten married again? You've been married twice already, and they were miserable failures," I thought to myself. We had already bought a big house in Jersey and we were going to move in right after the wedding. "Now you're married to a real straightforward woman who lives by God. No more hanky-panky and champagne parties," I mused. It's time to grow up and be a man.

Be a man? I had no idea what that meant. I had always lived in a child's world: Keeping that childlike innocence was really important to me. So all these doubts were going through my head, and now I felt guilty that it was Gigi's wedding night and we weren't even having sex because I was so freaked out. Gigi was really understanding.

"You seem scared, Peter," she said. "Do you regret marrying me?"

I didn't know how to answer. Meanwhile Gigi was depressed because she felt that she was paying for all of the mistakes I had made with other women. She didn't get a nice, elaborate wedding because I was concerned about having a woman who drains all my resources in my life. I was wrong. Later I'd feel bad that I denied Gigi the wedding she'd always envisioned.

The next day we flew home and I felt suffocated, sitting in coach between Gigi and her mother. Whoever made the arrangements had screwed up royally, because I always flew first-class, but here I was dying to have a scotch and soda, wedged between two people who were sober. "I can't even have a fucking drink? What did I get into?" I thought. So I sat on my hands and white-knuckled it, counting the hours until we landed.

Ironically, they would have been fine with me having a drink. It was my hangup.

Later that summer, KISS was set to go into the studio to record our new album. Both the fans and I were really excited; this was going to be the first time the four of us had collaborated on an album in twenty years. Ace and I were both working on songs diligently. But then, once again, our hopes were shattered. We found out that they didn't want Ace or me to play on the album. They were offering us $850,000 each not to play! I had heard that Paul once said he wouldn't play in a studio with us ever again. I guess now that was confirmed.

That was a lot of money for nothing, but I didn't want to just take the money and not play. It was never just about money for me, it was always about the music. Then Doc asked us to sign a paper saying that we played on the album. I told him I couldn't lie like that. "But the fans gotta feel you guys did the album together," Doc protested.

I sat down with Tommy Thayer (who would eventually play guitar on all of the tracks except for two) and wrote a couple of really good songs. One, "Hope," was a ballad that I wrote for Gigi, and, since the tour was going to be called the Psycho Circus Tour, we wrote "Psycho Circus," a cool tune that could have been the signature song on the album. Like they would have ever let me have that. I was set to come to the studio and play the songs for Gene and Paul, but that cocksucker Thayer snuck behind my back and brought them the demos before I could play them for them. Of course I was shot down, but I complained so much that they set up a meeting for me with the producer, Bruce Fairbairn. We met for lunch at the Bel-Air Hotel. He seemed like a nice guy, another Canadian like Ezrin. And he was also wired, I realized.

Bruce put the headsets on and listened to my stuff with his eyes closed, like he was into it. He already knew they weren't going to use any of it; they just wanted to placate me with this meeting, and that's what he did. He listened and said, "I like what I hear, Peter, there's a lot of emotion here, but I don't know if it fits in the KISS genre. I'll get back to you, I got to get back to the studio, we have a session today," he told me.

I'm thinking, "I should be at that fucking session. This is so disrespectful." Instead of Ace and me, they had their road manager Tommy Thayer playing guitar and a guy named Kevin Valentine playing drums. Now I was locked out of my own band's sessions. But then I get a call that Paul wanted me to sing a ballad that he wrote with Ezrin. If I sang it, they could tell people that I appeared on the album. I listened to the song, "I Finally Found My Way," and it was just a blatant attempt at another "Beth," except it sucked. The lyrics were about this pitiful, pathetic loser who finally finds his way back to God or Bob Dylan or some chick, who knows?

Bruce told me that I could do the song any way I wanted, so I went in and sang it as if it was a Sam Cooke song. I gave it a bluesy feel, I sang my heart out, and Bruce loved it. Next thing I knew, Paul called me.

"We heard you were down there recording," he said.

"Yeah, I wanted to get a feel for the song," I said.

"Well, we listened to it and you sound like Jimmy Durante."

This was Paul's attempt at a joke.

"What do you want, Paul?"

"I'm going to the studio, and you come down and I'll be right next to you in the room and make sure we do it the right way," he said. There was one note on the song that I couldn't really hit. So he wanted to come in and sing it with me so I could get it right.

"You mean your way. There's no right or wrong way, there's Paul Stanley's way."

I went back and sang the song and it was like going through a root canal. Paul stood there every fucking second: "No, Peter . . . like this."

It was the same old shit.

Then Ace called me. He really wanted a song on the album and he was breaking balls big-time, calling Gene every hour—"I want my fucking song on the album. I'm going to quit the band if I don't get a song." So they finally caved. Ace had written something called "Into the Void," which was perfect for the Spaceman, but it wasn't really a good song. Ace insisted that I come over to his apartment and rehearse with him because he wanted me to drum on at least one song on the album. That's what I loved about Ace. He always did seem to have my back.

So we went into the studio and Gene and Paul were standing there, like they're the producers, and we cut the track. It was a nightmare, and it was even worse when we tried to play it live, but Ace was appeased. He got a song on the album so he stood to make some money because it was going to sell well. Nobody was going to know that we weren't on it. But in fact, the album was subpar. There was a bad song from Ace, I sang a song at gunpoint, they got a substitute in for me so they're not getting that flaming fiery instinctual drumming that they had years ago, and the road manager is playing Ace's leads.

In October of 1998 we started the Psycho Circus Tour. Right off the bat, things started going wrong. The big gimmick for this tour was that we were going to have a huge 3-D monitor in the middle of the stage. During the show there would be previously recorded segments shown in 3-D, so from the audience it would look like Paul and Gene and Ace's guitars would be right in your face and my drumsticks would seem to be inches from your nose. But all that was based on the idea that you could get thirty thousand KISS fans to wear the cardboard glasses and that the glasses would work. Neither assumption was correct. The 3-D effects never seemed to work, and nobody wanted to be hindered from seeing the big picture of what was going on onstage. It made no sense. Why show some snippets of 3-D on a screen while the actual band was playing? So people just chucked their glasses, and we took a bath on that tour because the technology to do 3-D was super-expensive in those days. We worked hard to get it to work right to no avail.

Even though the 3-D effects hardly ever worked, I still loved being up on that screen. I began to get off on the power that huge image would have on the audience. One night I was playing and I was pointing my sticks at chicks in the audience and almost as if by magic, one by one, they lifted up their tops and flashed their boobs. So I started using it as a Harry Potter–type wand to get people to do things. Once this couple on the side of the stage were actually fucking and I pointed to them and the guy lifted his girl's dress. He had been boning her from the rear.

The tour rolled on, and we did a European leg, but when we got back to the U.S. we decided to pull the plug. Ticket sales were nowhere as good as the reunion had been. Besides, Gene and Paul were preoccupied with other things. Paul was up in Toronto playing the Phantom in a stage production of *Phantom of the Opera*. He was great. He should have stayed in theater. Meanwhile Gene was busy putting the finishing touches on our next film, *Detroit Rock City*.

His next film, to be more precise. In 1982, Tim Sullivan, a huge KISS fan, had befriended Gene when he interviewed him for *Fangoria,* a horror magazine. Ten years later, Tim was working with New Line, the hottest movie studio in California, so Gene pitched him a proposal for a KISS movie called *The Creatures of the Night*. It was the same old *Phantom of the Park* bullshit with talismans and superpowers. Tim and the New Line guys hated it.

At the same time, a few young filmmakers were writing a script that focused on the KISS fans, a much more creative idea. The main character was a drummer who was obsessed with me. It was like a Holy Grail story where the grail was my drumstick and the drummer had to retrieve it just like Lancelot had to find Excalibur. This script was called *Detroit Rock City.*

The script was sent to KISS's office for KISS to be a part of. Somehow Gene got wind of this and hijacked the script, made himself the producer, and got Barry Levine, one of our longtime photographers, to coproduce it with him.

It was such a good script that Tim got it green-lighted in two weeks at New Line. But for Tim to work on it, he had to get permission from Gene to be a producer. Gene gave it to him, but Tim wound up making a $50,000 producer's fee next to Barry's fee of $500,000. God knows how much Gene made.

Ace, Paul, and I didn't even know about the movie until we read about it in the *Hollywood Reporter.* After we met with Tim and the producers, I was excited. This wasn't some Hanna-Barbera pablum, this was a real movie with a director, Adam Rifkin, whom I had heard about and admired for his movie *Mousehunt*. I really wanted to work on it, but then Gene started fucking everything up.

He had them take out a scene where the kids meet us backstage because, according to him, "Ace and Peter can't act." Tim asked Ace and me to come up with some ideas for our own cameos. That idea got axed when Gene put down his big fat producer's foot. Then he told the other producers and the director that Ace and I were like children and we needed to be kept on a tight leash. But he also lumped Paul in with me and Ace. Word got back to Paul, and he got really pissed that he was being marginalized, too. By then I was used to being put on the same shitlist as Ace.

New Line started discussing the music for the film with Gene. He threw out any songs that weren't written by him and Paul. If they used "Beth," then they couldn't use the vocal, because then they'd have to pay me. We wanted an original song for the movie, not something from *Psycho Circus,* so Paul said he wanted to write it.

As they went into production, the New Line guys were getting harassed by Gene, who was pitching them all these other projects. He was licking every New Line asshole he could find, he was so desperate to break into Hollywood. I remember we'd all be in a limo and Gene would say, "Can we have some quiet in the car please? I'm expecting a call from Steven Spielberg." Of course the call never came. It took years for Gene to get a call from Hollywood. He finally got a reality show. Only it was his reality.

Tim and the director wanted us to record a new version of "Detroit Rock City" to use in the finale of the film. But Doc and Gene tried to give them the recording of that song from *Alive II.* They told Gene that it wouldn't work and, for the last time ever, the four of us got in the studio and recorded a new version of "Detroit Rock City." I did twenty-one takes in one day. Not bad for an old man, right?

The movie was completed, and it was testing through the roof. Now it was time for the director and Tim to hear the new song Paul wrote for the end credits. Gene called them into the studio, and they were shocked to see just Paul there. Ace and I never even knew about this new song. Gene sat them down and they were expecting some kick-ass rock anthem to end the movie, and all of a sudden they heard violins and Paul singing, "Wherever you are, I'll be there for you." There were no drums, no guitars: It was Paul and a karaoke machine doing a bad imitation of Steven Tyler. The song may have been okay for a remake of *Romeo and Juliet,* but it wasn't working here at all. The New Line guys didn't know what to say. Gene later told them that he hated the song, too, but that he had fucked Paul over so much that he told Paul that the end credits could be his domain. So they had to keep the song.

Now New Line wanted a music video. They wanted to include all of us in the video, but Paul and Gene nixed that. So now New Line had lost its KISS song and its KISS video. They wound up using Paul's lame song at the very end of the credits for twenty-five seconds. But the final "fuck you" was that the great new version of "Detroit Rock City" that we had just recorded—that New Line was convinced was going to help sell massive quantities of the soundtrack album—never made it onto the soundtrack. Doc accidentally gave them the master of the remix of "Detroit Rock City" from the *Double Platinum* album, and that was the version on the soundtrack. I'm still convinced this last trick was a ploy to keep them from paying Ace and me residuals.

By the time the movie was released, on August 13 of 1999, New Line was fed up with Gene's lies. He had promised an incredible KISS media blitz that would include a kick-ass single, a kick-ass video, clips from the movie playing at every KISS concert, postcards handed out at every show, all this tie-in promotion. It was all bullshit.

New Line arranged for a huge premiere in Westwood and we played a show in the street outside the theater. We were supposed to get paid to play, but of course we never did. A few days later, KISS received a star on the Hollywood Walk of Fame. That really meant a lot to me. When it was my turn to speak, I dedicated the award to my mom. That day I looked out into the audience and saw Tim, our producer, standing out in the audience with the fans. Gene and Barry Levine were posing with the star and carrying on backstage, but they made Tim, the man who brought the film to New Line, stand out on the street behind a barricade. He didn't exist for them anymore: They had used him and discarded him. I pulled him out of the crowd and brought him backstage. That's when I found out that it was Tim, not Gene, who got us the star in the first place. One more lie.

The movie came out to scathing reviews. But the reviews didn't really mention the movie—they were all focused on how this was another attempt by Gene to milk the KISS fans out of whatever money they had that they hadn't already spent on KISS condoms or KISS coffins. The negativity was a backlash against Gene's continual attempts to cash in on the band's success in lame ways.

Tim took the failure of the film hard. After a few months of licking his wounds he decided to visit Gene, maybe to get some closure. He went to Gene's house and Gene was sitting on his throne. He actually has a throne that he sits on in the middle of a room that's packed with memorabilia and is a shrine to himself.

Tim told Gene how sad the whole experience had been for him.

"You know, Gene, I've got to tell you that it's very upsetting to me, as a friend and as a KISS fan, when I read these interviews and you're just trashing Peter and you're trashing Ace. Sometimes as brothers you fight, but when you go out into the world you should still be a family. It's really tough when the critics are criticizing this movie and criticizing you, for you to just lash back by shit-talking Ace and shit-talking Peter, but also shit-talking KISS. I can't stand it when you say that KISS isn't a rock band, they're a rock brand. It's wrong."

Gene looked at Tim, who had poured out his heart, with amusement.

"Sullivan, you know what your problem is? You believe in all this," Gene said with glee.

But Tim was right. We dyed our hair, we gave our blood, we struggled and cooked for each other in seedy hotels because we were a band, not a brand. It's shocking and horrifying that Gene has forgotten that.

Right before the last few dates of the Psycho Circus Tour, Paul convened a meeting in his room before a show. The tour had been a disaster and was bleeding money.

"Things aren't going well on the tour," he said. "We don't want to, but we're going to have to pull the plug on the upcoming legs of the tour. But we have an idea. We're going to do a farewell tour, one more time around for everyone to see us. We probably won't make much, we may even lose money, but we think we should do it for the fans. Then we can leave the right way."

Who the fuck was he kidding? Gigi picked up on it right away. "They're full of shit. They're going to make a small fortune," she told me.

Of course, Ace and I had to sign new contracts, and we wound up getting less money than we had on the previous tours. I had been previously represented by the same lawyer who also represented both George Sewitt and Ace. I fired him because I became convinced that he never really had my best interests at heart.

My new lawyer was a young kid from Jersey, and he turned out to be a fucking idiot. Their lawyer, Bill Randolph, just ate him up and spit him out. My guy was in over his head, and I paid the price. It's on my mind every day of my life.

On February 14, 2000, we announced a farewell tour that would begin in March and run for two years. VH1 was sponsoring the tour, and they covered it almost every day. So it seemed to Gigi and me that this tour would be mammoth and make a fortune—for Gene and Paul, of course. By then I was so tired of fighting them over money I figured getting a nice salary would be enough. I'd retire and never have to see them again. But once we got out on the tour and I saw the packed houses every night, I got pissed. Ace and I were earning peanuts compared to them. Doc was making more money off the tour than Ace and I were. Every time they'd talk to me, they'd belittle me or correct me. That's what wives do, not band members. We were supposed to be brothers. I felt that deep down something was wrong.

Ace and I coped in different ways with the second-class treatment we were getting. A joint and a couple of beers after the show was the extent of my drug use. I wish I could say the same for Ace. He was a nightmare. Some nights it was a feat for him to even stand up on the stage. Each girlfriend he'd have on tour was worse than the last in terms of enabling him. One of the girls was into designer heroin, so that was fun: Ace falling into the jet, then falling out of the jet when we landed. I truly feel that if it wasn't for Gigi, Ace would be dead now. She would literally feed him and wipe his mouth—food was falling out of it, he was so fucked up. If she saw Ace about to nod out, she'd divert his face from the mashed potatoes. She'd get him a pillow so it looked like he was taking a nap and not nodding out. I'm thrilled to death that Ace is sober now, but he was just a mess on the farewell tour.

Onstage, Paul was up to his old tricks. He would constantly signal me to slow down the tempo and it looked like it was my fault, that I couldn't play in time. But Paul had to have been popping painkillers before the shows, because by then he had chronic debilitating hip, knee, back, and ankle problems. Of course, nobody knew that, and I certainly wasn't going to say anything about it in an interview. Gigi would get all frustrated when I wouldn't defend myself, but I had too much integrity to trash Paul then.

Shortly after this, I received probably the most devastating blow I'd ever suffered in my professional life. It started when Gigi was talking to Ace's girlfriend Betsy. Somehow money came up, and Gigi said that I was making forty thousand a show.

"No, fifty," Betsy corrected her.

"No, forty," Gigi stood her ground.

"No, fifty, it's in the contract," Betsy said, and gave her a piece of paper. Gigi ran to a copy machine and, heart racing, copied the document. The whole time they were talking, Ace was in the bathroom. Then Betsy went into the bathroom and the two of them were taking forever to get out. When Ace finally came out, Gigi confronted him.

"Are you making fifty thousand a show?" she asked him point-blank.

Ace wouldn't answer her.

A week later, Gigi had gone home and I was alone on the road. I got a call from Mac, one of Ace's bodyguards.

"Hey, Peter, Ace wants to talk to you."

"Well, why can't Ace call me?" I said.

"He's a little fucked up. He wants you to come up to his room, he's really upset and he wants to talk," Mac said.

I dropped whatever I was doing and went up to the room. Ace was sitting in the middle of the bed with a beer bottle in his hand. He looked smashed. My guess was alcohol and pills.

Mac saw me in and then left us alone in the room.

"Cat, I gotta tell you something," Ace said. "It's killing me and I can't live with myself anymore."

"What do you mean?" I asked.

"I've done something really wrong. I should never have done this, but money does strange things to people. I've been making a lot more money than you on the tour."

"Really?" I was shocked.

"Yeah," he said, and downed the beer, threw it on the floor, and opened another.

"They've been paying me ten thousand more a night than you," he said. "Plus I'm getting a piece of the merch."

"That's a nice chunk of change," I said. I didn't know what to say.

"I can't live with myself anymore. I see you up there smiling and breaking your ass. You and Gigi are really sweet to me and this is just wrong. I can't live this lie anymore."

I was so hurt that I thought I was going to take a heart attack. I didn't know how to react. Should I say something? Yell at him? Punch him out? I decided to just leave and go back to my room. On the way back, I could feel my blood pressure going up and I started to sweat and my hands got clammy and I felt this intense pain in the middle of my chest. I got back to the room, downed a beer, and took a Valium. Then I called Gigi to break the news to her. It confirmed what Betsy had told her.

Ace was a guy I would kill for. We were like brothers for over twenty years. I cried for hours. I was in shock. I had a deep sense of loss because I knew that I would never again feel the same way about Ace.

After his confession, Ace tried to patch things up by showing me checks he was getting, a hundred thousand here, sixty thousand there, and urging me to have my lawyer get me the same.

To add insult to injury, two months earlier we were playing Vegas and I was complaining to Paul.

"I can't take this shit anymore," I told him while we were walking down the hallway at the Palms. "You guys are fucking me at every turn."

Paul looked me in the eye and kissed me on the lips.

"Peter, I swear on my kids, there's nothing going on."

Gene told me the same thing. "I swear on my children, I will never fuck you over."

You're going to swear on your fucking kids? That's heavier than the earth to me. But it was a lie.

Ace's betrayal hurt me more because I loved the man, but this was the final straw. I wanted to pack up my shit and leave. All your life you wanted to be here, onstage in front of millions of people, dressed in a cool costume, everybody waiting on you hand and foot, and here I was wishing I was anywhere else in the world.

I called my attorney and he called Randolph and he told him that I was going home. Immediately they freaked because there were seven more shows left on this leg of the tour before we had a break before the trip to Tokyo.

We had to play a show, so while they negotiated, I tried to figure out how I could communicate to the audience that I had been fucked over without putting it in the press. It came to me while I was putting on my makeup. I would add a little teardrop under my eye. In prison, a teardrop signifies that you're tough because you had killed someone. But to me, it meant that they had fucked me over. I knew that our fanatical fans would pick up on such a subtle alteration of my makeup, especially when it's up there on the JumboTron screen.

Ted Nugent was our opening act, and his wife asked Gigi why I was wearing the tear. When Gigi told her, she told Ted.

"I can't believe those guys," he fumed, and then he went out and dedicated his show to me.

On September 29 in Columbus, Paul announced that this was the final night of the tour. When I sang "Beth," I prefaced it by saying, "This is the last time I'm singing this, so this comes from the heart to you." Nobody knew if the tour was going to finish up the last six dates.

That night I told my drum tech, "Start packing up my drums, and I don't mean for a trailer. I'm going to send a personal plane for all my gear."

I guess they took me seriously, because the next day Randolph came up with an extra ten grand per show for me for the last seven dates. That didn't come close to making up the half million dollars they owed me in salary just for that tour, but for now at least I was back to parity with Ace, I thought. But who knew about any other deals they had?

So for the last seven dates, we'd put on our makeup and nobody talked to one another anymore. Nobody laughed, there was no music playing in the room, it was all about just getting through these shows. The last show of the tour, in Charleston, South Carolina, Paul started smashing his guitar at the end, so I got up and while the riser was still high up in the air, I started kicking my drums off it. Everyone stood up and cheered and Paul thought the cheers were for him until he turned around and saw a huge floor tom-tom coming down at him. So he took his guitar, threw it down on the stage, and walked off. He must have kept walking, because I didn't see him or Ace or Gene when I went in to take my makeup off.

After the last U.S. dates, my contract expired. We began the negotiations by demanding that they pay me the half million dollars I had lost in salary on the last tour while I was making less than Ace. They told me to go fuck myself, then they took my contract off the table, and that was the end of it. I was perfectly willing to continue as long as I earned as much as Ace. They didn't care. Now they could bring back Eric Singer to replace me again. Even though KISS has continued touring even as you read these words, that truly turned out to be the farewell tour. That was the last time anybody saw the four original members of KISS together on the same stage.

CHAPTER NINETEEN

I was standing on third, sipping on a beer. The softball arced in and the batter swung and hit a grounder in the hole.

"Go, go!" our third-base coach said.

I threw the bottle down and took off toward the plate. The fielder scooped up the ball and threw home. I was safe by inches.

"You're out!" the umpire shouted.

"What the fuck are you talking about? I was safe by a mile!" I screamed back.

"You are out," he said, and turned his back on me.

I went ballistic, even though I was playing for Quinn's and not the New York Yankees. I picked up the bat that was near the batter's box and hit the umpire in the back. He went down like a shot. Then I hit him in the chest. When their catcher tried to intervene, I hit him and he went down. The other players tried to stop me, but I was swinging the bat like crazy, keeping them at bay. They were all scared shitless of me.

"*Cut! Cut!*" the director yelled. "What happened to the rest of you? You were supposed to gang up on him."

"He looked like he was really going to hit us with the bat," one of them said.

"He's not going to actually hit you and crack your skull. He's an actor, just like you. I want you guys to attack him. Peter, are you going to kill them?"

"Yup," I smiled.

"All right, let's do another take," the director said.

It was early in the morning and we were shooting the scene that introduces my character, Marty Montgomery, on *Oz*, one of the hottest shows on TV in the summer of 2001. I had been out of KISS for a few months when I told Gigi that maybe it was time for me to try to get some acting jobs. I had always wanted to act in a real role, not some Hanna-Barbera superhero crap.

"I know Tom Fontana," Gigi volunteered. "Do you want me to call him and we'll have dinner and see if we can get you on *Oz*?"

I thought *Oz* was the coolest show on the planet. Where else could you see beatings, stabbings, and guys with their schlongs hanging down to the floor walking around? What single woman or gay guy would miss that show?

I had heard about Fontana. He had done *St. Elsewhere* and *Homicide,* and I thought those shows were so far ahead of their time. Before anyone else, Tom raised important issues like AIDS when nobody else would touch it. He was a real rebel, a tough Italian kid. I was dying to meet him.

It turned out that Tom owned a bar in SoHo. So Gigi and I drove into the city and met him there. He was sitting there drinking a bourbon, wearing a leather jacket, turtleneck, and jeans. To me, this was like meeting Spielberg: I put Tom right up there with those guys.

We exchanged pleasantries and sat down at the table.

"So what do you want to do, Peter?" he asked.

"I would love to get on *Oz*," I said.

"Well, we're working on next season's scripts right now," he said. "Tell me a little bit about yourself."

I gave him a quick bio: Brooklyn kid, Italian-German-Irish family, got in with a gang, made zip guns, rumbled. I told him about all the heartaches and bullshit with KISS. He was taking it all in, not saying anything.

"When we used in get in fights back in the neighborhood, I used to be real good with a bat. I could do a job on someone with that. Matter of fact, I got one in the back of my car, just in case," I said.

"If we do work together, I want to go to acting school immediately. I know I can't just walk on the set and read my lines. This is an intense show and if I get a part, I know it's going to be an intense character, not some rock-star shit. So I'll need some acting lessons. It's not gonna be like getting onstage and singing 'I Want to Rock and Roll All Nite.'"

Tom looked impressed with my attitude.

A few weeks later, I got a call from Tom. He had a part for me on the premiere of the new season playing a two-bit criminal named Marty Montgomery, who's in Oz serving eight years for two counts of assault in the first degree stemming from that bat-swinging incident during the ball game.

I started taking acting lessons with a man named John Eyd at Actors Training Institute in New Jersey. John had studied with Meisner and Strasberg and Stella Adler. His studio was over a pet shop, so I was skeptical about him at first, but Gigi had taken some lessons with him and she thought he was a genius.

He was majorly into method acting, which was perfect for me because you can forget your lines and make it up as you go.

"Fuck the words," John would say. He was more concerned with the feeling, the emotion, the reality of the performance. But if you made up your lines, they better be great.

Gigi dropped me off the first time I went. After she left, John sat me down. He was a big guy, six foot three, two-hundred-some-odd pounds. He was Syrian with a big Arab nose and the most intense eyes you'll ever see.

John asked me if I had acted before, and I told him about *KISS Meets the Phantom of the Park*.

"Action is not acting," John said. "Anyone could fight with a monster. Acting is using words and gestures to convince the audience that you are who you say you are. You have to be authentic."

"I'm going to get up and walk over to the other side of the room. I want you to look at me and realize that I'm someone you really admire and you can't believe it's me. You're freaking out. That's an easy thing, right?" he said.

So he went over to the corner and I was sitting there making all sorts of expressions and he was looking at me and saying nothing. I felt like I was making a jerk out of myself.

"Are you done?" he finally said.

"Yeah."

"That was absolutely terrible. You've got to learn not to act. I don't want you acting. I want you to be."

I started seeing him twice a week. Our relationship immediately blossomed and I wound up taking lessons with him for two years and we're close friends to this day. He had some unique teaching methods. He didn't like the way I read scripts, so he had me reading every sign I saw as I drove. And it worked. I was getting better. After about a month, John thought that I was a natural. Which was just as well, because Tom had sent over the script and I was supposed to shoot my scenes in a few weeks.

My character was a quick-tempered lowlife wise guy who would do anything for a buck. We began by shooting my action scene out on the ball field. Tom wasn't there for that, but he did show up for my first scene in Oz. I was sitting in the cafeteria eating lunch when Dean Winters came up to me. His character had just killed a man, and he wanted me to rat out another guy who was innocent. He was going to slip me some money to help him.

My big line was, "You never even farted in my direction and I've been here for three years, now you want something from me?" My acting teacher told me that I should deliver the line just staring at my food until I say the word *fart*, and then look at Dean. Then go back to looking down at my food.

Sure enough, they rolled the camera and I was a nervous wreck. I rushed all my lines.

"Relax, Peter, just tell the story," the director said.

So we did another take, and when I got to "fart" I delivered the line just the way John told me to. Tom Fontana's face lit up. He knew that a coach had to have told me how to deliver that line.

For my next scene, Tom paired me with Ernie Hudson, the great character actor who played the warden. I went in and squealed on the innocent guy and convinced the warden that my conscience had been bothering me. We did it in two takes.

"Good job, my man," Ernie told me. "For a guy that's just coming into the ball park, I think you got a career here." Ernie and I bonded off the set, and became very good friends.

I got knocked off in the next episode. I try to renegotiate with Dean to get more money, and he tells me to meet him in the library. Then Dean tells the guy I squealed on that I was a rat. This character was played by Tommy Waites, who was in *Miami Vice* and *The Thing*. Great actor. Tom gave me scenes with three of the best actors on the show.

I'm in the library and Tommy's character comes in, slams the door, and stabs me in the neck with a pen. They had a tube going up my shirt so when the pen hit me, blood went spurting everywhere. I fall down and the guards rush in and take Tommy away.

"Take him to the infirmary," someone says. That was a signal that they might bring my character back: I may recover. But I told Tom that I might have to go back out with KISS. Later on, in the final season, someone asked, "How's that Montgomery guy doing?" And the other guy said, "He ain't going to sing no more."

Fontana told me that he had used everything I had told him when we first met in his restaurant in building my character. When I told him all the stories about how Gene and Paul fucked me over, he had me go to the warden because I couldn't keep it inside anymore. And when I told him that the pen was mightier than the sword with these guys, and I had been fucked over so many times by signing bad deals, he had me bumped off with a pen. And of course in the end I wasn't going to sing anymore.

Acting in *Oz* was a great accomplishment. I practiced and practiced and was able to learn six pages of a script at a time. That's a lot of words to learn and deliver. I remember coming home from the taping with Gigi and feeling so proud. I had hit a home run, I didn't fuck up once, and sitting there in the limo I was exhilarated: It was one of the best feelings of achievement I'd ever had, next to playing Madison Square Garden.

Gene publicly maintained that I was a part of KISS even after I left the group after the farewell tour. It wasn't like they were doing so well without me. In February 2002 they played at a Lane Bryant fashion show. In March they performed at a nudist resort in the West Indies. By then Ace's contract was running out, so he refused to do that show. And when it ran out, he left KISS for good.

Just after the New Year in 2003, I got a call from Doc. KISS was going to Australia to perform with a symphony orchestra and it was going to be recorded for a CD and DVD. They wanted me to play. Jesus, it just doesn't end with these guys, I thought to myself. I had heard that Paul had been divorced after the farewell tour and his wife had taken him to the cleaners. I really liked Pam. She was a pretty girl from Texas, much too hot for Paul. Her father was a high-ranking military man and her family were builders. Pam was smart, and they had a son together, but you could see that she and Paul weren't in love. There was a distance that you felt when they sat together. Part of it was because Paul was possessive and insecure. When they were apart, he'd call her every five minutes.

I think another part of the problem was that Pam met and married Paul during the years KISS were unmasked. She had never really seen him perform in makeup. I watched Pam when she came to the shows and I think she couldn't handle seeing the Starchild up there slapping his ass and making out with himself. She would split in the middle of the show. After a while, she didn't even come out to the shows and then Paul was living in Gene's guesthouse, and then it was "See ya." So Paul had a lot of money to make back.

So did I, actually. I had lost a lot in the market after 9/11. I hung up after Doc gave me the whole pitch and I thought, "Wait a minute. These guys just ripped me off for millions of dollars. We were feuding. Gene is calling me names in the press. Our fans had probably flipped out reading so much shit from Gene. Yes, no; I love him, I hate him."

Then my lawyer called me. He told me that they were going to give me 25 percent of the proceeds from the album and DVD. I was going to make pretty much what they were making. Now, that was great. That album could sell. And the idea of playing with a sixty-piece orchestra hooked me right there. I would have paid my own money to go and play with sixty people.

So the deal was sounding better and better. Then I heard that David Campbell, the great conductor whose son is Beck, was conducting. So this was the chance of a lifetime for me.

I started working with Sandy Gennaro, a drum coach who had played with Cyndi Lauper. I wanted to be a walking metronome: I didn't want to embarrass myself in front of all those people. We worked for four months, eight hours a day, on tempo. Now there was no way that Paul would be able to complain about my tempo.

We rehearsed in L.A. I was having a great time, playing my drums with twenty percussion guys banging away around me. I was well oiled from the tutoring. Every fill had to be precise, every hit had to be precise; everyone was feeding off the drums. I was so up for playing.

And then Gene reared his ugly head. We were arguing about something and I casually said, "Look it, what does it matter? As long as I'm getting my one quarter of the album, it'll all be good."

"What?" Gene said.

"I'm getting an even share for this album," I repeated.

"You are getting nothing for this album. You are getting a paycheck. Over my dead body will you see one fucking dime from this record," he pronounced.

I went into shock. I called my lawyer and he assured me that I would be getting 25 percent. Of course, eventually I didn't see a fucking dime from the record. I had been ripped off again.

I even got screwed at the show. Gene and Paul arranged everything for their benefit, so they gave "Beth" the wrong slot in the set and only gave me thirteen pieces instead of the full sixty-piece complement. But I did enjoy playing that show. There's something about a woman spreading her legs with a cello in between them that is so hot. When they're playing, their dresses bunch up way over their knees. One woman even played barefoot. I had a perpetual erection looking at those cello girls.

When all was said and done and we were back home in New Jersey, I told Gigi, "I can't do this anymore. I want nothing to do with these guys." Look at all the people they drove mad. Poor Eric Carr, the guy who first replaced me, was reduced to sitting in his hotel room naked with the blinds all drawn, drinking and refusing to come out. Bill Aucoin lost his whole empire on drugs. Sean went crazy. Howard Marks died a drunk. Neil Bogart died. They drove Mark St. John and Vinnie Vincent crazy. The list could go on and on. There was no way in hell that I would ever tour with those guys again.

And then Doc called. I didn't want to talk to him, so I put Gigi on.

They were going to go out on tour again, and they wanted me to come out. Gigi started negotiating with Doc. He told her that they had tried to get Aerosmith to go out with them but it had fallen through, so this wouldn't be a big tour. Naturally, they wouldn't be able to pay me much money.

"Well, what kind of money are you talking about?" she said. "You can pay him at least twenty-five thousand dollars a show?"

"They're not going to go for that, Gigi," he said.

"Well, you disrespected Peter and treated him like a second-class citizen throughout the entire reunion tour," Gigi said. "You didn't give him the right merch money, you didn't do a lot of things financially that you were supposed to do, and now you're telling me that you won't give him twenty-five thousand dollars a show? Doc, I've been to these shows. I see what kind of money you people make."

They talked back and forth for a while until finally our lawyer told us that Doc didn't want Gigi to call him anymore; he would only negotiate with the lawyer. "You've got to do this," my lawyer told me. "You can walk away after this and retire."

I don't know why I believed this guy. They had gotten the better of him on the Australian negotiations. I still didn't know who owned my Catman makeup and what had happened to it. But Doc and my lawyer worked out a new contract based on this being a small-cities tour.

I was in L.A. rehearsing when Gigi and I went to Paul Stanley's birthday party at his house. Everyone there seemed to be ecstatic. Gene and Paul were smiling from ear to ear, already counting their money. Doc was drinking champagne and getting plowed. Gigi started talking to some guy from Cleveland who seemed to be in the know and he told her that Tommy Thayer was going to play on the tour. She was dumbfounded and she came right over to tell me. I was furious. I had been told by Doc that Ace was going to be playing.

Then we got more news. We were sitting in the veranda area with Paul and his new girlfriend when Doc came over.

"What happened, Doc?" Paul asked, as if it was for our benefit. "How'd the phone call go?"

"I just got off the phone with Brian," Doc said, all smiles. "We just signed the deal with Aerosmith."

I grabbed Gigi's hand and clenched it so hard I thought I would break it. Gigi had to restrain me, I was ready to get up and punch that fat fuck Doc in the face. They had screwed me again. I had signed my contract after they told me that it would be a small-venue tour and they swore they didn't know who was going to be the opening act, so I had agreed to play for ten thousand dollars a night. Now we were going to play big venues and I was getting none of the merch and a lousy ten grand a show.

We ran out of that party and got back to the hotel and Gigi called my lawyer.

"You are such an asshole!" she yelled. "What the hell did you do to us? Peter is so mad at me."

I couldn't believe that I was right back where I didn't want to be. But I needed the money.

I was back in New Jersey getting ready to go out on tour when I got a call from Joe Perry, Aerosmith's guitar player.

"Peter, we're having trouble with the tour," he said. "Ace ain't coming. But we want the real KISS on the tour. Can you call Ace?" Joe asked me. "Maybe you can talk him into it."

It looked like the tour might fall apart. Aerosmith's drummer, Joey Kramer, didn't want to get on the same stage with us: He thought we were just buffoons. But I wasn't going to call Ace and beg him to come out on tour. As much as I felt betrayed by Ace, I still would have preferred having him play instead of Tommy Thayer. I hated playing that one show in Melbourne without Ace. And this was going to be half a year out of my life.

But I bit the bullet and went back to the rehearsals. At first they had talked about the opener alternating between us and Aerosmith, but now Aerosmith decided that we were going to open every show. If Ace wasn't there, Aerosmith didn't feel that they deserved to open for an imitation of KISS.

It was an interesting tour, but I missed Ace. Instead I had Tommy/Ace. Thayer just morphed into being Ace. He moved like Ace; he started coming into the dressing room and acting like he was a star, throwing his shit all over the place, ordering people around.

I would sit there while I was putting on my makeup and just ruthlessly bust his balls.

"You think you're a rock star? You're a piece of shit. You used to order my breakfast," I'd say.

Gene would snicker because he didn't have the balls to tell Tommy off himself.

"Like he's earned the right to be called a rock star," I'd continue. "He's a stand-in for Ace. He doesn't even have his own licks, and I'm supposed to respect this piece of shit?"

"Peter is complaining again," Gene would say.

Sure, I was complaining. I grew to hate that guy. Tommy would come up to me onstage and I would look the other way. I didn't even want to look at him, I despised him so much.

Then Tommy started sitting in on meetings with Gene and Paul that I wasn't even invited to. Doc would call for a meeting and never once did he ask me to attend. Here's a fucking punk ass-licker privy to more shit than me. It broke my heart. I laugh about it now, but it killed me then.

I even hated Tommy's playing. He would play Ace's leads perfectly, note for note. That was the problem. I loved the crudeness of Ace. Ace wore twenty-four million bracelets, skulls, and chains. He had a ring on every finger, one of them the same big skull ring that Keith Richards, his idol, wore. And when Ace played, you'd hear the jewelry jangling and slamming against the Les Paul. Ace was electrifying. But Tommy played like a schoolteacher, perfectly precise. That's not KISS. KISS was a loose, great band. Now we're perfect, all of a sudden. Now and then I'd fuck around and try something different and I'd get a look. It was the same fucking boring show night after night after night.

As disgruntled as I was, Gigi kept me focused. She had talked me into playing the tour in the first place.

"Babe, you're fifty-six years old. This is your last shot, whether it's ten grand or two grand. You're never going to play Madison Square Garden again. Do like Bruce Springsteen, enjoy your glory days. Go out, enjoy the crowd, enjoy the moment, because it will be the last time you'll have your rock-star moment."

She was right. I never really enjoyed touring in the seventies. We were on the road all the time and it was too much, too fast. Plus you couldn't enjoy anything with Gene and Paul. I certainly didn't enjoy the reunion tour because I was so upset that they hadn't changed. So this time I was determined to go out and have fun. I thought, "Do it for yourself, Peter. You are the Catman, you created that image, you bring people alive with that image, you heal people with that image, you've changed people's lives."

So I had the best time of my life playing for me, really enjoying the curtain drop and the spectacular bombastic roar of the crowd through my headgear. If you were lucky to be at any of those last shows, it was probably the best I ever played and the best I ever sang. I really was reminded why I picked up the sticks when I was a kid. I just felt magical and wonderful.

Until we hit Vegas. There I heard that Tommy Thayer was getting paid $25,000 a night.

"That motherfucker is not even a real member of the band, and you gave him more money than me?" I yelled at Gene and Paul.

We would travel in a little Winnebago to the gigs because Doc and Paco kept crying about how bad this tour was doing. But we sold out every night, and eventually it was one of the top-ten grossing tours that year. Yet we were cutting back on the food, getting cheaper stuff. Meanwhile Aerosmith was pulling up in four limos. It was just more of Doc and Paco's bullshit.

I did enjoy touring with Aerosmith. I had been friendly with Joe Perry for years, and he's just a wonderful guy. I'd often be sitting on my balcony in the hotel and Joe would be walking by.

"Hey, Joe, what's happening?" I'd yell down.

"Ah, just another day in paradise, Petey," he'd say.

I also liked Tom and Brad. Joey Kramer, their drummer, was an asshole. And Steven was Steven. Steven couldn't get enough of himself. He wanted attention so bad, he was even worse than Paul. Everywhere he was, he'd be loud, boisterous, laughing, making sure people noticed him. It was like Steven World. I'd be taping an interview, and out of nowhere Tyler would stick his head in and say, "*Heeeey,* what's happening there? Tyler here." Then he'd disappear.

Tyler was really nice to Gigi, though. He would go over to her every day and give her a hug. "Come here and give me my sugar today, girl," he'd say. And they would talk about sobriety. Deep down, he was a sweet guy. Aerosmith were the best. It was an honor to play with them.

I loved their crew. Their road manager, Charlie Hernandez, was phenomenal to me. He took better care of me than Doc and our crew did.

I was getting sick from all the smoke from our pyro because it would rise and I'd be immersed in it. It got so bad that I would literally have to come down at the end of the show wearing an oxygen mask. That didn't look too good, especially for a fifty-seven-year-old man. Gigi would constantly complain and ask for additional fans for me, but our road manager, Patrick, was so far up Gene and Paul's asses that he claimed he couldn't do anything—that Aerosmith was in charge of the stage. So Gigi went to Charlie Hernandez and he immediately put in two extra fans that blew the smoke away so I could breathe again.

It was so obvious on the tour that Paul was jealous of Tyler. Aerosmith had built a ramp in the front of the stage that went way out into the audience. Paul was itching to get on that ramp, but the law was that only Steven and Joe could use it. Paul wanted to fly on his swing over the audience, but it was too expensive to use this tour, so he had no leg up on Tyler. Plus Tyler was one of the best entertainers I've ever seen. He's not a good-looking man, but like Mick Jagger he just oozes sex with those big, pouty lips. He was the chick magnet that Paul only dreamed of being.

So Paul became crazier. He started doing all these bizarre antics. He started going on and on with his raps as if he was an evangelist. Shut the fuck up! Now and then I would bang a drum in the middle of one of his raps to annoy him so he would shut up. It got so bad, we started calling him the Preacher. I'd look at my watch and he'd be talking for five minutes.

Then he'd put his arms behind him, turn his back to the audience, and passionately make out with himself. His hands would be in his hair; he'd be rubbing his ears. I would want to hide. Then he'd go into the Crab, as we called it. He'd take his guitar and stick it between his legs and ride it around the stage and then he'd hump himself with the guitar. Then he'd switch it around so it looked like the guitar was humping him in the ass.

I wanted to shoot myself. To make things worse, he'd go crazy and run from one end of the stage to the other, slapping himself on the ass.

What the fuck does that have to do with rock 'n' roll? Gene would look at me and shrug. He would just work his end of the stage and let Paulie go crazy. Tommy would disappear and then later tell Paul how great he was. He was Paul's bitch. He was on twenty-four-hour call in case Paul wanted to go out and look at fabrics or blinds.

In all my years of watching performers from Jim Morrison to Mick Jagger to Steven Tyler, I'd never seen any star make out with themselves, stick a guitar up their ass, fuck the guitar, and then run around slapping their own ass. I didn't get it. Maybe if there was a song called "Slap My Ass," then it would make sense. Sometimes I wondered how he ever got girls. But he became a focal point for a lot of gay guys. They would congregate in a section in the front of the stage and just look up at him and drool.

That was partly because Paul used to stuff his pants. He had done it before, but on the Aerosmith tour it was chronic. I guess he wanted to have a bigger dick than Steven. One night I caught him from the corner of my eye putting something down there. All of a sudden he turned around—and let's just say I know this man's dick, and that wasn't this man's dick. Steven Tyler even commented on it.

"Jesus, Paul, how the fuck do you walk around with that? That's one hell of a weapon you've got," he said.

"Ah, some of us are blessed," Paul said.

Gene and I both almost fell off the couch.

"What the fuck is he talking about?" I whispered to Gene.

"She's wild, Peter, she's wild," Gene smiled. "She can't help herself."

We actually began calling Paul "Wild One."

The problem with the stuffing was that his dick was a different size every show. Check out photos of him from that tour. I could relate to him, though. Sometimes when I was about to go out and sing "Beth," I'd rub myself a little to make it bigger. Then I'd walk out and the spotlight would hit me and boing! You couldn't miss that thing in my spandex pants.

Paul wasn't just insecure about his dick size. One night Lenny Kravitz came to see us and he walked right past Paul and came up and greeted me—"My man, Peter!"—because when he was a kid he used to wear the Catman's makeup. Paulie's face just dropped.

As dysfunctional as my relationship was with Gene and Paul at the end, they were feuding just as bad. We were all eating together during the Aerosmith tour, and Gene and Paul were at each other.

"Why don't you guys just make up?" I suggested. "This is a fucking nightmare, you two guys going at it."

"Being around him is toxic to me," Paul said. "So just stay out of this—this is between me and him. We do business together, but he's toxic. I can't be near him."

Paul walked out of the room.

Gene seemed genuinely hurt. "I didn't know he thought I was toxic," he said. "I thought he loved me."

"He just insulted you," I said.

"No, he loves me," Gene maintained. He was totally delusional. Then again, Paul could insult Gene as much as he wanted as long as they were making money together. Their relationship deteriorated to the point where Doc had to be a buffer between the two of them.

The tour was supposed to end on December 18 at the Forum in Inglewood, outside of L.A. But they added a show in Fresno on December 20, which was my fifty-eighth birthday. If it hadn't been for Gigi, they wouldn't have even gotten me a cake. But right before the gig, they announced it was my birthday and a couple of hot girls brought out a big cake. I came down off the drums, took a bow, everybody sang "Happy Birthday" to me, and then they took the cake away. We finished the show and then I found out that they were going to take the jet back to L.A. and they had arranged for Gigi and me to stay over and then take an eight A.M. commercial flight from Fresno to New Jersey. So everybody, including the Ace imposter, was getting flown home by private jet, but I was being sent home like second-class baggage. Gigi was pissed. So she got on the phone and booked a Learjet for us. She loaded it down with champagne and food and even had the nice big birthday cake delivered right to the jet.

We all left the gig and got to the airport. There were two jets, side by side.

"Whose fucking jet is that?" Doc said.

"It's Peter's," Gigi said proudly.

"What?"

"We're not taking any commercial flight home. We've got our own jet."

It must have cost quite a pretty penny, but it was worth it just to see the look on those guys' faces.

Paul's girlfriend didn't even say good-bye; she just got on their jet. Paul turned to me and said, "See you in a couple of months, Peter. Have a Merry Christmas." Then Tommy came over. "Take care of yourself, Peter," he said, and followed right behind Paul.

Gene came over. "Stay in shape, Peter. We have to play Tokyo in a couple of months."

Then Doc came over to me. He began to talk, but I cut him off.

"Ahh, don't even fucking go there with me. Don't tell me you love me, don't fucking open your mouth. Just shut up and merry fucking Christmas to you too," I said.

Then our pilot came up. "Mr. Criss, are you ready to leave?"

"Absolutely," I said, and I popped the champagne bottle in front of Doc. Gigi and I went up the stairs and Doc went up his stairs and we both slammed the door. And we took off in opposite directions. In my mind, I knew that was my last fucking night with those bastards.

I sat back in the plush seat and felt like a million dollars. At least I was leaving on top. I didn't leave playing the Sandbox to forty inattentive people. I didn't leave clinging to the stage while the audience was saying, "Look how fat he got. And he's wearing a wig. And they're doing the same fucking songs for fifty years."

My reverie was interrupted by Gigi, who poured me another glass of champagne. She had showed her love for me, and that made me feel important.

"You should feel important," she said. "You are an equal member of that band, and when you step on that stage, people go crazy. You don't get it, but you're the shit."

She was right. I never really believed that. After all those years of emotional battering from them, I always felt lesser than. Gigi was there to tell me to stop thinking like that.

So I took another sip of the champagne and nibbled on the cake. Now we were on our way home to start our new life. And I was going to make my own album and document all the pain I endured and all the shit I had been through and all the love that Gigi had shown toward me. "It doesn't get better than that," I thought as we winged our way back home.

CHAPTER TWENTY

The minute I got home from the tour, I went to see my psychologist.
My life was so tangled and stressed from being fucked over and lied to and
deceived. I was harboring immense anger toward Gene, Paul, and Doc. I
even fantasized about packing a gun and taking a plane to L.A. and shooting the three cocksuckers.

I had been seeing this guy since the end of the Psycho Circus Tour. I
chose to see a psychologist instead of a psychiatrist because I didn't want
someone to prescribe me drugs that would numb my thinking and feeling. I wanted to talk to someone and work out my problems in a rational,
intelligent way. So we discussed the whole history of the band and how
diminished I felt coming back and working as an employee for something
I had built from scratch. Over the years we talked about Gene and Paul's
Machiavellian game playing, Ace's betrayal, and all the other bullshit.

Ever since I had rejoined the group, I had been subject to relentless
emotional battering from Gene and Paul. And on top of that, I had been
battered financially. Gene once told Gigi that he was still resentful that he
had to pay me a share of the group's proceeds after I left the group. Now
that I was rejoining the band from a position of weakness, they had me
right where they wanted me.

Some of it was my fault. I never should have allowed Ace's manager and
lawyer to represent me. They had been Ace's guys for years, why did I think
they would work in my best interests? Ace was always about "I should get

more than Peter" right from that opening negotiation in their lawyer's office.

But I was so damaged from my divorce and my IRS troubles and my carjacking and its painful aftermath that I was just an emotional wreck and a big, fat target. I had nobody on my side, except for Gigi and God.

The terms of our contracts were always unfair. In the downtime between tours, Ace and I were getting a monthly payment that was a mere fraction of what Gene and Paul were collecting. There were all of these ancillary revenue streams coming in—video games and big commercials like the "Got Milk" campaign and a major Pepsi ad. I never got my fair share of that money that was supposed to be pooled and distributed between all of us.

And when we hired an independent auditor who claimed that KISS owed me a tremendous amount for merchandise revenue in 1999 alone, all they offered me was a puny settlement. I didn't have the money to fight it, so I wound up taking the settlement for pennies on the dollar.

The worst blow was losing my makeup. The Catman was a character I created and I never knowingly signed over to them. I'm a musician. I want to play drums. I trusted my lawyers and my managers. And I feel that they didn't have my back on this issue. I regret the loss of my makeup to this day. So is it any wonder that I was ready to go out to L.A. and do damage to Gene and Paul and Doc?

But my psychologist helped me build my confidence up. My anger was overwhelming and was literally making me sick. We talked and talked and he helped me come to terms with the poor decisions I had made and the people I trusted. I should have been happy. I had a nice home and money in the bank. But money doesn't buy happiness, I don't give a fuck who you are. When you're taken advantage of over and over again, it damages you. And it was always over money. But money is what they're all about. So sad.

Then it all started again. In May of 2004 KISS was going to tour again, starting first in Australia and Japan. I was still under contract to them, but I hadn't heard from them one way or the other. Finally, the afternoon that my contract was set to expire, I got a call from Paul.

"You know your contract runs out today," he said.

"Yeah, I did notice that," I said.

"You didn't seem too healthy that last tour, Peter. You were coughing a lot. The corporation thinks that it might be for your benefit that you don't go out on the road again."

The corporation? The guy didn't even have the balls to take responsibility. He had to hide behind the corporation? Plus I was coughing because night after night I'd inhale all that smoke from the bombs. Yet they were so concerned that they didn't do anything about it until Gigi complained to Aerosmith's people, who were pissed off because the smoke was affecting Steven Tyler's throat.

"The corporation just thinks it's better for both of us that you don't come out," Paul continued. "You're not that young anymore."

Yeah, I was young enough the last seven years when I made them very wealthy men. Paul just relished calling me directly so he could personally cut my throat and taste the blood. I was lucky not to be going on that tour. Now they could rehire Eric and have Thayer imitate Ace and pay them peanuts. Good riddance. I guess the fans had the final word. In the States, they played to half-filled houses and had to cut the tour off prematurely, they were losing so much money.

It wasn't like I was just waiting on pins and needles for them to call me. I had begun my solo album. I had written about five songs on the Aerosmith tour and Angel, my guitarist in Criss, now living in China, started sending me new songs that needed lyrics.

I decided to do a CD of ballads and draw on my experience of the last few years. So I wrote a song about my daughter and a song about my ex. I had been in New Jersey when the world turned upside down on 9/11, and I wrote a song about that harrowing experience. The plight of those first responders to the Twin Towers hit me so hard that I volunteered and played for a concert that raised millions for the heroes of 9/11.

And then there was "Doesn't Get Better Than This."

"Old-time movies, up till three / Another night, just you and me / The trip was lonely but now we're here / Let's lock the door and disappear / It doesn't get better than this." It was about getting away from the bullshit and going into a different world once we closed that hotel-room door. I wrote a song called "Faces in the Crowd" about our fans, and how the spotlight should be shown out onto the audience's faces—because they really were the stars. I wrote a number of songs about Gigi.

I even wrote a song about Ace for the album: "Space Ace." You might think it was a tribute, but I was really writing about Ace's betrayal of me.

> Have you ever been locked in a spaceship? / And lost in your lies? / Flying high above the highways / still trapped in the skies / I know the meaning of success / oh, but you got to believe / Evil has a way of showing its face

I had put all my experiences of my last go-round into these songs and I just knew the fans would love the CD for its honesty.

I called Tall Man, my old bass player, and he came and stayed in my guest room in New Jersey so we could work on laying down the tracks. But working with Tall Man again was a disaster. I had come off years of touring so I was smoking hot: My chops were like nothing he had ever seen when I was with Criss. As soon as he started playing, I saw that he was sloppy and unsure of himself. He just couldn't jam anymore. Tall Man was one of the best bass players I had ever worked with, but now he had a kid, was raising the child as a single father, and had given up the bass. He felt uncomfortable, and I felt bad for him. I loved the guy, but it just wasn't working, so he went home. But not before he wrote some great music for the "Space Ace" song.

Meanwhile Angel was sending me stuff from China, and one song was better than the next. I was taking the music and writing lyrics and working on arrangements. By then I had met an engineer named Tom Perkins who seemed to be very knowledgeable, so I called him and he helped me get whatever equipment I'd need to record professionally.

When we had fifteen or so good songs, I flew Angel in from China. I had set up a small home studio so we could work there. We buckled down and worked eight hours a day. Now it was time to record, and Angel was a Pro Tools genius. He said that he could engineer the recording, but I wanted his brain on his guitar playing. We started out recording with just me and Angel, figuring that we'd add the bass later, which was a big mistake. But Angel could play enough bass to fake it. Tall Man was supposed to come back when he regained his chops, but he never did. We tried sending him the tapes so he could add his bass, but that didn't work out either.

So I went to New York and met with Paul Shaffer. Paul was an old friend, and he listened to the tracks that I wanted him to play on and loved them. He wound up offering to play for free—that's the kind of guy he is. But we did pay him.

Through Paul, we got the great bass player Will Lee. He didn't play for free. He had his fee and he was going to get it no matter what the gig was. But he was a world-class musician, so we bit the bullet. We went into a studio in New York and he was there for hours, playing bass on five tracks. When it was over, he came over to me.

"You know that 'Send in the Clowns' cover you're doing? I really dig it. I'll play on that for free," he said. So that became a special track with both Will and Paul playing on it. Paul also turned me on to Clifford Carter, who did all the string arrangements.

We went home and I recorded the vocals in my huge two-story-tall living room. The sound was brilliant. Then I decided that even though we had recorded the CD digitally, I wanted that warm analog sound. Thousands of dollars later, that was accomplished.

It was time to mix the CD. I soon realized that I didn't know how to do a mix with all these different elements. I was in a guitar band. Give me three guitars and a set of drums, and I could produce fine. But twenty strings and cellos and French horns, I don't know where the fuck I'm going. And Tom Perkins, the engineer, was in even further over his head. He was basically a sound engineer for dialogue. He didn't know how to mix music. I had hired two young engineers to assist, and they told me that Tom had no idea how to work with all this new technology: He was so old school. I was turning into a gestapo officer, screaming at Tom every time he fucked up. Lucky for me, Chris Jennings stepped up and engineered the rest of the album and we had the great George Marino, from Sterling Sound, master the disc. By the time we were done, the CD cost me at least a hundred grand.

In July of 2007, *One for All* was finally released. It had taken me three years to make it. My lawyer cut a really good distribution deal with a company called Megaforce and they did a good job, getting me into Best Buy and other big chains. I hired Lori Lousararian, a great publicist, and we broke our asses doing radio interviews, sometimes twenty a day. We had a signing at a record store in the Village and there were hundreds of people lined up around the block. Things seemed to be looking good, thanks to Gigi.

So imagine how devastated I was when the CD failed. I really believed it would sell. I thought the fans would want to scour the lyrics to see if there was any dirt in them. After all that work, the recording, going into the city to mix it, all that money, I was crushed. I never really wanted to wear all those hats. I'd rather be a member of a team than a boss any day. But I wasn't just one guy in a band, I was *the* guy, so this failure was all on me. I couldn't even blame the producer! I was the producer.

I was so depressed and Gigi thought that going to Hawaii might jar me out of my funk. But it was worse there. I went to my favorite spot, a big rock that overlooked the ocean, and I took my Walkman and listened to my album over and over again. I couldn't believe that it had tanked. There were such great songs on it, and great players. We covered my mom's favorite song, "What a Difference a Day Makes," with just Paul Shaffer, Will Lee, and me playing the brushes. I had cut Stephen Sondheim's "Send in the Clowns." Those wonderful lyrics—"Isn't it rich, isn't it queer / Losing my timing this late in my career? / And where are the clowns? There ought to be clowns / Maybe next year"—were a sly reference to KISS.

I had hired the best guns in the world, and I thought that I couldn't fail. So I sat on those rocks listening over and over again, and each song was like a knife twisting into my heart and my guts.

I went back to the hotel. Gigi was lying by the pool, and I told her that I wanted to go up and take a nap. But I didn't. I just wanted to be alone, and as soon as I darkened the room and lay down on that bed, I cried and cried like a baby. I became the most miserable man on Kauai, the most beautiful spot on the earth.

When we got back to New Jersey, I was still almost suicidal. And, to my discredit, I started taking things out on Gigi. She had worked very hard on the CD, doing tons of footwork and arranging flights and dealing with the publicist and the distribution company. It was stressful on both of us, and when the CD went nowhere I blamed Gigi and started talking about a divorce. It's true you always hurt the one you love. It was far from her fault. I found it very difficult to let go of my pain, even going back to my mother dying and my divorcing Deb. So all that shit came surfacing again, and it was a terribly stressful time for both of us.

But, to our credit, we went to marriage counseling and worked out our problems. Gigi was determined not to let me wallow in my misery. She pushed me to get right back in the studio and work on a rock CD. She had been getting tons of e-mails through my Web site asking for a rock album, so she had arranged for Angel to come back to New Jersey and start working again. I was still feeling the wrath of failure from the ballads CD, so I wasn't too into getting right back to work. But she went downstairs, put a lot of my memorabilia in storage, and hired some guys to build a nice big studio. I didn't want to record in a closet again: I wanted a room big enough for my whole drum kit.

I almost felt forced into this rock thing, but as Angel sent me song after song, it started lighting my pilot light up and the fire grew and my belly started feeling warm again. Angel and I worked on every arrangement, and the songs were shaping up great. Angel was possessed. He never stopped working. He'd spend hours in the guest house, sitting at the table, playing with his headset on, working on the material. Then he'd go, "Cat, I'm going downstairs to the studio to put down this stuff while I got it in my mind." I'd say, "Fuck it, I'm going to watch *The Simpsons,*" and he'd be down there working away.

I brought in Richie Scarlett, Ace's old guitar player, who I promised I'd use on one of my albums when we were on the Bad Boys tour. I made him play bass on some of the tracks. He had switched to bass for a while when he was playing with Leslie West, and he had become a great bassist. He was back to guitar, but I convinced him we needed a bass player, not another guitarist.

By October of 2007 we had thirteen great tracks, and all they needed was my vocals. But then fate intervened. Gigi was upstairs in the bathroom, finishing up a shower. She was toweling off and looked down and saw blood all over the place. At first she thought that her period had come, but then she sat on the bed to towel off her legs and when she got up the towel was just saturated with blood.

By the time she called me up, she was sitting on the toilet.

"I think I'm having a miscarriage," she told me. I looked at her and saw blood dripping down her legs, and when she got up, there were clumps of blood on the towel.

I flipped out. I had never seen anything like that in my life.

"We got to rush to the hospital, right now!" I screamed, and started running around the house like a chicken without a head, trying to get dressed. My whole brain just became mush.

"How about we just go to my gynecologist, who knows me, before we rush off to an emergency room, where I'll be waiting for hours?" she suggested.

She was thinking clearly, so we drove to her gynecologist's office. The office was in a converted house, and I was not impressed with the place when we got there. They took Gigi in right away and I was sitting out there, waiting and waiting, freaking out. The doctor finally came out and told me that they were going to do some tests on her.

A couple of days later, they called her and asked her to come into the office. When she got home, she sat me down and told me that she had cancer. It was an aggressive sarcoma that could spread rapidly through the body, but they had caught it early. Gigi seemed to be taking this okay, but I think she was just in shock. Here she was, just turning forty. You don't expect a diagnosis like this.

At first, I was in total denial. When she said, "I have cancer," all I could think was, Yeah, that's what they tell you so they can make extra money. I couldn't accept that the disease that took my mother was now attacking my wife. When the news sank in, I couldn't breathe. I felt like my heart was going to blow up in my chest.

I was so angry at God. How could he do this to a person who was so spiritual and helped so many people with their own problems with sobriety? Then I just got angry in general. I was angry at Gigi for getting it. I thought about the fact that she smoked cigarettes, the thing that killed my mother. Maybe the cigarettes caused this.

"How could you get cancer? Now you're gonna die and leave me alone," I said to her. I was such an asshole.

Ever since my grandmother took that diabetic stroke in front of me, I had no heart for dealing with people who were sick. But God forbid you don't take care of me when I'm sick: I'll kill you. I was that way with Lydia,

Deb, and Gigi too. If they got sick, it was "Take a fucking aspirin, have a bowl of soup, see you later."

But this time, besides being angry, I was really, really scared. I hadn't been that scared since I had gotten carjacked and I was sitting alone in my apartment. I just couldn't believe I was going to lose my wife at such an early age.

Gigi's men and women friends from her 12-step program were much more supportive than I was. They were calling morning, noon, and night. I always had issues with the whole 12-step thing, but if that's what it took to get Gigi off drugs and drinking, then God bless her. But the way they rallied around her gave me a whole new respect for them.

One day I came home from the gym and Gigi was talking with a friend. I figured they were discussing her cancer, so I went upstairs and took a shower. I was lying naked on the bed afterward and unconsciously checking myself, because if you wore spandex as much as I did you would notice things that don't belong there. So I felt my pecs and they were fine, but when I passed the towel over my left nipple, I saw stars. It felt like someone had popped a nail into it. Then I started messing with it and I felt a small lump behind the nipple.

Of course, my first paranoid thought was that I had cancer. Cancer was on our minds 24/7 then. But men don't get breast cancer, so I figured I had lifted weights at the gym and strained something. It was probably a cyst.

The next day, Gigi was scheduled to consult with Dr. Gae Rodke—a well-respected doctor in Manhattan—about her cancer, so she suggested I come along with her. Gigi went in and I was waiting when the nurse came over to me.

"Could you come in? The doctor wants to see you, too," she said.

I went back and Dr. Rodke explained to me what tests she wanted to do on Gigi. She had wonderful blue eyes and a reassuring smile and she really made me feel that everything was going to be okay with Gigi. Then she said, "Your wife mentioned that you have something on your breast. Would you mind if I look at it while you're here?"

I took my shirt off and she started futzing around with the nipple.

"Hmmm. Let me do something," she said.

She rubbed some lubricant on my left breast and did a quick sonogram.

"If you were my husband, I would send you to see my colleague Dr. Alex Swistel. He's over at Cornell, and he's a wonderful doctor. Let me call over and make sure he can see you right away."

Peter, what is she telling you? There must be something wrong here. She's sending you to see a heavy doctor, you get the message?

"I could come back . . ."

"Now, Peter," she said. She got Swistel's office on the phone and told them that she had a VIP patient and she'd like it if Alex could see me immediately.

We went right over to Cornell, and it was a beautiful building. We got to Dr. Swistel's suite and there's a big sign, BREAST CANCER RESEARCH. Now I was freaking out again. We sat down in the waiting room and I looked around—all women there, except for a couple of men who were there with their wives. I saw a very tall, beautiful young girl who had no hair and was wearing a scarf. She could have been a model, and here she was, dealing with this. Another woman was obviously on a lot of medication and was nodding out in her seat. All around there were women who looked drained of life, with sunken cheekbones and wigs. You just felt you were in a room of cancer, a room that no one should ever have to be in.

I was sitting there holding Gigi's hand, really nervous. They called me in, and Dr. Swistel introduced himself. He was like House: He had a whole bunch of young doctors following him around.

Swistel started feeling the nodule.

"Do you think it's breast cancer?" I spurted out.

"I don't know, but at this point I doubt it," he said, trying to reassure me.

Then one of the resident doctors started asking me a few questions. She was straight off the boat from Ireland, a beautiful brunette with green eyes.

"Do you feel any nausea?" she asked me in that thick Irish brogue. I had learned some dialects in acting school, so I answered her right back in a nice brogue. She gave me a great smile.

"I love the Irish," I said. "I have a shamrock tattoo. I'm half Irish, actually."

Gigi was not smiling. She was pissed that I was flirting in front of her.

Dr. Swistel told me to hang there: He was going to run a test and come right back. The Irish doctor followed him out.

"Don't get your hopes up," Gigi cracked. "She's only here for the day. You'll always have that wandering eye, huh, Peter? You will never change." We laughed about that Irish doctor the whole way home.

Swistel wanted to get a biopsy on the nodule and was going to have me make an appointment with someone at Cornell, but Gigi wondered if it would be all right to schedule with a doctor closer to our house in Jersey. I hated to come into the city, and she knew of a breast center nearby. Alex reluctantly agreed, so we made an appointment with this doctor in New Jersey.

We went to this hospital center. I was sitting in the room waiting for the doctor, and I was scared. All of a sudden the door opened and this very short doctor walked in. She was wearing a short skirt and black nylons, black stiletto heels.

This doctor knew who I was and was being flirty, and I flirted right back. And I felt the fire coming from my left side, where Gigi was sitting. Right away this doctor said something negative about Dr. Swistel, and that didn't sit right with us. But I let it go, and they took me inside for a mammogram and an ultrasound. Then it was time to do a needle biopsy. She sprayed something to numb my breast, then stuck a long needle into the nipple. It hurt like hell.

Now we had to sit and wait forty-five minutes for the results of the biopsy.

The doctor finally came over to me.

"So do I have breast cancer?" I cut to the chase.

"Oh, no. We got some stuff out with the needle, but it's just a cyst, nothing to worry about."

I leaned over and tapped her on the knee.

"All right," I said. "I was worried that I had cancer."

"That's very rare in men," she said. "But if it keeps hurting you, you should go back to Dr. Swistel and have it removed. Otherwise it'll probably go away on its own."

I left feeling like a million bucks. Some time later, Gigi got a call from

Dr. Swistel. The medical center in Jersey had never sent him the results of the biopsy. When he finally got the benign report, he called again and told Gigi that he wanted to take the nodule out just to be safe. So we made an appointment for the surgery.

We drove into the city and I felt great. I wasn't worried—they were going to give me the joy juice and put me out, I had the best doctor in the city, and it wasn't cancer anyway. So they put me out, and the next thing I knew I was waking up in the recovery room and Gigi and Dr. Swistel were standing over me. Everybody was smiling. Dr. Swistel wanted me to stay overnight as a precaution, but I told him how much I hated hospitals, so he let me go straight home.

A few days later, it was a Saturday morning and I was watching a horror movie, something I've done all my life. I heard the phone ring and then Gigi came in.

"It's Dr. Swistel. He wants to talk to you."

I picked up the phone.

"Are you sitting down or standing up?" he asked.

That's not a good thing to hear.

"I'm standing up," I said.

"Well, I think you ought to sit down," he said.

I sat down.

"What have you got, Alex?" I asked.

"It's not what I've got, my friend. You have breast cancer."

My heart fell out of my asshole onto the floor and stopped beating. I couldn't blink, I couldn't open my mouth. I felt like I'd never talk again.

"I know you must be in shock, but the good news is that you couldn't have come in at a better time. You caught it right at the beginning. I want you to come back in and I'll do another procedure and take your lymph nodes out just to be on the safe side. What do you think?" he said.

"Can we operate now?" I said. I just wanted that cancer out of my body.

We scheduled the surgery for the following week. My imagination ran wild. Both of us had cancer, and you could palpably feel the fear in the house. What a way to go, I thought. I did all those drugs, I shot people, I've been shot and stabbed, I've nearly died in car crashes, and now you're going to take me with breast cancer? Jesus Lord, of all things! I'd even buy ass cancer—I'd buy taking a big one and going "boom," and I'm gone. But breast cancer? What a sense of humor you've got.

I was walking around in a fog. Everything seemed surreal; time seemed to stretch out forever. It was like paying a visit to Jandel, Ace's home planet. Come the day of the surgery, I was a total wreck. Now I know that I'm going in for surgery for cancer, and if they don't get it all, I'm fucked. Gigi later told me that she'd never seen me look so frightened. Dr. Swistel got me a private room and they booked me under a phony name. I got there on time, but Alex had two emergencies, so he took them first and I was waiting around for six hours. I was trying to rest and calm myself down in the bed, but the nurse kept coming in every five minutes to take my blood pressure. Each time she looked at the pressure she shook her head and said, "It's got to go down. The doctor can't operate unless it goes down."

"Stay out of the room and his blood pressure will go down," Gigi said. "You're driving him crazy."

Finally, it was time for the surgery. Gigi was next to me as they walked me into the operating room. I really thought that I would never see her again, that I would die on the operating table. When we got to the door, I was cold to her. I didn't hold her and tell her that I loved her because I didn't want to let her know how afraid I was. I just said, "All right, see you later."

They put me on the gurney and wheeled me in and I saw the white coats and the big white mirror. Sure enough, they took my blood pressure and it was high.

"Alex, I'm scared shitless. I'm really afraid I'm not going to make it through this," I said.

"What are you talking about? It's going to be fine, Peter. Just relax," he said. He told his associate to give me a shot. Seconds later I was floating, my blood pressure was normal, and everything was kosher.

"So, you ready now?" Dr. Swistel asked.

"Yeah, whatever you want to do," I slurred.

"See, now that I got you stoned, you'll let me do anything," he smiled.

That was the last thing I remembered. Later, Alex told me that he took my nipple off, did a mastectomy, removed my lymph nodes, and sewed the nipple back on. He did such a great job. I have so much feeling left in my nipple that I can just rub it and get a boner.

Once again, I opened my eyes and there were Gigi and the doc standing over me in the recovery room. Of course, he suggested I stay in the hospital for the night, and naturally I told him I wanted to go home. He told me to wait an hour, and then I could leave. Meanwhile, he was thrilled with how the surgery went. My lymph nodes were clean as a whistle and the cancer was highly contained and not even at stage one, we caught it so early. So it was a nice ride back to Jersey.

Dr. Swistel had recommended that Dr. Daniel Smith do Gigi's cancer surgeries. She had two, and then she was given a clean bill of health. So we were both in remission. But except for a few close friends, we hadn't told anyone about our cancer battle. That was going to remain a secret in our home. Gigi especially felt that with me being in the limelight, we should keep it on the QT. I didn't want to deal with reporters: The one time I had the run-in with *Star* magazine was enough.

In October of 2009, two years after our diagnoses and after we both got clean bills of health, I was talking to Gigi one day.

"I'm always seeing these commercials on TV with women talking about breast cancer. But I've never seen a man come on TV and say, 'I had breast cancer and I beat it.' That irritates the shit out of me," I told her. "A man needs to step forward and say that men can die from this as well as chicks. A hundred and fifty thousand men a year die from breast cancer. I'm going to be the man that does that."

"You sure you want to do this?" she asked.

"Yes," I said. I had gone to church and prayed on this. I knew I had to go to the press and tell them that I had it and that I wasn't going to die because we caught it early.

So Gigi called my publicist in L.A. and she put the story out, and I went on *Good Morning America* and CNN and the story spread like wildfire. Then the phones hit, everyone wanted to interview me, talk to me, take pictures with me. Dr. Swistel called Gigi and told her that he had a patient come in who had seen me on TV talking about breast cancer. He was a huge fan and he said, "If Peter could say 'I had breast cancer and beat it' to millions of people, then I can go in and get it checked out."

Sure enough, he had breast cancer; Alex caught it early enough, so he was fine. Even my friend in L.A., Dr. Terry, called to say that he was getting men who came in and asked to have him check their breasts because of my going public. Terry was so proud of me.

Last year I did a lecture at a big hospital in New Jersey.

"I want to be the first man in history to change the literature in doctors' offices that treat breast cancer. All of the paperwork that you fill out is geared toward women. Give men a separate form where the questions relate to males. Most men are Joe Machos, we're all too tough to admit that we have cancer. We're like John Wayne: 'I got cancer of the lung? Hey, rip it out. I don't need that extra lung.' And we need our own commercial on TV, and I don't care if you pick me, but somebody should come on the tube and say, 'I'm a man, and I beat breast cancer.' There's nothing like that, and it isn't fair."

The audience was cheering.

"Third," I said, almost like a politician, "The ribbon. All pink. Bullshit. Maybe they can give us guys a quarter of the ribbon and make it blue." The place cracked up.

Every year I do a walkathon for breast cancer to raise money. My dentist sent in a grand one year. Did the band send anything? Not a fucking dime. They didn't even call me after I went public with my cancer. I really expected them to call. I thought they would display that much class to me, not only as their drummer but as a human being, as a man they've known for forty years. I tell you, and I mean this from God above, if it was any of them, I would be on the phone in a heartbeat, no matter what they did to me—and they've done a lot of shitty things to me. But that has nothing to do with death or dying or sickness. So it really hurt. I really thought Gene would call but he didn't. Paul didn't call. Paul was a fifty-fifty in my head. But I definitely expected Ace, without a shadow of a doubt. Gigi texted Ace to tell him that I had cancer and he texted back that he would say a prayer for me and call the next day. But he didn't. That really hurt me. But, as much as Ace has fucked me around, part of me still loves him.

My family called. Well, at least my sister Donna Donna and my brother, Joey. They were pissed off. "Why didn't you tell us, we would have been there." Donna Donna was angry she had to see it on television. They were right.

But one of the nicest calls came from Florida. The phone rang one day, and Gigi came into the room.

"It's Bill," she said.

"Bill who?"

"Bill Aucoin."

"Really!"

I picked up the phone.

"I am so proud of you," Bill started. "Number one, it's good to see you on television—of course, not the best circumstances, but I'm so happy you beat it. You need to go out into the world and let them see what a great guy you are. I think of you often and I love you very much."

My heart soared.

"I love you so much, Bill. Maybe I'll get down to Miami and we'll hook up."

"Absolutely. My favorite drummer, are you serious, that would be great," he said.

I hung up. It was such a good feeling that my old manager, the man who made me famous when I was twenty-four, said he loved me and was proud of me. That meant more to me than all of the other calls I got.

I have to take a mammogram every October, and that is decidedly not cool. Whoever designed that machine must have been from the Middle Ages, the days of stretching people and ripping them apart. The machine is like an elaborate vise. You get up against it and it opens and you stick your tittie into it and then it comes up from under you and closes and holds your tit in place.

The first time I did it, I was freaking out.

"Don't hurt me," I told the lab assistant.

"Don't worry, I've been doing this for thirty-five years. I'm a pro," she told me. "But it is a little uncomfortable."

Uncomfortable? My nipple felt like it was being ripped out of its socket. It took her three tries before she got a good image, and when she released me from that machine, I felt such joy. Now I really appreciate what women have to go through every year.

Looking back on it, Gigi's cancer saved my life, for sure. If she hadn't raised my awareness of cancer, I probably would have just thought nothing of that little lump behind my nipple. And if she hadn't been referred to Dr. Rodke by my shoulder surgeon, Dr. Alton Barron, then I would never have gone with her and I wouldn't have found the great Dr. Swistel. How many doctors are proactive like him, checking up on the biopsy report? We later found out that the doctor in Jersey used the wrong needle and didn't probe far enough. A lot of people urged me to sue her and level the whole hospital. Gigi and I mulled it over for a long time. I told her that making money like that was blood money.

"Fine, we'll donate it right back to cancer research," Gigi said.

But then I thought about the impact on the doctor's career. She must have studied for twenty years to get where she was, and I would ruin her reputation in a second. I didn't know if I could sleep after that. Then I thought that she shouldn't be doctoring if she couldn't do her job right. What if she misdiagnosed other people? I went with that for a while, trying to convince myself.

"You'd better make up your mind now. There's only a few days left to file if you want to go that route," Gigi said.

I knew I couldn't do it. I had received a miracle and I wasn't going to ruin it by getting money. Just writing about my experiences in this book was enough. Now I wasn't only raising awareness about male breast cancer, I was raising awareness about bad diagnoses, too.

Having gone through all this, I have a whole different outlook on the big C. Maybe giving me cancer was God's way of showing me what an insensitive, selfish prick I was in dealing with Gigi's cancer. And now that we both battled it and made it, God willing, to the other side, we have an unbreakable bond between us. Facing cancer together truly made us inseparable soul mates, and we're closer now than ever. I guess God does work in mysterious ways.

CHAPTER TWENTY-ONE

Whenever I talk to people about my spiritual beliefs and tell them how I relate to God, they tell me that I should write a book about my religion because I have a unique relationship with my maker. It didn't start out that way. I was born and raised in a traditional Catholic setting. I was baptized at All Saints. I went to the same Catholic school my mother did.

My first issues with the organized church came when it was time for me to go to confession. We had to go every Saturday afternoon at four o'clock. You'd go into a dark box. The priest was sitting next to it and pulled open the screen. Then you confessed your sins, listing them one by one.

Then he talked. "You know it's not good to masturbate. It can lead to other dysfunctional behavior, so say twenty Our Fathers and don't do it again. And it's bad to say the f-word, so say three Hail Marys . . ."

He went on and on, sentencing me for each offense. After a while, I thought this was a bunch of shit. So I started lying, just to get a rise out of him.

"Hey, Father, I couldn't help myself, I beat the shit out of a guy last weekend. I wouldn't let him up and I kicked his teeth in. And I smoked my mother's cigarettes . . ."

But I couldn't get a reaction from him. He just calmly told me to do my Hail Marys.

After a while I started believing that I should confess directly to God.

Not that I don't respect priests but I just felt that there shouldn't be a middleman. So I talked to my mother.

"Ma, this whole confession shit don't fly with me. If I want to talk to God, I can just talk to him, right?"

"Absolutely," she said. "As long as you go to church, I'm happy."

I've always said my prayers, though, every night, ever since I was a little kid. I stuck to the rules of the church. I'd bless my father, bless my mother, bless my grandmother and my sisters and brothers. Then I'd do four Hail Marys, two Our Fathers, and an act of contrition. It was a genius way of getting kids to fall asleep. By the time I got to Hail Mary number two, I was gone. I hardly ever made it to the Our Fathers.

Even when I was going to Catholic school and suffering those horrific punishments at the hands of the nuns, my belief in God remained unshakable. I have a childlike faith that is impenetrable. I know that there's a higher power, somebody who pulls strings and has literally saved my life many times. I knew that it wasn't God who was throwing me in the closet in school; it wasn't God who was rapping my knuckles raw. It was these frustrated nuns.

Then, when I was a teenager, I got a visit from another kind of female authority figure. At the same time that I was being made to sit in my own feces by these nuns and my faith was being tested, one night I was lying in bed about to fall asleep when I felt a presence in the room. I was almost afraid to look because I knew it was something strong. My heart was beating through my pajamas. When I finally looked, my breath was taken away. It was Mother Mary. She was standing in a blue-and-white aura and she had a crown of gold on her head that glimmered. She looked like a porcelain goddess. There wasn't a wrinkle or an imperfection on her face. She just stood there with a Mona Lisa–like smile, a look of pure contentment, and I was in awe. She made me feel that everything was going to be okay, that I shouldn't be shaken by what I was experiencing in school.

I felt that I had been touched by God. And ever since that night, I had immense faith. I believed in God, end of story. Nobody could shake my crown. I didn't tell my parents about what had happened. I thought they would just say it was a dream. I went back to Catholic school and still hated and feared it, but I endured it because we were taught that Jesus endured pain. I think suffering is embedded in Catholics. When I finally left Catholic school for public school, my tormentors changed from the nuns to the bullies. I really believe that my faith in a loving God got me through that year of getting beat up every day outside of school.

In my mid-twenties I broke away from the formal rules of the church and began talking to God directly. That made me feel much better, and I think that's the ultimate goal of any religion: inner peace. I don't care how you get to it—you can be Jewish, Protestant, Buddhist, whatever, it's all fine with me.

In a way, I think that my rebellion was part and parcel of the times that I was living through. I was growing my hair, getting called a fag and getting beat up for it, and protesting what I thought was an unjust war. I saw people running around proclaiming "free love" and "peace," and it was rubbing off on me. When the Beatles sang, "All you need is love," I started looking at God as love. So why did I need to go through some rigamarole to get his attention?

Even when I was on the road with KISS and I was having orgies, I'd make sure to say my prayers every night. I used to call them my guilt prayers. By the end of the night there'd be three naked girls passed out in the room, but I'd be praying.

"Forgive me, Father. I'm an adulterer. I know I'm married, but I can't help it. I'm young, God, and they won't leave me alone. I know I'm doing wrong, but I'll try to do better. I won't do three, I'll only do one. I'm trying." And then I'd say a Hail Mary and the next morning I would throw them out of the room. But it would happen all over again the next night. There'd be naked people all around the room, someone passed out in the tub with the water overflowing. A girl and a guy would be passed out on the bed and she'd have her leg over the bed with her panties hanging off her ankle.

And I'd say, "Jesus, I know this doesn't look good. I promise I'll get rid of them all. I know you might not want to let me into heaven, but it could be worse, right? I could be a killer; I could sell drugs to children."

That's when my bargaining with the Lord started. I'd try to work out a deal with him that maybe it would be okay to do certain things as long as I didn't really go over the line.

But I did go over the line. I hit bottom in rehab. Before that, I was living like a rich pig in Darien, doing enormous amounts of blow. I still prayed a little bit, but my prayers weren't sincere. I wasn't really talking to the Man, I was just hearing myself talk to him. But when that angel came to me in my room at the rehab, I just felt like I had regained my soul. So from that low point I got back on track and my faith helped me get through the rough years of my mother's death, my divorce, the carjacking.

Then I came back to Mother Mary. I was on the balls of my ass and I owed millions to the IRS. I used to bring my Mitsubishi to get repaired in Santa Monica, and driving around the neighborhood I found a big church called St. Monica's. So I went in and figured that I should start praying to Mary. She had helped me get through those crises when I was back in school.

"Mary, I owe three million dollars, my face has been bashed in, I tried to kill myself. You've got to help me, you can't let me stay like this. I don't know what to do anymore, I'm at the end of my rope. You've got to give me a miracle." And I got it. A few weeks went by and George Sewitt called me and told me that we were going to do *MTV Unplugged*. You know the rest of the story.

I realized that my mother wore a Mary medal her whole life. (In fact, I wear it now.) Then I realized that I could never say no to my mother. So I figured that if Mother Mary came around and said, "Look, I need you to do me a favor," what is Jesus going to do? Say, "No, I don't have time. I have other miracles to perform"? No, he's gonna take time out for her.

I'd be a liar if I said that my faith was so strong that doubt never crept in. I certainly doubted God when I got my cancer diagnosis. That whole time I just felt numb. When I was cured and when I later found out that Gigi had beat her cancer, too, I never really felt grateful to God. I was going to church twice a week to pray but the only emotion I felt was anger. I was angry that Gigi and I had both gotten cancer, and I felt guilty that I had beaten it when so many great people die from the disease.

One day I was at my local church and I got on my knees and prayed. Then I went over and sat in the booth with my rosaries. The church was empty and all of a sudden, it just hit me. I felt such shame for not showing God any gratitude for saving us both from dying.

I sat there and I heard, "You ingrate. You come in my house and doubt me? How dare you? I saved your wife, I saved your life. How can you be so selfish?"

Tears started pouring out of me and I cried like I had never cried in my entire life. My stomach hurt from crying so much. I felt like I was about to throw up. A woman came into the church, but I didn't care. I got down on my knees and wailed, "I'm sorry, I'm sorry. I should be so grateful to you." She turned around and ran right out of the church. I must have cried for an hour easily. I finally settled down and I felt like a new man, like I had been cleansed. I left the church and drove home and I felt like I had taken forty tranquilizers, I was so calm. I really felt that God had touched me.

Surviving everything, including the cancer, should have given me some insight and made me appreciate this glorious immaculate conception, should have made me dance on flowers every day and think, Oh, my God, I'm so happy to be alive! But that's not in my personality. Over the last fifteen years, I've become a more serious Peter Criss, a deeper Peter Criss. I made a lot of mistakes when I was wasted on drugs, but I've also had my trust violated so many times. Trust was the most important code on the streets. Trust, honor, integrity, respect—all those things were very sacred to me. Then the trust was violated—by the mother of my daughter, by my manager, by my bandmates—all these people to whom I really gave the keys to my heart. So I have barbed wire around my heart, scars from the rock 'n' roll wars. I've got battle fatigue.

My life's been in a lot of turmoil lately. I haven't really been active creatively since the CD I put out five years ago. I haven't been in front of the public eye to hear that clapping—which is the true addiction, not the drugs. So I start feeling worthless and useless. Doing this book has stirred up some deep, deep feelings. I've been having weird dreams about Debra, and dreaming about Lydia and my daughter. Then I had a nightmare where some guy was chasing me and wanted to stab me. I've been opening doors to things that I haven't talked about in years, scary things. But as an artist I know that it won't work unless you put every fucking bit of your heart and soul into it.

I got up the other day and my brain just felt so overloaded; I felt so depressed. Then I went to the gym, and that didn't help. For the last few days I've been so melancholic and angry. I get to the point where I really want to bolt. Maybe take a trip up to New York, check in to a hotel, get room service, see a show, just get away from it all. But I've learned that what you've got goes with you. You go to Paris, you'll still have the same problem when you wake up in Paris. So the other day I was like, "I don't want to be here, I don't want to see you, I don't want to play my drums anymore. That rock album could burn in there, it's never going to get done." I felt like I was getting sucked into this great black void.

Then I was sitting in my studio and I looked at a picture of my daughter with my granddaughter. My relationship with my daughter has been very rocky over the years. It kills me that we don't have a loving presence in each other's lives. Then it gets worse and worse and I start having a panic attack and my heart starts beating really fast and then I'm not even thinking clear and I'm working on pure anger. All of a sudden I hate myself for not doing what I said I was going to do, work all week on my album, be happy and be positive. So now I've got a crown of shit, and I call it the Jesus process, where the crown gets really heavy and I feel the pain and I'm ready to take that gun and stick it in my mouth and say, "Fuck it, because there's really nothing left here anyway for me." And then I think, Am I a manic depressive? Maybe I'm bipolar? Finally I say, "You know what? I'm going to go to church. I've got to go talk to the Man and try to calm down or I'm going to take a heart attack." Even then I'm thinking, So I'm going to say a few Hail Marys, and who are you kidding, this shit is going to keep going.

But the minute I open the door and walk in, it hits me in the ass and I bless myself and I'm in this place of total quiet and beauty. And I think, You don't even see the guy, but you believe in the guy and he has a lot of these houses, all over the world. There are Jewish houses he owns, Protestant houses and Catholic churches. Talk about having houses built for you—no rock star will ever have houses built like this. And it makes me very humble and I realize how grand and how strong God is. So do I believe in him? Yes. Do I doubt him? Yes. I do doubt God a lot at times, and I talk to him about it.

So I go into the church and I do an Our Father, a Hail Mary, and an act of contrition and then I go, "Father, I ain't doing well. I'm ready to kill myself. I have such pain. I just had an anxiety attack like I can't tell you.

And my body hurts. I just feel like I want to die. I mean, look at the shit going on with me. I really miss my daughter and my granddaughter a lot. The holidays just went by again, and I didn't see her. You have to help me with this. My writer's going to be at the house in an hour. Doing this book is so painful. Do you understand, God? I want you to talk to me and make me feel better."

And as I'm saying all this, I start getting answers.

"Oh, really? You got some pain? Your breast is hurting? The one you had the cancer in that you caught just in time so now you're in my church, which you wouldn't be if you didn't get it just in time? That problem? The one that some people die from?"

I start realizing I have nothing to say.

Then I get, "So where are you living?"

"Oh, I got a nice house with a swimming pool," I answer.

"Really? Do you know that fourteen million people are out of work? Do you know that some people live in a tiny cubicle and now they've lost their jobs so they can't even pay their rent? And you're bitching? How'd you get here? What are you driving?"

"Well, I have a BMW."

"A BMW? You could have a little Corolla. Okay, you got any money in the bank?"

"Yeah."

"So you're coming in here bitching to me about your minute little problems, Peter. You've come in my house many times and told me about some serious problems: when you your mother had cancer, when your wife had the cancer, when you had cancer, when your band ripped you off, when your best friend hurt you. I'd rather hear these problems than see you having a panic attack the last two days, hating yourself, wanting to jump through the window. 'Oh God, no one loves me. I'm not worthy of this world. I feel like a dot on the wall.' I'm not going to give you any pity or any mercy. Be grateful. Get out of it and be happy and leave my house with a smile and realize you're walking out, not going out in a wheelchair."

And it works. I've been praying that way for a long, long time, and I know if something ain't broke, don't fix it. Whatever way I talk to that man up there, I've had a pretty good run. I should have been dead many,

many times. I should have been on skid row at times. I should have OD'd many times. I should have been shot by one of my wives. I should have come to my end like all the other rock stars that I've seen die in these ways. I should have been a casualty of these wars, but for some reason I'm not.

So I can't really feel any regrets. I almost died from drugs, I almost died in car crashes, I had cancer. Did I learn? Abso-fucking-lutely. I drive like an old lady now. I wouldn't ever dream of doing serious drugs again. I wrecked some cars, I wrecked some rooms, I wrecked some marriages. And I paid for all that.

As much anger as I still harbor for the way the band fucked me over, I realize that the Christian thing to do is to forgive them. I'm working on that. To forgive is to live, and I intend to live a lot longer. It's not healthy to hold on to that anger and let it fester.

I'm also trying to work through my anger toward Ace. I loved Ace. I would have cut off my arm for Ace, and he betrayed me like Judas for some pieces of silver. I was crushed by that. We were both street kids, he knew the code. His actions were so reprehensible that I'm sure that's one of the reasons that he doesn't even talk about the reunion and farewell tours in his book.

So I'm working on forgiving them. But am I still hurt? Yeah. Does it still bother me? Yeah. Will it always bother me? I don't know. I hope that I don't take these feelings to my grave.

There was a time when I loved those guys. The other day I woke up and looked in the mirror and—for a second—I missed the band. The more I thought about it, the more I realized that I missed being *in* the band. I missed the greasepaint, the bombs, the excitement, the fans. I certainly didn't miss the aggravation and the backstabbing and the petty games that were so toxic I had to go and run and hide in my room every night. I still need help with the hatred that I feel for lawyers and the business people who rob you with a fountain pen.

What people forget is that I was no hero and certainly no superhero. Underneath that Catman makeup was little Peter Georgie Criscuola from Williamsburg. When I go to sleep these days, I'm still wearing my cowboy pajamas. And I say my prayers. Some things never change. But I have. And I thank God that he's never left me.

PHOTO CAPTIONS

Page 366

- 1st row, *left to right*:

    Paul and I having fun in May of 1979.

    Paul and I really having fun!

    The Reunion, backstage with Lenny Kravitz.

- 2nd row, *left to right*:

    Ed Trunk, a real down-to-earth guy.

    Tommy Lee and me. I love Tommy Lee.

- 3rd row, *left to right*:

    With John 5, one of my best friends.

    Marky Ramone and me at CBGB.

- 4th row, *left to right*:

    Louie Bellson, Mr. Remo, and me at Blue Note in California. An honor to be in such
      greatness.

    Backstage with the legendary Tony Bennett. I was so honored.

- Page 367, *clockwise from top left*:

    On European signing tour in Prague. I was with Steve Campbell, Nico, Joe Marshall, and
      Peter Arquette.

    Dreams come true. Me behind Gene Krupa's drums at Zildjian.

    Top of the world. At the Super Bowl rehearsal in Miami.

    Having a ball being myself on the Farewell Tour.

    Gigi and me in Cape Anne, one of my favorite places in the world. When I pass, this is
      where my ashes will be spread.

    Gigi and me in our favorite place in Hawaii.

    In front of my house after a snowstorm, 2005.

    Super Bowl, 1999, with the coolest lady, Cher, and my beautiful wife, Gigi.

time to go into a new phase and enjoy the rest of my years. I really don't want to put on spandex and scream "Black Diamond" anymore.

But I still play drums every day. And I write songs. Whether I put them out eventually doesn't really seem to matter—I'm a musician first and foremost. I'm always going to be in my studio, putting in the time, jotting down lyrics.

I've always wanted a house on the water and now Gigi and I are building one. And I'm going to have an art studio so I can get back to painting. I learned a lot writing this book and I think I have a children's book and a screenplay in me too. And I would still love to act. I've had and have a wonderful life.

So now I'm going to reap the fruits of all my labors. Go fishing, do some sketching, maybe just watch the river flow behind the house. Despite all the bad things that have happened to me, they're all water under the bridge now. My life has been a lot like that classic Bob Seger song "Turn the Page." Life goes on, within you and without you, some other wise men said. They also said the love you take is equal to the love you make. Simple words, but true.

I'm blessed to have a good wife like Gigi and a shelter cat we adopted named Fanny. I can't wait to see Fanny run around the new house. I've got a lot to be grateful for, and I thank my loving God who keeps this old cat's heart beating.

that was so unique and compelling that it became a band that put on events, not just shows. We created a rock 'n' roll circus with the members flying through the air, spitting fire, and levitating a hundred feet up. We were a band, not a brand.

We resonated with our fans because, in the beginning, we were just like them. I was a skinny kid with big ears and dark circles under my eyes, the kid who had to join a gang to protect himself from getting beaten up every day. All four of us understood what it was like to be the underdog, and in us our fans found hope whether they were white, black, green, orange, whether they were gay or straight. We told them to lift up their heads and be proud of who they were. And they did. They are the KISS Army.

I loved my band. There was nothing better in my whole life. KISS was the band I always wanted to be in. I gave my heart and soul to KISS—in the beginning and even in the end, and my heart is with them still today. I blew out both my rotator cuffs from drumming my ass off, and I had hand surgery because my tendons were literally hanging off my fingers. I couldn't even hold my sticks, I had to tape them to my hands, but still I played. After all, you wanted the best, and I gave you the best.

So how can I be negative? How many people came from the gutters of Brooklyn and achieved their dream of playing that great cathedral of entertainment, Madison Square Garden? I know I made my parents proud. I will always see their faces in the crowd as long as I live. And I'm proud that I influenced untold thousands to pursue their dream and pick up their sticks or guitars and play music.

I'm prouder still about the work I do to fight cancer. Every October I hit the streets with thousands of people and march to raise money for breast cancer research. I'm a spokesperson in raising awareness of male breast cancer. There's not a platinum record or lifetime achievement award that can touch the news that a person's life has been saved because he heeded my warnings, went to his doctor and got treated in time.

It's funny when I look back to when I first started playing music. I remember telling my mom that all I wanted in life was a cute white-picket-fenced house and a gold .45 record on the wall. Well, I got a lot more than that. I achieved things beyond my wildest dreams. So now it's

EPILOGUE

Life goes by so fast. I often look back at my life and ask myself: did I do enough? Did I say enough? What am I leaving behind, a Cat face and the band KISS? Did I really make my parents happy and proud of me? Was I a good dad? I keep questioning myself more and more. I think everyone does that as they get older.

I'm getting older and closer to the box, and I don't really want to be a grumpy man. I don't really want to keep on holding on to that pain. I'm trying to forgive to live, but it isn't always easy.

Sometimes when I get melancholy, Gigi comes over to me and grabs my face and says, "I hear you bitching, but you amaze me. You've almost been killed, you've been through hell and back, but you're here. Babe, you're a survivor and I love you to death and so does God. You have changed so many people's lives for the better. What a blessing." She's right. I am a survivor. I think that comes from growing up on the streets of Brooklyn. Everybody has a breaking point. I've been beaten up and stabbed and shot at, and I've made it through. My first two marriages went sour, but I got through them with the help of God. Somehow I even summoned up the strength not to pull that trigger when I was sitting on the floor in Hollywood with the debris of my life scattered around me.

Maybe some of that strength came from having created something that will never be duplicated. KISS was a special band. There will never be another band like my band. It took special chemistry to create something